Frugal Innovation in Entrepreneurship

Reshmi Manna
MIT World Peace University, India

Ankit Singh
LINTL Clothing Private Limited, India

IGI Global
Scientific Publishing
Publishing Tomorrow's Research Today

Vice President of Editorial	Melissa Wagner
Director of Acquisitions	Mikaela Felty
Director of Book Development	Jocelynn Hessler
Production Manager	Mike Brehm
Cover Design	Phillip Shickler

Published in the United States of America by
IGI Global Scientific Publishing
701 East Chocolate Avenue
Hershey, PA, 17033, USA
Tel: 717-533-8845
Fax: 717-533-7115
Website: https://www.igi-global.com E-mail: cust@igi-global.com

Library of Congress Cataloging-in-Publication Data

Names: Manna, Reshmi, 1978- editor.
Title: Frugal innovation in entrepreneurship / edited by Reshmi Manna, Ankit Singh, Krishna Dixit.
Description: Hershey, PA : Business Science Reference, an imprint of IGI Global, 2024. | Includes bibliographical references and index. | Summary: "The primary objective of the book "Frugal Innovation in Entrepreneurship" is to offer a thorough examination of frugal innovation ideas and their use in promoting entrepreneurial endeavors. This book attempts to explore by using a wide range of successful case studies, empirical research, a meta-analysis of prior literature, and the identification of theoretical underpinnings to assess the influence of frugal innovation"-- Provided by publisher.
Identifiers: LCCN 2024038344 (print) | LCCN 2024038345 (ebook) | ISBN 9798369340509 (hardcover) | ISBN 9798369351338 (paperback) | ISBN 9798369340516 (ebook)
Subjects: LCSH: Entrepreneurship.
Classification: LCC HB615 .F78 2024 (print) | LCC HB615 (ebook) | DDC 338/.04--dc23/eng/20240923
LC record available at https://lccn.loc.gov/2024038344
LC ebook record available at https://lccn.loc.gov/2024038345

British Cataloguing in Publication Data
A Cataloguing in Publication record for this book is available from the British Library.

Table of Contents

Detailed Table of Contents

Frugal innovation considers societal and operational challenges as starting points for innovative solutions that could serve as drivers of sustainable development. Prior research, however, has done little to understand firm level requirements to set-up a frugal innovation-based business. In this article, we established a link between frugal innovation and the sustainable business model concept. More specifically, the research questions are: 1) How do societal and operational pressures together influence business activities and 2) how can these pressures be assessed analytically? We present an analytical framework that can be used in assessing frugal innovations for long-term sustainability and we demonstrate the functioning of the framework with the empirical analysis of three case firms.

The concept of frugal is attributed to products, process, services and systems to develop under resource-constraints, customers are at the center of the development of accessible, adaptable, affordable and appropriate comfortability. Various concepts have been associated interchangeably with the term 'Frugal innovation' in the field on entrepreneurship. This includes the word 'Jugaad innovation' because of the transformation of limited and scared resources from complexity to simplicity on meeting the need of the beneficiary Also because of the ability to solve complex problems of its rigidity of high-cost to affordability, logistic climax to accessibility, portability and mobility, the term adopted was 'Reverse Innovation' which as reinventing or creating viable resources that will seen as comfortability to the consumers.

The study explores the intersection of frugal innovation, circular economy, and environmental entrepreneurship for sustainable development. Given the dearth of resources, increasing pollution and global warming, with an increasing demand for goods and services because of increasing global population, development and sustainability need to go hand in hand. The book chapter focuses on this research gap and identifies policy level recommendations based on case examples of best practices and applications at a global scale. The major recommendations of the study are an assessment of the factors influencing entrepreneurs to engage in the circular economy by adopting best practices, namely, using recycled and repurposed material, as well as application of longevity, repairability and recyclability potential, among others. One of the critical findings of our study includes the adoption of the principles of responsible investment in furthering environmental entrepreneurship. We propose future research areas to enhance the body of knowledge on the theme.

In an age marked by resource constraints, environmental concerns, and a growing awareness of social responsibility, the intersection of frugal innovation and ethical consumerism emerges as a pivotal pathway toward sustainable development. This chapter aims to explore the synergies between frugal innovation and ethical consumerism, offering insights into how these two concepts can collectively contribute to sustainability and global prosperity. The example of a social enterprise explains how ethical consumerism and frugal innovation can go hand in hand. The environment-friendly sanitary napkins are made by rural women through locally sourced raw materials. This socially conscious strategy empowers women, encourages participation in the community, and supports sustainable business practices. This is an example of how ethical consumerism and frugal innovation work together to create positive social change.

In the dynamic landscape of entrepreneurship, resources are finite and challenges are omnipresent, the ability to innovate amidst constraints becomes paramount. This chapter presents an exploration of leveraging frugal innovations as catalysts for entrepreneurial success. The chapter delves into understanding frugal innovation, tracing historical evolution, and emphasizes the importance of embracing constraints for innovation. By shifting mindsets and adopting problem-solving techniques, entrepreneurs can reframe limitations as opportunities for growth. The chapter explores practical strategies for frugal innovation, the lean startup methodology and minimum viable product development, accompanied by case studies across various industries. It highlights best practices and lessons learned from successful frugal innovators, emphasizing scalability, sustainability, and importance of collaborative ecosystems. The chapter equips readers with knowledge and tools necessary to navigate resource-constrained environments and foster sustainable entrepreneurial growth through frugal innovations.

Frugal Digitalisation has proven to be a strategic approach which emphasizes on Cost effectiveness, simplicity, and optimized performance level. Harnessing Digitalisation frugally for MSMEs is an appropriative strategy for the firm's sustainability. Rapidly changing technologies and VUCA environment are emerging as the biggest business challenge and digitalisation of MSMEs has become essential these days. This chapter provides an overview of Frugal innovations that can digitalise MSMEs for their sustainability and, understanding ongoing digital transformations of MSMEs. It also explains the digitalization strategies tailored for MSMEs from adopting cloud computing and SaaS to building an online presence and leveraging e-commerce platforms also the key topics in the field. The chapter provide case studies of successful frugal digitalisation that illustrate real-world scenarios, offering lessons learned and best practices for MSMEs embarking on their digital adoption.

This chapter delves into frugal innovation in rural Indian entrepreneurship, tracing its roots, principles, and applications. Through qualitative research, it explores how frugal solutions, inspired by the Indian concept of jugaad, address social and economic challenges. Findings illustrate how these innovations improve access, productivity, and sustainability in sectors like healthcare, agriculture, and education. Collaboration among stakeholders is highlighted as vital for scaling these initiatives and promoting inclusive rural development.

This chapter undertakes an examination of primary data sourced from interviews conducted with educators and principals from rural South African educational institutions. The purpose of this chapter is to investigate and comprehend the ramifications of Information and Communication Technologies (ICTs) within these scholastic settings, with a particular emphasis on the viewpoints and encounters of those directly engaged in such educational instruction. Against the background of frugal innovation in entrepreneurship and employing a qualitative analysis of the interview data, this chapter endeavors to unveil the salient themes encapsulated within the respondents' narratives. This, in turn, furnishes invaluable insights into the existent state of ICTs within rural educational establishments, the attendant challenges encountered, and the prospective scope for subsequent integration and advancement.

In a world confronted with multifaceted challenges in healthcare, agriculture, and education, frugal innovation emerges as a beacon of hope, offering affordable and accessible solutions to address pressing societal needs. This chapter explores the principles and applications of frugal innovation in social technological domains, emphasizing its transformative potential in bridging the gap between technology and underserved communities. Through an in-depth examination of case studies,

Preface

INTRODUCTION

"In a world where 'doing more with less' is not just a necessity but a virtue, frugal innovation has emerged as a beacon for resilient entrepreneurship."

In a time when there are pressing global concerns such as climate change, resource depletion, growing inequality, and rapid technological disruption, the value of innovation has become increasingly essential in discussions regarding inclusive growth and sustainable development. On the other hand, traditional conceptions of innovation frequently fail to consider the realities of low-resource environments and grassroots people. An approach known as "Frugal Innovation in Entrepreneurship" is emerging as a response to these gaps, which are desperately required. This book combines contemporary concepts, cutting-edge research, and extensive case-based observations on how individuals and businesses worldwide are redefining innovation. It examines these concepts through the lens of affordability, accessibility, flexibility, and appropriateness.

Frugal innovation is a proactive strategy that leverages constraints as a source of creative inspiration rather than merely reacting to a scarcity of resources. The concept of frugal innovation emphasises simplicity, local relevance, and sustainability instead of relying on solutions that need significant resources. It does this to establish a transformative foundation for entrepreneurial endeavours, particularly in impoverished countries, underprivileged areas, and industries that historical inefficiencies have hindered. This book delves into the facets of frugal innovation related to social enterprise settings, political issues, technical developments, and business structures.

Relevance in Today's World

The book corresponds with a seismic shift in the global entrepreneurial landscape. Recovery from a pandemic, climatic catastrophes, geopolitical upheaval, and a renewed focus on the Sustainable Development Goals (SDGs) all call for the adoption of new paradigms of innovation that are resilient, inclusive, and innovative. That is precisely what the frugal invention concept provides. In doing so, it addresses the dilemma between expansion and sustainability by offering approaches that are not only practical financially but also ethically. The chapters that amplify the examples in this book respond to the current needs that are being presented all over the world. These examples range from microenterprises in India to social technologies in Africa and digitally transformed building patterns in industrial sectors.

Frugal Innovation and MSMEs: Empowering Startups and Business Acceleration

Micro, Small, and Medium Enterprises (MSMEs) form the backbone of most global economies, especially in emerging markets. Yet, these enterprises often operate with limited financial, technological, and human resources. Frugal innovation is a practical and strategic approach for MSMEs to overcome constraints while achieving meaningful growth.

For startups, frugal innovation fosters agility and resourcefulness from the outset. It encourages entrepreneurs to develop minimum viable products (MVPs), pilot low-cost business models, and refine their offerings based on real-time feedback. These practices reduce risk and enhance the chances of early success.

In established MSMEs, frugal innovation enhances operational efficiency, lowers production costs, and allows businesses to pivot quickly in response to market shifts. It drives value creation through customer-centric and need-based innovations while often tapping into local resources and community knowledge.

Moreover, frugal innovation opens doors to new markets—especially in underserved and low-income segments—by offering affordable, accessible, and appropriate solutions. By democratising innovation, it supports business acceleration and contributes to inclusive and sustainable economic development.

The chapters in this book are replete with real-world examples where MSMEs and startups have leveraged frugal principles to overcome adversity, scale responsibly, and generate lasting impact.

The Role of Institutions and Academia

Educational institutions and universities are critical in nurturing the spirit of entrepreneurship and innovation among students and aspiring entrepreneurs. Through teaching, research, and mentorship, they form the intellectual bedrock upon which future business leaders are developed. Frugal innovation, emphasising practicality, resourcefulness, and inclusivity, is an ideal pedagogical model in this endeavour.

This book is a key resource for educators and curriculum developers seeking to embed real-world, sustainable innovation models into entrepreneurship education. By incorporating insights from this volume, institutions can train students to adopt a problem-solving mindset that embraces constraints as opportunities rather than limitations.

Furthermore, research scholars working on various dimensions of innovation—social innovation, grassroots innovation, digital transformation, and sustainable entrepreneurship—will find this book a rich source of empirical data, theoretical insights, and global case studies. Each chapter contributes to the expanding literature on frugal innovation, offering fresh perspectives and unexplored intersections with policy, business strategy, and technology.

Through this integration into academic settings, the book informs and inspires. It encourages students, educators, and researchers to reimagine innovation in a way that is grounded in local realities and aligned with global aspirations.

Chapter Overviews

Authors from all over the world submitted many chapter proposals for the book. After a rigorous blind peer review process and carefully considering how well each contribution aligned with the book's essential principles, ten chapters were selected for publishing in their final form. When viewed as a whole, these chapters offer a perceptive examination of how effective utilisation of cost-effective innovation could boost entrepreneurial endeavors, facilitating the acceleration of enterprises and enabling a sustainable worldwide effect.

Chapter one discusses the paradigm shift that frugal innovation represents for the success of entrepreneurs, as elucidated by Prachita A. Patil, Smruti A. Patre, and Yogesh Deshpande. This study investigates the relationship between environmentally responsible business structures and inventive, frugal innovation. This chapter's framework explains how operational and social dynamics lead to long-term sustainable innovation. A comprehensive study of three case studies is offered to establish this framework. To gain an understanding of the foundations of frugal entrepreneurship, it provides the necessary background information.

The second chapter addresses social entrepreneurship and frugal innovation. A. Orugba and Harry Ovharhe pioneered the ideas of Ultrapreneurs and Social Extrapreneurs as seasoned businesspeople. The chapter's explanation of the complex meanings of terms like "reverse innovation" and "jugaad" will make it easier for the reader to understand the socioeconomic effects of frugal innovation meant to help people experiencing poverty.

Chapter three discusses "Frugal Innovation, Circular Economy, and Environmental Entrepreneurship" by Supriya Singh and Subrat Sarangi, establishing linkages among three critical domains: environmental stewardship, circularity, and frugality. Using global case studies and regulatory principles, the authors propose a framework that businesses may use to integrate economic efficiency with environmental conscience.

The fourth chapter, "Frugal Innovation and Ethical Consumerism," by Oly Mishra, investigates the junction of ethical consumerism and frugal innovation to produce solutions that are both sustainable and socially responsible. This chapter contains a case study on environmentally friendly sanitary napkins to shed light on how ethical corporate practices and community empowerment can coexist.

Thriving on Constraints by Radhika Sharma explores how constraints can be turned into opportunities for creativity in its fifth chapter. To encourage business owners to adopt cost-effective and efficient ideas, it gives them workable approaches such as the Lean Startup methodology and minimum viable product development. This allows them to turn challenges into opportunities.

The adoption of frugal digitisation by micro, small, and medium-sized firms (MSMEs) is examined by Jayasankar Prasad C. and Lekshmi Krishna S. in chapter six, "Big Ideas, Small Businesses." This chapter looks at digital solutions, such as software as a service (SaaS), to ensure the long-term viability of micro, small, and medium-sized enterprises (MSMEs) and cloud computing. Additionally, case studies are shown that demonstrate the implementation of technologies that are both cost-effective and disruptive.

The seventh chapter of Siddharth Misra and Subhajit Bhattacharya's book Driving Change investigates the notion of frugal innovation in rural entrepreneurship in India. The chapter, which examines the ways in which rural business owners tackle problems pertaining to education, agriculture, and healthcare, is based on the history of jugaad.

Bongi G. Mahlangu and Leila Goosen present a qualitative investigation on the influence that information and communication technologies (ICTs) have on schools in rural South Africa in chapter eight, entitled "Empowering Rural Communities and Schools for Frugal Innovation and Entrepreneurship." Clarification is provided regarding the structural issues, as well as how innovative design that is both creative and economical can propel development in underdeveloped regions, notably in the fields of education and business.

The importance of creating cost-effective healthcare, education, and agriculture innovations is emphasised in chapter nine, titled "Tech for Good: Frugal Innovations in Social Technologies" by Ravi Shankar Saripalle and Jayasri Sai Venkata Angara. This chapter highlights the scalability of social technology when it is established on thrift principles by utilising appealing case studies such as Cropin and Karkinos Healthcare to demonstrate this scalability.

Vinay Simoga Baburao and Premasish Roy examine digital transformation in the pipeline construction industry in chapter ten, "Digital Transformative Trajectories." By analysing the factors that drive and hinder technology adoption, this chapter illustrates the significance of cost-effective innovation within traditional small business contexts. Consequently, it broadens the discourse to encompass heavy industries.

LAST THOUGHT

This book bridges the gap between research and practical significance in the field of frugal innovation, and as a result, it is situated at the intersection of theory and practice. Rather than viewing restrictions as obstacles, we aim to empower a new crop of entrepreneurs, scholars, and change-makers who perceive boundaries as opportunities to innovate sustainably. This will be accomplished by mixing a variety of voices and perspectives from multiple dimensions.

The contribution that the book provides is threefold. It offers a multidisciplinary viewpoint on frugal innovation, ranging from the industrial sector's digital revolution to grassroots entrepreneurship. Second, by basing our analysis on empirical findings and real-world case studies, we fill key research and policy gaps, making this volume theoretically solid and pragmatically helpful. Thirdly, the many locations ranging from India to South Africa, from rural communities to high-tech corporations, demonstrate frugal innovation's global significance and importance.

The influence of this book lies not only in the things that it clarifies but also in the things that it permits. Our work aims to provide legislators with the ability to develop inclusive innovation plans, assist educators in improving curricula, encourage corporations to embrace innovative problem-solving strategies, and encourage further academic study in this rapidly increasing field. In conclusion, "Frugal Innovation in Entrepreneurship" provides a vital and current story. It creates a narrative that emphasises the connection between entrepreneurial activities, sustainability, equity, and innovation and shows contempt for the limits already in place.

As we move deeper into the twenty-first century, the principles of frugal innovation are becoming more essential than ever. In contrast to innovation models that rely heavily on abundant capital and sophisticated infrastructure, frugal innovation demonstrates that ingenuity, community engagement, and contextual relevance can lead to equally powerful—if not superior—results. It invites a mindset shift among innovators, urging them to look at what they have and how best they can use it to solve real problems.

Importantly, frugal innovation also aligns with global sustainability goals. Encouraging minimal waste, energy efficiency, and socially responsible business models champions a regenerative approach to entrepreneurship. Whether a rural farmer using a solar-powered irrigation system in India or a small African enterprise delivering healthcare using mobile platforms, the reach and relevance of frugal innovation transcend industries and geographies.

This book seeks to initiate fresh dialogues, stimulate practical applications, and cultivate a global community of innovators dedicated to creating a better, more equal society through frugality-driven business.

This compilation is a timely and significant addition to the existing body of knowledge on entrepreneurship and innovation, and it is a source of great joy for us as editors to be involved in its production. Not only will the concepts given contribute to the advancement of intellectual discourse, but we are confident that they will also stimulate actual ground-based practical reform. We invite scholars, practitioners, and students alike to embrace frugal innovation as a transformative approach that recognises limitations not as obstacles but as opportunities to create impactful and lasting change.

Editorial Note

The editors have travelled far to view the numerous and highly contextual stories developed due to our authors' work. The variety of ideas presented in this collection highlights the adaptability and importance of frugal innovation in today's discussion of entrepreneurship. These ideas range from rural creativity and grassroots business models to social innovations that technology facilitates.

Our inspiration came from the high quality of the entries submitted from all across the world, highlighting the global significance of this matter. The selection of the final chapters from the pool of entries needed careful consideration, and we are confident that the selected pieces offer depth and variety. To choose each chapter, editors considered its intellectual value and ability to inspire action and practical application.

Our editorial mission has always been to bridge the gap between the commercial and academic worlds and promote scalable, inclusive, and meaningful innovation. By publishing this book, we hope to provide a new generation of academics and company owners with the tools necessary to introduce frugal innovation into educational institutions, corporate boardrooms, policy tables, and underprivileged communities.

Chapter 1
Frugal Innovation: A Paradigm Shift for Entrepreneurial Success "Necessity is the mother of all inventions"!

Prachita A. Patil
Dr. Ambedkar Institute of Management Studies and Research, Nagpur, India

Smruti Rahul Patre
Symbiosis Institute of Business Management, Nagpur, India & Symbiosis International University (Deemed), Pune

Yogesh Deshpande
Department of Humanities and Social Sciences, Visvesvaraya National Institute of Technology, Nagpur, India

ABSTRACT

Frugal innovation considers societal and operational challenges as starting points for innovative solutions that could serve as drivers of sustainable development. Prior research, however, has done little to understand firm level requirements to set-up a frugal innovation-based business. In this article, we established a link between frugal innovation and the sustainable business model concept. More specifically, the research questions are: 1) How do societal and operational pressures together influence business activities and 2) how can these pressures be assessed analytically? We present an analytical framework that can be used in assessing frugal innovations for long-term sustainability and we demonstrate the functioning of the framework with the empirical analysis of three case firms.

DOI: 10.4018/979-8-3693-4050-9.ch001

INTRODUCTION

The Latin term "frugalis" from the middle of the 16th century is where the word "frugal" originated. Frugal is defined by the Oxford Dictionary as "sparing or economical as regards money or food." When there were few financial resources available in the old world, frugal living was a virtue. This is still true in most of today's emerging economies. The concept of "frugal innovation" is not new, despite the term's recent adoption.

In an era where resources are scarce and the need for sustainable solutions is growing, frugal innovation has become an attractive approach to company and product creation. This idea is all about accomplishing more with less, not only in terms of money but also in terms of effectively using resources like time, energy, and materials. It contradicts the conventional story of innovation, which frequently depends on large sums of money and sophisticated technologies. Rather, frugal innovation emphasizes cost, accessibility, and simplicity; this makes it particularly pertinent in developing economies where limitations serve as catalysts rather than as impediments to invention.

The ability to produce high-quality goods and services within budgetary, material, or infrastructure limits is known as frugal innovation, and it has become increasingly popular in a variety of fields, such as business, economics, and sustainable development. Frugal innovation is a powerful approach to solving the global concerns of affordability, accessibility, and sustainability. Its origins lie in practices seen in emerging nations, where scarcity frequently spurs creativity and invention.

Frugal innovation is based on the idea of accomplishing more with less, or seeing limitations as possibilities rather than roadblocks. This strategy makes necessary goods and services available to underprivileged groups worldwide, which not only encourages inventiveness but also democratizes invention. Three key elements are at the heart of frugal innovation: simplicity in design, cost efficiency, and flexibility to a variety of socioeconomic and cultural circumstances.

The field of frugal innovation is dynamic and diversified, shaped by a variety of contextual elements including cultural norms, legal frameworks, and socioeconomic realities. Entrepreneurial endeavours that prioritize agile development, fast prototyping, and scalable solutions that are specially designed to address regional need are frequently the source of successful inexpensive inventions. The strategic benefit of inexpensive innovation in attaining market penetration and promoting sustainable development is highlighted by case studies of trailblazing frugal innovators such as Tata Nano and Aravind Eye Care.

Frugal innovation has inherent challenges, despite its potential. Critical difficulties requiring sophisticated tactics and cooperative efforts from all stakeholders include assuring sustainable scalability, negotiating complicated intellectual property landscapes, and maintaining quality standards while minimizing costs. Furthermore, improving the efficacy and scalability of thrifty innovations is made easier and harder by the incorporation of digital technologies.

Frugal innovation provides a unusual viewpoint in a world where invention is frequently connected to costly resources and technology. This mindset, which emphasizes innovation, resourcefulness, and simplicity, has the ability to completely change the way we approach problem-solving. Finding creative methods to accomplish more with less is the essence of frugal innovation, which has the ability to solve some of the most important problems of the day. Frugal innovation has the ability to drastically affect the society we live in, from combating poverty and inequality to addressing environmental degradation and climate change.

The academic discussion around frugal innovation has been gaining relevance in both emerging and advanced economies (Agarwal and Brem, 2017; Agarwal et al., 2017; Crisp, 2014; Lim and Fujimoto, 2019; Melkas et al., 2019; Pisoni et al., 2018). Frugal innovation is understood as the process of reducing complexity and costs during the design and development of smart solutions (product/services) to meet the needs of low-income customers (Zeschky et al., 2011) and generate institutional change in their societies (Karnani, 2007). Frugal innovations have been supported by an inclusive approach of contributing with social innovations to the development of new products/services that meet societal needs (Chataway et al., 2014; Lorentzen, 2010; Murray et al., 2010).

Stimulating frugal innovations requires building up strategic capabilities throughout the various university dimensions (individual, research group, faculty, or university), in order to ultimately institutionalize social and frugal innovation logics within the mission of universities (Benneworth and Cunha, 2015; Rasmussen and Borch, 2010).According to Hossain et al. (2016, p.113), FI is a resource-scarce solution that has been developed and used under financial, technological, and material or other resource constraints, yet it is good enough to meet the needs of underserved customers who would otherwise be un-able to afford the existing products and services. FI has emerged as a solution to social challenges (Hossain et al., 2021), and many aspects of FI link to sustainability (Albert, 2019).

According to Gul, et al., (2021), frugality is a formative construct that encompasses four dimensions: basic quality, cost of consumption, simplicity, and sustainability thus uplifting the future strategies the mission of this book chapter is to highlight the context of simplicity, sustainability optimizing the future resources. Frugal innovation is the process of developing low-cost products, methods, and designs that are affordable to low-income consumers. Frugal innovations are often simple, built by the people who need them most, and use fewer resources than alternative products. They are often created in resource-constrained environments, such as developing countries, and are often built with locally sourced materials. The concern of this chapter is to highlight the major parameters of frugal innovation with entrepreneurial issues and taking the challenges into consideration.

The conceptual framework presented in this research creates a structured model by combining the insights and knowledge already in existence. The framework describes the essential elements of frugal innovation, points out important problems and difficulties, suggests clever ways to get around obstacles, and suggests future avenues of inquiry to further the discipline. The five aspects and various models in this framework are intended to provide a thorough guide for researchers, practitioners, and policymakers who wish to use frugal innovation to promote inclusive growth and sustainable development on a global scale. This is achieved by methodically organizing the multifaceted dimensions of frugal innovation.

FRUGAL INNOVATION

Frugal entrepreneurs explore untrodden paths in resource constrained environments where institutional voids, weak intellectual property protection and a lack of support structures are commonplace (Mair et al., 2012). Frugal innovation is defined as the creation of high-quality products and services under constraints of cost, material, or infrastructure, typically targeting underserved populations (Zeschky et al., 2011; Bhatti, 2012). Its core characteristics include cost optimization, simplicity in design, and adaptability to diverse contexts (George et al., 2016).

Efficient and effective innovative ways and solutions are mandatory to solve existing complex issues (Mushtaq, et al., 2021), and Frugal Innovation is a way to accomplish this goal. Tunio, et al., (2021) suggest considering the following three criteria to define frugal innovation: substantial cost reduction, concentration on core functionalities, and optimized performance level. Policymakers largely ignore the consumers within sustainable innovation. To address poverty at the grassroots level, Shaikh, et al., (2021) argue that the market-based approach has proven challenging when serving low-income customers, whereas a sustainable business model approach has shown promising results. Frugality is also an important issue for western countries, however (Aurangzeb, et al., 2021). It is widely accepted that innovation diffuses from the developed to the developing countries, from high-income customers to the low-income ones (Rogers &Greenhalgh, 2010). FIs, in contrast, diffuse in the opposite direction. Tunio and Shaikh, (2020) argue that the diffusion of FIs mainly shows four patterns. They label them as local, proximity, distance, and global diffusion. In general, FIs diffuse from low income customers to high-income ones, from developing countries to developed ones. However, before reaching the more developed countries, they diffuse through neighbouring or distant countries with similar socioeconomic settings. When an innovation is successfully used in developing countries and then trickles up to developed countries, it is called reverse innovation. Diffusion is defined as the process through which an innovation spreads over time through markets, and it depends on several factors. Both individual and cultural factors are important for an innovation's diffusion. We know that advertising plays an important role in diffusing new products. Our extensive search and review of the extant literature reveal that studies into the diffusion of FIs and similar innovations in the context of developing countries are largely absent (Shaikh, and Tunio, 2020).

Entrepreneurial Strategies

Frugal innovation is increasingly recognized as a strategic approach for startups and corporations alike to achieve competitive advantage through rapid prototyping, agile development, and cost-effective scaling (Iansiti and Levien, 2004; Radjou et al., 2012). Case studies of successful frugal innovators like Aravind Eye Care and Tata Nano illustrate effective entrepreneurial strategies (Govindarajan and Trimble, 2012).

Impact on Sustainability

The intersection of frugal innovation and sustainability is explored in terms of resource efficiency, environmental impact, and socio-economic benefits (Schaltegger and Lüdeke-Freund, 2011; Michelini and Fiorentino, 2012). Frugal innovations often promote sustainable practices by reducing waste and energy consumption.

Challenges and Risks

Critical assessments acknowledge challenges such as maintaining quality standards, navigating intellectual property rights, and scaling amidst resource constraints (Brem and Wolfram, 2014; Radjou et al., 2015). These challenges highlight the need for nuanced strategies and regulatory support.

Figure 1. 1-5'aspects of sustainability (Author)

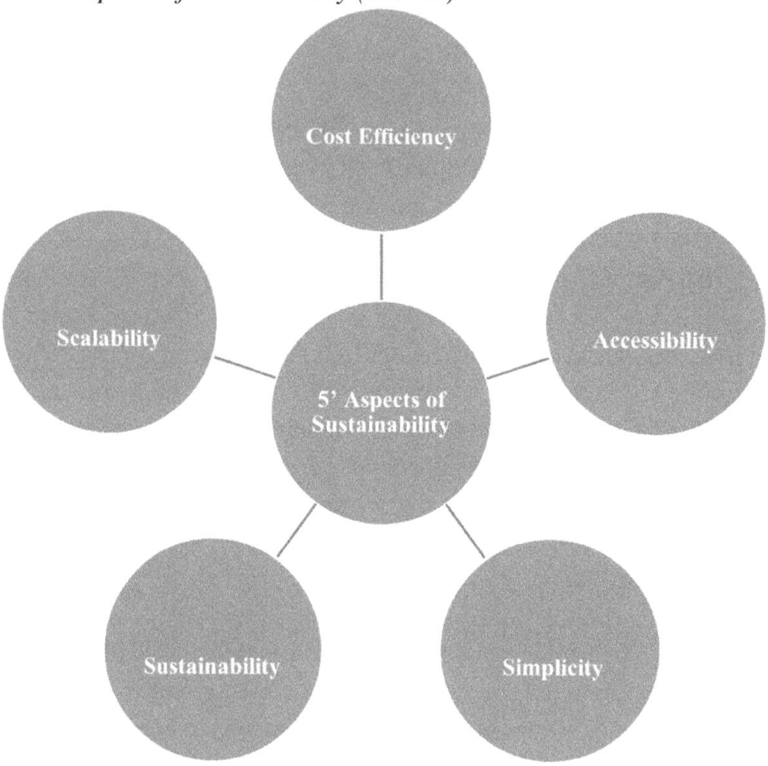

Cost Efficiency: The primary goal is to minimize costs without compromising on quality. This often involves rethinking design, materials, and production processes.

Accessibility: Frugal innovation aims to make products and services accessible to a broader audience, including those at the bottom of the economic pyramid.

Simplicity: Solutions are designed to be simple, easy to use, and maintain, ensuring they can be adopted by individuals with varying levels of technical expertise.

Sustainability: Often, frugal innovations focus on sustainability, utilizing local resources and environmentally friendly practices.

Scalability: These innovations are designed to be scalable, allowing them to be adapted and expanded to meet growing demand.

LITERATURE REVIEW

Frugal innovation advocates the idea of being innovative while simultaneously saving resources (Pisoni et al., 2018). At first, frugal innovation was viewed as an innovative approach to generating new applications, and it even allowed the creation of previously unexplored or unserved markets in the promising low-end market segment (e.g. Farooq, 2017; Leliveld and Knorringa, 2017; Tiwari et al., 2016b; Weyrauch and Herstatt, 2016a). Some of these researchers suggest attributes that consist of developing products and services for substantially lower costs, offering limited features, ease of use, and good value-for-money, with a focus on low-income customers (Agarwal and Brem, 2012; Bhatti, 2012; Brem and Ivens, 2013; Economist, 2009; Zeschky et al., 2011b). However, the development of the literature showed that frugal innovation is not only for the bottom of the pyramid (Hossain, 2018a; Pisoni et al., 2018; Tiwari et al., 2016b). Companies from developed countries are adopting frugal innovations to reach unserved resource-constrained markets or those customers worried about waste excess (Rosca et al., 2017b).

Bound and Thornton (2012) defined frugal innovations as a unique innovation strategy that responds to resource constraints—financial, material, or institutional—and turns them into advantages. According to Pawlowski (2013), the goal of frugal innovation is to develop highly scalable solutions with core functionality at lower prices.

Frugal innovation is a decade-old concept gaining increasing prominence in academic and practitioner-based discourse. It is defined in many ways, including a popular and comprehensive definition: "a resource-scarce solution (i.e., product, service, process, or business model) that is designed and implemented despite financial, technological, material or other resource constraints, whereby the outcome is significantly cheaper than competitive offerings (if available) and is good enough to meet the basic needs of customers who would otherwise remain under served" (Hossain et al., 2016, p. 133). Technical prowess alone is not sufficient for sustainable innovation, but FIs integrate both prowess and sustainability (Annala et al., 2018; Endres et al., 2022; Molina-Maturano et al., 2020; Pisoni et al., 2018) in fulfilling the needs of low-income customers in developing countries (D'Angelo and Magnusson, 2020; Levanen ¨ et al., 2022).

FI has led to frugal entrepreneurship, which involves creating a venture based on frugal products (Hossain and Sarkar, 2021). Despite the criticism, FI is widely accepted as a promising concept for developing affordable products for underserved customers, particularly those in developing countries, thereby contributing to Sustainable Development in rural areas (Pansera and Owen, 2015).Frugal output refers to the final delivery – the final product or service – and its features, such as robustness, simplicity, adequate quality, sustainability, proper packaging and low price (Khan, 2016; Farooq, 2017; Weyrauch and Herstatt, 2017). Frugal output also considers the affordability of products and services and can be understood as the recognition of consumer needs and how much they will pay for products and services (Borchardt et al.,2018).

Frugal innovation includes new processes, business models, products, and services. This decreases the negative impact on the environment, requires minimal usage of resources, and is affordable (Gupta & Wang, 2008). Extensive literature concurs with the significant importance of entrepreneurial bricolage in pursuing opportunities in a resource-constrained environment (An, Zhao, Cao, Zhang, & Liu, 2018; Witell et al., 2017).

Khavandkar et al. (2023) Provides comprehensive overview and future research directions for frugal innovation. Gupta and Sharma (2022) Identifies key models and adoption factors of frugal innovation across different contexts. Rao and Abraham (2021) positively impacts firm performance through cost savings and customer satisfaction. Singh and Kapoor (2020) indicates econometric analysis that Frugal innovation contributes significantly to economic growth in emerging markets.

Prabhu and Roberts (2019) Proposes strategies for scaling frugal innovations while maintaining affordability and quality. Rai and Singh (2018) suggested that Frugal innovations contribute to sustainable development by promoting resource efficiency and social equity.

According with Kumar and Lim (2017) suggested that Mobile money innovations have transformed financial inclusion in emerging markets. Schumacher et al. (2016) suggested that Business model innovation can significantly reduce water and energy consumption in manufacturing. Kumar et al. (2024) Provides a comprehensive overview of frugal innovation and proposes future research directions. Lee and Choi (2023) Studies that Frugal innovations contribute significantly to achieving Sustainable Development Goals (SDGs) by promoting resource efficiency and social equity. According with Das and Dutta (2022) entrepreneurs in emerging markets use frugal innovation to achieve rapid growth and market penetration. Sharma and Mishra (2021) Proposes a framework for integrating digital technologies into frugal innovation practices to enhance scalability and impact. Verma and Sood (2020) stated that Frugal innovations in renewable energy enhance access and affordability, contributing to sustainable development. Agarwal et al. (2019) demonstrate effective healthcare innovations tailored for low-income countries, improving access and affordability.

DEFINITIONS

Table 1. Definitions of frugal innovation

Definitions of frugal innovation	Reference
Frugal innovation literature has several overlaps with sustainable entrepreneurship outcomes.	Shahid, M. S., Hossain, M., Shahid, S., & Anwar, T. (2023).
Frugal innovation as a source of sustainable entrepreneurship to tackle social and environmental challenges	Journal of Cleaner Production,406,137050.
Gupta argued that 'frugal innovation is a new management philosophy, which integrates specific needs of the bottom of the pyramid markets as a starting point and works backward to develop appropriate solutions which may be significantly different from existing solutions designed to address needs of up market segments'.	
FI as having, '...low to medium sophistication, medium sustainability, and medium emerging market orientation'	Brem and Wolfram

BENEFITS OF FRUGAL INNOVATION

Frugal innovation offers several benefits:

Affordability: Enables access to essential goods and services for low-income populations (Govindarajan and Trimble, 2012).

Inclusive Growth: Facilitates economic participation and social inclusion by addressing unmet needs (Rai and Singh, 2018).

Sustainability: Promotes resource efficiency and reduces environmental impact through innovative practices (Schumacher et al., 2016).

Cost Savings: FI reduces expenses, benefiting both consumers and organizations.

Inclusive Growth: Reaching underserved populations.

Market Expansion: Tapping into new markets.

Environmental Impact: Minimizing resource use.

DIMENSIONS OF FRUGAL INNOVATION

Figure 2. Dimensions of frugal innovation (Author)

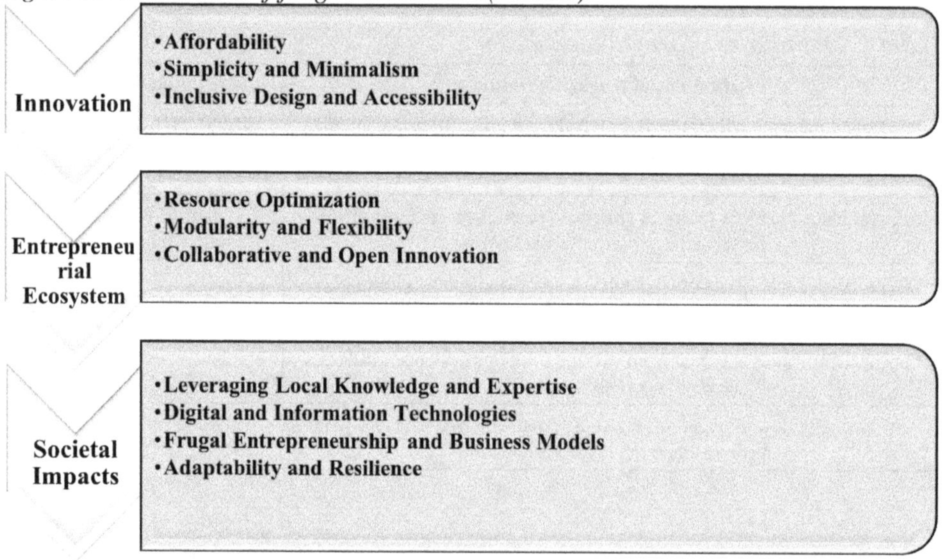

Affordability: At the core of frugal innovation is the emphasis on affordability, ensuring that products and services are accessible to a wide range of consumers, particularly those in low-income or resource-constrained environments.

Simplicity and Minimalism: Frugal innovations often prioritize simplicity and minimalism in design and functionality, focusing on essential features and functionality to reduce complexity and costs. This approach not only lowers production and maintenance costs but also enhances usability and accessibility for end-users.

Resource Optimization: Frugal innovators leverage existing resources, materials, and infrastructure creatively to minimize waste and maximize efficiency. This may involve repurposing or recycling materials, optimizing energy and water usage, or adapting technologies to local contexts to minimize resource consumption and environmental impact.

Modularity and Flexibility: Frugal innovations are often designed with modularity and flexibility in mind, allowing for easy customization, repair, and scalability.

Leveraging Local Knowledge and Expertise: Frugal innovators tap into local knowledge, skills, and resources to co-create solutions that are tailored to the specific needs and contexts of target communities. This involves collaborating with local stakeholders, including end-users, entrepreneurs, and community organizations, to ensure relevance and acceptance of innovations.

Digital and Information Technologies: Frugal innovation harnesses the power of digital and information technologies to overcome traditional barriers to access and affordability.

Inclusive Design and Accessibility: Frugal innovators prioritize inclusive design principles to ensure that products and services are accessible to diverse user groups, including people with disabilities, elderly individuals, and those with limited literacy or technical skills. This involves considering diverse user needs, preferences, and constraints throughout the design process.

Collaborative and Open Innovation: Frugal innovation thrives on collaboration and open innovation models that involve sharing knowledge, resources, and expertise across organizational boundaries. Open-source software, crowdsourcing platforms, and collaborative networks enable innovators to leverage collective intelligence and accelerate the development and diffusion of frugal solutions.

Frugal Entrepreneurship and Business Models: Frugal innovation extends beyond product and technology development to encompass innovative business models and entrepreneurial approaches that create value for both customers and society. This may involve adopting lean start up methodologies, social entrepreneurship models, or inclusive business models that integrate social and environmental objectives with financial sustainability.

Adaptability and Resilience: Frugal innovations demonstrate adaptability and resilience in the face of dynamic socio-economic and environmental conditions. They are designed to withstand uncertainties and shocks, including changes in market demand, regulatory environments, and resource availability, while remaining responsive to evolving user needs and preferences.

PROPOSED MODEL

Figure 3. Conceptual framework (Author)

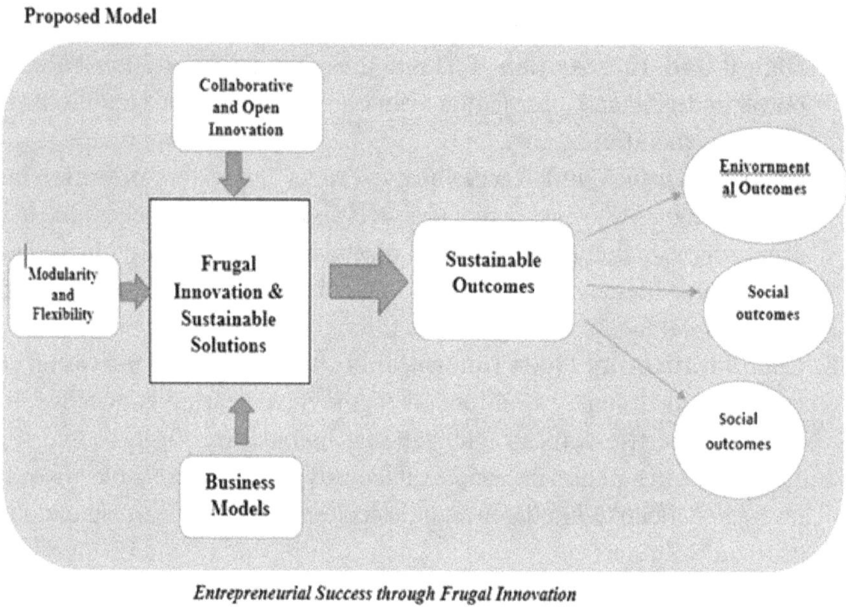

Frugal Innovation and Economic Development

The term "frugal innovation," also known as "constraint-based innovation," "jugaad" in India, or "shanzhai" in China (Wooldridge, 2010), refers to a broad category of diverse activities spanning multiple industries, including methods, procedures, and results (Bhatti and Ventresca, 2012, 2013). Therefore, it is better to think of frugal innovation as a new innovation mentality, method, and outcome that takes use of institutional gaps and resource limitations to refute costly R&D expenditures while benefiting underserved consumers. According to Bhatti and Ventresca (2013), frugal innovation is essentially the means and ends of doing more for more people while using less.

With the likely impact of natural disasters being felt in the form of huge losses due to flooding, storms, forest fires and alarming shrinkage of the natural pole caps, forest areas, due to global warming, the pressure to effectively use the available ecological resources in a most beneficial manner for the sustenance, growth and current consumption is likely to increase in the future (Ravichandran, R., Kulshrestha, P., & Nadig, A., 2022). Frugal innovation stands as a potent force for economic development, particularly in regions grappling with limited resources and infrastructural constraints. Its significance lies in its ability to render essential products and services accessible and affordable to a broader swath of society, including those marginalized by financial barriers. By focusing on simplicity and cost-effectiveness, frugal innovations expand market opportunities, fostering inclusive growth and propelling individuals into the formal economy. Moreover, they fuel grassroots entrepreneurship, generating employment opportunities and bolstering local economies.

First, to achieve successful societal engagement, entrepreneurial universities must adopt leadership and governance systems that promote an organizational culture oriented towards frugal innovation (Heaton et al., 2019; Leih and Teece, 2016). It implies including social partners, by giving them a voice on the university board/committees, or at least to introduce the stakeholders' vision as part of the university strategies (Benneworth and Jongbloed, 2010; Natalicchio et al., 2018). Recent research suggests that a stronger engagement of stakeholders from civil society democratizes the decision-making process; results in closer alignment between scientific priorities and social needs; accelerates the diffusion of research outputs; and enhances trust and transparency (Cope et al., 2018; Olsen et al., 2016; Willyard et al., 2018).

Although the involvement of multiple agents is widely recognized as a key factor for the success of frugal innovations (Altmann and Engberg, 2016; Annala et al., 2018; Leliveld and Knorringa, 2018; Martı´nez et al., 2018; Tiwari and Herstatt, 2012), the contribution of universities on frugal innovation is underrepresented in the existing literature (Bayuo et al., 2020; McKelvey and Zaring, 2018). Over the past two decades, the literature has legitimised the significant contributions of entrepreneurial universities through the generation of human capital, graduate/academic entrepreneurs, as well as the dissemination/commercialisation of knowledge that contributes to strengthening societal, economic and technological development (Audretsch, 2014; Guerrero and Urbano, 2012; Guerrero et al., 2015; Guerrero et al., 2016a; Klofsten et al., 2019).

CHALLENGES TO FRUGAL INNOVATION

The real challenge for frugal innovation is to introduce *something new or different* (innovating) whilst being *sparing* with resources (frugal). Frugal innovation and entrepreneurship, while holding significant promise for economic development and social inclusion, also face several challenges that need to be addressed. These challenges include:

Limited Access to Capital: Frugal entrepreneurs often struggle to access traditional financing due to their unconventional business models or lack of collateral. This limits their ability to scale their ventures or invest in research and development.

Regulatory Barriers: Complex regulatory frameworks and bureaucratic hurdles can impede the growth of frugal ventures, particularly in sectors such as healthcare and energy where stringent regulations are in place.

Intellectual Property Issues: Protecting intellectual property rights can be challenging in frugal innovation, especially in markets where enforcement mechanisms are weak. This may deter entrepreneurs from investing in innovation for fear of imitation or infringement.

Infrastructure and Logistics: Inadequate infrastructure, such as unreliable electricity or poor transportation networks, can hinder the distribution and delivery of frugal products and services, increasing costs and limiting market reach.

Skills and Capacity Building: Frugal entrepreneurship requires a unique set of skills, including resourcefulness, adaptability, and a deep understanding of local contexts. However, there is often a lack of training and capacity-building programs tailored to the needs of frugal entrepreneurs.

Market Fragmentation: Frugal ventures may struggle to achieve economies of scale due to fragmented markets and heterogeneous consumer preferences, making it challenging to achieve profitability and sustainability.

Resistance to Change: Frugal innovation may face resistance from established players in the market who are invested in traditional business models or technologies. Overcoming inertia and convincing stakeholders of the value proposition of frugal solutions can be a significant challenge.

Cultural and Social Barriers: Sociocultural factors may pose challenges to the adoption of frugal innovations, particularly in conservative or traditional societies where new ideas or technologies are met with scepticism or resistance.

Quality and Reliability Concerns: Frugal products and services are often perceived as inferior in quality or reliability compared to their more expensive counterparts. Building trust and credibility in the market can be a challenge for frugal entrepreneurs.

Long-term Sustainability: Ensuring the long-term sustainability of frugal ventures beyond the initial stages of innovation and entrepreneurship poses a significant challenge. Balancing affordability with profitability while maintaining social and environmental impact requires careful management and strategic planning.

CRITICISM OR DRAWBACKS OF FRUGAL INNOVATION

Here are some arguments that could be made from a sceptical perspective:

Quality Compromises: Critics may argue that the relentless focus on affordability in frugal innovation could lead to compromises in product or service quality. This could result in substandard goods that fail to meet consumer expectations or even pose risks to health and safety, particularly in critical sectors like healthcare or infrastructure.

Sustainability Concerns: Frugal innovations, while often celebrated for their resource efficiency, may not always prioritize long-term environmental sustainability. Rapid scaling and mass production of frugal products could exacerbate issues such as resource depletion, pollution, and waste generation, particularly if not accompanied by stringent environmental regulations and oversight.

Exploitation of Labour: Frugal entrepreneurship in some cases might rely on low-cost labour or informal employment arrangements, leading to exploitation of workers and perpetuating socioeconomic inequalities. This could undermine efforts to promote fair labour practices and decent work conditions, particularly in industries with high labour intensity and low-profit margins.

Market Saturation and Commodification: Critics may argue that the proliferation of frugal innovations could lead to market saturation and commodification, eroding the uniqueness and value proposition of these solutions over time. This could result in a race to the bottom in terms of pricing and quality, ultimately undermining the sustainability of frugal ventures and stifling innovation.

Dependency on External Support: Frugal entrepreneurs often rely on external support, such as grants, subsidies, or philanthropic funding, to sustain their ventures. Critics may question the long-term viability of frugal innovations if they are unable to become financially self-sustaining or if external support dries up, leading to a reliance on aid rather than fostering genuine economic development.

Limited Scalability and Impact: While frugal innovations may demonstrate success in localized contexts or niche markets, critics may argue that their scalability and broader societal impact remain limited. Scaling frugal ventures to reach larger populations or address systemic challenges may require overcoming significant barriers, including regulatory constraints, market fragmentation, and entrenched interests.

Ethical Dilemmas: Frugal entrepreneurship may raise ethical dilemmas, particularly in contexts where businesses operate in resource-constrained environments with vulnerable populations. Critics may question whether frugal entrepreneurs adequately consider the social and ethical implications of their ventures, including issues related to cultural sensitivity, community engagement, and unintended consequences.

Innovation Stagnation: In some cases, the pursuit of frugality in innovation could stifle creativity and innovation by prioritizing cost-cutting measures over breakthrough advancements. Critics may argue that the relentless focus on affordability may discourage investment in research and development or discourage risk-taking and experimentation, ultimately hindering long-term progress and competitiveness.

MAIN FOCUS OF THE CHAPTER

Frugal Innovations Comparison with Other Innovation Concepts

According to Bahadur & Doczi (2016), most aspects of frugal innovation may be classified into three categories: degree of performance, core functionality, and cost reduction. Based on this finding they developed three conditions for economic innovation: a large decrease in expenditures, a focus on only the necessary activities, and an ideal level of performance (Bahadur & Doczi, 2016). If an invention fits all three criteria at the same time it should be dubbed frugal. These three requirements offer a more complete picture of how economic innovation works (Dhraief et al., 2018). For instance, all three requirements must be met at the same time, which may be tough. This has practical implications: while creating cost-cutting innovations, it is vital to analyse all three aspects to establish precisely what makes a new product or service less expensive. Agarwal et al. (2017) use terminology like indigenous innovation, Gandhian innovation, reverse innovation, jugaad innovation, grassroots innovation, catalytic innovation, and constraint-based innovation to distinguish frugal innovation from similar concepts (Bahadur & Doczi,2016).

Figure 4. Types of innovations (Costa, 2018)

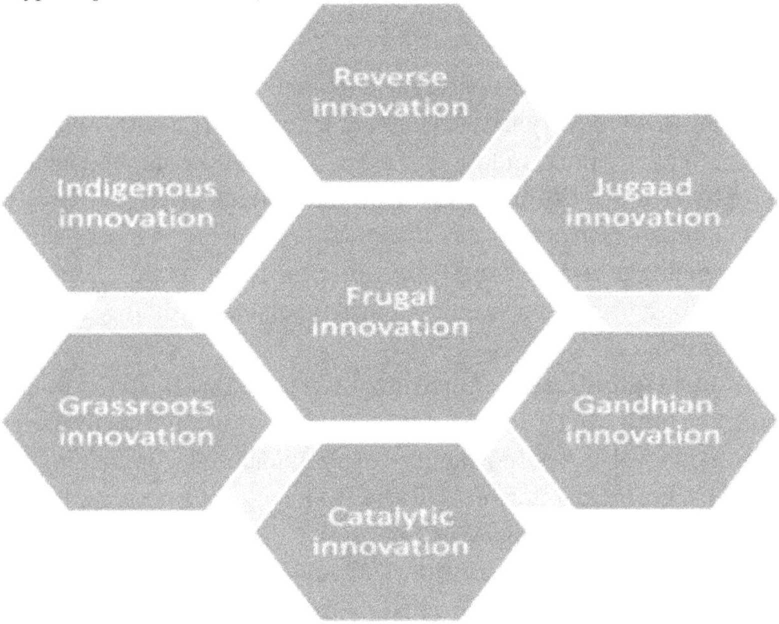

Source: Costa (2018)

ISSUES, CONTROVERSIES AND PROBLEMS AIM OF THE PROPOSAL

This study aims to review the frugal innovation and its paradigm shift for entrepreneurship in order to understand the main sources, characteristics, and aspects, as well as the input, success factors that dwelves with frugal innovations (FIs).

OBJECTIVES OF THE PROPOSAL

To provide an overview of the concept of frugal innovation and its evolution.
To study the key principles, characteristics, opportunities and challenges associated with frugal innovation.
To discuss the implications of frugal innovation for entrepreneurs, businesses, and society.

MAJOR PARAMETERS /DIMENSIONS OF FRUGAL INNOVATION

Affordability: At the core of frugal innovation is the emphasis on affordability, ensuring that products and services are accessible to a wide range of consumers, particularly those in low-income or resource-constrained environments.

Simplicity and Minimalism: Frugal innovations often prioritize simplicity and minimalism in design and functionality, focusing on essential features and functionality to reduce complexity and costs. This approach not only lowers production and maintenance costs but also enhances usability and accessibility for end-users.

Resource Optimization: Frugal innovators leverage existing resources, materials, and infrastructure creatively to minimize waste and maximize efficiency. This may involve repurposing or recycling materials, optimizing energy and water usage, or adapting technologies to local contexts to minimize resource consumption and environmental impact.

Modularity and Flexibility: Frugal innovations are often designed with modularity and flexibility in mind, allowing for easy customization, repair, and scalability.

Leveraging Local Knowledge and Expertise: Frugal innovators tap into local knowledge, skills, and resources to co-create solutions that are tailored to the specific needs and contexts of target communities. This involves collaborating with local stakeholders, including end-users, entrepreneurs, and community organizations, to ensure relevance and acceptance of innovations.

Digital and Information Technologies: Frugal innovation harnesses the power of digital and information technologies to overcome traditional barriers to access and affordability.

Inclusive Design and Accessibility: Frugal innovators prioritize inclusive design principles to ensure that products and services are accessible to diverse user groups, including people with disabilities, elderly individuals, and those with limited literacy or technical skills. This involves considering diverse user needs, preferences, and constraints throughout the design process.

Collaborative and Open Innovation: Frugal innovation thrives on collaboration and open innovation models that involve sharing knowledge, resources, and expertise across organizational boundaries. Open-source software, crowdsourcing platforms, and collaborative networks enable innovators to leverage collective intelligence and accelerate the development and diffusion of frugal solutions.

Frugal Entrepreneurship and Business Models: Frugal innovation extends beyond product and technology development to encompass innovative business models and entrepreneurial approaches that create value for both customers and society. This may involve adopting lean startup methodologies, social entrepreneurship models, or inclusive business models that integrate social and environmental objectives with financial sustainability.

Adaptability and Resilience: Frugal innovations demonstrate adaptability and resilience in the face of dynamic socio-economic and environmental conditions. They are designed to withstand uncertainties and shocks, including changes in market demand, regulatory environments, and resource availability, while remaining responsive to evolving user needs and preferences.

FRUGAL INNOVATION AND ECONOMIC DEVELOPMENT

With the likely impact of natural disasters being felt in the form of huge losses due to flooding, storms, forest fires and alarming shrinkage of the natural pole caps, forest areas, due to global warming, the pressure to effectively use the available ecological resources in a most beneficial manner for the sustenance, growth and current consumption is likely to increase in the future (Ravichandran, R., Kulshrestha, P., & Nadig, A., 2022). Frugal innovation stands as a potent force for economic development, particularly in regions grappling with limited resources and infrastructural constraints. Its significance lies in its ability to render essential products and services accessible and affordable to a broader swath of society, including those marginalized by financial barriers. By focusing on simplicity and cost-effectiveness, frugal innovations expand market opportunities, fostering inclusive growth and propelling individuals into the formal economy. Moreover, they fuel grassroots entrepreneurship, generating employment opportunities and bolstering local economies. These innovations often prioritize sustainability and resource efficiency, mitigating environmental degradation while driving economic progress. For instance, initiatives like M-Pesa in Kenya have revolutionized financial inclusion, while companies like d.light Design provide affordable solar energy solutions, both enhancing livelihoods and fostering economic resilience. Similarly, innovative healthcare models like those pioneered by Aravind Eye Care System in India offer high-quality services at a fraction of the cost, improving health outcomes and reducing the financial burden on patients. Such examples underscore the transformative potential of frugal innovation in unlocking economic opportunities and advancing societal well-being.

CHALLENGES TO FRUGAL INNOVATION

The real challenge for frugal innovation is to introduce *something new or different* (innovating) whilst being *sparing* with resources (frugal).

Frugal innovation and entrepreneurship, while holding significant promise for economic development and social inclusion, also face several challenges that need to be addressed. These challenges include:

Limited Access to Capital: Frugal entrepreneurs often struggle to access traditional financing due to their unconventional business models or lack of collateral. This limits their ability to scale their ventures or invest in research and development.

Regulatory Barriers: Complex regulatory frameworks and bureaucratic hurdles can impede the growth of frugal ventures, particularly in sectors such as healthcare and energy where stringent regulations are in place.

Intellectual Property Issues: Protecting intellectual property rights can be challenging in frugal innovation, especially in markets where enforcement mechanisms are weak. This may deter entrepreneurs from investing in innovation for fear of imitation or infringement.

Infrastructure and Logistics: Inadequate infrastructure, such as unreliable electricity or poor transportation networks, can hinder the distribution and delivery of frugal products and services, increasing costs and limiting market reach.

Skills and Capacity Building: Frugal entrepreneurship requires a unique set of skills, including resourcefulness, adaptability, and a deep understanding of local contexts. However, there is often a lack of training and capacity-building programs tailored to the needs of frugal entrepreneurs.

Market Fragmentation: Frugal ventures may struggle to achieve economies of scale due to fragmented markets and heterogeneous consumer preferences, making it challenging to achieve profitability and sustainability.

Resistance to Change: Frugal innovation may face resistance from established players in the market who are invested in traditional business models or technologies. Overcoming inertia and convincing stakeholders of the value proposition of frugal solutions can be a significant challenge.

Cultural and Social Barriers: Sociocultural factors may pose challenges to the adoption of frugal innovations, particularly in conservative or traditional societies where new ideas or technologies are met with skepticism or resistance.

Quality and Reliability Concerns: Frugal products and services are often perceived as inferior in quality or reliability compared to their more expensive counterparts. Building trust and credibility in the market can be a challenge for frugal entrepreneurs.

Long-term Sustainability: Ensuring the long-term sustainability of frugal ventures beyond the initial stages of innovation and entrepreneurship poses a significant challenge. Balancing affordability with profitability while maintaining social and environmental impact requires careful management and strategic planning.

Maintaining Quality Standards: Balancing cost reduction with maintaining adequate product/service quality (Brem and Wolfram, 2014).

Scaling and Replication: Challenges in scaling innovations beyond initial markets while maintaining affordability and effectiveness (Mishra and George, 2018).

Intellectual Property Rights (IPR): Navigating complex IPR landscapes and ensuring fair distribution of benefits (Radjou et al., 2015).

SOLUTIONS AND RECOMMENDATIONS

There are following solution to overcome the challenges for sustaining in frugal innovation.

Collaborative Partnerships: Engaging with local communities, governments, and NGOs to enhance distribution networks and market reach (Prabhu and Robertson, 2019).

Agile Development: Iterative prototyping and rapid testing to refine products/services based on user feedback (Iansiti and Levien, 2004).

Digital Integration: Leveraging digital technologies (e.g., AI, IoT) to optimize processes and enhance scalability (Sharma and Mishra, 2024).

Collaboration: Engage with local communities, NGOs, and governments.

Design Thinking: Iterative, user-centric approach.

Modularity: Building solutions in components for flexibility.

Frugal Mind-set: Prioritize simplicity and efficiency.

Figure 5. Solution and recommendations (Author)

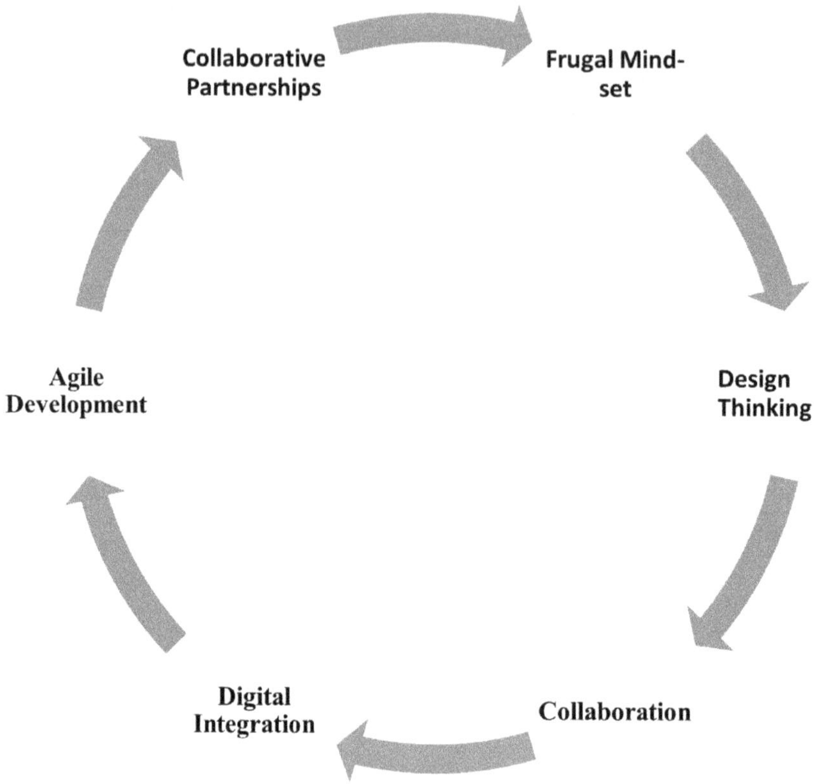

CRITICISM OR DRAWBACKS OF FRUGAL INNOVATION

Here are some arguments that could be made from a sceptical perspective:

Quality Compromises: Critics may argue that the relentless focus on affordability in frugal innovation could lead to compromises in product or service quality. This could result in substandard goods that fail to meet consumer expectations or even pose risks to health and safety, particularly in critical sectors like healthcare or infrastructure.

Sustainability Concerns: Frugal innovations, while often celebrated for their resource efficiency, may not always prioritize long-term environmental sustainability. Rapid scaling and mass production of frugal products could exacerbate issues such as resource depletion, pollution, and waste generation, particularly if not accompanied by stringent environmental regulations and oversight.

Exploitation of Labor: Frugal entrepreneurship in some cases might rely on low-cost labor or informal employment arrangements, leading to exploitation of workers and perpetuating socioeconomic inequalities. This could undermine efforts to promote fair labor practices and decent work conditions, particularly in industries with high labor intensity and low-profit margins.

Market Saturation and Commodification: Critics may argue that the proliferation of frugal innovations could lead to market saturation and commodification, eroding the uniqueness and value proposition of these solutions over time. This could result in a race to the bottom in terms of pricing and quality, ultimately undermining the sustainability of frugal ventures and stifling innovation.

Dependency on External Support: Frugal entrepreneurs often rely on external support, such as grants, subsidies, or philanthropic funding, to sustain their ventures. Critics may question the long-term viability of frugal innovations if they are unable to become financially self-sustaining or if external support dries up, leading to a reliance on aid rather than fostering genuine economic development.

Limited Scalability and Impact: While frugal innovations may demonstrate success in localized contexts or niche markets, critics may argue that their scalability and broader societal impact remain limited. Scaling frugal ventures to reach larger populations or address systemic challenges may require overcoming significant barriers, including regulatory constraints, market fragmentation, and entrenched interests.

Ethical Dilemmas: Frugal entrepreneurship may raise ethical dilemmas, particularly in contexts where businesses operate in resource-constrained environments with vulnerable populations. Critics may question whether frugal entrepreneurs adequately consider the social and ethical implications of their ventures, including issues related to cultural sensitivity, community engagement, and unintended consequences.

Innovation Stagnation: In some cases, the pursuit of frugality in innovation could stifle creativity and innovation by prioritizing cost-cutting measures over breakthrough advancements. Critics may argue that the relentless focus on affordability may discourage investment in research and development or discourage risk-taking and experimentation, ultimately hindering long-term progress and competitiveness.

TARGET AUDIENCE

This chapter is intended for entrepreneurs, business leaders, policymakers, researchers, and students interested in understanding the concept of frugal innovation and its implications for entrepreneurial endeavours. It will serve as a valuable resource for those seeking insights into innovative strategies for navigating resource constraints and driving sustainable growth in today's dynamic business environment.

LIMITATIONS AND FUTURE RESEARCH DIRECTIONS

1. Scaling and Replication

Future research should explore strategies for scaling frugal innovations beyond initial markets while maintaining affordability and quality (Mont, 2020). Comparative studies across different sectors and regions can provide insights into effective scaling practices.

2. Innovation Ecosystems

Investigating the role of innovation ecosystems—comprising entrepreneurs, investors, government agencies, and NGOs—in fostering frugal innovation is crucial (Mohan and Banerjee, 2020). Understanding ecosystem dynamics can facilitate supportive policies and collaborations.

3. Digital Technologies

The integration of digital technologies such as AI, IoT, and blockchain presents opportunities to enhance the effectiveness and scalability of frugal innovations (O'Neil and Dubé, 2018). Research should explore the impact of digitalization on frugal innovation processes and outcomes.

4. Impact Measurement

Developing robust frameworks for assessing the socio-economic impact of frugal innovations is essential (Verganti and Öberg, 2013). Metrics should capture improvements in access to essential services, income generation, and environmental sustainability.

5. Policy and Governance

Examining the role of policy frameworks and governance structures in supporting or hindering frugal innovation initiatives can inform policy recommendations (Bhatti and Ventresca, 2013). Comparative policy studies across countries can highlight best practices and regulatory challenges.

SOME BUSINESS MODELS ASSOCIATED WITH FRUGAL INNOVATION:

1. Reverse Innovation Model

Govindarajan, V., & Trimble, C. (2012), This model involves innovating in emerging markets and then scaling those innovations back to developed markets. It emphasizes adapting products or services designed for low-resource settings to serve similar needs in more affluent markets.

2. Low-Cost Business Model

Prahalad, C. K., & Mashelkar, R. A. (2010). Companies under this model focus on reducing costs across the entire value chain, from design to distribution, while maintaining acceptable quality standards. This allows them to offer products and services at significantly lower prices than competitors.

3. Frugal Engineering Model

Bhatti, Y. (2012). Frugal engineering involves simplifying product designs and using locally available materials to create affordable solutions. It emphasizes efficiency, minimalism, and practicality in design and manufacturing.

4. Jugaad Innovation Model

Radjou, N., Prabhu, J., & Ahuja, S. (2012). Originating from India, jugaad innovation refers to improvisational and flexible approaches to problem-solving with limited resources. It emphasizes rapid prototyping, iteration based on user feedback, and finding unconventional solutions.

5. Pay-Per-Use Model

Taneja, S., & Bhushan, B. (2017). This model involves offering products or services on a pay-per-use or subscription basis, which reduces upfront costs for consumers. It aligns the cost of usage with the value derived, making it more accessible to a broader range of customers.

6. Partnership and Co-Creation Model

Weyrauch, T., & Herstatt, C. (2017) This model involves collaborating with various stakeholders, including local communities, NGOs, governments, and other businesses, to co-create solutions that address local needs and leverage local knowledge.

7. Ecosystem-Based Model

Nambisan, S., & Nambisan, P. (2008). How In this model, companies build ecosystems of partners and suppliers to share resources, knowledge, and infrastructure, reducing costs and accelerating innovation cycles.

CONCLUSION

Frugal innovation represents a dynamic field with significant implications for entrepreneurship, sustainability, and inclusive development. By addressing current themes and proposing future research directions, this literature review contributes to advancing our understanding of how frugal innovation can foster economic growth and societal well-being in an increasingly interconnected world.

This study has several limitations. "Frugal innovation" was the sole keyword used to search articles, so some relevant papers may not have been included in this study. This study also considered articles written only in English. FI is dominant in local contexts, especially in developing countries, and valuable publications may exist in languages other than English. Including these non-English publications may well bring a richer understanding of FI. In addition, the search may have overlooked some articles that explored the same phenomenon using different terms, even though a very comprehensive search approach was applied. Considering these limitations and the synthesis of the literature, this study provides research agenda.

Frugal innovation is experiencing a contextual shift and is progressively emerging as a complementary approach to combat the global challenges. Although there is growing interest and efforts to understand, design and develop FIs with the aim of mitigating problems efficiently and effectively, there still remains the challenge of conceptualising and characterising FI due to its significant overlap with other innovation types. But perhaps this is due to the diversity in definition for other concepts which feature in the definition of FI such as sustainability, low income and good-enough. Defining FI as a concept should not deter from focusing on its core aim. Identifying an FI may be best achieved by comparing it to an incumbent alternative, rather than against an ill-defined concept. There is merit in developing a common understanding of FI to support strategies for its successful acceptance and diffusion globally.

In a world marked by growing resource constraints, swift technological advancements, and societal challenges, the concept of frugal innovation appears as a shining example of hope. Through its importance on simplicity, affordability, and flexibility, frugal innovation not only offers practical solutions to pressing problems but also fosters transformative change across business and societal landscape. In conclusion, this chapter will focus on the significance of frugal innovation as a transformative approach in the entrepreneurial background. The chapter will conclude with reflections on the future trajectory of frugal innovation and its implications for entrepreneurship in an ever-changing world.

REFERENCES

Agarwal, N., & Brem, A. (2017). Frugal innovation-past, present, and future. *IEEE Engineering Management Review*, *45*(3), 37–41. DOI: 10.1109/EMR.2017.2734320

Agarwal, N., Grottke, M., Mishra, S., & Brem, A. (2017). A systematic literature review of constraint- based innovations: State of the art and future perspectives. *IEEE Transactions on Engineering Management*, *64*(1), 3–15. DOI: 10.1109/TEM.2016.2620562

Albert, M. (2022). Assessing the sustainability impacts of frugal innovation–A literature review. *Journal of Cleaner Production*, *365*, 132754. DOI: 10.1016/j.jclepro.2022.132754

Altmann, P., & Engberg, R. (2016). Frugal innovation and knowledge transferability. *Research Technology Management*, *59*(1), 48–55. DOI: 10.1080/08956308.2016.1117323

An, W., Zhao, X., Cao, Z., Zhang, J., & Liu, H. (2018). How bricolage drives corporate entrepreneurship: The roles of opportunity identification and learning orientation. *Journal of Product Innovation Management*, *35*(1), 49–65. DOI: 10.1111/jpim.12377

Annala, L., Sarin, A., & Green, J. L. (2018). Co-production of frugal innovation: Case of low cost reverse osmosis water filters in India. *Journal of Cleaner Production*, *171*, S110–S118. DOI: 10.1016/j.jclepro.2016.07.065

Audretsch, D. (2014). From the entrepreneurial university to the university for the entrepreneurial society. *The Journal of Technology Transfer*, *39*(3), 313–321. DOI: 10.1007/s10961-012-9288-1

Baud, I. (2016). Moving towards inclusive development? Recent views on inequalities, frugal innovations, urban geo-technologies, gender and hybrid governance. *European Journal of Development Research*, *28*(2), 119–129. DOI: 10.1057/ejdr.2016.1

Bayuo, B., Chaminade, C., & Go¨ransson, B. (2020). Unpacking the role of universities in the emergence, development and impact of social innovations – a systematic review of the literature. *Technological Forecasting and Social Change*, *155*, 1–11. DOI: 10.1016/j.techfore.2020.120030

Benneworth, P., & Cunha, J. (2015). Universities' contributions to social innovation: Reflections in theory & practice. *European Journal of Innovation Management*, *18*(4), 508–527. DOI: 10.1108/EJIM-10-2013-0099

Benneworth, P., Pinheiro, R., & Sanchez-Barrioluengo, M. (2016). One size does not fit all! New perspectives on the university in the social knowledge economy. *Science & Public Policy*, *43*(6), 731–735. DOI: 10.1093/scipol/scw018

Bhatti, Y. (2012). Frugal innovation: An accessible innovation concept for Africa's social and economic development. *International Journal of Engineering and Science Invention*, *1*(2), 18–27.

Borchardt, M., Pereira, G., Viegas, C., Reolon, D., Xavier, Y. and Battaglia, D. (2018). Providing goods to the base of the pyramid: opportunities for micro, small and medium-sized local producers, *Journal of Small Business Strategy*, Vol. 28 No. 2.

Bound, K., Thornton, I.W., 2012. Our Frugal Future: Lessons from India's Innovation System.

Chataway, J., Hanlin, R., & Kaplinsky, R. (2014). Inclusive innovation: An architecture for policy development. *Innovation and Development*, *4*(1), 33–54. DOI: 10.1080/2157930X.2013.876800

Cope, A. P., Barnes, M., Belson, A., Binks, M., Brockbank, S., Bonachela-Capdevila, F., Carini, C., Fisher, B. A., Goodyear, C. S., Emery, P., Ehrenstein, M. R., Gozzard, N., Harris, R., Hollis, S., Keidel, S., Levesque, M., Lindholm, C., McDermott, M. F., McInnes, I. B., & Isaacs, J. D. (2018). The RA-MAP consortium: A working model for academia – industry collaboration. *Nature Reviews. Rheumatology*, *14*(1), 53–61. DOI: 10.1038/nrrheum.2017.200 PMID: 29213124

Corsini, L., Dammicco, V., & Moultrie, J. (2021). Frugal innovation in a crisis: The digital fabrication maker response to COVID-19. *R & D Management*, *51*(2), 195–210. DOI: 10.1111/radm.12446

Crisp, L. (2014). Mutual learning and reverse innovation: Where next? *Globalization and Health*, *10*(1), 1–4. DOI: 10.1186/1744-8603-10-14 PMID: 24673828

D'Angelo, V., & Magnusson, M. (2020). A bibliometric map of intellectual communities in frugal innovation literature. *IEEE Transactions on Engineering Management*, *66*, 653–666.

Dabić, M., Obradović, T., Vlačić, B., Sahasranamam, S., & Paul, J. (2022). Frugal innovations: A multidisciplinary review & agenda for future research. *Journal of Business Research*, *142*, 914–929. DOI: 10.1016/j.jbusres.2022.01.032

Delfa, B. (2020). *Innovación frugal: más con menos para un mundomejor*. The Conversation.

Endres, M., Bican, P. M., & Wollner, ¨. T. (2022). Frugal innovation with Scrum: How can Scrum be used to develop resource-efficient innovations in developed world companies? *Journal of Cleaner Production*, •••, 130871. DOI: 10.1016/j.jclepro.2022.130871

Farooq, R. (2017). A conceptual model of frugal innovation: Is environmental munificence a missing link? *International Journal of Innovation Science*, *9*(4), 320–334. DOI: 10.1108/IJIS-08-2017-0076

Farooq, R. (2017). A conceptual model of frugal innovation: Is environmental munificence a missing link? *International Journal of Innovation Science*, *9*(4), 320–334. DOI: 10.1108/IJIS-08-2017-0076

Fischer, B., & Guerrero, M., Guimon,́ J., Schaeffer, P.R. (2020). Knowledge transfer for frugal innovation: Where do entrepreneurial universities stand? *Journal of Knowledge Management*, *25*, 60–379.

Fischer, B., Guerrero, M., Guimón, J., & Schaeffer, P. R. (2021). Knowledge transfer for frugal innovation: Where do entrepreneurial universities stand? *Journal of Knowledge Management*, *25*(2), 360–379. DOI: 10.1108/JKM-01-2020-0040

Friedman, M. (1962). *Capitalism and Freedom*. The University of Chicago Press., DOI: 10.1016/j.jclepro.2020.121456

Govindarajan, V., & Trimble, C. (2012). *Reverse Innovation: Create Far From Home, Win Everywhere*. Harvard Business Review Press. DOI: 10.5437/08956308X5506003

Guerrero, M., & Urbano, D. (2016a). The impact of triple helix agents on entrepreneurial innovations' performance: An inside look at enterprises located in an emerging economy. *Technological Forecasting and Social Change*, *119*, 294–309. DOI: 10.1016/j.techfore.2016.06.015

Guerrero, M., & Urbano, D. (2016b). The transformative role of universities: determinants, impacts, and challenges, in Leita˜ o, J. and Alves, H. (Eds), Entrepreneurial and Innovative Practices in Public Institutions, *Springer*, Cham, pp. 1-17.

Gupta, A., & Wang, H. (2009). *Getting China and India Right: Strategies for Leveraging the World's Fastest-Growing Economies for Global Advantage*. Wiley.

Gupta, A. K., & Wang, H. (2008). Global Enterprise 2020: Five factors that will give you the edge in the race to access the world's most rapidly developing markets. *Chief Executive-New York*, *234*, 32.

Heaton, S., Siegel, D. S., & Teece, D. J. (2019). Universities and innovation ecosystems: A dynamic capabilities perspective. *Industrial and Corporate Change*, *28*(4), 921–939. DOI: 10.1093/icc/dtz038

Hossain, M. (2018). Frugal innovation: A review and research agenda. *Journal of Cleaner Production*, *182*, 926–936. DOI: 10.1016/j.jclepro.2018.02.091

Hossain, M. (2020). Frugal innovation: Conception, development, diffusion, and outcome. Journal of Cleaner Production, Volume 262, 2020, 121456, ISSN 0959-6526.

Hossain, M. (2020). Frugal innovation: Conception, development, diffusion, and outcome. *Journal of Cleaner Production*, *262*, 121456. DOI: 10.1016/j.jclepro.2020.121456

Hossain, M., & Sarkar, S. (2021). Frugal entrepreneurship: Profiting with inclusive growth. *IEEE Transactions on Engineering Management*, *70*(11), 3812–3825.

Hossain, M., Simula, H., & Halme, M. (2016). Can frugal go global? Diffusion patterns of frugal innovations. *Technology in Society*, *46*, 132–139. DOI: 10.1016/j.techsoc.2016.04.005

Karnani, A. (2007). The mirage of marketing to the bottom of the pyramid: How the private sector can help alleviate poverty. *California Management Review*, *49*(4), 90–111. DOI: 10.2307/41166407

Khan, R. (2016). How frugal innovation promotes social sustainability [Sustainability]. *Sustainability (Basel)*, *8*(10), 1–29. DOI: 10.3390/su8101034

Klofsten, M., Fayolle, A., Guerrero, M., Mian, S., Urbano, D., & Wright, M. (2019). The entrepreneurial university as driver for economic growth and social change-key strategic challenges. *Technological Forecasting and Social Change*, *141*, 149–158. DOI: 10.1016/j.techfore.2018.12.004

Knizkov, S., & Arlinghaus, J. C. (2020). Frugal processes: An empirical investigation into the operations of resource-constrained firms. *IEEE Transactions on Engineering Management*, *683*, 667–684.

Knorringa, P., Peša, I., Leliveld, A., & van Beers, C. (2016). Frugal innovation and development: Aides or adversaries? *European Journal of Development Research*, *28*(2), 143–153. DOI: 10.1057/ejdr.2016.3

Koerich, G. V., & Cancellier, E. L. P. D. L. (2020). Frugal Innovation: Origins, evolution and future perspectives. *Cadernos EBAPE.BR*, *17*, 1079–1093.

Leih, S. and Teece, D. (2016). Campus leadership and the entrepreneurial university: a dynamic capabilities perspective, *Academy of Management Perspectives*, Vol. 30No. 2, pp. 182-210.

Leliveld, A., & Knorringa, P. (2017). Frugal Innovation and Development Research. *European Journal of Development Research.* Advance online publication. DOI: 10.1057/s41287-017-0121-4

Leliveld, A., & Knorringa, P. (2018). Frugal innovation and development research. *European Journal of Development Research*, *30*(1), 1–16. DOI: 10.1057/s41287-017-0121-4

Leva¨nen, J., Hossain, M., Lyytinen, T., Hyva¨rinen, A., Numminen, S., & Halme, M. (2015). Implications of frugal innovations on sustainable development: Evaluating water and energy innovations. *Sustainability (Basel)*, *8*(1), 4. DOI: 10.3390/su8010004

Lev¨anen, J., Hossain, M., Lyytinen, T., Hyv¨arinen, A., Numminen, S., & Halme, M., 2016.

Levänen, J., Hossain, M., & Wierenga, M. (2022). Frugal innovation in the midst of societal and operational pressures. *Journal of Cleaner Production*, *347*, 131308. DOI: 10.1016/j.jclepro.2022.131308

Lim, C., & Fujimoto, T. (2019). Frugal innovation and design changes expanding the cost-performance frontier: A schumpeterian approach. *Research Policy*, *48*(4), 1016–1029. DOI: 10.1016/j.respol.2018.10.014

Lim, C., Lee, J. H., Sonthikorn, P., & Vongbunyong, S. (2021). Frugal innovation and leapfrogging innovation approach to the Industry 4.0 challenge for a developing country. *Asian Journal of Technology Innovation*, *291*(1), 87–108. DOI: 10.1080/19761597.2020.1786707

Lorentzen, J. (2010). Low-income countries and innovation studies: A review of recent literature. *African Journal of Science, Technology, Innovation and Development*, *2*(3), 46–81.

Mair, J., Marti, I., & Ventresca, M. J. (2012). Building Inclusive Markets in Rural Bangladesh: How Intermediaries Work Institutional Voids. *Academy ofManagement Journal*, *55*(4), 819–850. DOI: 10.5465/amj.2010.0627

Martínez, N., Dutrénit, G., Gras, N., & Tecuanhuey, E. (2018). Actores, relaciones estructurales y causalidad en la innovación inclusiva: Un caso de telemedicina en México. [Actors, structural relationships, and causality in inclusive innovation: A case of telemedicine in Mexico]. *Innovar (Universidad Nacional de Colombia), 28*(70), 23–38.

McKelvey, M., & Zaring, O. (2018). Co-delivery of social innovations: Exploring the university's role in academic engagement with society. *Industry and Innovation, 25*(6), 594–611. DOI: 10.1080/13662716.2017.1295364

Melkas, H., Oikarinen, T., & Pekkarinen, S. (2019). Understanding frugal innovation: A case study of university professionals in developed countries. *Innovation and Development, 9*(1), 25–40. DOI: 10.1080/2157930X.2018.1437687

Merriam-Webster. (2016). Frugal. EnDiccionario online Merriam-Webster. (11e ed.).

Molina-Maturano, J., Bucher, J., & Speelman, S. (2020). Understanding and evaluating the sustainability of frugal water innovations in M'exico: An exploratory case study. *Journal of Cleaner Production, 274*, 122692. DOI: 10.1016/j.jclepro.2020.122692

Murray, R., Caulier-Grice, J., & Mulgan, G. (2010). *The Open Book of Social Innovation*. NESTA and The Young Foundation.

Nahi, T. (2016). Cocreation at the base of the pyramid: Reviewing and organizing the diverse conceptualizations. *Organization & Environment, 29*(4), 416–437. DOI: 10.1177/1086026616652666

Nambisan, S., & Nambisan, P. (2008). How to profit from a better 'virtual customer environment'. *MIT Sloan Management Review, 49*(3), 53–61.

Natalicchio, A., Ardito, L., Petruzzelli, A. M., & Giudice, M. D. (2018). The origins of external knowledge inflows and the impact of university technologies. *R & D Management, 49*(4), 639–651. DOI: 10.1111/radm.12354

Olsen, A.Ø., Sofka, W. and Grimpe, C. (2016). Coordinated exploration for grand challenges: the role of advocacy groups in search consortia, *Academy of Management Journal*, Vol. 59No. 6, pp. 2232-2255.

Pansera, M., & Owen, R. (2015). Framing resource-constrained innovation at the 'bottom of the pyramid': Insights from an ethnographic case study in rural Bangladesh. Technol. *Technological Forecasting and Social Change, 92*, 300–311. DOI: 10.1016/j.techfore.2014.10.004

Pawlowski, J. M. (2013). Towards born-Global innovation: The role of knowledge management and social software. *Proceedings of the European Conference on Knowledge Management,* ECKM, 2(January), 527–534.

Pisoni, A., Michelini, L., & Martignoni, G. (2018). Frugal approach to innovation: State of the art and future perspectives. *Journal of Cleaner Production, 171,* 107–126. DOI: 10.1016/j.jclepro.2017.09.248

Prabhu, J. (2017). Frugal innovation: Doing more with less for more. *Philosophical Transactions. Series A, Mathematical, Physical, and Engineering Sciences, 375*(2095), 20160372. DOI: 10.1098/rsta.2016.0372 PMID: 28461436

Prahalad, C. K., & Mashelkar, R. A. (2010). *The New Age of Innovation: Driving Cocreated Value Through Global Networks.* McGraw-Hill Education.

Prathap, G. (2014). The myth of frugal innovation in India. *Current Science, 106*(3), 374–377.

Radjou, N., Prabhu, J., & Ahuja, S. (2012). *Jugaad Innovation: Think Frugal, Be Flexible, Generate Breakthrough Growth.* Jossey-Bass.

Rasmussen, E., & Borch, O. J. (2010). University capabilities in facilitating entrepreneurship: A longitudinal study of spin-off ventures at mid-range universities. *Research Policy, 39*(5), 602–612. DOI: 10.1016/j.respol.2010.02.002

Ravichandran, R., Kulshrestha, P., & Nadig, A. (2022). Frugal Innovation for Economic Development-A Perspective Study. *The Management Accountant Journal, 57*(5), 53–57. DOI: 10.33516/maj.v57i5.53-57p

Rosca, E., Arnold, M., & Bendul, J. C. (2017a). Business models for sustainable innovation – an empirical analysis of frugal products and services. *Journal of Cleaner Production, 162,* S133–S145. DOI: 10.1016/j.jclepro.2016.02.050

Rosca, E., Bendul, J., & Arnold, M. (2016). (in press). Business models for sustainable innovation – an empirical analysis of frugal products and services. *Journal of Cleaner Production.*

Schaltegger, S., & Ho¨risch, J. (2015). (in press). In search of the dominant rationale in sustainability management: Legitimacy-or profit-seeking? *Journal of Business Ethics.*

Shahid, M. S., Hossain, M., Shahid, S., & Anwar, T. (2023). Frugal innovation as a source of sustainable entrepreneurship to tackle social and environmental challenges. *Journal of Cleaner Production, 406,* 137050. DOI: 10.1016/j.jclepro.2023.137050

Taneja, S., & Bhushan, B. (2017). Business models for frugal innovation in emerging markets: The role of pay-per-use schemes. *Technovation*, *68*, 57–70.

Tata, R. N., & Matten, D. (2016) Corporate community involvement in the 21st century. In: D. Barton, D. Horva'th, M. Kipping (eds) Re-Imagining Capitalism: Towards a Responsible, Long-Term Model. Oxford University Press (Forthcoming). Available at *SSRN*: https://ssrn.com/abstract=2740687

Tiwari, R., & Herstatt, C. (2012). Frugal innovation: A global networks' perspective [Swiss Journal of Business Research and Practice]. *Die Unternehmung*, *66*(3), 245–274. DOI: 10.5771/0042-059X-2012-3-245

Tiwari, R., & Herstatt, C. (2012a). Assessing India's lead market potential for cost-effective innovations. *Journal of Indian Business Research*, *4*(2), 97–115. DOI: 10.1108/17554191211228029

Weyrauch, T., & Herstatt, C. (2016). What is frugal innovation? Three defining criteria. *Weyrauch and Herstatt Journal of Frugal Innovation*, *2*(1), 1. DOI: 10.1186/s40669-016-0005-y

Weyrauch, T., & Herstatt, C. (2017). What is frugal innovation? Three defining criteria. *Journal of Frugal Innovation*, *2*(1), 1–17. DOI: 10.1186/s40669-016-0005-y

Weyrauch, T., & Herstatt, C. (2017). Frugal innovation in emerging markets: The role of partnerships and co-creation. *International Journal of Technology Management*, *75*(1-4), 23–42.

Willyard, C., Scudellari, M., & Nordling, L. (2018). Partners in science. *Nature*, *562*(7725), 24–28. DOI: 10.1038/d41586-018-06858-4 PMID: 30283120

Winterhalter, S., Zeschky, M. B., Neumann, L., & Gassmann, O. (2017). Business models for frugal innovation in emerging markets: The case of the medical device and laboratory equipment industry. *Technovation*, *66*, 3–13. DOI: 10.1016/j.technovation.2017.07.002

Witell, L., Gebauer, H., Jaakkola, E., Hammedi, W., Patricio, L., & Perks, H. (2017). A bricolage perspective on service innovation. *Journal of Business Research*, *79*, 290–298. DOI: 10.1016/j.jbusres.2017.03.021

Zeschky, M., Widenmayer, B., & Gassmann, O. (2011). Frugal innovation in emerging markets. *Research Technology Management*, *54*(4), 38–45. DOI: 10.5437/08956308X5404007

ADDITIONAL READING

Hindocha, C. N., Antonacci, G., Barlow, J., & Harris, M. (2021). Defining frugal innovation: A critical review. *BMJ Innovations*, *7*(4), 647–656. DOI: 10.1136/bmjinnov-2021-000830

Ratten, V., & Dana, L.-P. (2019). *Societal entrepreneurship and competitiveness*. Emerald Publishing. DOI: 10.1108/978-1-83867-471-720191002

KEY TERMS AND DEFINITIONS

Sustainable Development: Sustainable development (2002) defines sustainable development by referring to 'economic development, social development and environmental protection as interdependent and mutually reinforcing pillars' (p. 2). Therefore, sustainable development is a process for growth and progress, with the goal of creating sustainability by balancing between economic, social and ecological aspects (dovers and handmer, 1992).

Frugal Innovation: Frugal innovation can be defined as a product, service or a solution that emerges despite financial, human, technological and other resource constraints, and where the final outcome is less pricey than competitive offerings (if available) and which meets the needs of those customers who otherwise remain un-served'. Frugal innovation is a new management philosophy, which integrates specific needs of the bottom of the pyramid markets as a starting point and works backward to develop appropriate solutions which may be significantly different from existing solutions designed to address needs of up market segments' .frugal innovation is a new management philosophy, which integrates specific needs of the bottom of the pyramid markets as a starting point and works backward to develop appropriate solutions which may be significantly different from existing solutions designed to address needs of up market segments'.

Resource Constraints: Resource constraints refer to limitations or restrictions on the availability of resources such as time, money, materials, or human capital. These constraints can pose challenges and impact the planning, execution, and success of various projects, initiatives, or operations. However, resource constraints also encourage creativity, innovation, and efficient resource utilization. By carefully managing and prioritizing available resources, organizations can optimize their outcomes and achieve their goals effectively within the given limitations.

Resource Mobilization: Resource mobilization refers to the process of gathering and allocating the necessary resources, such as financial capital, human capital, materials, and technology, to support a particular project, initiative, or organization. It involves identifying and securing resources from various sources, such as investors, donors, government funding, or internal budget allocations. Effective resource mobilization requires strategic planning, networking, and effective communication to engage stakeholders and convince them to contribute their resources. By mobilizing resources efficiently, organizations can enhance their capacity to achieve their objectives and drive positive change.

Entrepreneurship: Entrepreneurship is the process of identifying, creating, and pursuing opportunities to develop innovative ideas into successful businesses or ventures. It involves taking calculated risks, assuming full responsibility for the outcomes, and being proactive in adapting to changes and challenges. Entrepreneurs possess qualities such as creativity, resilience, and a strong drive to bring their ideas to fruition. They play a crucial role in driving economic growth, job creation, and innovation in society. Successful entrepreneurs not only create value for themselves but also contribute to the overall development of industries and communities. Through their vision, determination, and ability to mobilize resources, entrepreneurs shape the future and drive positive change.

Chapter 2
Frugal Innovation and Social Entrepreneurship Among Social Extrapreneurs and Ultrapreneurs

Harry Orugba Ovharhe
https://orcid.org/0000-0002-3631-498X
University of Port Harcourt Teaching Hospital, Port Harcourt, Nigeria

ABSTRACT

The concept of frugal is attributed to products, process, services and systems to develop under resource-constraints, customers are at the center of the development of accessible, adaptable, affordable and appropriate comfortability. Various concepts have been associated interchangeably with the term 'Frugal innovation' in the field on entrepreneurship. This includes the word 'Jugaad innovation' because of the transformation of limited and scared resources from complexity to simplicity on meeting the need of the beneficiary Also because of the ability to solve complex problems of its rigidity of high-cost to affordability, logistic climax to accessibility, portability and mobility, the term adopted was 'Reverse Innovation' which as reinventing or creating viable resources that will seen as comfortability to the consumers.

DOI: 10.4018/979-8-3693-4050-9.ch002

INTRODUCTION

Think frugal, grab opportunity and ensure sufficiency to eliminate scarcity of wants while synergizing capability to transform available limited resources into meaningful product, process and services that will be beneficial to all that lacks through innovation.

Innovation is viewed as an essential tool for boosting inclusive programme, economic growth and development, lowering poverty, zero-hunger, reducing cost of living and raising living standards as picture in the sustainable development goals (Ovharhe, 2022, 2023; Ovharhe, Okolo, 2022; Ovharhe & Chukwemeka, 2023; Ovharhe & Abada, 2023, 2024). Regardless of the educational background of the innovators, innovations are occurring all throughout the community, nation and globe. These innovations are typically spurred by the desire to use locally accessible technologies and resources to address local problems or increase the effectiveness of services or operations. These kinds of advances rely more on thrifty resources and support systems than on large investments in research and development. These low-cost inventions are catching up to big businesses to form an inclusive innovation ecosystem (Nimmagadda *et al.*, 2024; Usman, Kess-Momoh, Ibeh, Elufioye, Ilojianya & Oyeyemi, 2024).

Innovation is the brain-box of creating goods and services to satisfied human wants. Ovharhe (2024) fashion out that Joseph Schumpeter, Christensen, Jean-Baptiste Say, Peter F, Drucker and Charles Lead beater who published "The Rise of the Social Entrepreneur" are in accord that entrepreneurs are innovators which are pacesetters that thread to create dramatic changes in the environment to track and pursue entrepreneurship opportunities for betterment of mankind wellbeing and wellness. Ovharhe (2024) coined that innovation is the process of developing new and better ways of doing things, from developing new tangible and intangible ideas to improving existing ones. Innovation can be sparked by a variety of factors, including new innovative technologies, changing customer needs, and emerging market trends in the entrepreneurship world, institutions and society at large. Innovation involves identifying a customer or market need, developing a product, process, technology, structure and service that meet such need, and then creating a business model that allows the product or service to be sold and scaled.

Entrepreneurs are the individuals who take on the risks and challenges of starting a new business, and they are the ones who bring new products and services to the emerging market through innovation (Usman et al., 2024). For innovation to be authenticated in dealing with limited resources and tackling environmental challenges for better livelihood of individuals, communities, national and global economics issues, the social entrepreneurs need to synchronize frugal innovation for accomplishment of social mission (Ovharhe & Akandu, 2024).

Ovharhe & Chibuike, (2024) pointed out that frugal innovation is an inclusive entrepreneurship concept that focuses on making life suitable for less privilege, inequitable salary gap and unnerved community and individual with quality, abundance, comfort, care and social proof on the drive of social entrepreneurs' dreams and mission to accomplish in the globe. Social entrepreneurs are fundamental in trying to wipe hunger and achieve zero poverty as giant social innovator, but limited resources are fundamental pitfalls and bottlenecks act as syndrome. To overcome this syndrome the concept of frugal innovation must emerge to orchestrate the activities of the social entrepreneurs to accomplish its entrepreneurial journey and mission (Ovharhe & Akandu, 2024).

Social entrepreneurship is distinct from the concept of entrepreneurship, yet still shares several similarities with its business cousin. Jean-Baptiste Say, a French economist, in Ovharhe (2024) opined that an entrepreneur is a person who undertakes an idea and shifts perspectives in a way that it alters the effect that an idea has on society. An entrepreneur is further defined by 'J. B. Say' as someone who shifts economic resources out of an area of lower and into an area of higher productivity to generate high output. The difference between "entrepreneurship" and "social entrepreneurship", however, stems from the purpose of creation and innovation. Social entrepreneurs seek to transform societies at large, rather than transforming their profit margin, as classic entrepreneurs typically seek to do (Rahmanti & Subandi, 2024). Social entrepreneurs use a variety of resources to bring societies into a better state of well-being.

In this frame, because the world of social entrepreneurship is relatively new, there are many challenges facing those who delve into the field. Firstly, social entrepreneurs are trying to predict, address and creatively respond to future problems and often face difficulties in identifying the right problems to solve (Dee, 2024; Ovharhe, 2024). Unlike most business entrepreneurs, who address current market deficiencies, social entrepreneurs tackle hypothetical, unseen or often less-researched issues, such as overpopulation, environmental pollution, unsustainable energy sources and food shortages to mitigate mortality syndromes (Ovharhe & Woko, 2024a, b; Ovharhe & Odepeli, 2024). Funding successful social businesses on merely potential solutions can be nearly impossible as investors are much less willing to support risky ventures. If entrepreneurs are able to receive funding from investors, the challenges might stop with balancing both the social and business aspects of the entrepreneurship.

The lack of eager investors leads to the second problem in social entrepreneurship that entangles the bedrock of the pay gap. Elkington and Hartigan noted that the salary gap between commercial and social enterprises remains the elephant in the room, curtailing the capacity of social enterprises to achieve long-term success and viability. Social entrepreneurs and their employees are often given diminutive or non-existent salaries, especially at the onset of their ventures (Glasbeek, Wicker & Schad, 2024). Thus, their enterprises struggle to maintain qualified, committed and competent employees. Though social entrepreneurs are tackling the world's most pressing issues for mankind sustainability, survival and success, they must also confront skepticism and stinginess from the very society they seek to serve (Ovharhe & Akandu, 2024).

Another reason social entrepreneurs are often unsuccessful is because they typically offer help for those least able to pay for it. Capitalism is founded upon the exchange of capital (most obviously, money) for goods and services. However, social entrepreneurs must find new business models that do not rely on standard exchange of capital in order to make their organizations sustainable. This self-sustainability is what distinguishes social businesses from charities, which rely almost entirely on donations and outside funding (Rahmanti & Subandi, 2024).

Social entrepreneurship operandi's is integrated with social proof, social capital and social mission. The simple understanding of the expression is that social proof is sweet tales and positive testimonies derive as optimum accomplishment from the project. On the other hand, social capital could be easily seen as mutual understanding, trust, norms, value and trust (Ovahrhe, Okolo, Woko & Igbokwe, 2022).

Social entrepreneurship field is so enormous; hence a specialty professional ought to delve into jugaad to accomplish the operational and strategic goals of meeting the demand among those that do not have sufficient supply to satisfy their needs (Miller, 2024; Ovharhe & Abada, 2024). The professional are extrapreneurs' and ultrapreneurs' that deem fitted to solve the problem of frugal innovation because of their ability, capability and capacity they have. Also, their experience and competence in the entrepreneurship world has given them the functional managerial acumen to display their talent since they have the enthusiasm, creativity, resources and dream to accomplish in their entrepreneurial journey and social mission. It is a win-win among ultrapreneurs, social extrapreneurs and beneficiaries in the community and nations they seek to serve.

Additionally, it's the dream of joy and mutual accomplish for the extrapreneur and ultrapreneur with the social enterprise to achieve the purpose of jugaad innovation. Their business will enjoy profit and positive interface relationship with the community (Calo, Sancino & Scognamiglio, 2024). Thus, for the concept of frugal innovation to come to light, the vehicle needed is social entrepreneurship to convey the social mission that is pivoted with social extrapreneurship and ultrapreneurship.

Cuhadar and Rudnák (2022) hinted frugal innovation as it is known in this sense as reverse innovation refers to the practice of rejuvenated cost-effective solutions and possible remedies that address the needs of resource-constrained and emerging markets, often leveraging limited resources to create high-value quality products or services. Striking the equilibrium of any nation to navigate the right direct to enjoy a boom economic prosperity for wellbeing and wellness to human likelihood, green social entrepreneur ought to drive the ecosystem to preserve environment where the society can habitat in safety, low cost-effectiveness and affordability.

However, in the plight of competitive edge, innovation is the key to enterprise, sustainability, survival and success (Ovharhe, 2022, 2023, 2024). But frugal innovation is a species of new breed that drives social entrepreneurs in entrepreneurship opportunities planet (Ovharhe & Abada, 2024; Ovharhe & Woko, 2024a, b). Frugal innovation is a stem that anchor on several fields such as in academic, entrepreneurship, engineering, production, human resource, R&D strategies, marketing strategies, management support, and environmental aspect and massively embracing machine learning, big data analytics, internet of things and artificial intelligence. All variety of fields have its own specialty on frugal innovation with specific harmonized approach towards navigating to yield same results and outcome on quality, simplicity, cost-effectiveness, penetration pricing, durability, mobility and affordability.

Strategically, frugal innovation has gained traction in elevating innovation on entrepreneurship economies as a "scare resource solution" that focuses on producing cost-effective products, process and services (Le et al., 2022). Frugal has paradigm shift focus toward achieving meaningful sustainability development and growth, comfort, resilience, trust, mutual relationship among beneficiaries with the help of social entrepreneurs and its social extrapreneurs and ultrapreneurs.

The frugal innovation capability of a firm is determined by intellectual capital and leadership characteristics like ultrapreneurship and social extrapreneurship (Cuhadar and Rudnák, 2022). For instance according to Le in Rehman et al., (2024), coined that the leadership patterns of ultrapreneurs and social extrapreneurs are precursor for inducing frugal innovations among the community, countries and enterprise. The Environmental munificence issues and concerns about critical scarcity of resources needed by (one or more) firms operating within an environment that can be orchestrated or rejuvenated by the key social entrepreneurs actors for good (Ovharhe & Akandu, 2024). Hence, frugal innovation is pointed at the centre of value creation which in the long-term leads to wealth creation (Ovharhe & Chibuike, 2024; Farooq in Rehman et al, 2024).

Frugal innovation as reverse innovation is about the synchronization of syndicates where communities combine with the social entrepreneur's actors (social extrapreneurs and ultrapreneurs) that create team effort to arrive at possible solutions to navigate product, process and service in the emerging market to satisfied needs that are beneficial to the society. It is combined outcome of internal intelligence developed by the enterprise and external intelligence sourced from the outsider (Bonnici, Klijn & Nowack, 2024). Miller (2024) stresses that customer need must be considered and assessed before frugal innovation should swing into action to avoid failure of the operations. This is while social entrepreneurs should intervene with need assessment framework using asset mapping and strength-based approach with vibrant key actors like social extrapreneurs and ultrapreneurs. Shehzad *et al* (2022) are in support that, it is the key actors like social extrapreneurs and ultrapreneurs intelligence sources in alignment with the communities that help enterprise team performance to acquire frugal innovation (Sharma, Dubey & Rana, 2024). This is while community need assessment and baseline study is of extremely necessity before the commencement of Frugal engineering optimum process startup as a development guide and direction to achieve targeted goals that is specific (Ovharhe & Chibuike, 2024).

In 2012, Yasser Ahmad Bhatti make strong argument that the theory of frugal is attributed to products and services that are developed under resource constraints, customers are at the centre of the development of accessible, adaptable, affordable and appropriate products. To elaborate this, Jason Miller in 2024, fashioned that frugal Innovation is about doing more with less in resource constrained business environments. The 'Bull' Miller (2024) expands that frugal innovation orchestrates simplicity, affordability, and sustainability, turning limitations into opportunities for growth and impact to individual, society, enterprise and environment. Through this insight of tentacles, extrapreneurs and ultrapreneurs can explore how businesses across the globe should harness frugal innovation to navigate resource constraints, bottlenecks and pitfalls by fine-turning new pathways to sustainability, survival and success.

Based the discussion, this review focused on how frugal innovation could be achieved using the social entrepreneurship actors like ultrapreneurs and social extrapreneurs by considering sensitive actions on resource-constraint, business innovation model, bottom of pyramid, environmental munificence and innovation technology.

CONCEPT OF FRUGAL INNOVATION

Various concepts have been associated interchangeably with the term 'Frugal Innovation' in the field on entrepreneurship. This includes the word 'Jugaad Innovation' because of the transformation of limited and scared resources from complexity to simplicity on meeting the need of the beneficiary (Miller, 2024; Dawood, 2023). Also because of the ability to solve complex problems of its rigidity of high-cost to affordability, logistic climax to accessibility, portability and mobility, the term adopted was 'Reverse Innovation' which reinventing or creates viable resources that will see as comfortability to the consumers. Additionally considering the process of developing design on new prototype for suitability, acceptability and mobility the concept employed was ‘Frugal Engineering’ (Milthon, 2024).

In essences, whatever it may be called by respective stakeholders’ frugal innovation is centered on sorting out solutions as possible remedies to complex problems by optimizing limited available resources as entrepreneurship opportunities to innovate needs capable of satisfying consumers from its original fundamentals. Also, frugal innovation is the process of identifying and grabbing entrepreneurship opportunities focusing on meeting the needs of its beneficiary in the long-term with more appropriate convenience, care, comfort and satisfaction the end users.

Frugal innovation bears the inclusive entrepreneurship features to help those that have the inability to spend monetary resources to meet up with their need with customer benefits of proportional quantity and quality (Dabić, Obradović, Vlačić, Sahasranamam & Paul, 2022). The quantity is very important because the essence enables the poor families to satisfy their loves ones and homely stakeholders with abundance.

Nimmagadda *et al.*, (2024) connotes that the Latin term “frugalis” from the middle of the 16th century is where the word “frugal” originated. Frugal is defined by the Oxford Dictionary as “sparing or economical as regards money or food.” When there were few financial resources available in the old world, frugal living was a virtue. This is still true in most of today's emerging economies. The concept of “frugal innovation” is not new, despite the term's recent adoption.

‘Frugal’ been termed as ‘jugaad,’ emanated from Hindi colloquial use of words which is seen as ‘an innovative solution,’ groom out of ingenuity and resourcefulness. Jugaad is the centre of frugal innovation, as it rejuvenated social entrepreneurs to fathom a creative thinking spirit outside the box by fine-tuning an unimaginable solution as possible remedies to sort out challenges. Frugal innovation exceeds knowledge application; it went beyond the normative knowledge which leads to imagination on invention, creation and innovation. Albert Einstein says that imagination is greater than knowledge. Frugal innovation focused on transformable imagination that yields valuable on process, product, administrative, technology and market above the threshold (Ovharhe & Chibuike, 2024b).

The essence of frugal innovation is the diversion of complexity to simplicity on the product, process, services and system for betterment of the society at large. The simplicity entails utilization of socio-economic resources that are scare to be viable affordability and accessibility that will be at the benefit and satisfactory content of the end users (Le *et al.*, 2024). This is the trail of monetary resources to meet demand from supply. Frugal innovation has the tendency to streamline supply chain to tally with demand of the right quality, quantity, taste, benefit and satisfaction for the customer benefits when it’s enshrined by social entrepreneurs, which involves the social extrapreneurs and ultrapreneurs. Frugal innovation beams the spectrums of light to the community, developing nations and countries with dearth of unmet needs.

According to Farooq (2017), frugal innovation can be defined as a zero-based approach to solving customer's problems by arriving at homegrown solutions/ offerings which are simple, sustainable and extremely affordable leading to fast adoption by target customers. The global economy will face major challenges over the next few decades in terms of meeting the needs of seven billion people, including the currently unmet basic needs of large numbers in developing countries. In same view, frugal innovation is the ability to generate greater value for customers at the bottom of the pyramid while significantly reducing the use of abundant resources (Weyrauch & Herstatt, 2017).

Hossain, Shahid and Park (2024) defined frugal innovation as a resource-scarce solution designed and implemented despite resource-constraints, whereby the outcome is significantly cheaper than competitive offerings (if available) and is good enough to meet the basic needs of customers who would otherwise remain underserved.

As noted by León, Pichardo, Carrillo and Santiago (2024), frugal innovation has been defined as the (re)designing products, process, procedure, services, systems, and business models in order to reduce complexity and total lifecycle costs, and to enhance functionality of emerging market growth, while providing high user value and affordable solutions for relatively low-income customers. Gupta and Wang (2009) dramatized frugal in engagement of three perceptive; raw material, environment and low cost as innovation which pursuit to create products, services, processes, and business models. Raw material envisages the process of frugal engineering. The raw materials are factors that show what constitute the productivity index from the input to output stage. The final product of innovation is affected by the raw material been utilized on the entire process. The raw material should not be compromised because of its fashion the beauty, quality and perception of productivity. The visibility of the finished product is bent on the efficacy of the raw material. The composite of the raw material are what constitute the determinant of the prototype and finished product (León et al., 2024) Environmental munificence fathoms the scarcity and available infrastructure obtainable for the enterprise which warrants failure or success. These might also be attributed to cheap or expensive labor, material, and atmospheric climax of attracting or frustrating investor such as the social entrepreneurs' actors (ultrapreneurship and social entrepreneurs).

Low cost is the factor that is determined by the pricing; it is the juicy aspect of the frugal. If the input of economic resources such as raw material, labor, technology, rent, fittings and fixture are cheap, then the pricing can be low whereby the goods and services can be affordable. But if it of the reverse, the opposite will be obtain. Frugal innovation laid emphasis on affordable products, process and services in emerging markets (Miller, 2024).

Dabić et al., (2022) enlarged that jugaad deals with the modeling product, service, process and business model with limited available resources to meet consumer's needs. It is at the point that utilizing scare resource of finance, technology, material and human to pursuit the unmet needs to the benefit of customers. Jugaad, at any point in communal needs utilized innovation of new social entrepreneurship model of innovation to transform challenges that are in the state of pitfalls and bottleneck to solve customer's problem despite the limitation of scare resources (Hossain, Levänen & Wierenga, 2021). Generically, in the perspective of the innovator's framework, frugal is in the for front of dealing with scarce resources that evolves within the community on using available monetary resources to meet ends need from saving and momentary supplies of income flow (Hossain, 2018).

Principles Of Frugal Innovation

Frugal innovation is guided by several fundamental principles that help social enterprise harness its power effectively. These principles include: (Nimmagadda et al., (2024); Velananda, Dissanayake & Wickramasinghe, 2022):

- **Simplicity**: Frugal innovation focused on simplification of the product, processes, systems, and procedure with business models. By simplifying things, MSMEs, conglomerates and multinationals can reduce costs and make their products and services easily accessible to a broader customer base.
- **Affordability**: The goal of jugaad innovation is to create products, processes and services that are low penetration pricing and affordable for end users at all levels of income generating streams in the marketplace.
- **Sustainability**: Frugal innovation in all developing nations indulge in sustainability, survival and success by encouraging enterprises in using limited resources efficiently and minimizing waste with lean entrepreneurship effect (Chubuike & Ovharhe, 2022; Chibuike, Ovharhe & Abada, 2022; Ovharhe & Okolo, 2022). This benefits not only the environment but also helps reduce costs and increase long-term profitability.
- **Flexibility**: Jugaad innovation encourages enterprises to be flexible, dynamic, risk culture, remote working, green entrepreneurship and adaptable in their approach (Ovharhe, Woko & Ezeocha, 2021; Ovharhe, Woko & Ogolo, 2021; Ovharhe & Igbokwe, 2021). This enables them to quickly respond to changes in the enabling market challenges and customer needs, giving the enterprise a competitive edge with the approach of social entrepreneurship orchestrated by social extrapreneurs and ultrapreneurs.

In extension of the concept, Radjou et al., (2012) establish six principles that characterize frugal innovation:

1. Seek opportunity in adversity: Hossain, Levänen & Wierenga (2021) review on pursuing frugal innovation for sustainability at the grassroots level, which is fundamental, baseline framework for social entrepreneurs to identify, grabbed and pursue opportunities that which have meaningful sustainable tendency for growth and development in the environment.
2. Do more with less: Miller (2024) stresses adopting frugal innovation fosters the more accomplishment on mitigating constraints and boosting positively environmental munificence for the beneficiaries.
3. Think and act flexibly: Think frugal globally and acting locally as pacesetters in the entrepreneurial journey and dreams (Ovharhe & Chibuike, 2024).
4. Keep it simple. Ovharhe and Igbokwe (2021) centered on simplicity of the process of entrepreneurship to achieve competitive advantage towards client satisfaction.
5. Include the margin: Ovharhe et al (2021) sees innovation of the process, product, market and technology creates marginal transformation the impact individuals and community with controllable risk culture on strategic risk and operational risk.
6. Follow your heart: Khare, Ghura and Agrawal (2024) examine the scaling of a social enterprise through legitimacy which in turn spreads the values of the organisation and creates a deeper impact in society.

Specifically, jugaad innovation is the ability to generate significantly more business and societal value while significantly reducing the use of scarce resources (Radjou & Prabhu, 2013). The terms 'jugaad innovation,' frugal engineering,' or 'reverse innovation' are commonly used interchangeably with frugal innovation (Miller, 2024). Frugal innovation is reducing the extra features or sophistication of products, services, processes and systems as a result of minimizing the cost. Usually, this refers to removing nonessential features from durable goods, such as cars or mobiles, to sell in developing countries using affordable prices.

Dawood (2023) posits that frugal innovation is the ability, capability and capacity to do more with less that is, to create significantly more business and social value while minimizing the use of diminishing resources such as energy, capital and time (Rajou & Prabhu, 2015). Frugal innovation is streamlining and cutting excessive cost of the nonessentials by downsizing the services and product cost. On this basis, it focuses on durability, reachability, affordability, convenience, quality and taste of customer satisfaction. Frugal products do not mean cheaper quality, but products and services of acceptable quality, lower features, and low-end prices.

Challenges and Setback of Frugal Innovation

While frugal innovation offers many advantages, it also comes with its own setback and challenges. Some of these include: Milthon (2024)

Limited Resources: Jugaad innovation requires social enterprise, conglomerate and multinational to work with limited resources and constraints. While this can foster creativity, it can also restrict the scope of innovation and make scaling operations more difficult.
Quality Concerns: Balancing affordability with quality can be a challenge in jugaad innovation. Companies must ensure that their products and services meet the required standards and customer expectations while keeping costs low.
Cultural Barriers: Jugaad innovation often involves thinking outside the box and challenging established norms. This can encounter resistance in some corporate cultures, making it challenging to implement frugal innovation initiatives.
Market Acceptance: Jugaad innovation may face challenges in gaining market acceptance, especially in markets where customers are accustomed to high-quality and high-priced products. Convincing customers of the value and quality of frugal innovations can be a hurdle for companies.

Frugal Innovation and the Way Forward

In the paradigm shift of social entrepreneurship perspective, frugal innovation entails those strategies and tactics employed to manage limited resources on demand and supply of product, process and service in the emerging market environment (Weyrauch & Herstatt, 2017). There are always problems in an ecosystem when there is a rise in demand and insufficient supplies to meet the needs of the consumers. This might lead to a hike in pricing that calls for urgent attention and intervention to avoid social vices, catastrophe and calamity in the environment. This is how social entrepreneur are needed to readdress the situation using ultrapreneurs and social extrapreneurs to quench the turbulence in the environment to normalcy (Velananda et al., 2022).

The instrumental tools needed to manage this socio-economic crisis are frugal innovations. Frugal innovation approach has the capability and capacity to maintain balances in the environment by pivoting product, services and processes with equilibrium pricing on lower cost and better quality through optimization of resources at performance leverage which is beneficial and satisfactory to all stakeholders. Miller (2024) propounded that frugal innovation approach on managing depressed ecosystem in communities and nations has gained traction not only as a doctrine of necessity in emerging markets but also as a competitive edge in under-developed, developing and developed economies, challenging business enterprises to creative thinking on innovation models.

The origins of frugal innovation can be traced back to resource-constrained environments in local communities, where necessity sparked creativity and ingenuity. Entrepreneurs and companies in these settings have had to find ways to meet consumer needs with minimal resources, leading to innovative solutions that are both cost-effective and sustainable. This approach contrasts sharply with traditional innovation models that often rely on heavy investment in research and development, extensive use of materials, and complex technologies (Miller, 2024).

The principles of frugal innovation center on three key elements: simplicity, affordability, and sustainability. Simplicity involves reducing complexity in products and services, making them easier to use and maintain. Affordability ensures that innovations are accessible to a broader segment of the population, addressing the needs of cost-conscious consumers. Sustainability focuses on minimizing environmental impact, using fewer resources, and creating products that are durable and recyclable (Velananda et al., 2022).

Frugal innovation also emphasizes the importance of understanding customer needs deeply, often requiring businesses to engage closely with their target markets to identify what is truly essential (Weyrauch & Herstatt, 2017). This customer-centric approach helps in eliminating unnecessary features and focusing on what adds real value, leading to solutions that are not only economically viable but also highly relevant to consumers' lives.

The adoption of frugal innovation has the potential to transform industries by making products and services more accessible to underserved populations. It challenges the notion that innovation must be resource-intensive, opening up new avenues for growth and development. As businesses around the world embrace this approach, frugal innovation is becoming a key driver of sustainable development, economic inclusivity, and environmental stewardship, marking a significant evolution in the way companies innovate in response to the challenges of the 21st century.

Mitigating Frugal Innovation Challenges

Frugal innovation is propelled by a combination of global economic shifts, technological advancements, and a growing awareness of environmental sustainability. These forces converge to create a fertile ground for innovations that require minimal resources yet offer significant value and impact (Miller, 2024).

Economic shifts play a pivotal role, especially as companies face the dual challenge of reaching emerging markets and adapting to the budget constraints of cost-conscious consumers worldwide. The economic landscape is increasingly characterized by volatility and uncertainty, prompting businesses to seek more adaptable and resilient models of operation. Frugal innovation emerges as a response to this need, offering a pathway to sustainable growth that relies on ingenuity rather than on extensive capital investment (Velananda et al., 2022; Nassani, Sinisi, Mihai, Paunescu, Yousaf & Haffar, 2022).

Technological advancements have democratized access to information and tools that enable frugal innovation. The digital revolution, in particular, has lowered barriers to entry for inventors and entrepreneurs, allowing them to design, prototype, and market solutions with unprecedented speed and efficiency. Mobile technology, cloud computing, and social media have facilitated collaboration and sharing of ideas across borders, further fueling the development of frugal innovations that can be scaled globally.

The increasing emphasis on sustainability and responsible consumption is another critical driver. As consumers become more aware of the environmental impact of their purchases, there is a growing demand for products and services that are not only affordable but also eco-friendly. This shift in consumer preferences challenges businesses to rethink their processes and products, prioritizing sustainability and efficiency over luxury and excess. Frugal innovation, with its focus on minimizing waste and maximizing resource efficiency, aligns closely with these values.

Furthermore, the rise of socially responsible investing and the emphasis on corporate social responsibility encourage companies to incorporate frugal innovation into their strategies. Investors are increasingly attracted to ventures that promise not only financial returns but also positive social and environmental impact. This trend supports the development of frugal solutions that address the needs of underserved populations and contribute to the broader goals of sustainable development (Miller, 2024).

The driving forces behind frugal innovation reflect a broader shift in global business and societal trends. Companies that understand and embrace these dynamics can leverage frugal innovation to not only navigate the challenges of a resource-constrained world but also to lead the way in creating value-driven, sustainable, and inclusive solutions.

Concept of Social Entrepreneurship

The term 'social entrepreneur' is credited to William Drayton who won best leader in America News and Global Report in 2005 because of his tremendous impact and social changes attributed to him. However, the term was noticed in 1972. Social entrepreneurs are revealed to be an individual or enterprise that seeks to identify business opportunities that pursuit meaningful sustainable impact in society at large and the entrepreneurship world. However, the word social entrepreneur was observed to be interchangeable with the word 'social innovator' by the founder because of the idea of innovativeness to solve problems that impacted positive change in society (Glasbeek et al., 2024). Social entrepreneurs indulged in concept like 'product innovation', 'process innovation', 'service innovation, administrative innovation', 'technology innovation' and 'market innovation', all attributed to the betterment of sustainability, survival and success of mankind.

All social changes drive through various forms of innovation to establish her mission growth which is transformed into the dreams of entrepreneurship. Every societal change drive needs social entrepreneurship to activate the process for humanity and entire mankind to benefit. Social entrepreneurship is facilitators of goods and services for mankind's fitness. For the world to become a better place for mankind to exist, social entrepreneurship is needed because of the propensity to harmonize tribes, kindred, languages and culture. This creates great demarcation among social entrepreneurship and others from the pattern of operations. Unlike corporate entrepreneurship that focus on the pursuit of profit maximization and wealth maximization, social entrepreneurship considers the environment and people first on creation and innovation skills before indulging on profit maximization and survival of the enterprise (Bonnici et al., 2024).

Social entrepreneurship is a tentative wing of entrepreneurship which navigates through innovation of social enterprise creation that drives social economic changes in society, industries and individuals (Ovharhe, 2024). Social entrepreneurship is pivotal to the sustainable development goals of the people, planet and profit by creating credible stable atmospheric conditions for mankind. Social entrepreneurs pursue business opportunities to establish wellness and wellbeing by providing social resolutions on social change, social problems, social remedies, social care, social satisfaction and social proof in the environment at large (Rahmanti & Subandi, 2024). The optimum targeted purpose of social entrepreneurship to identify pursuit and establish social change with meaningful sustainable development through business enterprise.

Hence social entrepreneurship enlargement issues and concern are based on four key factors such as community, not-for-profit making enterprise, transformation on meaningful development and global attention to social business in line with sustainable development goals (Glasbeek et al., 2024).

The not-for-profit making enterprises are based on creation and innovation of products, processes, market, technology and administrative changes to benefit mankind in terms of the people, profit and planet (Bonnici et al., 2024).

Another consciousness of social entrepreneurship is the mindset of investing in relationships. Social entrepreneurship on investment in relationships tends to place high value towards social capital and social networking. Social capital is the ability to invest in trust, mutual relationship, norms, standard conformity and value (Ovharhe et al., 2022).

The president of Russia pointed is global view with respect to Africa, that they may not experience prosperity and wealth as expected because the lack 'trusts. In this same light, United Nation environment unit pointed out that while Africans are poor is because they lack the investment of 'trust'. Social entrepreneurship is the field that needs to address poverty in most nations. The perception and attitude of leadership in under development countries can be addressed if they adopt the concept of social entrepreneurship.

Social networking is the branching network of generating innovation skills through connectivity to various social enterprises, corporate enterprises, multinationals, conglomerates and corporations for support to the mission. That is to say that social entrepreneurs have the potency of pragmatism, social awareness, collaboration and adaptability on their social mission. In the act of networking social entrepreneurs can be community-based size where they may focus within a particular area one time after the other. It may be systematic operations, but they must think globally and act locally (Ovharhe, 2024).

Context of the Problem

Dees, J. G., articulated that social entrepreneurship is a result oriented innovative leader with a tendency to create and transform possession. Social entrepreneurs work in career and professional fields to solve critical social problems by achieving social proof and social mission. Michael Young an exponential vibrate entrepreneur was among the first most successful social enterprise creator in the western nations (Bonnici et al., 2024). He pioneered and innovate news ideas in enterprises that is based on health care, social welfare and schools to solve social problems.

In the mode to solve social problems and challenges in the environment, social entrepreneurs delve into developing innovative skills and creative thinking to ensure there is social care and satisfaction among every stakeholder in various sectors like community, business, health, even modern technology on artificial intelligence. All these are easy to achieve through intensive collaboration on social networking and synchronization of all stakeholders whereby the mission on frugal or inclusive entrepreneurship can be achieved. Social entrepreneurs always intend to predict and create possible solutions to address current and future problems that affects humanity wellness and wellbeing (Rahmanti & Subandi, 2024). Social entrepreneurs ensure that solving problems has meaningful sustainable development and long-term impact among stakeholders in the business, community and global structure (Glasbeek et al., 2024). Unlike most intrapreneurs, corporate entrepreneurs and serial entrepreneurs who focus on addressing business environment pitfalls and bottleneck through market research and data analytics, social entrepreneurs are actors who imbibe the strength based approached to rejuvenate complex issues on poverty, hunger, over population, food shortages, environmental pollution, unsustainably energy provision, soft loan on small businesses and mitigating environmental pollution factors threading business opportunities. Nevertheless, frugal innovation led to an approach to entrepreneurs and intrapreneurs challenges being affected by infant mortality, maternal mortality and life expectancy (Ovharhe & Woko, 2024a,b; Ovharhe & Odepeli, 2024; Rahmanti & Subandi, 2024).

More so, social entrepreneurs are energetic to accomplish her entrepreneurial journey and dreams with utilization of its collaboration of social capital and social networking to ensure their client needs are met, this is while frugal innovation is of great synchronization with social entrepreneurship. To achieve this, that calls for key actors to facilitate the process such as ultrapreneurship and extrapreneurship, because the good thing about these special breeds of social entrepreneurship preferred investing in relationship rather than driving for personal monetary achievement. Hence, relationship management and client satisfaction come first before any other factors. If this is so for all entrepreneurs' frugal innovation would not be paramount issues and concerns. Thus, the world calls for many social entrepreneurs that specialize in ultrapreneurship and extrapreneurship.

Without government intervention and partnership with non-governmental agencies it may seem impossible for the pursuit of social entrepreneurship. The alternative networking to facilitate the social mission of the social entrepreneurs is to collaborate with ultrapreneurs and intrapreneurs. This is while the like Nicholas Telsa failed in the pursuit of the social mission free energy project he beckoned on, because it all seems to the investor like J. P. Morgan that he is pursuing asupportfor risky venture that will not be profitable in the long-term. Not all entrepreneurs have the potency and orientation to possess the enthusiasm of becoming social entrepreneurs. Even several investors that assisted with funding financially failed communally and globally to think like social entrepreneurs talk less of executing the implementation process. The funds have been diverted for other unreasonable concerns not traceable to influence livelihood and wellbeing of humanity.

Hence, the fundamental problem society has is lack of sincere social entrepreneurs that will cultivate the spirit of ultrapreneurs and extrapreneurs in the entrepreneurship world. United Nations agency; USAID, World Bank, UNESCO, UNICEF among others has made all means possible to achieve frugal innovation to come to a meaningful sustainable and development light to enrich and satisfy mankind but of no avail (Ur, Anwar, Antohi, Ali, Fortea & Zlati, 2024). Sometime 'trust' and 'mutual understanding' have become a critical issue to contend with, meaning lack of social capital is a critical problem among enabling community, nations and environment at large.

Nevertheless, the inability to fund social entrepreneurship program in the less developed nations or poor rural community create a lacuna which lead to inequity of social justice that have a negative resultant effect on generating criminal element, kidnapping, banditry, terrorism and theft in the society. Also, the bridge on pay gap among the commercial and social enterprise is not awesome to talk about because if a pipe of water or oil passes through the community when they are poor, hungry and thirsty, the individual in such a neighborhood might be tempted to do the contrary (i.e. pipeline vandalism, thuggery). The bottom line is to activate all corridors accessible for the ultrapreneur and extrapreneur to delve in, to network and sort out every negation challenge that cripples community and nations hunger, poverty, poor industrialization and strategic alliance in productivity of meeting needs.

In this light, Elkington and Hartigan pointed out that salary gap among highly capitalized conglomerate, multination, corporation and social enterprise remains the elephant in the room, curtailing the capacity of low wealthy social enterprises to achieve long-term success and viability in the business environments (Bonnici et al., 2024). This is because social entrepreneurs and their resource people are often given diminutive or non-existent salaries with low motivation, intrinsic satisfaction and extrinsic satisfaction, mostly at the onset of their enterprise ventures. Thus, the enterprise cannot sustain competent and qualify personnel that leads to frequency in employee turnover without been able to replace such competent, experienced and skilled personnel from the labor market. This might be devastating, unawesome and irritating because the society that are struggling to bring out from perplex state makes them find themselves to become a victim of such scenario. Social entrepreneurs and their employees may find themselves in depression, anxiety, mental burnout, discouragement and disappointment. it is the origin of injelititis and cynicism among social entrepreneurs which is absurd to nature and mankind (Ovharhe, 2022; Ovharhe, 2023; Ovharhe & Chukwuemeka, 2023).

Additionally, critical problems encountered by social entrepreneurs are high levels of indebtedness from their client for not be able to pay back at the time when financial resources are needed to sustain and survive the enterprise success. In this era of merchandizing function, capitalism is the brightness of the business language. Entrepreneurs on normal stands seek to maximize wealth and profitability. Even 'Stanta Claus' at the Yule Tide season needs financial resources to buy its gift before he can distribute it within stipulated period of timeliness.

However, social entrepreneurs' continuous operations should figure out modalities of business model for sustainability, survival and success of the enterprise which may not depend on client funds (Bonnicci *et al.*, 2024). Hence, social entrepreneurs' enterprise having certain items being practiced in the financial position such as provision for reserve capital, undistributed income, contingency, sinking fund and their likelihood that do not rely on standard exchange of capital in order to make their organizations sustainable. This self-sustainability is what distinguishes social enterprise merchandizing functions from charitable ventures that depend on donations and external fund sourcing. Hence, to achieve a suitable environmental platform for social entrepreneurs' operation, the social extrapreneurs and ultrapreneurs need to come in to change the game with new style and pattern paradigm.

Social Extrapreneurship

Extrapreneurship as species on new breed of entrepreneurship world seeks to identify problems and develop models to pursuit and provide possible solutions for future benefits. Social Extrapreneur are seen as social innovation giant and champion in the entrepreneurship world which have the capacity, character and competence because of experiential practices they have encountered overtime in transformation and development of enterprise. Extrapreneurs are the extraordinary individuals who strive to create and innovate as entrepreneurs, intrapreneurs working within organizations, product managers, transformation leaders or investors. Extrapreneurs focus on learning, unlearning and relearning from business leaders to innovate new dimensions from the existing framework to change the future so the world would become a better place. Extrapreneur delve into complex, competitive and chaotic climax in the business world and actualized remedies by learning new stills, pattern and style to achieve higher goal. Extrapreneur via learning, unlearning and relearning scanned the business environment to solve the unmet need by positioning suitable strategies and tactics in the marketplace. Extrapreneur are apt to learning from historical performance of industries leading and bleeding syndromes on the entrepreneurial journey of sustainability, survival and success in the business world by learning directly from high profile expert (CFTE, 2024).

Extrapreneurs coined their healing stream in the business world through learning from the world most experience talented expert in the related field and gain insight from the world most innovative enterprise and build networking globally (Ovharhe, 2023, 2024, CFTE, 2024).

It can be said to be similar with job of prolific consultant. One major difference between the two terms is that extrapreneurship usually involves immigration of the talent. Intrapreneurship and extrapreneurship as new concepts of social entrepreneurship bound to become parts of humans' daily living and business (Ovharhe, 2022, 2023; Chibuike & Ovharhe, 2022).

Social entrepreneurship as fundamental rock and spiral cords to social extrapreneurship is all the rage in creativity, invention and innovation skills. Social extrapreneurship is pivoted on social impact through enterprise is lauded by world leaders in the polity, policy makers and enterprise practitioners. Social extrapreneurship is the moving train of not only should you do well, but you should do sustainable good as well that develop the society at large. Social extrapreneurship is the sound which drums reecho multifaceted plight of business in the marketplace.

University of Cambridge Centre for Social Innovation lightens the spectrum of extrapreneurship as a message that resonates with many aspiring entrepreneurs as well as social enterprise looking to make more impact increasingly like gold dust. Social extrapreneurship strapped for cash as opportunities from grants and benefits via public, not for profit making organization, social enterprise and corporate philanthropic.

Social entrepreneurship is not only lauded but invested in all dimensions to boost human livelihood. As the idea gained traction in the 2000s the public pound stimulated support organisations, training and academic courses as well as new financial institutions such as Big Society Capital, funds and socially motivated investors. Indeed, the public pound (local and national) has been crucial throughout the history of social entrepreneurship in stimulating creativity and momentum.

A notable and intensifying trend over the last decade has been the rise of social extrapreneurship, the bringing together of ideas, people and resources by working across or beyond organisational boundaries to create social impact. A good example is the growth of social incubators.

The rise of extrapreneurs introduces a higher level of flexibility to the labor market as a whole, but also it is a sign of the "job for life" economy further crumbling away. Maybe one can view it as a compromise, but as with the realities of the gig economy, Unions will need to decide whether to fight it or to embrace extrapreneurialism in a realistic manner and work out how to ensure more constructive and sensible regulation.

Rooijen (2024) averred that as strongly postulated by Forbes, 9 business out of 10 failed due to a lot negligence factors on product, process, administrative issue and lot more. In same light, Harvard Business School statistically revealed that 30-40% business failed with 80% not able to yield a return on investment. This is a catastrophe in the business world that needs the presence of extrapreneurs to drive a change. The approach of social extrapreneurs is different from entrepreneur and intrapreneur. Social extrapreneur are goal targeted individual with embedded expertise and problem solvers. Social extrapreneur causes action through changes of ideology and educating their client for achievement of goals purposefully. However, most extrapreneur were once intrapreneur, that is while extrapreneur has a lot of experience and expertise when compared to intrapreneur. Hence, for frugal innovation to be sustainable, the talents of extrapreneur are needed utmost for growth and development. Extrapreneur functions greatly with more dealings on societal values and dreams accomplishment.

Social entrepreneurship is a very exciting venture in the business world that actualizes societal dreams and mission with great influence compensation and benefits. Due, to the negation feedback on failure from the socio-economic attributes it calls for an alternative functions. The alternative functions is to focus on social extrapreneur that possesses a corporate blend with intrapreneurs and entrepreneurs which seeks to change the mental reasoning and creating thinking of employers, academicians and likelihood stakeholders for the future scenario learning. Extrapreneur have potentials to create dramatic change with the start-up failure rates of up to 90 percent in economic and high pricing in the social enterprise (Rooijen, 2024).

For individuals in the edge of start-up or currently running their own business, the extrapreneurs are pressure stream of enterprise. For any social enterprise to be sustainable there must be an action present of extrapreneur that will enable the organization to fly not to fail. The strength of an extrapreneurship model presence to propel a team or organization to accomplish targeted goals and mission cannot be compared to that of intrapreneurship and entrepreneurship. This is because extrapreneurs do not just have passion, but they have a drive and self-propelling force of fusion, vision and enthusiasm. Extrapreneurship utilizes strength-based approach to boost enterprise, community and national challenges by leading the way with healthiness of direction.

Extrapreneur directs available resources to meet the unmet needs of society on basis of its strength. The strength base approach sees the untapped resources of any society that has a positive resultant effect on the livelihood of the nations. Social extrapreneur breathe fresh breath to any society they find themselves because the engage with new purposeful and meaning life stream that gives mankind hopefulness and happiness.

Social entrepreneurship is not only lauded but invested in. As the idea gained traction in the 2000s the public pound stimulated support organizations, training and academic courses as well as new financial institutions such as Big Society Capital, funds and socially motivated investors. Indeed, the public pound (local and national) has been crucial throughout the history of social entrepreneurship in stimulating creativity and momentum.

A notable and intensifying trend over the last decade has been the rise of social extrapreneurship, the bringing together of ideas, people and resources by working across or beyond organizational boundaries to create social impact. A good example is the growth of social incubators. Social incubators began appearing in the USA and Canada in the late 2000s and were given an impetus in England in 2012 by the Cabinet Office's Social Incubator Fund.

Cambridge Social Ventures, for instance, was created by three charitable organizations and a business school. It offers business advice, office space, loans and training. However, its real impact for aspiring social entrepreneurs is the growth of a 'social ecosystem' nestled within the wider Cambridge entrepreneurial and social ecosystems, of experienced entrepreneurs (social or otherwise), organizations, investors, students and SIE graduates who provide invaluable (and freely given) support and open doors to give our social ventures an incredible start on their journey (Cambridge Centre for social Innovation, 2024).

Social incubators illustrate the social extrapreneurship of advocate organizations and the state. In combining ideas and resources into funded programs, it stimulated regional and local social extrapreneurs to experiment and build new support mechanisms for social entrepreneurship.

Extrapreneurship was originally used as a concept to explain activity leading to corporate spin outs as distinct from intrapreneurship (creating new opportunities within an organization) and entrepreneurship (creating new ventures outside extant organizations.

Dave Algoso recently highlighted the rise of a different sort of extrapreneur in the international development sector who works beyond organizational walls. He argues that; 'extrapreneurs' create things in a space that transcends any one agency. Extrapreneurship is a partnership approach that goes beyond co-ordination or co-branding. It starts with the network and leverages the factors above to create a disproportionately greater development impact (CFTE, 2024).

While the concept of extrapreneurship did not get much traction outside the 1990s entrepreneurial literature, reconceptualized in the contemporary context captures the idea of extra-organizational action which facilitates creative combinations of ideas, people, places and resources for impact. In the social context it is a concept that compliments social entrepreneurship and social intrapreneurship.

At the Centre for Social Innovation, we have seen a rise in interest in creating social impact through creating new social ventures and within corporate and public organizations amongst students and our local community. Our emphasis is on social impact through any appropriate organizational form or business model rather than a particular organizational form or model.

Indeed, the opportunities to make systemic changes through working within big organizations (public or private) is immense, as is the potential impact. To some it may be less attractive than the perceived glamour of the lone and heroic social entrepreneur and is potentially frustrating as big organizations are often slow to change, but the fact remains that big organizations are already having a huge impact (for better or worse) and there is an imperative to help them do better quicker or do well and do good.

Creating a social ecosystem is one way to achieve the opportunities of better livelihood. An ecosystem of people, places and resources that can stimulate, support and sustain, brings together social entrepreneurs and intrapreneurs. In other words, acting as social extrapreneurs is vital formation on the spirit of frugal innovation (Rooijen, 2024).

So, social extrapreneurs can be characterized as working in and between organizations and networks not only to create novel solutions but to develop a range of support and sustenance mechanisms and social change ecosystems.

Social extrapreneurs can be found in government, academia, private sector and network organizations. They shoal and coalesce in the pursuit of social impact. They pull ideas, people and resources together to create the environment for doing well and good to ensure social entrepreneurs and intrapreneurs are stimulated, supported and sustained.

Social Extrapreneurship Interface with Frugal Innovation

The essence of social extrapreneurship interface with frugal innovation is to create hopefulness and happiness in the livelihood of an individual. Social extrapreneur has the soft passionate heart to assist communities to accomplish their needs and want. Extrapreneurs are the ‘game changers’ of frugal innovation dreams to come to light (Nassani *et al.*, 2022). Many entrepreneurs and intrapreneurs dreams focus on how to increase the market share, business expansion, sales territories but social extrapreneur always make gains for a new dimension by satisfying the social needs of the society with social proof to climb and grab better opportunities.

Extrapreneurs do not just utilize their time frame and economical resources to satisfy their client but indulge in strategic alliance with interested stakeholders to meet the needs of the society needs. Social extrapreneur are high risk takers against all odds. They do not think more about profitability rather they focus more on sustainability and survival of human wellbeing and wellness.

Many are familiar with the term’s “entrepreneurship” and, to a lesser extent, “intrapreneurship”. However, extrapreneurship is a new term that is slowly but surely gaining traction and is related to both. In an ideal scenario, extrapreneurship represents the best of both intrapreneurship and entrepreneurship worlds with the goal being to deliver current services or products, or to boost a certain metric, be it productivity, efficiency or profitability.

According to Jason Clay, Senior VP at WWF, extrapreneurs can be described as “change agents” that “solve problems by moving between companies, organizations and sectors, spreading ideas and solutions from one to another like bees pollinating flowers”.

It is no secret that large multinational corporations that offer “jobs for life” are quickly becoming outdated and the idea of companies keeping on tens of thousands of staff members is fast becoming obsolete. This is where extrapreneurs come in, with promises of delivering existing services offered by the mother organization, without the company contracting it to full-time staff. However, both parties have skin in the game which works to ensure both cooperate accordingly to get the best results possible, with this structure feasible in public, private and charitable sectors.

Such organizations will lend both professional and financial resources to extrapreneurs to give them the best possible chance to succeed. In return, they will guarantee a certain level of results or change. For example, an organization in the public sector may be under heavy pressure to reduce its workforce. Instead of expensive outsourcing, existing staff may be given an extrapreneurial arrangement which reduces costs but also ensures that key staff will not simply be made redundant.

In addition, these extrapreneurs are also free to seek additional clients elsewhere to earn more income and make full use of their additional time and resources. This arrangement is beneficial to the company as they retain the services of staff that know the culture and organization, while the extrapreneurs benefit from the flexibility and the safety net offered by a long-term agreement while they pursue additional clients or income. Both parties guarantee each other a minimum level of trade and guarantees, creating a win-win scenario for all.

Extrapreneurship can also transform existing companies that have deep-rooted cultures but who are looking to change perceptions. For example, the World Wildlife Fund (WWF) has begun offering adventure travel packages run by extrapreneurs, of which a portion of proceeds contributes to the conservation of the very places would-be tourists visit. While such travel goes against the original values of the WWF, there is little doubt that an extrapreneurial venture with various vendors offered the change they desired without upsetting the applecart, and at a lower cost than handling the transition themselves which would include sourcing, hiring, and training full-time staff.

Could extrapreneurship offer a more stable solution than pure entrepreneurship? The numbers would suggest so, with Shikhar Ghosh, a senior lecturer at Harvard Business School, suggesting that around 30-40% of businesses fail completely, with a staggering 80% unable to project a return on investment. If failure is to be defined as falling short of a goal, a stunning 90-95% of companies fulfill this criterion.

The safety nets that extrapreneurship provides let established companies revamp and revise their outlook while maintaining their current targets. Problems faced by such large organizations may take too much effort to fix on their own, which is where extrapreneurs can find their niche and connect the dots between global organizations for large-scale change. This also allows burgeoning entrepreneurs to get their feet wet, or seasoned intrapreneurs to spread their wings and fly with a higher chance of long-term sustainability.

ULTRAPRENEURSHIP

Ultrapreneur is like also an intrapreneur in such a way that they are part of an existing enterprise either large or small. Ultrapreneur is an enterprising or entrepreneurial fellow, but his innovation commences within the organization itself and whose impacts may extend beyond the organization to which he or she is directly a part e.g. realizing new opportunities such as forming a subsidiary organization (Medium, 2024).

Unlike the term entrepreneur (defined here), the term Ultrapreneur is essentially made up. Even though you won't find the term in the English dictionary as with many other modern terms, the word Ultrapreneur is quickly becoming adopted by entrepreneurs of all kinds and attributed a meaning. Someone who has exceeded in their undertaking as an entrepreneur but also has a profound effect on their family, community, country or humanity.

A holistic approach encompassing all aspects of one's life including entrepreneurship, health and wellbeing, family, spirituality, morality and mentality which come together to provide supreme balance. An ultrapreneur have the self-starter, self-motivated and self-efficacy on specific things they do. The definition of ultrapreneur is someone who has many profit-generating pursuits at once (Nigel, 2024). However, it is my belief that what is more important that simply adopting a meaning for a word, It's important to separate the 'definition' of a word and what it actually 'means' to 'you' (Ovharhe, 2023; Nigel, 2024).

There's a definition of the word 'love' and then there's what it means to everyone. Thus, the same thinking can or indeed should be applied to the terms fitness of ultrapreneur. The meaning of these words is what gives ultrapreneur power, rather gives the power to change their reality.

An "ultrapreneur" is a term used to describe an entrepreneur who is highly successful and innovative, often pushing the boundaries of traditional business practices (Shifana, 2024). Ultrapreneurs are known for their ability to create and lead highly successful ventures that have a significant impact on their industries or even society as a whole (Medium, 2024).

On the other hand, an "entrepreneur" refers to a person who starts a business or organization, taking on financial risks in the hope of profit (Ganapati, 2024). While entrepreneurs can also be highly successful and innovative, the term "ultrapreneur" often implies a level of achievement and influence beyond what is typically associated with entrepreneurship. In essence, the difference lies in the scale, impact, and level of innovation associated with the ventures led by ultrapreneurs compared to those led by entrepreneurs (Nigel, 2024).

Ultrapreneurship and Frugal Innovation

If you want to start a business and get rich, there is no difference. What differentiates you is one's attitude (Ganapati, 2024). An entrepreneur starts a business and goes all the way to make it a success with the aid of frugal innovation (Nassani *et al.*, 2022). An ultrapreneur is someone committed to making the business as big as possible as soon as possible. He is an entrepreneur with a goal. The goal of an ultrapreneur is to make as much as possible as quickly as possible. An ultrapreneur is usually unconcerned about the business running smoothly and profitably in the long run. He is not looking for a company to manage and grow; he is looking for a business he can sell and takes a big check from at the end of a year or two. Ultrapreneurs want to be rich, and they want to be rich now (Ganapati, 2024).

Ultrapreneurs can be seen as ultimate elite entrepreneurs who are focused on creating a positive impact as well as job creation (Shifana, 2024). Mindfulness and ability to quiet the mind describe an ultrapreneur compared to an entrepreneur who is comparatively restless.

Ultrapreneur is relatively a new English word not found in any dictionary. An ultrapreneur possesses a holistic approach encompassing all aspects of one's life including entrepreneurship, health and wellbeing, family, spirituality, morality and mentality which come together to provide supreme balance (Ganapati, 2024).

Frugal Engineering and Technology Innovation

Frugal engineering is the concept emerging to problem-solving that focuses on creating thinking of simplicity, affordable, and resource-efficient solutions about intangible and tangible products (Hossain *et al.*, 2023). Frugal engineering focused on fine-tuning problems associated with people in resource constraint issues which enable them to perform better within limited resources. It is stated that frugal engineering empowers businesses to unleash the potential of innovative ideas and technologies by adopting simplicity, cost-effectiveness, and creativity (Qin, 2024).

Furthermore, Qin (2024) explored a critical discussion on how to unleash frugal engineering via internet of things (IoT) and artificial intelligence (AI) on boosting the entrepreneurship world quality, low cost-effectiveness, durability using SEM approach by SmartPLS. The result acknowledged that IoT and AI are valid predictors of frugal innovation. Hence social entrepreneurs in alignment with ultrapreneurs and social extrapreneurs should design semantic models with capacity, ability and capabilities to achieve frugal engineering to champion the competitive parity in today's technological-oriented era. Additionally, this revealed that acceptance of technology-oriented innovativeness on product, process, service, administration and emerging market is imperative where social entrepreneurship indicators like ultrapreneurship and social extrapreneurship could dramatize interface with innovative technologies like IoT and AI models into practices.

From the description of the structural equation model (SEM) by SmartPLS as illustrated by Qin (2024) it portrays that the future is safe on developing fabricated engineering design on prototype of product that has credible quality, affordability, durability, low cost and benefits to customer desire.

Frugal engineering has drawn international recognition with strong influence in the macro economies of developed, under-developed communities and developing nations. The emerging market systematically has benefits enormous development from frugal engineering via positioning new or diversified products and services that stimulate more entrepreneurship entries for multinationals, conglomerates and corporations, MSMEs growth and development (Ovharhe & Akandu, 2024; Ovharhe & Chibuike, 2024).

Frugal engineering fine-tunes present and future entrepreneurship opportunities that create emerging market demand in the supply chain system of countries with stimulates growth. This has stimulated optimistic socio-economic transformation in the rural and urban communities of nation with job creation, value creation, wealth creation and employment creation for the now and then of the society exposure generally.

Prolific Prof. Iman Khamis in 2024, explored dynamic feasible trend on "applications of artificial intelligence, deep learning and big data", which orchestrates frugality strategic alliance with artificial intelligence (AI) could boost social innovator strength to be the giant that mitigate constraints to advantageous environment munificence for community wellness, wellbeing and livelihood (Murphy, 2024). This ignites the spirit of innovator giants like the social extrapreneur and ultrapreneurs to delve into full capacity of frugality in the environment.

Professor Fahri Özsungur an accelerated emerging technology innovator giant in entrepreneurship, redeemed that "innovators will miss the mark without AI". This dramatized while AI has championed industrial tactics to develop insight, enabling foresight, pursuit and kneel resource constraints for betterment environment munificence in emerging market structure (Özsungur, 2024).

Purposefully for the betterment of communities, the synergy among artificial intelligence (AI) and the Internet of Things (IoT) adopted by social entrepreneurs brain players such as ultrapreneurs and social extrapreneurs has create tremendous transformation in the quality of mankind livelihood by addressing the threats and challenges in resource-constrained conditions, mostly in developing and under developing countries (Giuggioli & Pellegrini, 2023; Park, Rosca & Agarwal, 2022).

Nevertheless, the role of machine learning, data analytics, data coding, artificial intelligence (AI) and the Internet of Things (IoT) is noteworthy that offers numerous social entrepreneurship opportunities to augment positive expression and impact of frugal solutions in various aspect of opportunistic and exposure granted to communities globally (Govindan, 2022).

Data science, deep learning, IoT, clearer services, personalized solutions, affordable automation, data analytics, data virtualization, machine learning and AI are key drivers of frugal engineering in innovative technology. These technologies perform multi-dimensional functions to ensure the sustainable business innovative model, based on pyramid (BOP), resource-constraints and environmental munificence work simultaneously with achieving the goals of frugal engineering (Onsongo, Knorringa & Beers, 2023; Park et al., 2022).

This is cross sectional to various fields associated with frugal engineering that are vital to communities in developing and developed nations such healthcare diagnostics, predictive maintenance, academic functions, block chain, fintech, biotech and energy functionalities.

By making frugal engineering viable and worthwhile, the beneficiary in communities must experience simplicity, affordability and quality of the goods and services from the limited resources available in the environment. Social extrapreneur and ultrapreneurs should use technology innovation to create a global change in the community.

Technology innovation such as AI-based communication connects remote community clusters has the capability and ability to translate language for global reach of frugal solutions. Technology innovation allows frugal engineering models to perform effectively and efficiently well managing fewer resources and addressing challenges within the developing economies in order to provide optimistic solution that have positive impact and meaningful sustainable development (Govindan, 2022). In the same tail, innovation technology performs critical features in frugal engineering by networking and connecting via devices by enabling data-driven solutions for the organizations, community and individuals (Qin, 2024).

Deep learning, big data, data science, AI and IoT enhance efficiency in critical aspect of mankind which includes social infrastructure, agri-preneurship, healthcare, and capitalization, optimizing resource optimization and cost minimization (Ovharhe & Chibuike, 2024). Technology innovation facilitates remote monitoring and control of instrumentation that augments predictive maintenance and enhances lifespan. In healthcare, technology innovation empowers telemedicine, e-health, data virtualization, data science, deep learning and remote patient monitoring, which fine-turns it services to unmet needs clustering in the community (Ovharhe & Abada, 2024). Furthermore, Ovharhe (2024) argued that by synchronizing technology innovation (Data science, deep learning, IoT, clearer services, personalized solutions, affordable automation, data analytics, data virtualization, machine learning and AI) been aligned with frugal engineering in the communities the simplicity, affordability, cost minimization and quality product solutions can be on measureable metrics, as advantage to marginalized communities which is capable of providing possible remedies to global issues in resource-constrained and environments munificence. This enumerates that technology innovation plays imperative roles in frugal engineering as competitive edge and means of social mission accomplishment in the resource-constraint environment for sustainability, survival and success of mankind livelihood (Ovharhe & Abada, 2024; Qin, 2024; International Centre for frugal Innovation, 2024).

In this light, on brightening the future trend UCMB (2024) orchestrates program on internet of things (IoT) and artificial intelligence (AI) to augment frugal engineering in various pathways on academic institutions, society, business enterprise and environmental benefits for mitigating constraints. This is to iron out that frugal engineering is strictly about mitigating constraints which pill up obscurity and neglect visibility in the communities, industries and environments on limited socio-economic resources. Frugal engineering glows the environment and ecosystem of community, business enterprises and nations with illuminating light on coats of many colors that lead to positive emotions and upwards spirals. To shield the constraints on society and nations ecosystem, Miller (2024), calls for social entrepreneur in anchor spirit of extrapreneur and ultrapreneur to delve into the transformative power, strength, momentum and synergy of frugal engineering, a testament to human ingenuity and resilience in the face of adversity.

RESOURCE CONSTRAINTS

Resource is the most vital instrument for input and determinant of output in any business venture be it human, product, process, services, market and technology. Transformation of resources from one stage to another to become projected goals needs innovation. Innovation is the act and ability of transforming resources from one state to another state by achieving the pre-determination objectives from the design and framework.

Resource constraints are bottlenecks, pitfalls, limitations and barriers that affect the opportunistic venture and allocation of required resources necessary to accomplish targeted goals within specific timeline and scope. Frugality in this clause must be defined within the framework and scope of the specific project to meet the social missions and dream of the entrepreneurial journey.

For entrepreneurs to delves into the process of blending resources to meet the needs of client of consumers at quality, low costing estimation, durability, affordability and comfortability, without much consideration of profit maximization, return on asset (ROA), return on equity (ROE) and return on interest (ROI) within short-term frame instead of long-term, the presence of social entrepreneurs actors are needed.

The social entrepreneurs in this context are deemed to be ultrapreneurs and social extrapreneurs. Both possess trait, potential and competence to drive resources in tradition or sustainable business model to accomplish great tasks in the community settings by achieving much despites pitfalls on resource-constraints.

Hossain, Shahid and Park (2024) agreed that the resource-based view (RBV) network the entrepreneurial mechanisms through which an enterprise gains optimum competitive advantage by obtaining distinctive and superior resources, and subsequently, translating these resources into capabilities that deliver better value for customers and bolster the firm's value appropriation. The resource-based perspective has been applied to frugal entrepreneurs to understand how they mobilize human, financial, and social resources and capabilities in a resource-constrained environment to realize their innovative and entrepreneurial aspirations. Frugal entrepreneurs employ diverse strategies in developing markets, such as fostering partnerships with local actors to create products or collaborating with non-traditional stakeholders to overcome local constraints (Hossain, Park & Shahid, 2023).

A lack of resources prevents many people from engaging in entrepreneurship. In developing countries in particular, entrepreneurs often encounter several constraints, such as lack of raw materials and advanced machinery, underdeveloped information technologies, and a shortage of local technological expertise. Nevertheless, some entrepreneurs transform these resource limitations into opportunities, such as through partnerships. Moreover, the constraints in developing countries lead some firms to offer affordable products thanks to their low production costs (Park et al., 2022).

The RBV is mainly grounded in well-established markets that are characterized by intense competition, and it has been less commonly applied from the perspective of frugal innovation. A key limitation of the RBV is that we know little about how to configure resources to best realize their potential for creating value in various other contexts, such as in developing markets. Consequently, its managerial relevance is somewhat limited when we consider the process of configuring resources to create value in those countries, which are characterized by resource scarcities that significantly impact resource-management practices.

FRUGAL INNOVATION MODEL

Bhatti and Ventresca in Velananda, Dissanayake and Wickramasinghe (2022). Expatiate on the frugal innovation model with three paradigm shift in the frugal innovation model as itemized below; viz:

1. Market affordability constraints.
2. Resources scarcity, constraints

3. Institutional void or complexities

Figure 1. Frugal innovation model (Bhatti and Ventresca, 2013)

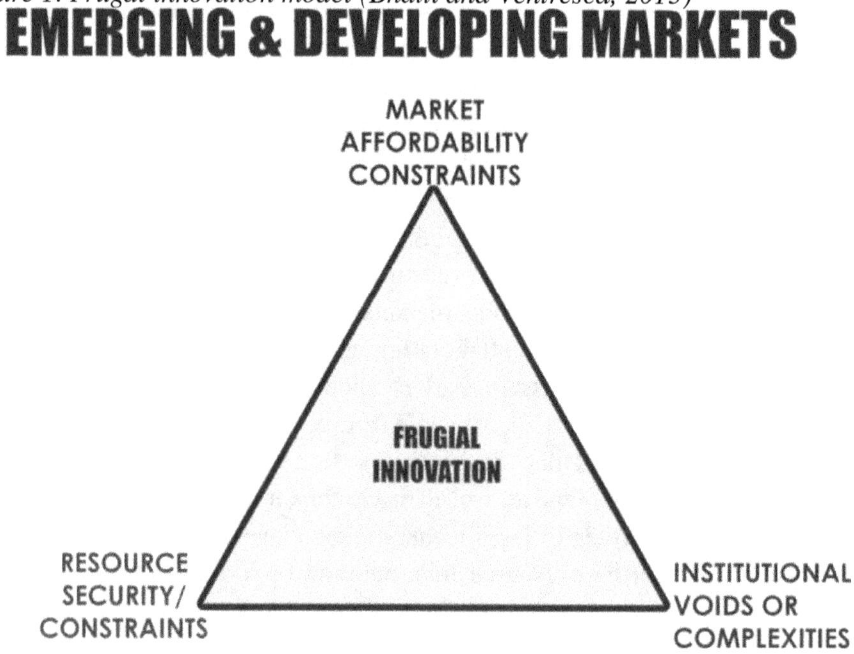

The first model of frugal innovations in connection to the financial side was created by Bhatti and Ventresca in Velananda, Dissanayake and Wickramasinghe (2022). The strategy concentrates on three concepts that are crucial for understanding frugal innovation. The first is the limited variety of resources that are offered. The customers' limited purchasing power further limits activities. The second aspect of frugal innovation is the result of emerging markets. There are many people who find it difficult to meet their basic needs and who have little money to spend on goods and services. The third reason is that a lack of institutions creates an environment where it is difficult to distinguish between official and informal politics and commercial transactions.

Frugal innovation should be seen as transfer of wealth to community, nations and environment instead of being used as a means of generating profitability for the organization. The first model of frugal innovations in connection to the financial side was created by Bhatti and Ventresca (2013). The strategy concentrates on three concepts that are crucial for understanding frugal innovation. The first is the limited variety of resources that are offered. The customers' limited purchasing power further limits activities. The second aspect of frugal innovation is the result of emerging markets. There are many people who find it difficult to meet their basic needs and who have little money to spend on goods and services. The third reason is that a lack of institutions creates an environment where it is difficult to distinguish between official and informal politics and commercial transactions.

Business modeling has emerged as an important topic in management scholarships, with it gaining significant momentum in recent years. A business model's significance can be understood through the central role it plays in explaining an enterprise competitiveness and leading edge instead of bleeding edge, numerous evidence between business model and entrepreneurship opportunity (Ovharhe & Chibuike; Ovharhe & Woko, 2024a,b). The term “business model” has no single universal definition, but the underlying concept mainly comprises three main components: value proposition, value creation, and value capture (Miller, 2024).

Business models are critical instrumental tools used as pragmatic, framework and dashboard to navigate the strategic goals of enterprise in the MSMEs, corporations, conglomerates and multinationals. Onsongo, Knorringa and Beers (2023) sees business models as the activities enterprise undertakes to create value for a specific market, and the mechanisms of capturing value. This means business models are strongly associated with value capture, value creation and wealth creation that drive entrepreneurship opportunities (Ovharhe & Woko, 2024a,b; Ovharhe & Saturday, 2024). Business models have credible interface with dynamism, adaptability, competitiveness, and turbulence in the entrepreneurship world which aims to satisfy and render benefits to society. Business model is a practical guide to entrepreneurship entry and exit that defined enterprise sustainability, survival and success towards meaningful sustainable development to the enterprise, society and nations (Ovharhe & Chibuike, 2023; Ovharhe & Abuda, 2023a,b).

Aligning with sustainability and competitive advantage with the business model creates the mindset of developing Base of Pyramid (BOP). In this light, focused will be drawn to business model innovation towards creating possible solutions to society and nations with socio-economic view where social entrepreneurs will be employed the ultrapreneurs and social extrapreneurs to delve into creative thinking of innovativeness on product, process and services to position the unmet needs in enabling communities. This is the bridge established by Onsongo, Knorringa and Beers (2023) to build frugal business model innovation as strong correlates in the base of the pyramid.

Base of the pyramid (BOP) markets are associated fine-tuning strong unique challenges and entrepreneurship opportunities, in particular, severe resource constraints and environmental munificence that call for innovative towards fashioning solutions as possible remedies locally and globally (Hossain, Shahid & Park, 2024). This shows that with the mergers of BOP, sustainable business model and frugal innovation social entrepreneurs should think globally and act locally to achieve credible results (Ovharhe, 2024; Ur, Anwar, Antohi, Ali, Fortea, & Zlati, 2024).

In the tail of these, Prahalad and Hammond in Vázquez-Pacho and Payaud (2024) who coined the term, BOP concept, have been defined on basis of per capita income at or below US$1500 or US$2000 *per annum*. The BOP market has also been enumerating with metrics on the household poverty threshold of US$1 or US$2 per day. BOP businesses in the enterprise environment were described as aligned with entire communities, nations and continents as in Africa, Asia and Latin America. However, the discourse has evolved to focus on customer, community and geographical segments been characterized by strong resource constraints and poor market access among clusters.

To serve these markets, social entrepreneur actors; ultrapreneurs and social extrapreneurs must fashion out how they can augment rejuvenated products and services which are of the right quantity, simplicity, affordability, durability, maintain functionality, and are affordable to low-income estimated customers. Frugal innovation offers a paradigm shift for individuals, communities and low-income countries to be of utmost beneficiary. Frugal business models maintain communal functionality by sustaining the delivery of low-cost, high-quality of products to BOP emerging markets, and through frugal business model innovation, which foster enterprise search for the optimal balance between wealth creation, value creation and value capture (León, Pichardo, Carrillo & Santiago (2024). This boosts the social extrapreneur and ultrapreneurs capacity to balance the drives to collaborate with stakeholders to create value and pursuit of entrepreneurship opportunities in the emerging markets.

Social extrapreneur and ultrapreneurs recognized the relevance of business models to employed possible solutions in BOP markets with the frugal business model innovation. With the softness of heart, social extrapreneur and ultrapreneurs in the spirit of social entrepreneurship are expert to develop new business models suitable for markets with pending issues of unmet need position in their community cluster. With application of frugal innovation, BOP and the business model social extrapreneur and ultrapreneurs should avoid failure to capture the dynamic nature of business models as possible solution and remedies to bridge the gap among low-income community globally that exhibited hunger and extremely poverty because the instrument of the business model could shift to value creation, value capture and wealth creation in the communities.

Based of Pyramid (BOP)

Based or bottom of Pyramid (BOP) could be regarded as a market-based model of meaningful socio-economic development which projected assurance to simultaneously alleviate widespread poverty and hunger while providing growth and profits for socio-entrepreneurs, champiopreneurs, ultrapreneurs, serial entrepreneurs and socio extrapreneurs (Nimmagadda, et al., 2024; Ovharhe, 2022, 2023, 2024).

Frugal innovation consists of creating possible solutions based on the authenticated utilization of resources with essential quality, design, and functionality, offered to customers with lower purchasing power (Miller, 2024). Frugal innovation is concerned with value-sensitive design and marketing strategies that bring sophisticated products within the reach of relatively poorer consumers and developing economies around definite territories. Through re-engineering, re-modeling and re-inventing, value consumer products and dramatically lowering their unit consumer price, product mix which can be made affordable for the estimated four billion consumers at the Bottom or Base of the Pyramid (BoP). BOP is the fundamental issues and concern that lead to the breakthrough which pivoted frugal innovation on its sustainability, survival and success on the Notion of 5billions or 4billions leave less than 2USD per day. Thus, BOP (or bottom-of-the-pyramid) optimistic emerging market refers to the four billion to five billion people living on less than $2 per day. When businesses get involved in BOP economies, they can stimulate the creation of new process, services and product (Hossain, Shahid & Park, 2024).

Investigation by León, Pichardo, Carrillo and Santiago (2024) explained sustainable business models (SBMs) interface with traditional business model (BM) components aiming to address the needs of the poor towards exposing base of the pyramid (BoP). The base of pyramid seems to be unique in addressing communal issues on need on value creation and wealth creation which is direct proposition to the emerging markets to satisfy needs of client from the adoption of frugal innovation.

In the view of frugal innovation concept, the adoption of business models is a key instrument that designs a framework for sustainability, survival and success. Social entrepreneurs in alignment with ultrapreneurs and social extrapreneurs uses the business model to design and fathoms the frugal innovation needs to transform complexity into simplicity and flexibility on satisfying clients' needs that will be beneficial to their livelihood. The model could be utilize to delve into business analysis in technology such as internet of things, machine learning, data virtualization, big data analytics and artificial intelligence for better outcome of results in product innovativeness, process innovativeness, service innovativeness and market innovativeness with the aim of promoting targeted sustainable development in developing countries (Ovharhe, 2023; Ovharhe & Woko, 2021, 2022).

Entrepreneurship has remarkable potential for achieving sustainable development, but traditional firms are profit-oriented with little interest in sustainable development (Tufts Gordon Institute, 2024). Nevertheless, there is a compelling need for both ultrapreneur and social extrapreneur to strike a balance between profitability and their contributions to sustainability. With their novel business models, frugal enterprises have emerged as key players contributing to sustainable development in resource-constrained environments. Frugal innovation is considered a valuable source of sustainable entrepreneurship as rendered by ultrapreneurship and social extrapreneurship. This is obtainable, because ultrapreneur and social extrapreneur as frugal enterprises and social innovator are ventures that develop affordable products and services for low-income customers who are typically not deemed worthy of attention by multinationals, corporations and conglomerates.

Over recent decades, meaningful high-value sustainable development has arisen as a means for addressing the issues of poverty, zero-degree hunger, inclusive entrepreneurship, environmental damage, and social inequality. It essentially means that enabling communities and developing nations should satisfy their current needs without sacrificing the ability of future generations to satisfy their needs (Ovharhe & Chibuike, 2024; Millers, 2024).

The challenge is not simply providing stripped down versions of high-value products but instead providing value-sensitive innovations that are truly compatible with the unique circumstances of relatively poorer consumers, and to find ways to co-produce these innovations with local producers. For example, developing much cheaper and more robust weather stations in cooperation with African universities or improved access to micro-credit, ideas or innovation partners through digital platforms

International Centre for frugal Innovation (2024) set up a motion on frugal innovation during which student teams leverage their multidisciplinary on academic backgrounds to address challenges pertaining to crucial issues like climate change, food accessibility, clean water provision, health support, and waste management. Frugal innovation is center on need assessment of these critical issues and concerns which foster meaningful sustainable development on the global communities.

Exponential research by European Association of Development Research and Training Institutes

(2024) was embedded on hydraulic ramp pump, address water scarcity. The hydraulic ram pump, demonstrated in the Living Mountain Lab, is a popular technology that lifts water using the kinetic energy of flowing water, offering potential benefits for upland communities. However, improvements could be made on the production costs, efficiency, and simplification of manufacturing for easier maintenance and repair. Apart from access to water, isolated and peri-urban areas face difficulties in accessing fresh and safe food. Efforts in sustainable livestock, agriculture, and fisheries aim to ensure food security and improve livelihoods. Aquaponics, an innovative system combining plant, fish, and bacteria growth, ensures water efficiency and intensive production without chemical inputs. However, challenges with current models include high costs, sophisticated operation skills, constant monitoring, and the need for reliable backup systems and electrical support for uninterrupted operation.

Tufts Gordon Institute (2024) fast track the momentum of thought-provoking panel discussion on the concept of jugaad and frugal innovation which center staged on doing more with less. Doing more with less is the motherhood ideology of frugal innovation. The discussion was focused on the future of frugal innovation towards doing more despite resource constraints and environmental factors. Although, the concepts of jugaad and frugal innovation have been making many waves positively in the developing and under developing communities. The entrepreneurship world is fast track with resourcefulness and ingenuity at the midrange which poses the tendency to achieve extraordinary feats within tight budgets, showcase the power of doing more with less. The power of doing more with less is deposit on the adoption of frugal innovation.

Though, no community is born without any resources that are not noteworthy because all way all community needs lie beneath, within or above to sustain and survive them for success. Every community are encrypt with noteworthy substances with value which can transform them into immeasurable changes that are treasurable. This is while the call for social entrepreneurs is of necessity to beam the light of ultrapreneurs and social extrapreneurs to brighten the environment in the entrepreneurship world (Ovharhe, 2022; Ovharhe & Chukwuemeka, 2023). The entrepreneurship world boosts the leverage of the emerging market which offers a unique opportunity to delve into the new insights surrounding jugaad or frugal innovation that create goods and services that are affordable, flexible, simplicity, sustainability and comfortability.

Frugal engineering has gained innovative strength on motion, which is while Hindawi among others journal of engineering dedicated to research more scientific discovery on environmental assessment on air quality and mitigation strategy, variation of water temperature and evaporation, machine learning approach on environmental assessment, effect of heat transfer characteristics, utilizing local waste and artificial intelligence-based approach in intrusion detection. More so, frugal engineering poses a new concept on semi-automatic composition that consists of workstations and an automatic transfer system between the stations (Hindawi, 2024).

No community, challenging environment and nation can prosper efficiently in her ecosystem without the role of social extrapreneurship and ultrapreneurship (Ovharhe & Abada, 2024). This is enterprises that pivot all entrepreneurial functions, including the social entrepreneurship which anchors the ultrapreneur and social extrapreneur activities that foster the growth and development of any nation's economy. This growth and development are the architect of innovation with availability of resources and process to fine-turn affordable goods and services. One specific constraint identified is the absence of frugal innovation, characterized by the capacity and capability to develop novel products, processes, or services with minimal resources and cost-effectiveness (Hyypiä & Khan in Rehman, Anwar, Antohi, Ali,

Fortea & Zlati, 2024). In alliance to the bottleneck and pitfalls of these constraints, the emergence of frugal innovation is a turn-around strategy and tactic to redeem the entrepreneurship world.

APPROACHES TO FRUGAL INNOVATION AND SOCIAL ENTREPRENEURSHIP

GAGA Approach

Basically, the idiomatic expression 'go along to get along' (GAGA) concept as augmented in Vietnamese portrays a matching order force team spirit or compliance to establish status quo ante (Merriam-Webster, 2024). This promotes the spirit of orderliness to accomplish targeted goals among stakeholders to be in simple harmony on social mission. The social entrepreneur in conjunction with the ultrapreneurs and social extrapreneur should apply this approach in the frugal innovation. In this scenario all stakeholders (social enterprise and beneficiaries) must be in simple heartedness to accomplish specific targeted goals in unity of purpose.

The GAGA concept is an action phrase for ultrapreneur and social extrapreneur to swing into action to carry everyone in the society along to accomplish its task. Families, relatives, friends, colleagues and stakeholders in the community, society and nation must develop unity of purpose to have the interest of all to achieve the social mission. This could be addressing possible solutions on the socio-economic factors like products, services, distribution and logistics that is problematic to society. Also issues and concern about marketing, technology and pricing can be harmonized to have a single heartedness of interest to all stakeholders involved in the social mission.

Additionally, constraints to pricing, quality, taste, quantity and design that suitable to consumers happiness must not be left out. All stakeholders must engage on the GAGA concept, which unified the social entrepreneur agent (i.e. ultrapreneurs and social extrapreneurs) to the community and beneficiary at large. This is an inclusive concept that buttresses the livelihood pattern of the sustainable development goals (SDG) on achieving zero hunger and poverty elimination (Ovharhe & Chukwemenka; Ovharhe & Okolo, 2022).

The social entrepreneur instrumentations (i.e. ultrapreneurs and social extrapreneurs) uses the GAGA concept to maintain orderliness of peace, security and industrial harmony among stakeholder with smooth implementation of frugal innovation the sense of betrayal and stigmatization. The GAGA concept has a swing in communal acceptability of the frugal innovation proposition of quality, pricing, design, style and process. This is because GAGA creates strong mutual relationships and trust being established among all stakeholders. GAGA concept is instrumental to comfortability to all stakeholders to be at ease on go along to get along.

GAGA concept creates conducive atmosphere for frugal innovation practices in nations and communities. GAGA means working together with one purpose, dreams and vision at utmost to achieve specific target from the short-term and long-term.

> -Go along means to agree with all stakeholders in the social mission to synchronized syndicates
> -Get along means that the society and social entrepreneurs (i.e. ultrapreneurs and social extrapreneurs) unify with one mindset without any disagreements or problems that can be prejudice and jeopardize the interest of the entire social mission of frugal innovation.
> -Go along to get along means to agree with someone so the relationship will not have problems

In the nutshell GAGA specifically means to proceed or move along with understanding society's trust, norms, mutual relationship, standard and team cohesiveness that might be optimistic in positive feedback.

The companionship, cooperation and team agreement with the social entrepreneur (social extrapreneurs and ultrapreneurs) in the application of GAGA cannot be overemphasized because the benefits are so enormous. With GAGA adoption extrapreneur and ultrapreneur can mitigate better technology and environmental regulation challenges that will push the society to achieve meaningful sustainable development as benefits from the enterprise.

Needs Assessments Approach

Miller (2024) posits that in frugal innovation, assessing the customer needs is of major priority. There are, of course, different approaches to assessing the needs of customers in the frugal innovation. The identification of problems or needs to mitigate the challenges of resource constraints and environmental munificence is development of framework called "needs assessments" with served as instrumentation tools in providing possible solution as fundamental remedies. However, a growing number of community development leaders in the spirit of social entrepreneurs argue that the focus on "needs" may itself be problematic. They suggest that needs-focused assessments risk defining an organization, neighborhood, or community by its problems that generally require outside expertise and resources to "fix.". Thus, needs assessments can have an unintended effect on the relationship between the servers such as social innovators (i.e. ultrapreneurs and social extrapreneurs) and those being served (i.e. needy, communities), as well as a negative long-term impact on the community's own capacity to grow and develop (Roehlkepartain, 2008).

Ovharhe and Woko (2024) explored that as an alternative, especially in the less developed, developing communities and stakeholders with optimal charisma, potential and trait should be the focus. They further opined that with this charisma, potentials and trait of ultrapreneurs and social entrepreneurs, it could be recommend shifting the focus from identifying dying dreams, hopelessness, frustration, depression and misfortune to identifying resources, hopes, and dreams. Instead of asking, "What problems do you have that we can fix for you," a social entrepreneurs asks, what are your strengths, priorities, untapped resources, and hopes, and how can we build and grab the business opportunities in alliance with stakeholders toward the kind of social mission and community benefits by mitigating constraints, pitfalls, turbulence and environmental munificence beyond assessing the needs of children, youth, women and elderly.

Often when people first hear about strength-based assessments, they find it counterintuitive. After all, we assume that "service" should meet "needs," so you should focus on identifying those needs in the assessment process. However, by focusing on what is present (not missing) in a community young people have the potential to identify constructive service opportunities that can add value to a community, building on latent potential, without merely focusing on what is lacking. In this way the focus of the project is positively defined instead of being characterized by what may be perceived as a community weakness.

This shift changes the power dynamic between those "being served" and those "providing service." Instead of the neighborhood, organization, or community having needs that young people meet through service-learning, both the service-learners and the "recipients" of service offer resources, capacities, hopes, and priorities in a mutually reciprocal partnership.

John L. McKnight and his colleagues at Northwestern University were pioneers in shifting the focus of community assessment or mapping to emphasize strengths (McKnight & Kretzmann, 1996; Kretzmann & McKnight, 1993). For example, a needs assessment might document patterns of crime, unemployment, pollution, and economic blight within a neighborhood (all of which are present). In contrast, a strengths map of the same neighborhood might identify individual gifts and interests, available untapped resources, as well as the capacities of local organizations and associations (all of which are also present).

The difference, McKnight and Kretzmann (1996) contend, is that the latter map is the map a neighbor must rely on if it is to find the power to regenerate itself. Communities have never been built on their deficiencies. Building a community of prolific magnitude has always depended upon mobilizing the capacities and assets of a people and a place. In other words, needs assessments create "mental maps" that define people primarily in terms of their problems and challenges, fostering a cycle of dependency on outside services and resources (Beaulieu in Greco, Savage & Souza, 2024).

Social entrepreneurs are embedded with great deals of tasks in trying to optimize success in actualizing frugal innovation come to beam light of sustainability and survival. It is important to note that there are too many communities and national products that bean structure without meaningfully impact on the people. This is as a result of an inadequate need assessment program which impose unmet ideas on society with little or no consideration or people's traditions, beliefs, and needs. Frugal innovation to be of paramount flying colors during and after implementation, the market analysis and customer feedback is of 100% necessity. When social extrapreneurs and ultrapreneurs are engage in the society or particular community to perform meaningful sustainable development for betterment of the society, it would be painful if all effort is of no value due to nonjustifiable need analysis.

Sometime when frugal innovation is sponsored by multinational and corporate philanthropic as full corporate social responsibility, it will be shameful and detrimental to the corporate image of the social entrepreneur being represented by the ultrapreneur and social extrapreneur if inadequate need assessment is conducted to truncate the entire process as waste.

When such scenarios occur the society, mostly the youth interpret the supportive contribution as intrusive and exploitive, this might jeopardize mutual relationship and trust in social extrapreneurs and ultrapreneurs. Also, these possess threat on the social enterprise operations and their resources will be at stake. Although, when there are remedies, this pointed out the fact that most youth strength are being development socially, emotionally, mentally and spiritually to achieve maximum energy and strength (Boyatzis, 2024).

Strength-Based Approaches

With its foundation in social work, the strength-based approach is a "work practice theory" that focuses on an individual's self-determination and strength (Rahmanti & Subandi, 2024).

This type of approach builds on clients' strengths, seeing them as resourceful and resilient when they are in adverse conditions (Baird & Peterson, 2024). It is also centered on getting people to fine-tuned change in them.

Change happens depending on how each person handles themselves:

- Attitudes about their dignity
- Capacities
- Rights

- Quirks
- Similarities

The strength-based approach is centered on the idea that the client is the actor or agent of change. The approach is highly dependent on how the individual processes their thoughts and emotions. It allows for open communication, encouraging individuals to identify values and assemble their strengths and capacities. The strength-based approach allows a person to see themselves at their best the value they bring by just being themselves. They are encouraged to capitalize on their strengths rather than focus on negative characteristics. The strength-based approach examines not only the individual, but also their environment; for example, how systems are set up or power imbalances between a system or service and the people it is supposed to serve. In addition, the strength-based approach identifies constraints that might be holding back an individual's growth. These constraints might be social, personal, and/or cultural issues (Rahmanti & Subandi, 2024).

Rapp et al. as in accordance with Smith (2017); Pulla (2017); Jones (2017) suggested six standards for identifying a strengths-based approach. You can use this list when considering if the strength-based approach might be a good fit for your practice.

1. Goal orientation: It is crucial and vital for the client to set goals.
2. Strengths assessment: The client finds and assesses their strengths and inherent resources.
3. Resources from the environment: Connect resources in the client's environment that can be useful or enable them to create links to these resources. The resources could be individuals, associations, institutions, or groups.
4. Different methods are used first for different situations: In solution-focused therapy, clients will determine goals first and then strengths. In strengths-based case management, individuals first determine their strengths using an assessment.
5. The relationship is hope inducing: Hope is encouraged through finding strengths and linking to connections (with other people, communities, or culture).

Every community, individuals and nations are prolific with championship talent with their own strengths, resources, and hopes. It is the social innovators' duty to improve upon the choices the social extrapreneurs and giant ultrapreneurs make and encourage informed decisions (Ovharhe & Abada, 2024).

Firstly, Strength-based approach focuses on abilities, capabilities and capacities or gifts that are present in the community, not what is absent (Smith, 2017; Sabo & Trudeau, 2020). This idea connotes that frugal innovation must focus on issues and challenges that engulf around the environment and resource-constraint mostly which enable social entrepreneurs' actors like ultrapreneurs and social extrapreneurs to solve problems easily. Frugal innovators in social mission accomplishment (i.e. ultrapreneurs and social extrapreneurs) should inculcate abilities, capabilities and capacities of communities in prospective emerging environments to achieve the social mission purpose. The actual purpose is how to mitigate the effect of resource constraint and environmental munificence to ensure product, processes and service are affordable, low-cost syndrome, comfortable and quality oriented. Social entrepreneurs are much concerned with the threading potentials in communities when it comes to frugal innovation because you cannot innovate when there are no vacuum of gaps, it creates no meaning and waste of material, financial, energetic and timeliness resources. Innovation, creativity and invention are differences in notion, especially in frugal engineering (Ovharhe, 2024).

Bohach writes as agreed by Ovharhe and Woko, (2024a,b) that every community or society, no matter how there are obstacles and pitfalls that causes them to be deprived or disadvantaged they may feel, it is comprised of unlocked potential citizens with entrepreneurship opportunities who have an endless supply of unique, positive, and valuable abilities that are their gifts. Using their potential and talented gifts, a community's citizens can focus on areas of strength (the positive) rather than only focusing on areas of need (the negative) (Erika & Jo, 2024). Frugal innovation is the strength of community that overpowered the need of community because of the resource-constraint and environmental munificence. It is at this point that ultrapraneurs and social extrapreneurs utilized frugal innovation skills to transform the community by joint effort with the community counterpart to create the product, process and services out of the potential resources available in the community. This is the expertise spirit of transformation that augments the change and resilience that brightens the landmark and partway of the community to be satisfied with positive emotion and upward spiral.

Secondly, strength-based approaches stress local partnership among communities' social entrepreneurs on frugal innovation. Social extrapreneurs and ultrapreneurs should sustain citizen engagement for frugal innovation to be successful. The citizens of any community are in the best position to know the true strengths and capacities of their community's clusters, making them potential experts, because they are potential beneficiaries and not just clients as customers. This creates a paradigm shift that leads to a landmark for unleashing and sustaining community capacity, citizen engagement, and social capital where the entrepreneur could maximize wealth from the frugal innovation process in the short-term and long-term (McCashen, 2016). This might also provide room for customer funded business because the social entrepreneur might have the advantages and opportunities for the citizens to be treated as customers to maximize profitability.

Thirdly, strength-based approaches surface on formal institutional resources as well as individual, associational, and informal strengths and resources (Erika & Jo, 2024). Frugal innovation is the ability to generate greater value for customers at the bottom of the pyramid while significantly reducing the use of abundant resources by connecting across traditional sectors and boundaries, communities often discover previously unrecognized interests, talents, skills, and capacities that can be matched with needs or challenges in another part of the community.

Fourthly, strength-based approaches seek to link the strengths and priorities of all partners. Social entrepreneurs and her surveillance teams always seek to link synergy of all stakeholders to achieve growth. The social entrepreneurs being represented by the ultrapreneurs and social extrapreneurs are combined force that will be to groom the communities' social mission to come to land light by polishing the unlocked potential of young people to be converted to input resource to transformable product and services for commercialization on emerging markets and export in the future (Pulla, 2017; Rahmanti & Subandi, 2024). Social extrapreneurs and ultrapreneurs should listen to the community they need to develop the frugal innovation model that will serve for long-term by recognizing citizens' own priorities, talents, skills, and passions. The best frugal innovation is to link the priorities and resources of a community with the capacities and interests of the young people towards sustainable growth and development. This will be transformed to value creation, value capture and wealth creation because the respects for frugal innovation model always transform society even to the point of employment creation for those citizens of the community. This mutual engagement, respect, and commitment yields reciprocal benefits to everyone involved.

Asset Mapping

Asset mapping is a capacity-focused way of reimaging the place-making practice around the strengths and gifts that already exist in our communities (Baird & Peterson, 2024). By fixating on a community's problems, the solutions proposed by a traditional deficit approach rely on outside resources and experts rather than the deep knowledge and expertise of community leaders and residents. Although an asset-based approach may not fully remove the need for outside resources, it certainly makes their use more effective. By gathering the collective knowledge, skills, and resources of the community into one shared document, asset maps are designed to build connection and spark collaboration between individuals, organizations, and local government as your team works together to imagine new ways to shape the spaces and places you love (UCLA, Center For Health Policy Research,

2023). Asset mapping is based on tangible assets, people, recurring events, history and traditions and public services (Calo *et al,* 2024).

Community asset mapping is a strength-based approach to community development. The goal of asset mapping is to document a community's existing resources, incorporating these strengths into community development work. The process of asset mapping can include identifying the institutions, individuals, and citizen associations existing within communities that serve as positive resources (Baird & Peterson, 2024; Khare, Ghura & Agrawal, 2024). Approaching individuals and communities from an asset-based mentality empowers them to recognize their own strengths and capacities.

Asset mapping provides information about the strengths and resources of a community and can help uncover solutions. Once community strengths and resources are inventoried and depicted in a map, you can more easily think about how to build on these assets to address community needs and improve health. Finally, asset mapping promotes community involvement, ownership, and empowerment (Trasciani, Petrella & Richez-Battesti, 2024).

Yin Yang Philosophy

The Chinese philosophical principle is best to augment the complexity paradigm among duality that entrepreneurs encounter in the enterprise environment. The ideology of the Yin and Yang principle expresses the bond nature of business climax inseparability that exists in opposite dimension. This opposite dimension possesses forces that seem to be contradictory in parallel patterns in the business world. Stephan (2016) in considering the principle being common with African and Asian because of the religious tendencies support that the equality pair nature of the two concepts has striking forces that could affect an entity. An entity like a business enterprise faces tough times in making decision and formulating policies towards sustainability, survival and success on basis of the existing duality.

Kelvin (2020) augmented that the duality factor believes the 'Yin' is the receptive concept, while 'Yang' which is the active concept expresses striking opposite forces. In Africa, there are likelihood of the duality of raining season and dry season, in religious settings; fear and faith, and legal terms guilty/not guilty or truth/falsehood, In the entrepreneurship concept there is profit and loss, income and expenditure, wealth maximization and profit maximization, asset and liability, debit and credit, lazy entrepreneurs or strong entrepreneurs, enterprise weaknesses or enterprise strength, leading port-folio and bleeding port-folio. In a nutshell, the light gives energy and propels momentum rather than darkness. Yin-yang, meaning "dark and light" in the eyes of business philosophy in the entrepreneurial globe (Needham, 1956). This means negative forces and positive forces in the business environment are struggling to take up leadership. Hence, the "Yin" has a receptacle of the negative propensity forces, while the "Yang" has the propensity of navigating with the positive forces. Social entrepreneurs focus is to activate the Yang (positive) forces to mitigate the Yin (negative) forces to accomplish her targeted goals, vision and mission. This means enterprise should have high propelling forces on the Yang (income, profit, innovativeness, creativity) to override the Yin (expenditure, loss, mediocrity). Furthermore, entrepreneurs should have continuous improvement and focus on customer Yang (cognitive consonance) rather than Yin (cognitive dissonance).

Every ultrapreneur and social extrapreneur must bear in mind that the Chinese philosophy of Yin and Yang has great deal in the business enterprise success and survival (Kelvin, 2020). Opportunistic entrepreneurs especially, should be conscious of the Yin and Yang philosophy principles, not being over carried away with ballonic and fictitious profit mentality. The lack of consciousness of the Yin and Yang principle is while most frugal innovation failed in the market environment. This is because most social innovators only plan for profit and growth but never foreseen exigencies for the loss on a frugal basis. Social innovators should develop framework, metric and dashboard for both profit and loss plan on bench of resiliency spirit on sustainability, survival and success in the entrepreneurial journey. When this is done, they will not be taken by surprise by the occurrence of any business turbulence, mayhem, hazard, disaster, pandemic and catastrophe in the enterprise environment.

Application of Frugal innovation and Social Entrepreneurship

Yin represents black, while Yang depicts white. Yin could be better expressed as "Dark" and Yang should be seen as "Light". This is because generally in the layman perspective, "black" could be connote as "dark", on the other hand white could be term to be "light" (Roger, 2002).

Figure 2. Yin-Yang philosophy (Kelvin, 2020)

This is to settle that the "dark" represents resource-constraints, environmental challenges, poverty, hunger, social inequity etcetera, whereas, "light" represents frugal innovation, social entrepreneurs, social extrapreneurs and ultrapreneurs.

To understand, the yin-yang philosophy is to analyze better on in-depth breakdown, Yin and Yang's symbol. The black area representing yin, with the opposite white side representing yang. Baxter and Sagart (2014) acclaimed it is also known as the Taijitu, the Yin, or the dark side of Taijitu, is associated with everything bad, negative, sad. The Yang, or the light side of Taijitu, is associated with all things good, positive, happy among related others.

Collins (2024) says 'light is the brightness' that makes the social entrepreneurship sees the future, which glow the environment with growth and development by the adoption of ultrapreneurs and social extraprenurs mission strategies. Darley (2022) and Freedom (2020) up large that the spectrum of the light brightness is determined by its illumination, which means frugality has the power to shine light out of the darkness in the community. The darkness in the community could be poverty.

Therefore, in an algebraic formation dramatically, the yin-yang respectively represents: constraints-munificence; hunger-stuffed; expensiveness-affordability; poverty-wealth; hopelessness-resilience; complexity-simplicity; conventionalism-innovation; stress-wellbeing; darkness-light. The illustration revealed that every developing, underdeveloped and developed community always wants to experience the Yang to mitigate the Yin, which means to lighten up prosperity and greatness.

Hence, the light in this context could be reveal as social entrepreneurs (ultrapreneur and social extrapreneur) with striking balance with frugal innovation for sustainability, survival and success of the meaningful community growth and development. Thus, in algebraic terms ultrapreneur and social extrapreneur are an active co-efficient to social entrepreneurship which leads to the rapid growth of frugal innovation. So, for frugal innovation to excel, intensive propensity, velocity, acceleration and momentum needs to be energized that could create a driving force towards propelling social entrepreneurship to high altitude in the product, services, process, systems and emerging market growth in the action of social extrapreneurship and ultrapreneurship. This means frugal innovation utilizes social entrepreneurship as an instrument to conquer the darkness caused by resource constraint, environment forces, infrastructure and other critical factors of production. The marketplace is filled with darkness, because of the resource constraints, lack of infrastructure, hunger and poverty which engulf the environment's munificence. The darkness can be portrayed as those negative forces affecting the emerging market growth in the entrepreneurship planet that is not being inclined with social entrepreneurship characteristics such as innovation-skill, creativity, invention, passion, idea generation, risk culture, leadership, agile and agility among others (Ovharhe, 2022a).

Argumentatively, social entrepreneurs that are ignorance or not deem fit to learn, re-learn and un-learn they are bound to experience frustration, mental illness, trauma, disappointment, discouragement, depression, mental burnout and anxiety as roller coaster in the emerging market with darkness (Ovharhe & Chukwuemeka; Ovharhe, 2022,2023). If entrepreneurs lack social entrepreneurs' characteristics, the possibility of becoming successful in frugal innovation could not be easily ascertained. The Yin (darkness or resource constraints) and Yang (light or frugal innovation and social entrepreneur) principles strengthen spiral cords social extrapreneurs and ultrapreneurs to prevent the darkness of striving over the light the beneficiaries and community will experience light (Needham, 1956). Nevertheless, the Yank (light) needs high intensity with swift acceleration, velocity, momentum and elevation to overcome the storms of pandemic, turbulent, catastrophe, competition, and recklessness in the dark business world of resource constraints, high cost of living, inflation, inadequate infrastructure and environmental challenges.

CONCLUSION

Frugal innovation becomes a viable alternative for 'producing more with fewer resources. This type of innovation can help social entrepreneurs and her actors to generate a new product for new customers. Frugality is revolutionizing how businesses operate, enabling them to achieve more with less and drive success in the competitive current market. By embracing the principles of simplicity, affordability, sustainability, and flexibility, companies can create innovative solutions that are accessible to a broader customer base. While Jugaad innovation comes with its challenges and limitations, the benefits are undeniable. From cost savings and market expansion to increased competitiveness and environmental sustainability, frugal innovation offers numerous advantages for companies of all sizes and industries like ultrapreneurship and social extrapreneurship. Social entrepreneurship actors (social extrapreneurs and ultrapreneurs) possess all necessary innovation skills to transform the environment's munificence, resource constraints and emerging market into products, process and services which are affordable, accessible, durable and beneficial to the communities, nation and globe. The adoption of the frugal business model and approaches set to mitigate all negativism in the environment. With these there are strong correlations among social entrepreneur actors and frugal innovation to experience sustainability, survival and success.

Implications of the Study

The study focused on theoretical models and approaches such as the GAGA, Need Assessment, Strength-Based Approach, Asset Mapping Techniques, Frugal Innovation Business Model, Based of Pyramid (BOP), Innovation Technology. Yin-Yang philosophy, whereas practical implication on the constraints and environmental munificence factors.

Theoretical Implications

Basically, the idiomatic expression 'go along to get along' (GAGA) concept promotes the spirit of orderliness to accomplish targeted goals among less developed and developing nations to be in simple harmony on social mission. The social entrepreneur in conjunction with the ultrapreneurs and social extrapreneur should apply this approach in the frugal innovation. In this scenario all stakeholders (social enterprises and beneficiaries) must be in simple mindset to accomplish specific targeted goals in unity of purpose with the community.

The 'need assessment approach', implies recommending shifting the focus from identifying dying dreams, hopelessness, frustration, depression and misfortune to identifying resources, hopes, and dreams. Instead of asking, "What problems do you have that we can fix for you," a social entrepreneurs asks, what are your strengths, priorities, untapped resources, and hopes, and how can we build and grab the business opportunities in alliance with stakeholders toward the kind of social mission and community benefits by mitigating constraints, pitfalls, turbulence and environmental munificence beyond assessing the needs of children, youth, women and elderly.

'Strength-based approach' implies momentum drives on an individual's self-determination and strength, which enables individual and communities to use the environmental munificence to mitigates resource constraints and boost affordability of product, services and process as beneficiary to the society.

Asset mapping enhances the capacity-focused of reimaging the place-making practice around the strengths and gifts that already exist in our communities. This implies fixating on a community's problem; the solutions proposed by a traditional deficit approach rely on outside resources and experts rather than the deep knowledge and expertise of community leaders and residents.

Frugal innovation business models seek to address market affordability constraints, resources scarcity and institutional void or complexities. This implies the fundamental challenges and bottles with Based of Pyramid (BOP), that pursue meaningful assurance to simultaneously alleviate widespread poverty and hunger while providing growth and profits for socio-entrepreneurs, champiopreneurs, ultrapreneurs, serial entrepreneurs and socio extrapreneurs.

Technology innovation orchestrates programme on internet of things (IoT) and artificial intelligence (AI) to augment frugal innovation in various pathways on academic institutions, society, business enterprise and environmental benefits for mitigating constraints.

Yin-Yang philosophy fine-tuned duality encounter on positive and negative; food abundance and hunger; wealth and poverty; optimum environment munificence and resource constraints; positive mindset and hopelessness among others. This implies that social innovators should focus emphatically on the positive instrument to boost the wellness, wellbeing and livelihood of the communities. This opposite dimension possesses forces that seem to be contradictory in parallel pattern in the business world.

Practical Implications

Thinking about problems are constraints, but thinking about solution energizes munificence. Thinking about problems is problematic, thinking about solution orchestrates remedies. The study practically demonstrates that 'social innovators are the giant of frugality' that can rekindle complexity to simplicity on affordability constraint, resource scarcity constraint and void institution. The synchronization of innovation technology with artificial intelligence, internet of things, deep learning, big data analytic boost the environmental munificence in emerging markets in local communities and the society at large.

This enables social entrepreneur to inculcate ultrapreneur and social extrapreneur to innovation as the architect of rebranding goods and services to satisfied human wants as frugal engineering orchestrates to control and meet the markets demands. Hence, frugal innovation is seen as an inclusive entrepreneurship concept that focuses on making life suitable for the less privilege, inequitable salary gap and unnerved community and individual with quality, abundance, comfort, care and social proof on the drive of social entrepreneurs' dreams and mission to accomplish in the entrepreneurship globe.

To achieve the frugal innovation targeted goals, the social entrepreneur needs to synchronize the support of ultrapreneurship and social extrapreneurship to transform resource constraints and rejuvenate environmental munificence. This portrays "social innovators as the giant of frugality". The basis of this study is centered on how social extrapreneurs and ultrapreneurs with the spirit of social entrepreneurship break every barriers ground in the environment with strategies and tactics for innovation to be adopted and implemented.

Innovation is viewed as an essential tool for boosting inclusive program, economic growth and development, lowering poverty, zero-hunger, reducing cost of living and raising living standards in alignment with the sustainable development goals (SDG). Regardless of the educational background of the innovators, innovations are occurring throughout the community, nation and globe to ensure product, process and services are aligned with affordability, quality; mitigate constraints to advantageous environment munificence for community wellness, wellbeing and livelihood.

However, I think frugality pointed to achieve low-cost inventions is catching up to big businesses to form an inclusive innovative ecosystem. Innovation is the brain-box of creating goods and services to satisfy human wants. To address human needs, the rises of the 'Social Entrepreneur' are seen as innovators.

REFERENCES

Albert, M. (2022). Assessing the sustainability impacts of frugal innovation: A literature review. *Journal of Cleaner Production*, *365*, 132754. DOI: 10.1016/j.jclepro.2022.132754

Baird, L., & Peterson, M. (2024). Introduction to community asset mapping. https://www.innovatingjustice.org/sites/default/files/documents/asset_mapping.pdf

Baxter, W. H., & Sagart, L. (2014). *Old Chinese: A new reconstruction*. Oxford University Press., DOI: 10.1093/acprof:oso/9780199945375.001.0001

Bhatti, Y. A. (2012). What is frugal, What is innovation? Towards a theory of frugal innovation. DOI: . https://www.researchgate.net/publication/228121294_What_is_Frugal_What_is_Innovation_Towards_a_Theory_of_Frugal_Innovation#:~:text=The%20theory%20of%20frugal%20innovation,%2C%20affordable%20and%20appropriate%20products%22%2CDOI: 10.2139/ssrn.2005910

Bhatti, Y. A., & Ventresca, M. (2013). How Can 'Frugal Innovation' Be Conceptualized? (January 19, 2013). Available at *SSRN*: https://ssrn.com/abstract=2203552 or http://dx.doi.org/DOI: 10.2139/ssrn.2203552

Bohach, A. (1997). Fundamental principles of asset-based community development. *The Journal of Volunteer Administration*, *15*(4), 22–29.

Bonnici, F., Klijn, V., & Nowack, D. (2024). The state of social enterprise: A review of global data from 2013-2023.https://www3.weforum.org/docs/WEF_The_State_of_Social_Enterprise_2024.pdf

Boyatzis, C. J. (2024). Spiritual development during childhood and adolescence. In Miller, L. J. (Ed.), *The Oxford handbook of psychology and spirituality* (2nd ed., pp. 100–124). Oxford University Press., DOI: 10.1093/oxfordhb/9780190905538.013.5

Calo, F., Sancino, A., & Scognamiglio, F. (2024). Social enterprise and social entrepreneurship in the Public Administration (PA) a scholar field bibliometric analysis and some conceptual considerations. *Public Management Review*, *26*(10), 3013–3039. Advance online publication. DOI: 10.1080/14719037.2024.2311181

Cambridge Centre for social Innovation (2024). The rise of social extrapreneurship. https://socialinnovation.blog.jbs.cam.ac.uk/2015/12/04/the-rise-of-social-extraprenuership/The rise of social extrapreneurship

CFTE. (2024). What is extrapreneurship. https://courses.cfte.education/extrapreneurship-programmes/#:~:text=We%20define%20Extrapreneurship%20as%20the,managers%2C%20transformation%20leaders%20or%20investors.

Chibuike, C. U., & Ovharhe, O. H. (2022). Emergence of risk culture and lean culture in Nigeria during pandemic and crisis era: Using confirmatory analysis. *International Journal of Multidisciplinary Research and Growth Evaluation*, *3*(1), 263–271. DOI: 10.54660/anfo.2021.3.1.14

Chibuike, C. U., Ovharhe, O. H., & Abada, A. M. (2022). Synchronization of lean accounting alert and entrepreneurial sustainability among micro firms in Nigeria during pandemic and catastrophe: Using confirmatory factor analysis. *International Journal of Business and Management*, *10*(1), 1–13. DOI: 10.54660/anfo.2021.2.6.15

Cuhadar, S., & Rudnák, I. (2022). Literature review. *Sustain. Leadership*, *9*(3), 55–65. DOI: 10.18531/Studia.Mundi.2022.09.03.55-65

Dabić, M., Obradović, T., Vlačić, B., Sahasranamam, S., & Paul, J. (2022). Frugal innovations: A multidisciplinary review & agenda for future research. *Journal of Business Research*, *142*, 914–929. DOI: 10.1016/j.jbusres.2022.01.032

Darley, L. (2022). Red light in entrepreneurship. https://www.grin.com › document

Dawood, M. A. (2023). What is the frugal innovation model, and how does it work? https://growenterprise.co.uk/2023/02/09/what-is-the-frugal-innovation-model-and-how-does-it-work/#:~:text=Frugal%20innovation%20is%20reducing%20the,developing%20countries%20using%20affordable%20prices

Dee, E. (2024). MGE303 Social entrepreneurship 2024. https://www.scribd.com/document/719869450/MGE303-Social-Entrepreneurship-2024

Dictionary, C. (2024). Light. https://www.collinsdictionary.com/dictionary/english/light

EADI. (2024). Frugal innovation and development. https://www.eadi.org/network/eadi-working-groups/frugal-innovation-and-development

Effa, G. A., Ovharhe, O. H., Ezirim, A. C., & Igwe, S. (2023a). Procurement sustainability policy and logistics performance in Nigeria. [IJMCS]. *International Journal of Marketing and Communication Studies*, *7*(1), 56–72. DOI: 10.56201/ijmcs.v7.no1.2023.pg56.72

Effa, G. A., Ovharhe, O. H., Ezirim, A. C., & Igwe, S. (2023b). Strategic procurement initiatives and logistics performance in Nigeria. International Journal of Marketing and Communication Studies (IJMCS), 7(1), 38-55. DOI: . Erika, S., & Jo, N. (2024). What is Strenght–based approach. https://positivepsychology.com/strengths-based-interventions/DOI: 10.56201/ijmcs.v7.no1.2023.pg38.55

Farooq, R. (2017). A conceptual model of frugal innovation: Is environmental munificence a missing link? *International Journal of Innovation Science*, *9*(4), 320–334. DOI: 10.1108/IJIS-08-2017-0076

Freeman, M. A. (2020). Are entrepreneurs touched with fire. https://econa.net/wp-content/uploads/2020/08/Are-Entrepreneurs-Touched-with-Fire.pdf.https://www.linkedin.com/pulse/entrepreneurs-touched-fire-michael-a-freeman-m-d

Ganapati, L. S. (2024). What's the difference between an ultrapreneur and an entrepreneur? https://www.quora.com/What-s-the-difference-between-an-ultrapreneur-and-an-entrepreneur#:~:text=Ultrapreneurs%20can%20be%20seen%20as,entrepreneur%20who%20is%20comparatively%20restless

Giuggioli, G., & Pellegrini, M. M. (2023). Artificial intelligence as an enabler for entrepreneurs: A systematic literature review and an agenda for future research. *International Journal of Entrepreneurial Behaviour & Research*, *29*(4), 816–837. DOI: 10.1108/IJEBR-05-2021-0426

Glasbeek, L., Wickert, C., & Schad, J. (2024). Evaluating definitions of social entrepreneurship: A rulebook from the philosophy of science. *International Journal of Management Reviews*, *26*(3), 1–26. DOI: 10.1111/ijmr.12359

Govindan, K. (2022). How artificial intelligence drives sustainable frugal innovation: A multitheoretical perspective. *IEEE Transactions on Engineering Management*, *71*(1), 638–655.

Greco, M., Savage, L., & Souza, S. (2024). Asset mapping in a rural context: Asset based community development in collaboration with Cairo, Georgia. https://coss.fsu.edu/durp/wp-content/uploads/sites/9/2024/03/January-Final-Draft-1-1-compressed.pdf

Gupta, A., & Wang, H. (2009). *Getting China and India Right: Strategies for leveraging the world's fastest-growing economies for global advantage*. Wiley.

Hindawi (2024). Implementation of Frugal Innovation Approach in Moroccan Industry through the Development of a New Frugal System. https://www.hindawi.com/journals/je/2024/3971088/fig10

Hossain, M. (2018). Frugal innovation: A review and research agenda. *Journal of Cleaner Production, 182*, 926–936. DOI: 10.1016/j.jclepro.2018.02.091

Hossain, M., Levänen, J., & Wierenga, M. (2021). Pursuing frugal innovation for sustainability at the grassroots level. 2021;(May):374– 381

Hossain, M., Park, S., & Shahid, S. (2023). Frugal innovation for sustainable rural development. Technol. Forecast. Soc. Chang., 193, Article 122662

Hossain, M., Shahid, M. S., & Park, S. (2024). The business models of frugal enterprises for sustainable development in a constrained environment. *IEEE Transactions on Engineering Management, 71*, 3448–3463. DOI: 10.1109/TEM.2023.3342440

International Centre for frugal Innovation (2024). Student challenges 2023-2024 – LDE minor frugal innovation for sustainable global development. https://www.icfi.nl/news/student-challenges-2023-2024-lde-minor-frugal-innovation-for-sustainable-global-development

Jones, J. (2017). The two problems with the strengths-based approach. Dr. Jason Jones. Retrieved from https://drjasonjones.com/characterstrengthsapproach/

Kelvin, H. (2020). *Introduction to the theory of Yin-Yang*. Independent.

Khare, P., Ghura, A. S., & Agrawal, A. (2024). A process model of social enterprise scaling using the legitimacy lens. https://doi.org/. Journal of Social Entrepreneurship, 15(1)DOI: 10.1080/19420676.2024.2315933

Kretzmann, J. P., & McKnight, J. L. (1993). *Building communities from the inside: A path toward finding a community's assets*. Center for Urban Affairs and Policy Research, Northwestern University.

Le, P. B., Tran, D. T., Phung, T. M. T., & Vu, K. D. (2022). *Leadership and knowledge management practices for frugal innovation of firms in the emerging market: moderating role of collaborative culture*. Asia-Pacific J. Bus. Admin., DOI: 10.1108/APJBA-03-2021-0130

León, E. M., Pichardo, R. D., Tatiana Reyes-Carrillo, T. R., & Santiago, M. R. R. (2024). What is unique about sustainable business models for the base of the pyramid? *Business Strategy and the Environment, 3*(33), 2345–2366. DOI: 10.1002/bse.3609

McCashen, W. (2016, December 1). What is "the strengths approach"? Innovative Resources. Retrieved from https://innovativeresources.org/what-is-the-strengths-approach/

McKnight, J. L., & Kretzmann, J. P. (1996). *Mapping community capacity* (rev. ed.). Institute for Policy Research, Northwestern University., Retrieved from http://www .northwestern.edu /ipr/publications/papers/mcc.pdf

Medium (2024). Ultrapreneur.https://theultrapreneur.medium.com/the-meaning-of -the-word-ultrapreneur-de4036e1a4c4

Miller, J. (2024). Frugal innovation: Doing more with less in resource-constrained environments. https://www.linkedin.com/pulse/frugal-innovation-doing-more-less -environments-jason-miller-rdqgc/

Milthon, L. M. (2024).Frugal innovation: definition, principles, characteristics, and examples. https://innovaromorir.com/en/frugal-innovation-definition-principles -examples/

Murphy, K. P. (2024). On distillation of guided diffusion models. search/index_ htm_files/On_Distillation_Of_Guided_Diffusion_Models.pdf.https://interactive .cornish.edu › index_htm_files Murphy, K. P. (2024).

Nassani, A. A., Sinisi, C., Mihai, D., Paunescu, L., Yousaf, Z., & Haffar, M. (2022). Towards the achievement of frugal innovation: Exploring major antecedents among SMEs. *Sustainability (Basel)*, *14*(7), 4120. DOI: 10.3390/su14074120

Needham, J. (1956). *Science and civilization in China: History of scientific thought*. Cambridge University Press.

Nielsen, M. S. (2023). What is light. https://chromaviso.com/en/knowledge-about -light/what-is-light

Nigel, C. (2024). Five element of ultrapreneur. https://ultrapreneursuccess.com/ what-is-an-ultrapreneur/elements/

Nimmagadda, R. (2024). Frugal Innovation and Entrepreneurship. Proceedings of the 3rd International Conference on Reinventing Business Practices, Start-ups and Sustainability (ICRBSS 2023), Advances in Economics, Business and Management Research, 277.

Onsongo, E. K., Knorringa, P., & Beers, C. V. (2023). Frugal business model innovation in the base of the pyramid: The case of Philips Community Life Centres in Africa. *Technovation*, *121*, 102675. https://www.sciencedirect.com/science/article/ abs/pii/S0166497222002267 DOI: 10.1016/j.technovation.2022.102675

Ovharhe, O. H. (2022a). Sustainable development goals: Multicollinearity between therapeutic entrepreneurship and rehabilitation therapy among African nations. *International Journal of Small Business and Entrepreneurship Research, 10*(3), 1–59. DOI: 10.37745/ijsber.2013/vol10n3157

Ovharhe, O. H. (2022b). Sustainable development goals: Therapeutic entrepreneurship and entrepreneurship Injelititis among West Africa Countries. [WJEDS]. *World Journal of Entrepreneurial Development Studies, 7*(1), 87–113. DOI: 10.56201/wjeds.v7.no1.2022.pg87.113

Ovharhe, O. H. (2024). Business intelligence and innovation moderating roles on entrepreneurship and management using champiopreneurship approach. In K. Kankaew, P. Nakpathom, A. Chnitphattana, K. Pitchayadejanant, & S. Kunnapapdeelert (Eds.). Applying business intelligence and innovation to entrepreneurship advances in business strategy and competitive advantage (p. 171-223). IGI Global.com. DOI: 10.4018/979-8-3693-1846-1.ch009

Ovharhe, Orugba Harry & Abada, A. M. (2024). Creative accounting and entrepreneurship opportunities. [JAFM]. *Journal of Accounting and Financial Management, 10*(5), 175–190. DOI: 10.56201/jafm.v10.no5.2024.pg175.190

Ovharhe, O. H., & Abada, A. M. (2023). IFRS: Entrepreneurial exit and Entrepreneurial entre. *American Journal of Social Development and Entrepreneurship, 2*(2), 1–8. DOI: 10.54536/ajsde.v2i2.1578

Ovharhe, O. H., & Abada, A. M. (2023). *IFRS adoptions on entrepreneurship entry and entrepreneurship exit: The Nigeria experience from 2006-2017. 2(2)*. American Journal of Social Development and Entrepreneurship., DOI: 10.54536/ajsde.v2i2

Ovharhe, O. H., Ahunanya, V., & Woko, E. B. (2022). Consignment inventory system and entrepreneurial survival in Lagos State. *International Journal of Social Science & Management Research, 8*(5), 29–42. DOI: 10.56201/ijssmr.v8.no5.2022.pg29.42

Ovharhe, O. H., & Akandu, C. J. (2024). Innovation accounting and innovation entrepreneurship. [WJIMT]. *World Journal of Innovation and Modern Technology, 8*(2), 31–49. DOI: 10.56201/wjimt.v8.no2.2024.pg31.49

Ovharhe, O. H., & Chibuike, C. U. (2024a). Creative accounting and creative entrepreneurship. [JAFM]. *Journal of Accounting and Financial Management, 10*(7), 157–174. DOI: 10.56201/jafm.v10.no5.2024.pg157.174

Ovharhe, O. H., & Chibuike, C. U. (2024b). Innovation accounting and frugal innovation. [WJIMT]. *World Journal of Innovation and Modern Technology, 8*(2), 50–70. DOI: 10.56201/wjimt.v8.no2.2024.pg50.70

Ovharhe, O. H., Chibuike, C. U., & Abada, A. M. (2023). Lean Accounting And Lean Entrepreneurship. *American Journal of Social Development and Entrepreneurship*, *2*(2), 1–8. DOI: 10.54536/ajsde.v2i2.1578

Ovharhe, O. H., & Chukwuemeka, S. P. (2023). Sustainable Development Goals: Therapeutic Entrepreneurship and Mental Health Conditions. *British Journal of Multidisciplinary and Advanced Studies*, *4*(1), 81–119. DOI: 10.37745/bjmas.2022.0107

Ovharhe, O. H., & Igbokwe, E. L. (2021). Analytical intervention of remote working correlates on risk culture and entrepreneurial adaptability in South-South Geopolitical Zone, Nigeria: Covid-19 Perspective. *Journal of Education and Practice, IISTE*, *12*(3), 34–44. DOI: 10.7176/JEP/12-34-05

Ovharhe, O. H., & Odepeli, S. (2024). Environmental pollution and maternal mortality among female entrepreneurs. [IJGEM]. *International Journal of Geography and Environmental Management*, *10*(2), 170–195. DOI: 10.56201/ijgem.v10.no3.2024.pg170.195

Ovharhe, O. H., & Okolo, B. S. (2022). Sustainable development goals: Lean entrepreneurship and Green entrepreneurship. International Journal of Research and Scientific Innovation, 9(10), 59-71. ISSN: 2321-2705

Ovharhe, O. H., Okolo, B. S., Woko, E. B., & Igbokwe, L. (2022). Light entrepreneurship and customer funded business model. *International Journal of Social Sciences and Management Research*, *8*(5), 87–106. DOI: 10.56201/ijssmr.v8.no5.2022.pg87.106

Ovharhe, O. H., & Woko, B. E. (2024a). Environmental pollution and life expectancy among Intrepreneurs. [IJMEPR]. *International Journal of Medical Evaluation and Physical Report*, *10*(2), 9–32. DOI: 10.56201/ijmepr.v8.no3.2024.pg9.32

Ovharhe, O. H. & Woko, B. E. (2024b). Environmental pollution and infant mortality on entrepreneurial opportunities: A champiopreneurship approach. International Journal of Geography & Environmental Management (IJGEM), 10 (3), 144-171. D.O.I: DOI: 10.56201/ijgem.v10.no3.2024.pg144.171

Ovharhe, O. H., Woko, E. B., & Ezeocha, V. U. (2021). Remote working: Entrepreneurial risk and entrepreneurial survival in the micro firms in Niger-Delta, Nigeria (COVID-19 Pandemic Prospects). *International Journal of Small Business and Entrepreneurship Research*, *9*(4), 11–28. DOI: 10.37745/ijsber.2013/vol9n11-28

Ovharhe, O. H., Woko, E. B., & Ogolo, T. M. (2021). Competitive risk strategy and entrepreneurial satisfaction among fast moving consuming goods in Nigeria during covid-19 pandemic using confirmatory factor analysis. *International Journal of Multidisciplinary Research and Growth Evaluation*, *2*(6), 267–272. DOI: 10.54660/anfo.2021.3.1.14

Özsungur, F. (2024). Generating entrepreneurial ideas with AI. IGI Global.com (ISBN: 9798369334980) DOI: 10.4018/979-8-3693-3498-0

Park, S., Rosca, E., & Agarwal, N. (2022). Driving social impact at the bottom of the pyramid through the internet-of-things enabled frugal innovations. *Technovation*, *118*, 102381. DOI: 10.1016/j.technovation.2021.102381

Pulla, V. (2017). Strengths-based approach in social work: A distinct ethical advantage. International Journal of Innovation. *Creativity and Change*, *3*(2), 97–114.

Qin, W. (2024).How to unleash frugal innovation through internet of things and artificial intelligence: Moderating role of entrepreneurial knowledge and future challenges. 28(202) https://www.sciencedirect.com/science/article/pii/S0040162524000829 .https://doi.org/10.1016/j.techfore.2024.123286

Radjou, N., & Prabhu, J. (2013). *Frugal innovation: A new business paradigm.* INSEAD Knowledge.

Radjou N., Prabhu, J., & Ahuja, S. (2012). Jugaad innovation: Think frugal, be flexible, Generate breakthrough growth.

Rahmanti, V. N., & Subandi, H. (2024). Redefining Social Entrepreneurship as a Strategy to Strengthen the Social Welfare of SDGs. *Migration Letters : An International Journal of Migration Studies*, *21*(S2), 110–132. https://migrationletters.com/index.php/ml/article/view/644

Rehman, K. U., Anwar, R. S., Antohi, V. M., Ali, U., Fortea, C., & Zlati, M. L. (2024). Driving frugal innovation in SMEs: How sustainable leadership, knowledge sources and information credibility make a difference. *Frontiers in Sociology*, *9*, 1344704. 1344704.doi.org/10.3389/fsoc.2024.1344704 DOI: 10.3389/fsoc.2024.1344704

Roehlkepartain, E. C. (2008). Beyond needs assessments: Identifying a community's resources and hopes. https://www.search-institute.org/downloadable/2008-Roehlkepartain-Beyond-Needs-SL-NSLC.pdf

Roger, T. A. (2002). *Yin and Yang", in encyclopedia of Chinese philosophy* (Cua, A. S., Ed.). Routledge.

Rooijen, M. V. (2024). Extrapreneurs: A more sensible form of entrepreneurship. https://www.europeanbusinessreview.com/extrapreneurs-a-more-sensible-form-of-entrepreneurship/

Sabo, B., & Trudeau, V. L. (2020). A strengths-based approach to mental health recovery. *Journal of Psychosocial Rehabilitation and Mental Health*, *7*(1), 69–79.

Sharma, R., Dubey, D., & Rana, G. (2024). Impact of team building on organizational performance. *Migration Letters : An International Journal of Migration Studies*, *21*(S7).

Shehzad, M. U., Zhang, J., Alam, S., & Cao, Z. (2022). Determining the role of sources of knowledge and IT resources for stimulating firm innovation capability: A PLS-SEM approach. *Business Process Management Journal*, *28*(4), 905–935. DOI: 10.1108/BPMJ-09-2021-0574

Shehzad, M. U., Zhang, J., Alam, S., Cao, Z., Boamah, F. A., & Ahmad, M. (2022). Knowledge management process as a mediator between collaborative culture and frugal innovation: The moderating role of perceived organizational support. *Journal of Business and Industrial Marketing*, *38*(7), 1424–1446. DOI: 10.1108/JBIM-01-2022-0016

Shifana, M. (2024). What's the difference between an ultrapreneur and an entrepreneur? https://www.quora.com/What-s-the-difference-between-an-ultrapreneur-and-an-entrepreneur#:~:text=Ultrapreneurs%20can%20be%20seen%20as,entrepreneur%20who%20is%20comparatively%20restless

Smith, J. (2017). Strength-based interviews. PROSPECTS. Retrieved from https://www.prospects.ac.uk/careers-advice/interview-tips/strength-based-interviews

Stephan, F. (2016). *Religions in the modern world: traditions and transformations*. Routledge.

Trasciani, G., Petrella, F., & Richez-Battesti, N. (2024). Navigating Cross-Sector Partnerships: Innovative Strategies and Challenges for Work Integration Social Enterprises in France. *Journal of Social Entrepreneurship*, *15*(1), 1–22. Advance online publication. DOI: 10.1080/19420676.2024.2325706

Tufts Gordon Institute. (2024). Jugaad & Frugal Innovation: Is doing more with less the future of innovation? https://gordon.tufts.edu/news-events/events/jugaad-frugal-innovation-doing-more-less-future-innovation

UCLA, Center For Health Policy Research. (2023). Asset Mapping. https://healthpolicy.ucla.edu/sites/default/files/2023-08/tw_cba20.pdf

UCMB. (2024). IoT & AI for Frugal innovation 2024. https://www.unicampus.it/corsi/offerta-formativa/ucbm-academy/bootcamp-overview/iot-and-ai-for-frugal-innovation-2024

Ur, R. K., Anwar, R. S., Antohi, V. M., Ali, U., Fortea, C., & Zlati, M. L. (2024). Driving frugal innovation in SMEs: How sustainable leadership, knowledge sources and information credibility make a difference. *Frontiers in Sociology*, *9*, 1344704. DOI: 10.3389/fsoc.2024.1344704

Usman, F. O., Kess-Momoh, A. J., Ibeh, C. V., Elufioye, A. E., Ilojianya, V. I., & Oyeyemi, O. P.Favour Oluwadamilare Usman, & the Azeez Jason Kess-Momoh, & the Chidera Victoria Ibeh, & the Akinola Elumakin Elufioye, & the Valentine Ikenna Ilojianya, & the Oluwaseun Peter Oyeyemi. (2024). Entrepreneurial innovations and trends: A global review: Examining emerging trends, challenges, and opportunities in the field of entrepreneurship, with a focus on how technology and globalization are shaping new business ventures. *International Journal of Science and Research Archive*, *11*(01), 552–569. DOI: 10.30574/ijsra.2024.11.1.0079

Vázquez-Pacho, M.G., & Payaud, M.A. (2024), "From strategy to impact: how MNCs innovate their business models for social value in BoP contexts?", Journal of Strategy and Management, Vol. ahead-of-print No. ahead-of-print. DOI: 10.1108/JSMA-06-2023-0145

Velananda, Y. V., Dissanayake, D. M. R., & Wickramasinghe, C. N. (2022). Application of frugal innovations in a global context. *Asian Basic and Applied Research Journal*, *6*(3), 17–28.

Weyrauch, T., & Herstatt, C. (2017). What is frugal innovation? Three defining criteria. *Journal Frugal Innovation*, *2*(1), 1–17. DOI: 10.1186/s40669-016-0005-y

KEY TERMS AND DEFINITIONS

Resource Constraints: Resource constraints are bottlenecks, pitfalls, limitations and barriers that affect the opportunistic venture and allocation of required resources necessary to accomplish targeted goals within specific timeline and scope.

Environmental Munificence: Environmental munificence fathoms need assessment and asset mapping in the environment that mitigates scarcity and identified available infrastructure obtainable for the enterprise which warrants failure or success.

Frugal Innovation: Frugal innovation is the ability, capability and capacity to do more with less that is, to create significantly more business and social value while minimizing the use of diminishing resources such as energy, capital and time

Frugal Innovation Model: Frugal innovations model are critical business instrumental tools used as pragmatic, framework and dashboard to navigate the strategic goals of enterprise in the MSMEs, corporations, conglomerates and multinationals.

Social Entrepreneurship: Social entrepreneurship is a tentative wing of entrepreneurship which navigates through innovation of social enterprise creation that drives social economic changes in society, industries and individual.

Social Extrapreneur: Social Extrapreneur are seen as extraordinary social innovation giant and champion in the entrepreneurship world which have the capacity, character and competence because of experiential practices they have encountered overtime in transformation and development of enterprise.

Ultrapreneur: Ultrapreneur is an enterprising or entrepreneurial fellow, but his innovation commences within the organization itself and whose impacts may extend beyond the organization to which he or she is directly a part e.g. realizing new opportunities such as forming a subsidiary organization.

Based or Bottom of Pyramid: Bottom of Pyramid (BOP) could be regarded as a market-based model of meaningful socio-economic development which projected assurance to simultaneously alleviate widespread poverty and hunger while providing growth and profits.

Technology Innovation: Technology innovation is the design and development of new emerging trends of technology such as AI-based communication connects to remote community clusters that has the capability and ability to translate language for the global reach of solutions

Artificial, Intelligence (AI): AI: is technology evolution that designs algorithm language applications to solve complex problems to achieve deterministic goals.

Chapter 3
Frugal Innovation, Circular Economy, and Environmental Entrepreneurship

Supriya Singh
Mudra Institute of Communications, Ahmedabad, India

Subrat Sarangi
https://orcid.org/0000-0003-4597-3298
Mudra Institute of Communications, Ahmedabad, India

ABSTRACT

The study explores the intersection of frugal innovation, circular economy, and environmental entrepreneurship for sustainable development. Given the dearth of resources, increasing pollution and global warming, with an increasing demand for goods and services because of increasing global population, development and sustainability need to go hand in hand. The book chapter focuses on this research gap and identifies policy level recommendations based on case examples of best practices and applications at a global scale. The major recommendations of the study are an assessment of the factors influencing entrepreneurs to engage in the circular economy by adopting best practices, namely, using recycled and repurposed material, as well as application of longevity, repairability and recyclability potential, among others. One of the critical findings of our study includes the adoption of the principles of responsible investment in furthering environmental entrepreneurship. We propose future research areas to enhance the body of knowledge on the theme.

DOI: 10.4018/979-8-3693-4050-9.ch003

INTRODUCTION

As the world population continues to grow, there is an increasing demand for goods and services, leading to increasing waste. Waste and inefficient utilization of natural resources lead to pollution and global warming. Due to increasing pollution, there is a need to take corrective measures while considering development. Development is necessary to meet the demands of the increasing population. Prioritization of development is critical since it must be viable and sustainable. Various factors that lead to improper utilization of resources, like Environmental degradation, unequal opportunity, and rising inequality, are evident in our daily lives. To address these challenges mentioned above, such as inequitable and unsuitable allocation of resources, it is necessary to implement creative ideas and approaches that foster sustainability and equality. Hossain et al. (2016) defined "Frugal Innovation as a resource-scarce solution (i.e., the product, service, process or business model) that is designed and implemented despite financial, technological, material and other resource constraints, whereby the final outcome is significantly cheaper than competitive offerings (if available) and is good enough to meet the basic needs of customers who would otherwise remain un(der)served." When we extend the discussion on innovation, we also come across similar terms in extant literature. In the Western concept, disruptive innovation means replacing old technologies with new ones.

Similarly, in the Indian context, disruptive innovation follows the basic principle of "Jugaad Innovation," which means converting constraints into opportunities (doing more with less). "It is defined as a unique way of thinking and acting in response to challenges" (Radjou, Prabhu, & Ahuja, 2012). The second research theme in the study is the concept of Circular Economy, which is aligned with the principles of frugality and resource efficiency. It is defined as "A regenerative system in which resource input and waste, emission, and energy leakage are minimized by slowing, closing, and narrowing material and energy loops. Entrepreneurs use circular economy practices, which can be achieved through long-lasting design, maintenance, repair, reuse, remanufacturing, refurbishing, and recycling" (Geissdoerfer et al. 2017). The concept of circular economy complements the third theme of our research - Environmental Entrepreneurship. Environmental Entrepreneurship combines economic value creation with environmental stewardship (preservation and regeneration of the natural environment) (Isaak, 2002; Lenox & York, 2012; Schaefer, Corner, & Kearins, 2015). Despite the importance and popularity of these concepts among academicians, policymakers, entrepreneurs, and environmentalists, there is a lack of conceptual relationship between frugal innovation, circular economy, and environmental entrepreneurship.

Therefore, in this study, we try to investigate the points of intersection and interrelationships among Frugal Innovation (FE) (locally known as "Jugaad" in India), the Circular Economy (CE), and Environmental Entrepreneurship (EE) to demonstrate their potential and functional interaction, which helps in advancing sustainable development. Over the past few years, we have observed worsening environmental issues, including climate change, natural catastrophes, Arctic melting, and water scarcity. These problems have become so significant that they are now considered part of the list of substantial challenges society faces, known as Grand Challenges (Howard-Grenville et al., 2014). Global problems are described as grand challenges by researchers and practitioners, and they need innovation and scientific efforts to solve them. (George et al., 2016).

Moreover, principles of frugal innovation and circular economy are combined to develop sustainable, resource-efficient, and cost-effective solutions by environmental entrepreneurs (Hossain et al., 2023). By analyzing the interrelationship between frugal innovation, circular economy, and mutual support by environmental entrepreneurs, this study tries to investigate the potential of these concepts to develop economically feasible, socially responsible, and sustainable solutions. Using different case studies and literature reviews, we draw a conceptual framework combining frugal innovation and circular economy principles with environmental entrepreneurship. This research highlighted the importance of integrating these concepts in building a sustainable future. This study also gives direction for future research in this field.

THEORETICAL BACKGROUND

Effectuation theory by Saras Sarasvathy (2001) describes a problem-solving approach in entrepreneurship that involves making decisions and performing actions. You can identify the next best step with the available resources to achieve your goals. According to Dr. Saras Sarasvathy (Sarasvathy 2001), the theorist behind it compares it to the distinction between following a recipe and improvising a dinner using the ingredients you have on hand in your kitchen. Particularly applicable in situations where resources are limited, Effectuation Theory emphasizes using extant resources to create opportunities and influence outcomes. Resource optimization, sustainability, and problem-solving approach of this theory unify it with frugal innovation, circular economy, and environmental entrepreneurship. Effectuation theory-based frameworks help entrepreneurs utilize resources efficiently and Manage uncertainty. According to this theory, Individual identity is regarded as a precondition or means that initiates the entrepreneurial process. Thus, identity is perceived as a relatively stable precondition in the entrepreneurial process, which influences how entrepreneurs organize their preferences and make decisions in the ambiguous and uncertain environment of entrepreneurship (Sarasvathy & Dew, 2005). However, effectuation theory also allows for the possibility that an individual's identity could transform the entrepreneurial process due to interactions with new individuals, acquisition of fresh resources, and access to fresh opportunities. By prioritizing sustainability, minimal resources, and cost-effectiveness, this concept of effectuation aligns with frugal innovation principles. (Dawa & Marks, 2023; Hossain et al., 2023). Circular economy principles, mainly based on the 3R principles (reduce, reuse, recycle) (Rosca et al., 2017).

Sustainable entrepreneurship is associated with ecological disruption, implementing innovative solutions for businesses and economies that benefit society (Rosario et al., 2022). . Sustainable entrepreneurs are actors or companies contributing significantly to sustainable development through their core businesses (Schaltegger & Wagner, 2011). Sustainable entrepreneurship focuses on seizing opportunities to create innovative solutions that minimize social and environmental impacts while enhancing quality of life. With a solid commitment to sustainability, sustainable entrepreneurship encourages entrepreneurs to develop new products and services that simultaneously generate economic, social, and environmental value. The case examples below show how frugal innovation, circular economy, and environmental entrepreneurship maximize financial gains, reduce ecological problems, and benefit society with a sustainable business model. According to this hypothesis, sustainable corporate practices can be advanced by combining frugal innovation with circular economy principles (Shahid et al., 2023). Innovative and sustainable business practices must harmonize various business model components—including value proposition, value generation, and value capture (Ezeudu et al., 2022).

The theory of stakeholder engagement is the foundation of frugal innovation. "Stakeholder engagement is a systematic approach enterprises can adopt to actively involve, cooperate with, or provide information to their current stakeholders, individually or in combination. This process involves identifying, mapping, and prioritizing stakeholders to find the most effective communication techniques while optimizing the use of resources. Engaging stakeholders can help reduce possible risks and disputes with stakeholder groups, such as ambiguity, discontent, lack of agreement, lack of involvement, and resistance to change."[1] Frugal innovation requires diverse stakeholders' involvement in a collaborative effort to formulate resource-efficient and cost-effective solutions. Thus, stakeholder engagement is paramount (Ezeudu et al., 2022).

By encouraging information sharing and stakeholder collaboration, sustainability-focused leadership can enable eco-entrepreneurship and frugal innovation to coexist, following the Social Exchange Theory (SET) (Albert, 2019). When we go back to history, the origin of social exchange theory can be traced back to 1958 when American sociologist George Homans published an article titled "Social Behaviour as Exchange." Homans builds a framework on the combination of behaviorism and basic economics. "Social exchange theory is based on the relationship between two individuals based on cost-benefit analysis. The theory does not measure the relationship based on emotional metrics. Rather, it calculates the cost-benefit and uses logic and reasoning to determine the balance between relationships. The theory has several core assumptions regarding human nature and relationships. The initial assumption is that humans are eager to get rewards but avoid punishments. Another one is humans trying to get maximum with minimum efforts, i.e., what benefits me. The third assumption is that humans calculate their cost-benefit before engaging in any activity. If the cost exceeds the benefit, individuals try to avoid it. Finally, people know that 'payoffs' vary from individual to individual and within individual over time." [2]

These theories and models provide a comprehensive understanding and interconnectedness among frugal innovation, circular economy, and environmental entrepreneurship and show the potential for developing sustainable business models.

LITERATURE REVIEW

The previous research and publications about frugal innovation, circular economy, and environmental entrepreneurship provide a base for an overview of the literature and for building the proposed framework on these three concepts. Since we aim to find the intersection of these three concepts, we use the case study method (Yin, 1993). Different researchers have used the concepts of frugal innovation, circular economy, and environmental entrepreneurship in various contexts. Frugal innovation is an inclusive approach primarily used in developing countries to reduce the use of financial and natural resources to maximize the value of society. This concept emerges in a situation of scarcity, where new products can be made from available resources, such as cooking something delicious from the available ingredients in the kitchen. Prakash et al. (2024) state that frugal innovation gives affordable, cost-effective goods and services by reducing resource consumption. Frugal innovation also stated as "Jugaad Innovation" in India, is similar to indigenous concepts in other countries, such as "Gambiarra" or "Jeitinho" in Brazil, "Kanju" in parts of Africa, "Jua Kali" In Kenya, "Jiejian Chuangxin" in China, "DIY" (do it yourself) in the United States and "Systeme D" in France (Prabhu and Jain, 2015). Albert (2019) states that the relationship between frugal innovation and sustainability is closely linked. The term CE was first mentioned by Pearce and Turner (1990) in their work "Economics of Natural Resources and Environment," they discussed that the current economic system is a threat to the environment by continuously producing waste and pollution. So, the circular economy concept is gaining popularity among practitioners and academicians because it is seen as a practical solution for environmental entrepreneurs to implement the much-discussed idea of sustainable development (Ghisellini et al., 2016; Murray et al., 2017). Geissdoerfer et al. (2017) asserted that the system should be transformed into a circular one by considering waste as a source of more resources.

According to Frosch and Gallopoulos (1989), the prevailing linear extract-produce-use-dump model of material and energy flow in the current and traditional economic system is unsustainable. So, circular economy provides an alternative closed loop or cyclical model. Environmental entrepreneurship has emerged as a significant practice in addressing prevailing environmental issues (Cohen & Winn, 2007; Dean & McMullen, 2007). The first special issues dedicated to EE were published in 1998 in the J. of Organizational Change Management and in 2002 in Greener Management International. Entrepreneurs are key drivers and are crucial in addressing the Sustainable Development Goals (SDGs) globally, aiming to tackle social, economic, and environmental challenges by innovating new technologies. So, in this case, entrepreneurs adopt frugal innovation techniques to achieve the goal of circular economy. To solve the complex problems of today's world, the intersection of frugal innovation, circular economy, and environmental entrepreneurship provides sustainable and cost-effective solutions. It enables affordable and readily available solutions that effectively meet individuals' requirements, especially in developing countries.

METHODOLOGY

In this study, we followed the case study method of research, whereby we sourced a set of case examples across diverse themes about frugal innovation, circular economy, and environmental entrepreneurship. The case study method is a robust technique for similar research (Feagin, Orum, and Sjoberg, 1991). We used the collective method for our analysis (Stake, 1995) with several case examples describing entrepreneurs' applications of frugal innovation with a sustainability orientation. The unit of analysis in each case is the innovation adopted by the entrepreneur, demonstrating sustainability and contribution to a circular economy. We would like to mention that there was no primary data collected with respect to the cases, and the entire research is based on secondary sources followed by underlying themes associated with the topic of study (Yin, 1993).

Case Description

We have chosen a set of cases based on their appropriateness at the intersection of frugal innovation, circular economy, and environmental entrepreneurship. Our secondary research and comprehensive analysis thereof help us formulate our findings and arrive at the proposed framework (Refer to Figure. 1).

Figure 1. Proposed framework

Figure 1 Proposed Framework

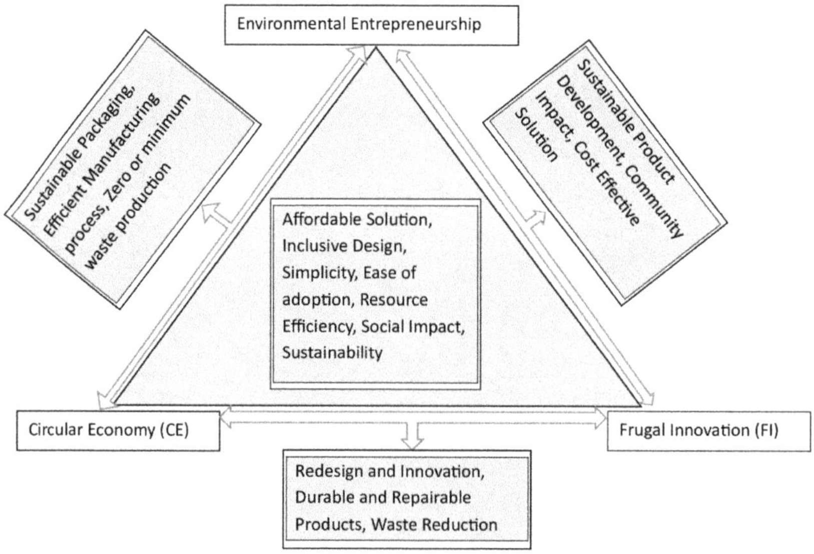

These case studies have been explained below-

Case Study 1: ecoBirdy- Sustainable Design Furniture

The case study is based on a furniture company named ecoBirdy. ecoBirdy was founded in 2018 in Antwerp by Vanessa Yuan and Joris Vanbriel. They created innovative technologies as a solution to environmental problems. They studied materials and innovated recycled plastic material named ecothylene. ecoBirdy uses discarded plastic and redesigns it into sustainable and ergonomic furniture. To introduce youngsters to the circular economy concept, they created the Rhino Lamp, Kiwi container, the iconic Charlie Chair and Luisa Table, a school program, and the storybook "Journey to a New Life." The crucial element of ecoBirdy is that their products intend to be recyclable at the end of their life, fostering their vision of a closed-loop system in plastic recycling. This shows how environmental entrepreneurship, resource recovery, recycling, and product and service design helped create a closed-loop system leading to a circular economy.

Case Study 2: Fairphone- Amsterdam-Based Electronic Company

This case discusses Dutch electronics manufacturer Fairphone, which designs and produces smartphones and headphones. Fairphone was founded by Bas van Abel, Tessa Wernink, and Miquel Ballester as a social enterprise company in 2013. Fairphone promotes sustainability by creating modular cellphones that are repairable and customizable by the user with lower maintenance costs. This case clearly aligns with the theme of this book chapter. This case shows the role of environmental entrepreneurs in designing their products and services that align with the notion of circular economy through frugal innovation techniques. The company aims to minimize its products' ethical and environmental impact by using fair trade, recycled, and conflict-free materials. It maintains fair labor conditions throughout its workforce and suppliers. Products are designed in such a way that they achieve a longer life span, which prevents accelerated obsolescence and massive waste generation. As of 2023, Fair Phone launched its new version, Fairphone5 (Shahhoseini et al.,2023).

Case Study 3: Cradle-to-Cradle (C2C)

Cradle-to-Cradle (C2C) is a method of creating products or processes that function more like a natural system. It is a holistic, economic, social, and industrial framework that aims to create an efficient and waste-free system. This method is intended to replace the linear extract-produce-use-dump approach by introducing the concept of "Everything is a resource for something else." This concept evolved from a low-waste, energy-conserving process. Like in nature, the waste of one becomes food for another; similarly, C2C-modeled products are made from materials that are already part of an existing use cycle, and at the end of life, another product is made from the same material of different types. This is based on the 3R (reduce, reuse, recycle) framework that explains circular economy. This concept of C2C aligns with the circular economy principles that eliminate the idea of waste. "Cradle to Cradle" is a registered trademark of McDonough Braungart Design Chemistry (MBDC) consultants.

Case Study 4: Loop- Elimination the Idea of Waste

Loop is a global platform for reuse managed by TerraCycle, an innovative social enterprise aiming to Eliminate the idea of waste. TerraCycle Global Foundation was formed in 2108. With the help of the national recycling platform, TerraCycle collects and recycles hard-to-recycle trash. It also helps manufacturers to integrate unique recycled content into their packages. By collaborating with brands and manufacturers, Loop strives to ensure that reuse is as accessible and convenient as single use. They established a circular reuse ecosystem that provided various products, including shampoo, coffee flasks, and other bottles (Ottosson and Oweini,2023). The concept of Loop is clearly based on the idea of circular economy. It helps companies shift from linear to circular systems by minimizing waste and creating a circular loop system. Loop system is based on the concept of durability. A loop product, on average, reduces 45% of greenhouse gas emissions compared to traditional in-store counterparts. Keeping materials in circulation improves supply chain resilience.

Case Study 5: Resortecs- Recycling Made Easy

Environmental entrepreneurs can source materials and resources locally to minimize environmental impact and align with circular economy and aligned practices. In this case, Resortecs (REcycling SORting TEChnologieS) is a pioneer in eco-design. Resortecs enables circularity in the fashion and textile industry through innovative design combining thermal engineering, eco-design, and chemical engineering. With the help of these innovative designs, it offers state-of-art solutions that empower the entire fashion and textile value chain to close the Loop. This example shows how environmental entrepreneurs capitalize on innovations that create circular economy practices that are profitable and sustainable. So, frugal innovation and circular economy practices are driven by environmental entrepreneurs.

RR: Other Case Examples

Developing new business models based on the collaborative economy and digital solutions: "Innovation strategies from a circular perspective are also often accompanied by developing new business models based on the collaborative economy and digital solutions for access to services. These business models r frugal innovation (fast, efficient, and affordable) and reinforce the firms' market image and differentiated positioning that could be threatened by frugal innovation." Environmental entrepreneurs can explore collaborative and digital-based business models that support circular economy principles. IKEA introduced a platform dubbed IKEA Home Smart, revolutionizing the approach to traditional business models where consumers now purchase artificial intelligence and use the Internet of Things powered hub, further incorporating a pay-for-subscription to access smart home services. This innovative model is not limited to collaborative and high-tech but is closer to a circular economy (Nussholz et al.,2024).

Environmental entrepreneurs can implement innovative approaches in agriculture to reduce soil erosion and increase crop yields. These methods support the circular economy's tenets by improving food security and promoting ecosystem regeneration. For example, Helvetas, a non-profit organization, has been working to develop innovative solutions for sustainable agriculture. They have implemented a project that transforms banana stems into valuable fiber raw materials for home textiles and sustainable packaging materials.[3]

Using Robotics and Artificial Intelligence (AI), environmental entrepreneurs can use robotics and artificial intelligence to expand sustainable practices. To improve seaweed farming, for example, startups like Samudra Oceans are utilizing these technologies, supporting the ideas of the circular economy. For instance, Samudra Oceans is a startup focused on improving seaweed farming by applying advanced technologies. By leveraging robotics and artificial intelligence, Samudra Oceans enhances the efficiency and sustainability of seaweed cultivation, aligning with the principles of the circular economy.[4]

Refill stations and reusable containers to refill stations for necessities like detergent, soap, and shampoo can help advance the circular economy. To lessen dependency on single-use plastic products and to promote trash reduction, startups like Algramo in Chile have installed refill stations where consumers bring reusable containers. For example, to reduce single-use plastics, Aldi UK and the UK Refill Coalition (which includes Go Unpackaged, Ocado Retail, and CHEP) are assessing an in-store refill system for dry products at their Solihull store and online.[5]

RISKS OF FRUGAL INNOVATION IN EMERGING MARKETS FOR A CIRCULAR ECONOMY

i. *Excessive resource consumption and waste generation:* Shorter product life cycles and excess resource consumption and trash generation may result from consumers' growing desire for economical, frugal goods, which could undermine the objectives of the circular economy. The present discourse highlights the conflict between the advancement of frugal innovation, which can lead to better livelihoods and a poverty reduction, and the degradation of environmental sustainability, which results from increased demand for frugal innovation.
ii. *Goods disposal*: Goods disposal is a significant issue faced by this world since increasing production of cheap and readily available goods may result in the easy and quick disposal of outdated and outdated goods. This practice undermines the concept of a circular economy inclined toward frugal innovation.
iii. *Issues with the ability to shift to a more balanced interaction of environmental and economic factors*: There are issues with the ability to do so, in addition to the necessity for inclusive, adaptable, and cost-effective innovation that may not fit in with current organizational structures and mentalities. This may create issues for the entrepreneurs to shift to the different modes of production.
iv. *Supportive institutions and policies*: Frugal Innovation in a circular economy may need helpful institutions and policies, particularly in developing nations where organizational and cultural resistance to change can be hindered. These possible hazards show how incorporating frugal innovation within the circular economy framework requires careful thought and balance, considering social and environmental factors.
v. *Limited purchasing power of consumers*: In developing countries, creating new job opportunities to increase purchasing power is still a significant challenge. In emerging economies, consumers usually have less purchasing power, making it challenging to adopt frugal innovations that require more upfront expenses or investments. Due to fear of failure, entrepreneurs hesitate to take rise to invest in these markets.
vi. *Inability to obtain funding for R&D investments*: "In emerging markets, innovation strategies are also affected by the level of reliability of institutions and infrastructure, which can entail delays, interruptions, or shortages." Inadequate infrastructure and financial resources might make creating and using cost-effective ideas more challenging.
vii. *Difficulties in expanding frugal innovations:* "For a long time, the main issue with frugal innovations has been their incapacity to grow, which limits their potential impact." Customers in emerging nations may not have the same pur-

chasing power, making it challenging to scale up frugal ideas and obtain the required economies of scale.

viii. *Challenges in striking a balance between enhanced wellbeing and environmental sustainability:* There is a "dilemma between the deterioration of environmental sustainability due to increased demand for frugal innovation and the improved wellbeing, better livelihoods, and poverty reduction that frugal innovation can provide." Achieving this balance in emerging areas with limited resources can be difficult.

These illustrations show how the restricted access to resources and purchasing power in developing countries can provide substantial obstacles to adopting frugal ideas within the circular economy framework, highlighting the need for innovative financing models and supportive policies to address these barriers.[6]

FRUGAL CIRCULAR ECONOMY SOLUTIONS IN DEVELOPING COUNTRIES

i. *Using locally accessible resources and materials:* "Companies emphasizing frugal innovation use in many cases locally accessible raw materials in their products, which reduces the need for transportation and hence lowers emissions." This lowers expenses and increases the accessibility of thrifty solutions for people with little purchasing power.

ii. *Using recycled and repurposed materials:* "Companies prioritizing frugal innovation also frequently employ repurposed materials in their manufacturing, offsetting waste generation in keeping with the concept of a circular economy." Reusing and recycling materials can help frugal inventions come at a lesser cost.

iii. *Considering longevity, repairability, and recycling potential*: "Longer lifespans are the goal of circular product design, averts rapid obsolescence and significant waste production. Additionally, the reduced customer maintenance costs associated with circular products' modularity—making them easier to repair—support frugal innovation's ecological and economic sustainability. This makes frugal innovations more accessible to people with lower incomes.

iv. *Creating new business models based on digital solutions and the collaborative economy*: "Creating new business models based on digital solutions and the collaborative economy for service access is frequently in tandem with innovation initiatives from a circular perspective. In addition to supporting frugal innovation—quick, easy, and inexpensive—these business models also uphold the companies' distinctive place in the market and image, both of which frugal innovation may compromise. These creative company plans can potentially increase the accessibility of frugal innovations.

MAKING USE OF TECHNOLOGICAL ADVANCEMENTS

i. *Health Cubed Inc.'s Health Cube in India:* This integrated, tablet-based, portable point-of-care diagnostic test device is a high-tech solution that demonstrates how technology can be an enabler for frugal innovation in the healthcare sector, catering to the needs of resource-constrained users.
ii. *Agatsa's pocket-sized 12-lead electrocardiogram* in India is another example of a high-tech medical device that highlights successful frugal innovation in the healthcare sector, targeting users' needs in emerging markets with limited resources.
iii. *Kodjo Afate Gnikou's $100 3D printer from electronic waste in Ghana:* This innovative solution highlights frugal innovation and the value of generating products from waste materials, aligning with the circular economy principles.
iv. *Qarnot's QH.1 high-performance computing server in India:* This server successfully applies frugal innovation that creates value from waste in a circular model by heating houses and buildings using "waste heat" from its microprocessors.
v. *Turning an old fridge into a disinfection chamber in Karnataka, India:* Researchers from the National Institute of Technology repurposed an old fridge to create a disinfection chamber, displaying a creative, low-cost solution that aligns with circular economy principles.
vi. *Developing a semi-automated, solar-powered pest-control device in India:* Scientists from the Indian Institute of Technology Kharagpur created a device that reduces the labor burden of small-scale farming, emphasizing sustainability and resource efficiency in agriculture.
vii. *Impossible Foods*: - Developing Plant-Based Meat Substitutes -The establishment of Impossible Foods aimed to provide consumers with the means to prevent climate change, preserve freshwater for flourishing natural habitats, and protect land for biodiversity. By developing a credible alternative to livestock, Impossible Food contributes to the long-term food security of established technologies. Impossible Food is renowned for its signature item, the Impossible Burger. This plant-based burger emulates the flavor of beef while employing a reduced number of environmentally detrimental products.

These examples show how resource-constrained populations' needs have been met. At the same time, environmental entrepreneurs have advanced ecological sustainability by using the concepts of frugal innovation and the circular economy to create affordable, sustainable solutions.

INTEGRATING PRINCIPLE RESPONSIBLE INVESTMENT (PRI) WITH SUSTAINABLE INNOVATION

"PRI, the preeminent advocate for responsible investment on a global scale, seeks to establish a comprehensive understanding of how investments are impacted by environmental, social, and governance (ESG) considerations. The PRI is critical in guiding organizations and investors toward ethical investment choices and sustainable practices in environmental entrepreneurship, frugal innovation, and the circular economy. Truly, the PRI is independent. It operates for no profit and encourages investors to use responsible investment practices to increase returns and manage risks more effectively; it engages with global policymakers but is not affiliated with any government; and the United Nations supports it but is not a subsidiary of it."

By adhering to the six Principles for Responsible Investment, one can implement various measures to address ESG concerns.

Principle 1: ESG concerns must be integrated into evaluating investments and formulating business decisions. Some of the possible courses of action under Principle 1 are mentioned below.

- Incorporate environmental, social, and governance (ESG) concerns into investment policy statements.
- Assist in advancing tools, measures, and analysis linked to environmental, social, and governance (ESG) factors.
- Evaluate the competencies of internal investment managers in integrating environmental, social, and governance (ESG) concerns.
- Evaluate the competence of external investment managers in integrating environmental, social, and governance (ESG) concerns.
- Request that investment service providers, such as financial analysts, consultants, brokers, research organizations, or rating businesses, incorporate ESG factors into their ongoing research and analysis.
- Promote scholarly and other investigations on this subject.
- Promote the implementation of ESG training for financial professionals.

Principle 2: ESG issues will be integrated into our ownership policies and practices, and we shall be active proprietors. The possible courses of action are as follows.

- Create and publicly share a proactive ownership policy that aligns with the principles.
- Engage in exercising voting rights or oversee adherence to voting policy (if delegated to an external party).
- Create an engagement capability by directly developing it or outsourcing the task.
- Engage in the process of formulating policy, regulations, and standards, including the promotion and safeguarding of shareholder rights.
- Submit shareholder resolutions that align with enduring environmental, social, and governance (ESG) factors.
- Interact with companies over environmental, social, and governance (ESG) problems.
- Engage in joint activities.
- Request investment managers to carry out and provide a report on engagement activities linked to environmental, social, and governance (ESG) issues.

Principle 3: Require the entities we invest to provide adequate disclosure regarding ESG issues. The possible courses of action are as follows.

- Request the implementation of uniform reporting on environmental, social, and governance (ESG) matters via instruments such as the Global Reporting Initiative.
- Request the integration of ESG (Environmental, Social, and Governance) problems into yearly financial reporting.
- Inquire with corporations about their adoption of or compliance with applicable norms, standards, codes of conduct, or international efforts (such as the UN Global Compact).
- Endorse shareholder initiatives and resolutions that advocate disclosing environmental, social, and governance (ESG) information.

Principle 4: Advocate for the investment industry's adoption and application of the principles above. The possible courses of action are as follows.

- Ensure that requests for proposals (RFPs) contain requirements directly related to Principles.
- Ensure that investment mandates, monitoring methods, performance metrics, and incentive structures are appropriately aligned. This includes ensuring that investment management systems reflect long-term time horizons as necessary.

- o Convey ESG (Environmental, Social, and Governance) requirements to investing service providers.
- o Reevaluate connections with service providers that do not satisfy environmental, social, and governance (ESG) requirements.
- o Assist in advancing methods for evaluating and comparing the incorporation of environmental, social, and governance (ESG) factors.
- o Advocate for regulatory or policy advancements that facilitate the application of the principles.

Principle 5: Collaborative efforts will be undertaken to optimize the efficacy of the principles' implementation. The possible courses of action are as follows.

- o Engage in networks and information platforms to exchange tools, combine resources, and utilize investor reporting for educational purposes.
- o Tackle pertinent developing concerns collectively.
- o Facilitate or endorse suitable cooperation endeavors.

Principle 6: Provide a report detailing our endeavors and advancements in implementing the sixth principle.[7] The possible courses of action are as follows.

- o Explain the integration of ESG (Environmental, Social, and Governance) issues into investment methods.
- o Provide information about current ownership activities, including voting, engagement, and policy dialogue.
- o Specify the obligations that service providers must fulfill in connection to the principles.
- o Engage in dialogue with beneficiaries regarding environmental, social, and governance (ESG) matters and the principles.
- o Provide a detailed account of the progress and accomplishments related to the principles by adopting a method where non-compliance is justified or explained.
- o Strive to ascertain the influence of the principles.
- o Utilize reporting to enhance awareness among a broader range of stakeholders.

RESULTS AND DISCUSSION

This chapter defines frugal innovation, circular economy, and environmental entrepreneurship. After that, different case examples are discussed to show how these terms are interlinked. Then, we discussed the risks and solutions for implementing frugal innovation techniques with circular economy principles. We also discussed how investors guided by PRI can support frugal innovation by funding companies that prioritize sustainability and inclusivity. Based on that, we have drawn a proposed framework showing their linkages. Our proposed framework explained how frugal innovation, circular economy, and environmental entrepreneurship are interconnected. This study mainly focused on secondary sources, including existing research papers and case studies. Figure 1 comes hereBased on several case study analysis and relevant literature, the proposed framework combines the essential ideas of frugal innovation, circular economy, and environmental entrepreneurship to explain how these can be collectively used to promote sustainable development and positive societal impact. As illustrated by the case example of Fairphone, entrepreneurs can adopt frugal innovation approaches to create affordable and resource-efficient solutions that address diverse consumer needs by adopting frugal innovation approaches. In the case example, ecoBirdy incorporates circular economy principles to ensure the sustainable development of its products, with a primary focus on waste management and effective resource utilization. This case study serves as a foundation for the convergence of environmental entrepreneurs with the circular economy concepts. Environmental entrepreneurs design and innovate products and services that enhance sustainable practices like Cradle-to-Cradle (C2C) and Loop. These case examples show how environmental entrepreneurs used frugal innovation techniques to provide solutions to today's world problems. This integrated approach in this proposed framework is followed to achieve significant community impact through inclusive design, affordable and sustainable solutions, ease of adoption, and efficient resource utilization. By combining economic and environmental objectives, the primary focus of this framework is to give an integrated approach to promoting sustainable development and addressing the issues of resource scarcity and environmental degradation with the help of entrepreneurs. Combining the efforts of environmental entrepreneurs with the circular economy objective gives solutions like Sustainable Packaging, Efficient Manufacturing processes, and Zero or minimum waste production. Also, entrepreneurs develop sustainable products that impact the community by providing cost-effective solutions. In this way, entrepreneurs adopt a frugal approach to tackle the problem of resource scarcity. Similarly, circular economy and frugal innovation approach are followed to redesign and innovate durable and repairable products by minimizing waste. These approaches collectively provide affordable, resource-efficient, economically, socially, and environmentally viable solutions.

CONCLUSIONS AND RECOMMENDATIONS

Based on our findings, we suggest the following areas for future research. First, this study is mainly based on secondary sources, so investigate and conduct the study, including primary sources, expert interviews, and surveys. Second, entrepreneurship impacts the welfare of society, the economy, and the environment, specifically how entrepreneurs can support sustainable practices in a circular economy. Highlighting the transition to sustainability, specify some essential competencies necessary for a frugal innovation in the developed countries. Third, it explores the incentives that drive entrepreneurs to participate in the circular economy by drawing data from countries like Finland, Norway, and Japan to understand what factors affect an entrepreneur's choice. Fourth, the interaction that propels sustainable practices underscores the significance of knowledge sharing, frugal innovation, and innovation capability in the context of value creation within the circular economy. Finally, an analysis of the impacts of economically viable energy technologies in developing nations, emphasizing the incentives that promote the implementation of energy-conserving practices, shall be one of the critical areas of future research that will enhance the body of knowledge.

REFERENCES

Albert, M. (2019). Sustainable frugal innovation-The connection between frugal innovation and sustainability. *Journal of Cleaner Production*, *237*, 117747. DOI: 10.1016/j.jclepro.2019.117747

Antolin-Lopez, R., & Montiel, I. (2018, July). Entrepreneurial collective responses to sustainability-related grand challenges. In Academy of Management Proceedings (Vol. 2018, No. 1, p. 11471). Briarcliff Manor, NY 10510: Academy of Management. DOI: 10.5465/AMBPP.2018.83

Cohen, B., & Winn, M. I. (2007). Market imperfections, opportunity, and sustainable entrepreneurship. *Journal of Business Venturing*, *22*(1), 29–49. DOI: 10.1016/j.jbusvent.2004.12.001

Conrad, A., & Schreiber, A. (2022). Circular Entrepreneurship: A pathway to circular entrepreneurship: An empirical study on how governmental institutions can improve the external environment of entrepreneurs.

Dawa, S., & Marks, J. (2023) An effectuation approach to sustainable entrepreneurship. *Journal of Entrepreneurship in Emerging Economies*, (ahead-of-print).

Dean, T. J., & McMullen, J. S. (2007). Toward a theory of sustainable entrepreneurship: Reducing environmental degradation through entrepreneurial action. *Journal of Business Venturing*, *22*(1), 50–76. DOI: 10.1016/j.jbusvent.2005.09.003

Desrochers, P. (2004). Industrial symbiosis: The case for market coordination. *Journal of Cleaner Production*, *12*(8-10), 1099–1110. DOI: 10.1016/j.jclepro.2004.02.008

Ezeudu, O. B., Agunwamba, J. C., Ugochukwu, U. C., & Oraelosi, T. C. (2022). Circular economy and frugal innovation: A conceptual nexus. *Environmental Science and Pollution Research International*, *29*(20), 1–16. DOI: 10.1007/s11356-022-18522-6 PMID: 34997516

Fischer, B., Guerrero, M., Guimón, J., & Schaeffer, P. R. (2021). Knowledge transfer for frugal innovation: Where do entrepreneurial universities stand. *Journal of Knowledge Management*, *25*(2), 360–379. DOI: 10.1108/JKM-01-2020-0040

Fonrouge, C. (2024). How to Change Entrepreneurs' Attitudes toward a Circular Economy: An Exploratory Framework to Reduce the Gap between Circular Intentions and Circular Actions. *Sustainability (Basel)*, *16*(5), 2048. DOI: 10.3390/su16052048

Geissdoerfer, M., Savaget, P., Bocken, N. M., & Hultink, E. J. (2017). The Circular Economy–A New Sustainability Paradigm? *Journal of Cleaner Production*, *143*, 757–768. DOI: 10.1016/j.jclepro.2016.12.048

George, G., Howard-Grenville, J., Joshi, A., & Tihanyi, L. (2016). Understanding and tackling societal grand challenges through management research. *Academy of Management Journal*, *59*(6), 1880–1895. DOI: 10.5465/amj.2016.4007

Ghisellini, P., Cialani, C., & Ulgiati, S. (2016). A review on circular economy: The expected transition to a balanced interplay of environmental and economic systems. *Journal of Cleaner Production*, *114*, 11–32. DOI: 10.1016/j.jclepro.2015.09.007

Hockerts, K., & Wüstenhagen, R. (2010). Greening Goliaths versus emerging Davids—Theorizing about the role of incumbents and new entrants in sustainable entrepreneurship. *Journal of Business Venturing*, *25*(5), 481–492. DOI: 10.1016/j.jbusvent.2009.07.005

Hossain, M., Park, S., & Shahid, S. (2023). Frugal innovation for sustainable rural development. *Technological Forecasting and Social Change*, *193*, 122662. DOI: 10.1016/j.techfore.2023.122662

Hossain, M., Simula, H., & Halme, M. (2016). Can frugal go global? Diffusion patterns of frugal innovations. *Technology in Society*, *46*, 132–139. DOI: 10.1016/j.techsoc.2016.04.005

Howard-Grenville, J., Buckle, S. J., Hoskins, B. J., & George, G. (2014). Climate change and Management. *Academy of Management Journal*, *57*(3), 615–623. DOI: 10.5465/amj.2014.4003

Isaak, R. (2002). The making of the ecopreneur. *Greener Management International*, *2002*(38), 81–91. DOI: 10.9774/GLEAF.3062.2002.su.00009

Korhonen, J., Honkasalo, A., & Seppälä, J. (2018). Circular economy: The concept and its limitations. *Ecological Economics*, *143*, 37–46. DOI: 10.1016/j.ecolecon.2017.06.041

Le Bas, C., & Czyżewska-Misztal, D. (2022). The economics of frugal Innovation: An integrative literature review. *Revue d'Economie Industrielle*, (4), 87–102. DOI: 10.4000/rei.11959

Lenox, M., & York, J. G. (2011). Environmental entrepreneurship.

Levänen, J., & Lindemann, S. (2016, June). Frugal innovations in circular economy: exploring possibilities and challenges in emerging markets. In *The International Society for Ecological Economics 2016 conference, transforming the economy: sustaining Food, water, energy, and justice. Washington DC, USA.*

López-Sánchez, J. Á., & Santos-Vijande, M. L. (2022). Key capabilities for frugal innovation in developed economies: Insights into the current transition towards sustainability. *Sustainability Science*, *17*(1), 191–207. DOI: 10.1007/s11625-021-01071-1 PMID: 35035587

Neumann, T. (2021). The impact of entrepreneurship on economic, social, and environmental welfare and its determinants: A systematic review. *Management Review Quarterly*, *71*(3), 553–584. DOI: 10.1007/s11301-020-00193-7

Numminen, S., & Lund, P. D. (2017). Frugal energy innovations for developing countries–a framework. *Global Challenges (Hoboken, NJ)*, *1*(1), 9–19. DOI: 10.1002/gch2.1012 PMID: 31565251

Nussholz, J., Assmann, I. R., Kelly, P., & Bocken, N. (2024). Circular Business Models for Digital Technologies in the Built Environment. A Circular Built Environment in the Digital Age, 245.

Ottosson, E., & Oweini, R. (2023). Developing a closed-loop supply chain to eliminate Single Use Plastic products: Implementing Circular Economy practices driven by EU commission directives.

Prabhu, J., & Jain, S. (2015). Innovation and entrepreneurship in India: Understanding jugaad. *Asia Pacific Journal of Management*, *32*(4), 843–868. DOI: 10.1007/s10490-015-9445-9

Prakash, N., Sharma, S., & Jindal, P. (2024). Entrepreneurship and Frugal Innovation for Realising SDGs in Global Context. In *Sustainable Development Goals: The Impact of Sustainability Measures on Wellbeing* (pp. 167–182). Emerald Publishing Limited. DOI: 10.1108/S1569-375920240000113A010

Radjou, N., Prabhu, J., & Ahuja, S. (2012). *Jugaad innovation: Think frugal, be flexible, generate breakthrough growth.* John Wiley & Sons.

Rosário, A. T., Raimundo, R. J., & Cruz, S. P. (2022). Sustainable entrepreneurship: A literature review. *Sustainability (Basel)*, *14*(9), 5556. DOI: 10.3390/su14095556

Rosca, E., Arnold, M., & Bendul, J. C. (2017). Business models for sustainable innovation–an empirical analysis of frugal products and services. *Journal of Cleaner Production, 162*, S133–S145. DOI: 10.1016/j.jclepro.2016.02.050

Rovanto, S., & Finne, M. (2023). What motivates entrepreneurs into circular economy action? Evidence from Japan and Finland. *Journal of Business Ethics*, *184*(1), 71–91. DOI: 10.1007/s10551-022-05122-0

Sarasvathy, S. D. (2001). Causation and effectuation: Toward a theoretical shift from economic inevitability to entrepreneurial contingency. *Academy of Management Review*, *26*(2), 243–263. DOI: 10.2307/259121

Sarasvathy, S. D., & Dew, N. (2005). Entrepreneurial logics for a technology of foolishness. *Scandinavian Journal of Management*, *21*(4), 385–406. DOI: 10.1016/j.scaman.2005.09.009

Schaefer, K., Corner, P. D., & Kearins, K. (2015). Social, environmental and sustainable entrepreneurship research: What is needed for sustainability-as-flourishing? *Organization & Environment*, *28*(4), 394–413. DOI: 10.1177/1086026615621111

Schaltegger, S., & Wagner, M. (2011). Sustainable entrepreneurship and sustainability innovation: Categories and interactions. *Business Strategy and the Environment*, *20*(4), 222–237. DOI: 10.1002/bse.682

Shahhoseini, A., Heydari, S., & Pedrammehr, S. (2023). Manufacturing and Assembly for the Ease of Product Recycling: A Review. *Designs*, *7*(2), 42. DOI: 10.3390/designs7020042

Shahid, M. S., Hossain, M., Shahid, S., & Anwar, T. (2023). Frugal innovation as a source of sustainable entrepreneurship to tackle social and environmental challenges. *Journal of Cleaner Production*, *406*, 137050. DOI: 10.1016/j.jclepro.2023.137050

Thompson, N., Kiefer, K., & York, J. G. (2011). Distinctions not dichotomies: Exploring social, sustainable, and environmental entrepreneurship. In *Social and sustainable entrepreneurship* (pp. 201–229). Emerald Group Publishing Limited. DOI: 10.1108/S1074-7540(2011)0000013012

York, J. G., & Venkataraman, S. (2010). The entrepreneur–environment nexus: Uncertainty, Innovation, and allocation. *Journal of Business Venturing*, *25*(5), 449–463. DOI: 10.1016/j.jbusvent.2009.07.007

Yousaf, Z., Panait, M., Tanveer, U., Cretu, A., Hrebenciuc, A., & Zahid, S. M. (2022). Value creation through frugal innovation, innovation capability, and knowledge sharing in a circular economy. *Sustainability (Basel)*, *14*(14), 8504. DOI: 10.3390/su14148504

Zeschky, M., Widenmayer, B., & Gassmann, O. (2011). Frugal innovation in emerging markets. *Research Technology Management*, *54*(4), 38–45. DOI: 10.5437/08956308X5404007

Zucchella, A., & Urban, S. (2019). *Circular entrepreneurship*. Springer International Publishing. DOI: 10.1007/978-3-030-18999-0

KEY TERMS AND DEFINITIONS

Frugal Innovation: The term frugal innovation or resource-scarce solution was initially discussed in the context of emerging economies where people who live at the bottom of the pyramid should have access to eco-friendly and affordable products and services. In recent times the term frugal innovation has transcended to developed countries too. In today's world, Frugal innovation means optimizing performance levels of industries in resource constraint situations so that it leads to sustainable cost reduction in core products and services.

Environmental Degradation: Environmental degradation means depletion of natural resources. In other words, environmental degradation means the depletion rate of environmental goods and services is more than the replacement rate because of natural and human activities. Environmental resources are getting polluted due to human interventions, which leads to the destruction of the ecosystem. There are various factors that lead to environmental degradation, i.e., Deforestation, pollution, climate change, etc.

Jugaad Innovation: Frugal Innovation is also known as "Jugaad Innovation" in India, which means quick-fix. It is a unique way of thinking in a challenging situation like natural disasters. It is a way to convert challenging situations into opportunities (doing more with less). It encourages out-of-the-box thinking, which is simple and creative, by making use of existing resources.

Circular Economy: The circular economy concept is a closed loop system that eliminates the idea of waste. It is based on the 3R principles (reuse, recycle, reproduce). It helps in reducing waste in the economy through a regenerative process. It is a solution to the linear extract and produce system by creating a close loop in which the waste of one can be reused as a raw material for others. It promotes resource efficiency by recreating them.

Environmental Entrepreneurship: This concept of environmental entrepreneurship emerges when there is a need to provide circular economy solutions to the market. Environmental entrepreneurs are also known as "Ecopreneurs" because they provide solutions to the market that promote sustainability. They are the key drivers for the frugal innovation techniques that create a circular economy that benefits overall society. They primarily focus on environmental benefits along with their profit.

Principle Responsible Investment (PRI): The principle for responsible investment is basically a network of all investors who promote responsible investment with the help of certain principles. The PRI is critical in guiding organizations and investors toward ethical investment choices and sustainable practices in environmental entrepreneurship: frugal innovation, and the circular economy. PRI integrates ESG (Environmental, Social, and Governance) factors into their consideration for their investment decision-making for more sustainable investments. The PRI is an independent body with no profit-seeking interests.

Sustainable Development: Sustainable development means aiming to meet the needs of the present generation without compromising the needs of the future generation. It is a holistic approach to development that encourages inclusive economic growth through innovation.

ENDNOTES

1 What is Stakeholder Engagement, and Why is it Important for Strategic Planning? https://www.smestrategy.net/blog/stakeholder-engagement-management-for-strategic-planning (accessed on 16 May 2024)

2 What Is Social Exchange Theory? https://socialwork.tulane.edu/blog/social-exchange-theory/ (accessed on 16 May 2024)

3 https://www.rural21.com/english/current-issue/detail/article/transforming-by-products-into-resources-circular-economy-approaches-for-agricultural-products.html (accessed on 11 May 2024)

4 https://www.startus-insights.com/innovators-guide/discover-5-top-artificial-intelligence-startups-advancing-the-circular-economy. (accessed on 11 May 2024)

5 https://www.responsiblebusinessnews.com/2023/11/20/aldi-stores-and-online-shopping-offer-a-refillable-option-for-dry-goods. (accessed on 11 May 2024)

6 https://www.linkedin.com/pulse/scaling-frugal-innovations-case-circular-economy-sheena-raikundalia (accessed on 11 May 2024)

7 https://www.unpri.org/about-us/about-the-pri (accessed on 11 May 2024)

8 https://www.thebetterindia.com/271662/best-innovations-by-indians-2021/ (accessed on 16 May 2024)

9 https://blog.jambo.cloud/10-reasons-why-effective-stakeholder-engagement-is-crucial (accessed on 16 May 2024)

[10] https://www.unepfi.org/ (accessed on 16 May 2024)

[11] https://www.climatepolicyinitiative.org/publication/updated-view-on-the-global-landscape-of-climate-finance-2019/ (accessed on 16 May 2024)

[12] https://www.unepfi.org/climate-change/tcfd/ (accessed on 16 May 2024)

[13] https://www.unpri.org/research/top-academic-resources-on-responsible-investment/4417.article (accessed on 16 May 2024)

[14] https://www.linkedin.com/pulse/role-policy-regulation-promoting-sustainable-consumption-santosh-g-7tzoc (accessed on 16 May 2024)

[15] https://odi.org/en/insights/three-tips-for-policy-makers-on-implementing-the-sdgs/ (accessed on 16 May 2024)

APPENDIX: SUPPLEMENTAL READINGS

- *10 Frugal Innovations by Indians That Give Simple Solutions to Big Problems.*
    - Sewage Pipe Home: Perala Manasa Reddy observed the problem of inadequate availability of potable water and sanitation amenities for the underprivileged during her time as a civil engineering student. As a result, she was motivated to research affordable housing alternatives further, and she stumbled onto dwellings constructed from sewage pipes, known as Pod-style homes. She created an Indian adaptation of the OPod, utilizing inexpensive, self-made structures constructed from repurposed sewage pipes. These structures have adjacent bathrooms, a kitchen, and bedrooms. This effectively addresses housing issues within the impoverished population.
    - Multi-Harvester: Deepak Reddy, a mechanical engineer hailing from Telangana, designed and constructed a multifunctional harvesting machine to assist farmers in cultivating land that had been uncultivated for several years. The terrain was abundant in substantial quantities of stone debris, posing a challenging task to remove and necessitating significant financial investment. Additionally, he discovered that vast expanses of such terrain are scattered throughout South India. It was vital to have cost-effective equipment to perform this duty, and he successfully designed such equipment. Additionally, it can gather crops.
    - Tupik Bed AC: Have you ever pondered the reason behind the need to cool the entire bedroom with an air conditioner solely to achieve comfortable sleep? Ravi Patel developed an energy-efficient air conditioning system that explicitly cools the bed. This compact air conditioner, weighing 13 kg, has a power use of 400 watts, equivalent to the energy usage of three light bulbs. It can also be easily installed by oneself, without the assistance of an expert, similar to a table fan.
    - Amphibious Bicycle: The intense want to reunite with his beloved prompted Muhammed Saidullah, a resident of Bihar, to become an inventor. To minimize the time spent waiting to see his wife, he constructed a versatile bicycle capable of operating on both land and water, making it amphibious. He traversed the Ganga on his bicycle to journey from Pahelaghat to Mahendrughat and bestowed the name "Noor" upon his two-wheeled vehicle in honor of his wife.
    - Mitti Cool: Mansukh Bhai Prajapati, a skilled artisan and innovator, is passionate about creating novel objects with clay. His most remarkable creation is a clay refrigerator that can keep food products for

an extended period without electricity. This inventor from Rajkot had their creation showcased at a conference hosted by the Centre for India and Global Business, Judge Business School, University of Cambridge, in the United Kingdom in May 2009.

- Jaipur Foot: Bhagwan Mahaveer Viklang Sahayata Samiti (BMVSS) is a non-profit organization located in Jaipur. Devendra Raj Mehta established it, providing thousands of needy individuals with complimentary prosthetic limbs. Mehta, a former IAS officer, experienced a near-fatal mishap in 1969 at Pokhran. Despite not experiencing limb loss, Mehta became aware of its financial burden, ultimately prompting the organization's establishment. Over 1.8 million people have profited from it thus far.
- Voice Box: Dr. Vishal Rao has developed a device priced at a little Rs 50 that can restore the voice of throat cancer patients. This doctor from Bangalore has created a voice prosthesis that is significantly more affordable than other options now on the market. The word 'Aum' is now accessible following its clearance by scientific and ethical committees. This device is essential for needy people, significantly improving their eating and speaking ability.
- Bullet Santi: A three-wheeled plowing apparatus constructed from a bicycle has become prevalent in Gujarat. This was developed by Mansukh Jagani, an individual engaged in farming. Due to his impoverished circumstances, he had to sell his bullocks; however, he desired to continue farming. Due to the challenges associated with managing and the high cost of livestock, he devised an idea that was well-received by fellow farmers. Now, plowing has become as effortless as taking a leisurely bike.
- Spandan: In 2016, Rajat Jain's close companion passed away due to a sudden stoppage of the heart. Subsequently, he was eager to expedite the development of a system capable of detecting cardiac issues. This individual from Dehradun quickly developed 'Spandan' - a compact ECG device the size of a matchbox that can identify cardiac irregularities in their early stages. By affixing electrodes to three specific locations on the patient's chest, it is possible to establish a connection between the device and a mobile phone. An application will be used to present the reading on the phone. It is rapid, efficient, and has the potential to preserve lives.
- Solar Rickshaw Home: Arun Prabhu, an architect from Tamil Nadu, was troubled by the unlawful encroachments in metropolitan areas and sought to discover a resolution to this issue. The 23-year-old

constructed a dwelling atop an autorickshaw, including a lavatory, entrance hall, rooftop area, living area, culinary area, and other necessary compartments. The configuration is easily transportable and specifically engineered to be affixed to any vehicle. Laborers, travelers, artists, and vendors view this concept as commendable, as the dwelling can also serve as a valuable resource during natural calamities.

- 10 Reasons Why Effective Stakeholder Engagement is Crucial.
    - Understand and align with your goals.
    - Identifying needs and concerns.
    - Build trust and credibility.
    - Get ahead of potential risks.
    - Make informed decisions.
    - Encourage innovation and creativity.
    - Smooth implementation and adoption.
    - Gain a social license to operate.
    - Stay compliant and avoid regulation headaches.
    - Strive for sustainability and long-term success.
- The UN-convened network of banks, insurers, and investors accelerates sustainable development.
- *Climate Policy Initiative*: - "Climate Policy Initiative's flagship analysis, the Global Landscape of Climate Finance ("The Landscape"), has provided the most comprehensive overview of global climate-related primary investment available since 2012. The Landscape aims to comprehensively track domestic and international investment from public and private sectors in activities that address and respond to climate mitigation and adaptation actions."
- *UNEP FI's Climate Risk and TCFD program* has led to the development of good practices to identify, measure, disclose, and manage climate risk in the financial sector. Working with over 100 banks, insurers, and investors since 2017, the program has created numerous tools, frameworks, and guides to accelerate the implementation of these good practices.
- *Top academic resources on responsible investment.*
- *The Role of Policy and Regulation in Promoting Sustainable Consumption.*
- *Three tips for policymakers on implementing the SDGs.*

Chapter 4
Frugal Innovation and Ethical Consumerism:
Navigating Sustainable Paths for Global Prosperity

Oly Mishra
https://orcid.org/0000-0002-5595-8705
Indian Institute of Foreign Trade, Kakinada, India

ABSTRACT

In an age marked by resource constraints, environmental concerns, and a growing awareness of social responsibility, the intersection of frugal innovation and ethical consumerism emerges as a pivotal pathway toward sustainable development. This chapter aims to explore the synergies between frugal innovation and ethical consumerism, offering insights into how these two concepts can collectively contribute to sustainability and global prosperity. The example of a social enterprise explains how ethical consumerism and frugal innovation can go hand in hand. The environment-friendly sanitary napkins are made by rural women through locally sourced raw materials. This socially conscious strategy empowers women, encourages participation in the community, and supports sustainable business practices. This is an example of how ethical consumerism and frugal innovation work together to create positive social change.

INTRODUCTION

In today's state of social, environmental, and economic challenges, the ideas of ethical consumption and frugal innovation represent revolutionary strategies that have great potential to promote sustainable development. Resource limitations and

DOI: 10.4018/979-8-3693-4050-9.ch004

the need for affordable solutions give rise to frugal innovation, which is based on the principle of accomplishing more with less. It entails making the most use of the resources at hand, coming up with original solutions to problems, and providing reasonably priced goods and services without sacrificing quality. With its minimal influence on the environment, waste production, and resource consumption, this strategy closely complies with sustainability standards. Ethical consumerism reflects people's and communities' growing awareness of the ethical and social implications of the things purchased by them. A positive change is being observed across industries by the consumer-driven desire for accountability and transparency, which motivates businesses to embrace sustainable practices. A potent synergy is produced when ethical consumerism and frugal innovation come together. Businesses may cut expenses, make the best use of their resources, and provide sustainable, reasonably priced solutions that appeal to ethical customers by adopting frugal innovation.

Businesses are incentivized by the market to prioritize sustainability in their operations via ethical consumerism. Businesses that use frugal innovation to create environmentally friendly products or use sustainable supply chain methods are more likely to draw in and keep moral customers. This positive feedback loop promotes ongoing innovation and progress toward sustainable objectives. Together, frugal innovation and ethical consumption have an impact on social and environmental results that go beyond the scope of individual firms. This synergy aids in waste reduction, environmental degradation mitigation, and resource conservation by encouraging responsible consumption and resource efficiency. Additionally, it promotes equitable economic growth by increasing access to necessities, especially in underprivileged areas.

The combination of ethical consumerism and frugal innovation offers a convincing route to sustainable development. This chapter will explain with the help of a case study and examples that demonstrate how these ideas can be successfully combined to promote good change, generate shared benefits, and accelerate the transition to a more affluent and sustainable future for all.

DEFINING FRUGAL INNOVATION

Frugal innovations are defined as new or significantly modified products, that are based on indigenous conditions and customer demands in developing and emerging markets (Lehner and Gausemeier, 2016; Albert, 2019). These innovations are characterized by their ability to reduce costs significantly, focus on core functionalities, and optimize performance (Mariano et. al, 2021). Frugal innovations start with the needs of the underprivileged and work their way up to address those requirements. It innovates the product with the necessary features and is mostly found in circumstances with limited resources. Furthermore, frugal innovation uses the resources available at hand to produce a new product and add value to it (Mishra, 2021a). Frugal innovations are more sustainable than alternatives and can diffuse from emerging countries to rich countries (Agarwal, and Brem, 2017). However, frugal innovation is still in a state of infancy from a theoretical perspective and lacks systematic approaches in practice (Hossain, 2018).

Researchers have also highlighted the disruptive and innovative potential of frugal innovations, which can generate new opportunities (McPhee et. al, 2018). Frugal innovations are associated with cost innovation, open innovation, sustainable innovation, and product innovation (Pisoni et. al, 2018). Overall, the previous literature suggests that frugal innovations are an emerging and promising area of research, with the potential to address the needs of underserved markets and drive sustainable development. While many scholars have provided definitions of frugal innovation, Prabhu et. al, (2017b) concept is the most relevant to the context of this study. It claims that frugal innovation uses fewer resources to provide solutions that are faster, better, and less expensive for a larger number of people. This definition reveals the true meaning of frugal innovation and is consistent with the case study covered in the research article. People living in underdeveloped areas should have access to and affordability of these frugal innovations (Prahalad, 2012).

THE POWER OF CONSTRAINTS

Frugal innovations leverage resource constraints to foster creativity, efficiency, and affordability in product development (Cai et. al, 2021). Constraint-based thinking drives the frugal product development process based on constraints. The main components of the constraint-based thinking approach are: (1) identifying current constraints; (2) conducting a root-cause analysis to ascertain the underlying causes of each identified constraint; (3) mapping each cause to the requirements of the product; and (4) developing a prototype or minimal viable product (Agarwal et. al, 2021).

Constraints shape our consumption patterns and behaviors in profound ways. Consumers seem to be locked in the current unsustainable consumption cycle due to market incentives, psychological conditioning, social norms, institutional frameworks, and cultural narratives (Scholderer and Grunert, 2005). However, constraints can also enable more ethical consumption by creating decision architectures that make sustainable choices easier (Lehner, et. al, 2016). Constraints-based thinking helps to identify and manage constraints and guide continuous improvement and change in organizations. (Kuruvilla, 2017). Ultimately, constraints enable and limit the agency of consumers (Hindocha, 2021). The power of constraints is that it leads to the possibility of radically restructuring those constraints. Recognizing constraints as productive forces open paths to reshaping consumption by redesigning the product (Ploeg et. al, 2021).

CHALLENGES IN SCALING FRUGAL INNOVATIONS:

The previous section refers to the power of constraints in developing frugal innovations. However, it is also true that one of the major challenges faced by frugal innovations is also due to resource-constrained environments. Previous literature has identified various challenges associated with scaling frugal innovations. The major obstacle is to control the costs while spreading the operations. Although resource and cost-efficient designs characterize frugal innovations, scaling them up frequently involves increased production costs, complex logistics, and the need for higher capital investment, all of which might compromise the initial innovation's frugal nature (Rao, 2013; Weyrauch & Herstatt, 2017).

The other problem is the innovation's ability to adapt to different markets and cultural contexts. Frugal innovations are typically tailored to specific local conditions and requirements, therefore it may be difficult to replicate the same success in other contexts. Low-resource areas also often lack infrastructure and institutional support, which could slow down the growing process. The necessity for constant innovation to meet the shifting demands of growing markets adds to the complexity (Bhatti, 2012; Zeschky et. al, 2014).

Maintaining consistency and quality control are additional problems when scaling frugal innovations. Because local manufacturing capabilities and resource availability can vary, it can be challenging to maintain the initial quality requirements as production increases (Brem & Wolfram, 2014). Furthermore, as frugal innovations are usually developed with less resources and it does not attract traditional investors who are doubtful about the profitability and scalability, acquiring finance and investments for scaling is sometimes difficult (Ray & Ray, 2011; Cunha et al., 2014). Significant obstacles may also arise from the protection of intellectual property and pressure from well-established businesses (Bound & Thornton, 2012; Soni & Krishnan, 2014).

DEFINING ETHICAL CONSUMERISM

Ethical consumerism refers to the collective behavior of consumers who choose products and producers based on ethical considerations like sustainability, justice, and fairness, to address global issues (Nakahara, 2017). It involves practices such as boycotts, "buycotts," and developing new discussions on market practices and exercising influence through purchasing decisions (Cıftcı, 2020). A conscious rejection or reduction of consumption techniques and behaviors is referred to as anti-consumerism. Opting against the prevailing consumer culture, which prioritizes materialism, excessive spending, and the never-ending need for new items, is a deliberate decision. People who practice anti-consumersim may do so for several reasons, including ethical objections to consumerism, environmental concerns, or the desire to improve their well-being. Purchasing second-hand or used goods, fixing and repurposing belongings, abstaining from unethical brands, and placing a higher value on relationships and experiences than material possessions are all examples of anti-consumption practices (Varman, and Belk, 2009). A counter-cultural movement known as "anti-consumption" urges people to consume with greater awareness and purpose while challenging the standards of consumer society. Anti-consumerism opposes excessive consumption and critiques its environmental, social, and cultural impacts, advocating for reduced consumption and a minimalist approach (Kasser, 2002). Ethical consumerism encourages responsible purchasing decisions based on sustainability, fair labor, and social justice (Micheletti & Stolle, 2007; Lewis, 2019). Both movements critique conventional consumerism but differ in their approaches, with anti-consumerism rejecting it outright and ethical consumerism seeking to reform it from within (Soper, 2007).

Research efforts to model ethical consumer decision-making have largely drawn from attitude-intention models while overlooking existing ethical decision-making models in business and consumer contexts (Eleni et. al, 2015). The attitude-behavior gap, where consumers claim ethical concerns but do not act accordingly, is a major issue in this field (Govind et. al, 2019). The attitude-behavior gap is evident in ethical consumerism, where consumers express concern for sustainability and social responsibility but do not consistently translate these attitudes into purchasing behavior (Joshi & Rahman, 2015). Factors contributing to this gap include higher costs of ethical products, limited availability, and insufficient information on the ethical credentials of products. Ethical consumption is more likely when consumers are receptive to ethical product information and consider it in making their purchasing decisions (Bray et. al, 2011). Consumer values are essential for engagement in ethical purchasing decisions. Trust in ethical advertising, and willingness to select ethical items are negatively correlated with egoistic values (Freestone, and McGoldrick, 2008). To improve the explanatory power of ethical consumer decision-making models, researchers have suggested incorporating models from the larger ethics and marketing literature. (Schwartz, 2016). Fair trade consumption, focused on products manufactured ethically for working conditions in developing countries, is a prominent area of ethical consumerism research (Elbeshbishi, and Al A'ali, 2020). Ethical consumerism refers to the practice of making purchasing decisions based on ethical considerations, such as social and environmental impact, sustainability, fair trade, and corporate social responsibility. It involves consumers actively seeking out and supporting products and brands that align with their values and beliefs, and avoiding those that are deemed unethical or harmful. Ethical consumerism, includes a variety of behaviours like buying locally and organic products to boycotting companies that engage in unethical business practices, can be viewed as a form of consumer activism where people use their purchasing power to advocate for positive change and hold businesses accountable for their actions (Carrington et. al, 2021). In general, ethical consumerism reflects a growing awareness and concern for the ethical implications of consumption choices as well as a desire to make a positive impact on society and the environment.

Among all the definitions given in the previous literature, the most relevant and apt definition of Ethical Consumerism is that of Degli Antoni and Faillo (2022) which emphasizes that Ethical Consumerism is a voluntary decision by consumers to buy goods and services while aims to positively affect certain social and/or environmental issues.

GOVERNMENT POLICIES AND ETHICAL CONSUMERISM

Government regulations that support sustainable practices can have a big impact on ethical consumerism. Stricter environmental laws guarantee that businesses use environmentally friendly production methods, which creates a demand for sustainable goods (Testa et al., 2016). As businesses work to satisfy legal requirements and customer expectations, policies that support corporate social responsibility can also encourage them to embrace ethical practices (Kitzmueller & Shimshack, 2012). Furthermore, monetary rewards like subsidies for environmentally friendly technology and fines for disregarding sustainability guidelines can further sway business decisions in favor of moral production (Delmas & Toffel, 2004).

Government public awareness campaigns and educational programs are essential for encouraging ethical consumption. These efforts can change consumer behavior by educating people about the social and environmental effects of the products they buy, leading them to make more moral decisions (McDonald & Oates, 2006). Additionally, certification programs, like organic or Fair-Trade labels, give customers trustworthy information to help them make moral decisions (Pelsmacker, Driesen, & Rayp, 2005). These regulations not only urge businesses to uphold strict standards of social and environmental responsibility but also promote ethical consumption, which eventually results in a more sustainable economy. Government policies in India that support sustainable and ethical business practices have greatly boosted ethical consumerism. The Ministry of Environment, Forest, and Climate Change (MoEFCC) has implemented the Extended Producer Responsibility (EPR) policy, mandating producers to manage post-consumer product disposal, particularly in electronics and plastics (MoEFCC, 2016). By encouraging companies to implement sustainable practices and consumers to make knowledgeable, environmentally friendly decisions, these policies foster an atmosphere favorable for ethical consumption.

RELATION BETWEEN FRUGAL INNOVATION AND ETHICAL CONSUMERISM:

Since frugal innovations provide sustainable solutions that are affordable for a larger audience, especially those in underdeveloped nations, they naturally align with the values of ethical consumption (Khan, 2016; Rosca et. al, 2018). The concept of frugal innovations encompasses both grassroots and sophisticated types, with advanced frugal innovations being systematically created through rigorous application of scientific methods (Rao, 2018). These innovations demonstrate the creativity and understanding of their inventors because they were developed despite resource limitations. These kinds of innovations address the demanding requirements of science, engineering, and related knowledge domains in addition to being economically viable, which makes them long-term answers to today's problems (Dabić et. al, 2022). Frugal innovations often face a consumer decision-making gap, where consumers recognize the value and benefits of these products but are hesitant to purchase due to perceived quality issues, lack of brand recognition, or uncertainty about performance (Mukherjee, 2018). This gap is prevalent in emerging markets, where consumers may be price-sensitive yet skeptical about low-cost innovations.

Frugal innovations have the potential to significantly contribute to ethical consumerism by promoting the use of environmentally friendly products and encouraging sustainable consumption behaviors (Prabhu, 2017; Panser and Sarkar, 2016). Frugal innovations are in line with ethical consumerism ideals, which emphasize the significance of making purchases that have a good influence on society and the environment, by emphasizing simplicity and the efficient use of resources (Rosca et. al, 2018; Dima et. al, 2022). Frugal innovation is being incorporated into ethical consumption in several areas, such as the creation of low-cost, accessible items that don't sacrifice sustainability or quality (van Beers et. al, 2020; Tesfaye and Fougère, 2022). For example, cost-effective innovations in the healthcare industry have increased the accessibility of medical services and products to marginalized communities, in line with ethical consumerism's focus on social justice and equity. Conscious consumer decisions encourage the creation and use of products that are made with sustainability in mind, which has a substantial impact on product life cycles. This includes goods that are made using recycled materials, consume less energy during production, and last longer, all of which minimize waste and the need for frequent replacements.

The adoption of sustainable methods in production processes is a part of the idea of frugal innovation as it aligns with ethical consumers' preference for products and reduces environmental damage. This strategy not only meets the immediate needs of cost-conscious consumers but also promotes responsible consumption and manufacturing practices. A possible means to sustainable production and consumption is the combination of ethical consumerism with frugal innovations. Frugal innovations can make a substantial contribution to ethical consumerism ideals and the promotion of a more sustainable and fair global economy by concentrating on developing solutions that are affordable, sustainable, and driven by values (George et. al, 2012; Bhatti and Prabhu, 2019).

By promoting economic self-sufficiency and environmental sustainability, ethical consumerism and frugal innovation can greatly strengthen rural communities. In rural areas, the establishment of local manufacturing facilities fosters entrepreneurship and the creation of jobs (Gbolarumi et al., 2021). It ensures that local women manage and actively engage in production processes by offering them education and training in sustainable practices (Shen et al., 2017). Local resources are used to create eco-friendly products that reduce environmental effects while providing reasonably priced solutions (Moorhouse & Moorhouse, 2017). Community empowerment is further enhanced by using inclusive marketing tactics (Mendoza, & Thelen, 2008), financial inclusion through microfinance (Egharevba et al., 2016), and leveraging government and NGO support (Joung, & Park-Poaps, 2013). Through the integration of low-cost, basic technology and the utilization of digital channels to expand their market reach, rural enterprises can thrive in a consumer-driven economy, ensuring resilience, self-reliance, and prosperity (Choe & Roberts, 2011).

The concepts of frugal innovation and ethical consumerism are closely related since they both seek to solve resource limitations and advance sustainability. Using as few resources as possible, frugal innovation aims to produce high-quality, reasonably priced goods. It frequently makes use of readily available materials and low-tech technology. This strategy adheres to ethical consumerism's guiding principles, which emphasize making purchases that promote social and environmental well-being, by lowering production costs while also making necessities more affordable for low-income consumers (Bhatti et. al, 2013; Pisoni, Michelini, & Martignoni, 2018). According to earlier research (Bhatti et. al, 2013; Radjou, Prabhu, & Ahuja, 2012), frugal innovations can have a big social impact by empowering marginalized communities through local entrepreneurship and employment creation. This promotes economic self-sufficiency and lowers poverty. By selecting environmentally and socially conscious products, ethical consumers—who are becoming more and more concerned with the sustainability and social impact of their purchases—support these innovations and create demand that pushes more companies to embrace frugal innovation practices (Sharma & Iyer, 2012). Businesses are encouraged to create reasonably priced, ecologically friendly products that satisfy the demands of ethical consumers, which can lead to a more sustainable and inclusive economy (Rosca, Arnold, & Bendul, 2017; Weyrauch & Herstatt, 2019; Hossain et. al, 2022). For example, frugal innovation in the healthcare industry has made it possible to create medical gadgets that are affordable and endorsed by moral consumers, improving access to healthcare in low-income areas (Bhatti et al., 2013; George et al., 2012). This integration considers not just the immediate social needs but also contributes to long-term sustainable development (Rosca, Arnold, & Bendul, 2017).

FRUGAL ENTREPRENEURSHIP

The method of creating and managing a business profitably and effectively—often with little funding—is known as frugal entrepreneurship (Michaelis et. al, 2020). It entails keeping an eye on costs, streamlining processes, and coming up with innovative ways to accomplish objectives on a shoestring (Hossain & Sarkar, 2021).

Sustainable, straightforward, and scalable business models are of utmost importance to frugal entrepreneurs, who frequently use lean techniques, bootstrapping, and creative problem-solving to spur expansion (Hossain, 2022). With this strategy, they can reduce waste and maximize available resources, prioritize profitability and cash flow; promptly adjust to shifting market conditions, and create a solid, long-lasting business by developing their competitive advantage (Laker, 2023; Shahid et. al, 2023). Since resources are generally limited in startups, small businesses, and social enterprises, frugal entrepreneurship is especially pertinent to these sectors. It is an attitude that propels business owners to be inventive, adaptable, and resourceful, which results in long-term success.

To understand the connection between frugal innovation and ethical consumerism, several gaps in existing literature need to be addressed. There is a need for context-specific studies (Kutaula et, al. 2024), longitudinal research (Chan et al., 2024; Gupta et al., 2024), and gain a deeper understanding of consumer psychology and motivation. Additionally, exploring interdisciplinary approaches (Carrington et. al, 2021), detailed case studies (Nangia et. al, 2023), and investigations into consumers from different demographics can provide comprehensive insights into how these concepts intersect and promote sustainable development (Belbağ et al., 2019; Perera et al., 2018). The case study that follows addresses the gap and shows a context-specific application within the realm of frugal innovation and ethical consumerism.

CASE STUDY

The social enterprise chosen for this study has been working on manufacturing and providing sanitary napkins of the best standard to the rural women of North India. The social entrepreneur established Vyomini in the outskirts of Delhi in 2016 to empower underprivileged and rural women. Like many other rural places in India, the people of this area confront numerous difficulties, such as restricted access to economic, educational, and medical facilities. Due to a lack of affordable menstrual hygiene products, women in these regions frequently experience health problems and social stigma. As there are fewer opportunities in the industrial or service sectors and the local economy is predominantly agrarian, it is challenging for women to obtain employment. To address these problems, Vyomini offers training and employment in the manufacturing of biodegradable sanitary napkins. In addition to encouraging good menstrual hygiene, this program gives women financial independence, enabling them to end the cycle of poverty. Using natural fibers from the local forests, such as jute and banana, is consistent with the company's commitment to environmental responsibility and sustainability. This all-encompassing strategy encourages sustainable behaviors while assisting in raising the standard of living for women living in rural areas. The company also provides education on menstrual health and hygiene to further support women's empowerment and wellbeing. The social entrepreneur aimed to remove 'period poverty' (Mishra et. al, 2020). It was decided that the rural women would manufacture sanitary napkins using locally available fibers. This way it became affordable for rural women. By sourcing raw materials locally, the social enterprise reduces transportation costs and the environmental impact associated with importing materials. The decentralized approach to manufacturing aligns with frugal innovation principles of optimizing resource utilization and minimizing production costs. Apart from providing them with sanitary napkins, the social entrepreneur also trained them in the sanitary napkins manufacturing process. This way, it has ensured that rural women became independent through entrepreneurship. The social enterprise has been working under plenty of constraints. So, they used easily accessible materials and simple production processes to create an affordable, biodegradable sanitary napkin. This strategy addressed the issue of period poverty by making the product accessible and affordable for women living in rural areas. It exhibited a frugal innovation strategy by concentrating on creating a product with the minimum possible expenses and resources.

The manufacturing approach is by its very nature economical and morally motivated. Through the establishment of decentralized manufacturing plants in rural areas of Rajasthan, and Haryana, the social enterprise empowers local communities and lowers costs, particularly for women from poor backgrounds. By utilizing local resources and knowledge, this decentralized model conforms to the ideas of frugal innovation and facilitates easier scaling and localized production. The use of natural fibers and adherence to ISO standards demonstrate their commitment to sustainability, guaranteeing both customer safety and environmental friendliness for their products. This meets consumer expectations for environmentally friendly and sustainable products by demonstrating an ethical approach to product sourcing and production. It provides sanitary napkins at a discounted price, with prices starting at $0.03 per napkin. With this pricing strategy, ladies from lower-income backgrounds can purchase the products. It therefore shows the values of frugal innovation by putting cost first without sacrificing quality and meeting market demands with reasonably priced solutions.

The other broader initiatives of the social enterprise include setting up vending machines in educational institutions and conducting awareness programs on menstrual health, demonstrating a commitment to social impact and ethical consumerism. By fostering awareness and education on menstrual hygiene, the social enterprise not only sells its products but also contributes to community welfare and empowerment. The social enterprise gives local communities' women economic empowerment by including them in the manufacturing and distribution processes. It encourages social involvement and economic independence. This way it actively promotes women's empowerment and community development. It encourages awareness of menstrual hygiene and expands access to sanitary products. This demonstrates its' dedication to enhancing the health of both its customers and the communities in which it operates.

In the case of Vyomini, several specific aspects of ethical consumerism are observed. One important aspect of ethical consumerism is environmental sustainability (Lubowiecki *et. al*, 2021). Vyomini produces biodegradable sanitary napkins using natural fibres like banana, jute, and cotton. This focus on eco-friendly materials reduces the environmental impact compared to conventional sanitary products that often contain non-biodegradable components. Ethical consumerism can be achieved by embracing both dimensions of sustainability and consumers need to have a sense for both social and environmental issues (Hosta, & Zabkar, 2021). Vyomini empowers rural women by involving them in the manufacturing process. This not only provides employment opportunities but also enhances their economic independence. The initiative fosters community development and improves the social standing of these women. The sanitary napkins produced by Vyomini are designed to be safe and healthy alternatives to conventional products that may contain harmful chemicals. By using natural and non-toxic materials, Vyomini ensures that its products are safe for women's health. This addresses the health and safety aspect of ethical consumerism (Hossain & Rakib, 2024).

Vyomini's products are made affordable for low-income rural women who otherwise might not be able to afford sanitary napkins. This aspect of accessibility is crucial in addressing menstrual hygiene management in marginalized communities

(Rana, 2024). Vyomini conducts awareness programs and education campaigns about menstrual hygiene. This aligns with the ethical consumerism principle of informed consumption (Strong, 1996), where consumers are educated about the benefits and importance of using safe, eco-friendly products (Gillani, & Kutaula, 2018; Freestone & McGoldrick, 2008). Vyomini's business model involves and benefits the local community directly. By creating a decentralized manufacturing process, the enterprise ensures that the economic benefits remain within the community (Long & Murray, 2013), promoting local development and self-sufficiency (Papaoikonomou, & Alarcon, 2017). Vyomini adheres to fair labor practices, ensuring that the women involved in the manufacturing process work in safe conditions and receive fair wages. This ethical approach to production contrasts with exploitative labor practices seen in some other manufacturing sectors (Uusitalo, & Oksanen, 2004; Berkey, 2021). Vyomini maintains transparency in its operations, ensuring that consumers are aware of the product ingredients, production processes, and the social impact of their purchases. This transparency builds consumer trust and aligns with the values of ethical consumerism (Kang & Hustvedt, 2014; Lee et. al, 2017; Schulte et. al, 2021). These aspects collectively demonstrate how Vyomini integrates ethical consumerism into its business model, promoting sustainable and socially responsible practices that benefit both the environment and the community.

Thus, this social enterprise is an example of frugal innovation and ethical consumerism. It maximizes impact without making significant financial inputs by utilizing human capital and community networks. It integrates ethical consumerism in different aspects of its operations from manufacturing procedures, product development, community outreach, and advocacy initiatives. With a focus on fair trade, sustainability, empowerment, and social impact, the social enterprise gives ethical consumers the chance to support a company that shares its values and makes a positive contribution to society. It embraces frugal innovation principles and effectively addresses social challenges, promotes economic empowerment, and offers sustainable solutions to improve women's health and well-being.

Vyomini had to face several challenges to achieve its goal to end period poverty. The major challenge was to secure funding. Though the initial funding was raised through government schemes and personal investments, however, sustaining and expanding the business required continuous financial support, which was difficult to obtain (Mair & Marti, 2009). The process of creating and producing biodegradable sanitary napkins presented technical difficulties. It was up to Vyomini to do research, find appropriate natural fibers, and create an economical manufacturing method. It took a lot of time and work to work with scientists and engineers to develop a straightforward, scalable production procedure. Furthermore, logistical planning and overcoming infrastructural constraints were necessary while establishing manufacturing units in rural areas (Bhatti et al., 2018). Another difficulty was gaining the trust of customers and breaking into the market for a new product, particularly in rural areas. In comparison to well-known brands, women in these communities frequently had doubts regarding the efficacy and quality of new sanitary napkins. To persuade customers of the product's worth and dependability, Vyomini had to spend money on product demos, awareness campaigns, and feedback gathering. Vyomini had to train women in the rural areas to produce and market sanitary napkins. This required developing comprehensive training programs and overcoming barriers such as low literacy levels and limited technical skills among rural women. The success of the social enterprise depended on ensuring that these women could run and manage the industrial facilities.

The relevant consumer behaviors in the case of Vyomini include a desire for reasonably priced, environmentally friendly goods, demonstrating a dedication to sustainable consumption even in economically challenged populations (Hindocha, 2021; Shen et al., 2017). A growing concern for environmental impact can be seen in the desire to switch from conventional to biodegradable sanitary napkins (Thφgersen, 1999). Furthermore, the impact of educational and awareness campaigns on menstrual hygiene highlights how crucial it is for customers to make well-informed decisions (White et. al, 2012). According to Johnstone and Tan (2015), Vyomini's strategy incorporates rural women in the manufacturing process, which fosters a sense of ownership and trust in the product. As such, community participation and peer influence play essential roles in this process. These actions demonstrate how frugal innovation and ethical consumerism are compatible and show how affordable, environmentally friendly solutions can satisfy the needs of both the environment and underserved populations (Carrington et. al, 2014). In the context of frugal innovations like Vyomini, addressing the attitude-behavior gap involves building trust through quality assurance, transparency, and effective communication of the product's social and environmental benefits. For instance, Vyomini's strategy of involving local women in manufacturing and using biodegradable materials directly appeals to ethical consumers while also ensuring affordability (Brem & Wolfram, 2014). This dual focus can help bridge both the decision-making and attitude-behavior gaps, fostering greater adoption of frugal and ethical products.

In the case of Vyomini, there is a multifaceted relationship between frugal innovation strategies and consumer behavior that shows how creative, economical solutions can impact and change consumer behavior. Frugal innovation strategies can significantly influence consumer behavior, particularly in developing markets where affordability and sustainability are key concerns. Frugal innovations can meet consumer needs at low cost without compromising on quality (Nature, 2023) or environmental impact which resonates with the principles observed in the case of Vyomini. The consumers' willingness to adopt these innovations is often driven by their perceived value and sustainability benefits. In the case of Vyomini also, the concept of frugal innovation aligns with ethical consumerism to empower rural communities through affordable, sustainable solutions. By creating reasonably priced, biodegradable sanitary napkins, Vyomini directly addresses rural women's financial limitations and encourages them to choose environmentally friendly products that they might not otherwise have considered reasonable. This is in line with the frugal innovation principles (Radjou & Prabhu, 2015; Mishra, (2021b), which stress adding value through resource-efficient solutions customized to marginalized populations' needs. According to Harris et al. (2020), frugal innovation frequently entails developing useful, reasonably priced items that appeal to customers with limited resources. This is especially important for Vyomini, whose menstrual hygiene products are made from sustainable, low-cost ingredients. Bhatti and Prabhu (2019) had demonstrated how frugal innovations might influence ethical consumer behavior by lowering the cost and increasing the accessibility of eco-friendly items. This is consistent with Vyomini's objective to support sustainable purchase patterns among rural consumers and menstrual hygiene.

CONCLUSION

By influencing consumer preferences towards products that are environmentally friendly and ethically manufactured, ethical consumerism plays a vital role in boosting demand for sustainably built and frugal goods. Consumers' purchase habits have changed because of their increased understanding of and concern for environmental issues, favouring goods that reduce environmental harm and advance social welfare. Additionally, environmentally friendly production techniques including using renewable energy sources and cleaner production processes are promoted by ethical consumption, which helps producers lessen the influence of their products on the environment. Customers minimize their consumption's negative effects on the environment, eliminate waste, and increase demand for environmentally friendly products by making thoughtful decisions. This in turn motivates companies to use more eco-friendly procedures and to develop in ways that support a more sustainable future.

REFERENCES

Agarwal, N., & Brem, A. (2017). Frugal innovation-past, present, and future. *IEEE Engineering Management Review, 45*(3), 37–41. DOI: 10.1109/EMR.2017.2734320

Agarwal, N., Oehler, J., & Brem, A. (2021). Constraint-based thinking: A structured approach for developing frugal innovations. *IEEE Transactions on Engineering Management, 68*(3), 739–751. DOI: 10.1109/TEM.2020.3042929

Albert, M. (2019). Sustainable frugal innovation - The connection between frugal innovation and sustainability. *Journal of Cleaner Production, 237*, 117747. DOI: 10.1016/j.jclepro.2019.117747

Belbağ, A. G., Üner, M. M., Cavusgil, E., & Cavusgil, S. T. (2019). The new middle class in emerging markets: How values and demographics influence discretionary consumption. *Thunderbird International Business Review, 61*(2), 325–337. DOI: 10.1002/tie.21980

Berkey, B. (2021). Ethical consumerism, democratic values, and justice. *Philosophy & Public Affairs, 49*(3), 237–274. DOI: 10.1111/papa.12191

Bhatti, Y., Khilji, S. E., & Basu, R. (2013). Frugal innovation. In *Globalization, change and learning in South Asia* (pp. 123–145). Chandos Publishing. DOI: 10.1016/B978-0-85709-464-3.50007-6

Bhatti, Y., & Prabhu, J. (2019). Frugal Innovation and Social Innovation: Linked Paths to Achieving Inclusion Sustainably. In George, G., Baker, T., Tracey, P., & Joshi, H. (Eds.), *Handbook of Inclusive Innovation: The Role of Organizations, Markets and Communities in Social Innovation*. Edward Elgar. DOI: 10.4337/9781786436016.00031

Bhatti, Y. A. (2012). *What is Frugal, What is Innovation? Towards a Theory of Frugal Innovation*. University of Oxford.

Bhatti, Y. A., Basu, R., Barron, D., & Ventresca, M. J. (2018). *Frugal Innovation: Models, Means, Methods*. Cambridge University Press. DOI: 10.1017/9781316986783

Bhatti, Y. A., & Ventresca, M. (2013). How can 'frugal innovation' be conceptualized? *Available atSSRN* 2203552.

Bound, K., & Thornton, I. (2012). *Our Frugal Future: Lessons from India's Innovation System*. Nesta.

Bray, J., Johns, N., & Kilburn, D. (2011). An exploratory study into the factors impeding ethical consumption. *Journal of Business Ethics*, *98*(4), 597–608. DOI: 10.1007/s10551-010-0640-9

Brem, A., & Wolfram, P. (2014). Research and development from the bottom up - Introduction of terminologies for new product development in emerging markets. *Journal of Innovation and Entrepreneurship*, *3*(1), 9. DOI: 10.1186/2192-5372-3-9

Cai, Q., Ying, Y., Liu, Y., & Wu, W. (2019). Innovating with limited resources: The antecedents and consequences of frugal innovation. *Sustainability (Basel)*, *11*(20), 5789. DOI: 10.3390/su11205789

Carrington, M., Chatzidakis, A., Goworek, H., & Shaw, D. (2021). Consumption Ethics: A Review and Analysis of Future Directions for Interdisciplinary Research. *Journal of Business Ethics*, *168*(2), 215–238. DOI: 10.1007/s10551-020-04425-4

Carrington, M. J., Neville, B. A., & Whitwell, G. J. (2014). Lost in translation: Exploring the ethical consumer intention–behavior gap. *Journal of Business Research*, *67*(1), 2759–2767. DOI: 10.1016/j.jbusres.2012.09.022

Chan, R. Y. K., Sharma, P., Alqahtani, A., Leung, T. Y., & Malik, A. (2024). Mediating role of cultural values in the impact of ethical ideologies on Chinese consumers' ethical judgments. *Journal of Business Ethics*, *191*(4), 865–884. Advance online publication. DOI: 10.1007/s10551-024-05669-0

Choe, K. A., & Roberts, B. H. (2011). *Competitive cities in the 21st century: Cluster-based local economic development*. Asian Development Bank.

Cıftcı, D. (2020). Political Consumerism: Discussion on the Motivation of Boycotting and Buycotts. *Dördüncü Kuvvet Uluslararası Hakemli Dergi*, *3*(1), 39–55.

Cunha, M. P., Rego, A., Oliveira, P., Rosado, P., & Habib, N. (2014). Product Innovation in Resource-Poor Environments: Three Research Streams. *Journal of Product Innovation Management*, *31*(2), 202–210. DOI: 10.1111/jpim.12090

Dabić, M., Obradović, T., Vlačić, B., Sahasranamam, S., & Paul, J. (2022). Frugal innovations: A multidisciplinary review & agenda for future research. *Journal of Business Research*, *142*, 914–929. DOI: 10.1016/j.jbusres.2022.01.032

Degli Antoni, G., & Faillo, M. (2022). Ethical consumerism and wage levels: Evidence from an experimental market. *Business Ethics, the Environment & Responsibility*, *31*(3), 875–887. DOI: 10.1111/beer.12447

Delmas, M. A., & Toffel, M. W. (2004). Stakeholders and environmental management practices: An institutional framework. *Business Strategy and the Environment, 13*(4), 209–222. DOI: 10.1002/bse.409

Dima, A., Bugheanu, A. M., Dinulescu, R., Potcovaru, A. M., Stefanescu, C. A., & Marin, I. (2022). Exploring the research regarding frugal innovation and business sustainability through bibliometric analysis. *Sustainability (Basel), 14*(3), 1326. DOI: 10.3390/su14031326

Egharevba, M. E., Eguavoen, A., Azuh, D., Iruonagbe, T. C., & Chiazor, I. A. (2016). Microfinance and poverty reduction strategy for promoting national development: The challenge of social/financial inclusion. *Social Sciences, 11*(22), 5373–5386.

Elbeshbishi, A. N., & Al A'ali, E. A. (2020). Fair trade and ethical consumerism: A complementary perspective. In *Ethical consumerism and comparative studies across different cultures: Emerging research and opportunities* (pp. 101–125). IGI Global. DOI: 10.4018/978-1-7998-0272-3.ch007

Eleni, P., Paparoidamis, N. G., & Chumpitaz, R. (2015, October 21). Modelling Ethicality in Consumption: Bridging the Literature on Ethics. *Thriving in a New World Economy*. Springer International Publishing. DOI: 10.1007/978-3-319-24148-7_65

Freestone, O. M., & McGoldrick, P. J. (2008). Motivations of the ethical consumer. *Journal of Business Ethics, 79*(4), 445–467. DOI: 10.1007/s10551-007-9409-1

Gbolarumi, F. T., Wong, K. Y., & Olohunde, S. T. (2021, February). Sustainability assessment in the textile and apparel industry: A review of recent studies. []. IOP Publishing.]. *IOP Conference Series. Materials Science and Engineering, 1051*(1), 012099. DOI: 10.1088/1757-899X/1051/1/012099

George, G., McGahan, A. M., & Prabhu, J. (2012). Innovation for inclusive growth: Towards a theoretical framework and a research agenda. *Journal of Management Studies, 49*(4), 661–683. DOI: 10.1111/j.1467-6486.2012.01048.x

Gillani, A., & Kutaula, S. (2018). An introduction to special issue: Sustainability and ethical consumerism. *Management Decision, 56*(3), 511–514. DOI: 10.1108/MD-03-2018-949

Govind, R., Singh, J. J., Garg, N., & D'Silva, S. (2019). Not walking the walk: How dual attitudes influence behavioral outcomes in ethical consumption. *Journal of Business Ethics, 155*(4), 1195–1214. DOI: 10.1007/s10551-017-3545-z

Gupta, R., Chandrasekaran, D., Sen, S., & Gupta, T. (2024). Marketing to bottom-of-the-pyramid consumers in an emerging market: The responses of mainstream consumers. *Journal of Business Ethics*, *191*(4), 739–755. Advance online publication. DOI: 10.1007/s10551-024-05664-5

Harris, M., Bhatti, Y., Buckley, J., & Sharma, D. (2020). Fast and frugal innovations in response to the COVID-19 pandemic. *Nature Medicine*, *26*(6), 814–817. DOI: 10.1038/s41591-020-0889-1 PMID: 32393803

Hindocha, C. N., Antonacci, G., Barlow, J., & Harris, M. (2021). Defining frugal innovation: A critical review. *BMJ Innovations*, *7*(4), 647–656. DOI: 10.1136/bmjinnov-2021-000830

Hossain, M. (2018). Frugal innovation: A review and research agenda. *Journal of Cleaner Production*, *182*, 926–936. DOI: 10.1016/j.jclepro.2018.02.091

Hossain, M. (2022). Frugal entrepreneurship: Resource mobilization in resource-constrained environments. *Creativity and Innovation Management*, *31*(3), 509–520. DOI: 10.1111/caim.12502

Hossain, M., Agarwal, N., Bhatti, Y., & Levänen, J. (2022). Frugal innovation: Antecedents, mediators, and consequences. *Creativity and Innovation Management*, *31*(3), 521–540. DOI: 10.1111/caim.12511

Hossain, M., & Sarkar, S. (2021). Frugal entrepreneurship: Profiting with inclusive growth. *IEEE Transactions on Engineering Management*, *70*(11), 3812–3825. DOI: 10.1109/TEM.2021.3088589

Hossain, M. T., & Rakib, M. D. (2024). Evaluating the effectiveness of the social marketing mix: a study of social marketing dynamics in Godrej Bangladesh. https://urn.fi/URN:NBN:fi:amk-2024052918106

Hosta, M., & Zabkar, V. (2021). Antecedents of environmentally and socially responsible sustainable consumer behavior. *Journal of Business Ethics*, *171*(2), 273–293. DOI: 10.1007/s10551-019-04416-0

Johnstone, M. L., & Tan, L. P. (2015). Exploring the gap between consumers' green rhetoric and purchasing behaviour. *Journal of Business Ethics*, *132*(2), 311–328. DOI: 10.1007/s10551-014-2316-3

Joshi, Y., & Rahman, Z. (2015). Factors affecting green purchase behaviour and future research directions. *International Strategic Management Review*, *3*(1-2), 128–143. DOI: 10.1016/j.ism.2015.04.001

Joung, H. M., & Park-Poaps, H. (2013). Factors motivating and influencing clothing disposal behaviours. *International Journal of Consumer Studies*, *37*(1), 105–111. DOI: 10.1111/j.1470-6431.2011.01048.x

Kang, J., & Hustvedt, G. (2014). Building trust between consumers and corporations: The role of consumer perceptions of transparency and social responsibility. *Journal of Business Ethics*, *125*(2), 253–265. DOI: 10.1007/s10551-013-1916-7

Kasser, T. (2002). *The High Price of Materialism*. MIT Press. DOI: 10.7551/mitpress/3501.001.0001

Khan, R. (2016). How frugal innovation promotes social sustainability. *Sustainability (Basel)*, *8*(10), 1034. DOI: 10.3390/su8101034

Kitzmueller, M., & Shimshack, J. (2012). Economic perspectives on corporate social responsibility. *Journal of Economic Literature*, *50*(1), 51–84. DOI: 10.1257/jel.50.1.51

Kuruvilla, S. J. (2017). Theory of Constraints and the Thinking Process. *International Journal of Business Insights & Transformation*, *11*(1).

Kutaula, S., Gillani, A., Gregory-Smith, D., & Bartikowski, B. (2024). Ethical Consumerism in Emerging Markets: Opportunities and Challenges. *Journal of Business Ethics*, *191*(4), 651–673. DOI: 10.1007/s10551-024-05657-4

Laker, B. (2023, May 28). *How frugal entrepreneurship can be a competitive advantage*. Forbes.https://www.forbes.com/sites/benjaminlaker/2022/05/05/how-frugal-entrepreneurship-can-be-a-competitive-advantage/

Lee, M. S., Seifert, M., & Cherrier, H. (2017). Anti-consumption and governance in the global fashion industry: Transparency is key. *Governing corporate social responsibility in the apparel industry after Rana Plaza*, 147-174.

Lehner, A. C., & Gausemeier, J. (2016). A pattern-based approach to the development of frugal innovations. *Technology Innovation Management Review*, *6*(3), 13–21. DOI: 10.22215/timreview/971

Lehner, M., Mont, O., & Heiskanen, E. (2016). Nudging–A promising tool for sustainable consumption behaviour? *Journal of Cleaner Production*, *134*, 166–177. DOI: 10.1016/j.jclepro.2015.11.086

Lewis, T. (2019). Ethical Consumption: Practices and Perspectives. *Journal of Consumer Ethics*, *3*(1), 45–62.

Long, M. A., & Murray, D. L. (2013). Ethical consumption, values convergence/divergence and community development. *Journal of Agricultural & Environmental Ethics*, *26*(2), 351–375. DOI: 10.1007/s10806-012-9384-0

Lubowiecki-Vikuk, A., Dąbrowska, A., & Machnik, A. (2021). Responsible consumer and lifestyle: Sustainability insights. *Sustainable Production and Consumption*, *25*, 91–101. DOI: 10.1016/j.spc.2020.08.007 PMID: 32864405

Mair, J., & Marti, I. (2009). Entrepreneurship in and around institutional voids: A case study from Bangladesh. *Journal of Business Venturing*, *24*(5), 419–435. DOI: 10.1016/j.jbusvent.2008.04.006

Mariano, E. B., Mariano, E. B., & Silva, H. M. R. (2021). Pro-poor innovations to promote instrumental freedoms: A systematic literature review. *Sustainability (Basel)*, *13*(24), 13587. DOI: 10.3390/su132413587

McDonald, S., & Oates, C. J. (2006). Sustainability: Consumer perceptions and marketing strategies. *Business Strategy and the Environment*, *15*(3), 157–170. DOI: 10.1002/bse.524

McPhee, C., Schillo, R. S., Earl, L., & Kinder, J. (2018). Inclusive Innovation in Developed Countries. *Technology Innovation Management Review*, *8*(2), 3–6. DOI: 10.22215/timreview/1134

Mendoza, R. U., & Thelen, N. (2008). Innovations to make markets more inclusive for the poor. *Development Policy Review*, *26*(4), 427–458. DOI: 10.1111/j.1467-7679.2008.00417.x

Michaelis, T. L., Carr, J. C., Scheaf, D. J., & Pollack, J. M. (2020). The frugal entrepreneur: A self-regulatory perspective of resourceful entrepreneurial behavior. *Journal of Business Venturing*, *35*(4), 105969. DOI: 10.1016/j.jbusvent.2019.105969

Micheletti, M., & Stolle, D. (2007). Mobilizing Consumers to Take Responsibility for Global Social Justice. *The Annals of the American Academy of Political and Social Science*, *611*(1), 157–175. DOI: 10.1177/0002716206298712

Ministry of Environment. Forest and Climate Change (MoEFCC). (2016). Extended Producer Responsibility. Retrieved from https://pib.gov.in/PressReleaseIframePage.aspx?PRID=1579741

Mishra, O. (2021a). Principles of frugal innovation and its application by social entrepreneurs in times of adversity: An inductive single-case approach. *Journal of Entrepreneurship in Emerging Economies*, *13*(4), 547–574. DOI: 10.1108/JEEE-07-2020-0247

Mishra, O. (2021b). Design thinking and bricolage for frugal innovations during crisis. *Journal of Innovation Management, 9*(3), 1–26. DOI: 10.24840/2183-0606_009.003_0002

Mishra, O., Sharma, R., & Agrawal, B. (2020). Facilitating women prosperity with higher purpose at Vyomini. *South Asian Journal of Business and Management Cases, 9*(2), 198–207. DOI: 10.1177/2277977920905820

Moorhouse, D., & Moorhouse, D. (2018). Sustainability in the fashion industry. *Clothing Cultures, 5*(1), 3–5. DOI: 10.1386/cc.5.1.3_1

Mukherjee, S. (2018). Frugal innovation: Aligning theory, practice, and public policy. *Journal of Management Science, 10*(1), 15–31.

Nakahara, H. (2017). *International Trends in Ethical Consumerism. Material Cycles and Waste Management Research*. Japan Society of Waste Management Experts., DOI: 10.3985/mcwmr.28.261

Nangia, P., Bansal, S., & Thaichon, P. (2023). Doing more with less: An integrative literature review on responsible consumption behaviour. *Journal of Consumer Behaviour, 23*(1), 141–155. DOI: 10.1002/cb.2163

Nature. (2023). Why the world needs to foster frugal innovation. *Nature, 620*(7970), 312-313. DOI: 10.1038/d41586-023-03816-7

Pansera, M., & Sarkar, S. (2016). Crafting sustainable development solutions: Frugal innovations of grassroots entrepreneurs. *Sustainability (Basel), 8*(1), 51. DOI: 10.3390/su8010051

Papaoikonomou, E., & Alarcon, A. (2017). Revisiting consumer empowerment: An exploration of ethical consumption communities. *Journal of Macromarketing, 37*(1), 40–56. DOI: 10.1177/0276146715619653

Pelsmacker, P. D., Driesen, L., & Rayp, G. (2005). Do consumers care about ethics? Willingness to pay for fair-trade coffee. *The Journal of Consumer Affairs, 39*(2), 363–385. DOI: 10.1111/j.1745-6606.2005.00019.x

Perera, C., Auger, P., & Klein, J. (2018). Green consumption practices among young environmentalists: A practice theory perspective. *Journal of Business Ethics, 152*(3), 843–864. DOI: 10.1007/s10551-016-3376-3

Pisoni, A., Michelini, L., & Martignoni, G. (2018). Frugal approach to innovation: State of the art and future perspectives. *Journal of Cleaner Production, 171*, 107–126. DOI: 10.1016/j.jclepro.2017.09.248

Ploeg, M., Knoben, J., Vermeulen, P., & van Beers, C. (2021). Rare gems or mundane practice? Resource constraints as drivers of frugal innovation. *Innovation (North Sydney, N.S.W.)*, *23*(1), 93–126. DOI: 10.1080/14479338.2020.1825089

Prabhu, J. (2017a). Frugal innovation: Doing more with less for more. *Philosophical Transactions. Series A, Mathematical, Physical, and Engineering Sciences*, *375*(2095), 20160372. DOI: 10.1098/rsta.2016.0372 PMID: 28461436

Prabhu, J., Tracey, P., & Hassan, M. (2017b). Marketing to the poor: An institutional model of exchange in emerging markets. *AMS Review*, *7*(3–4), 101–122. DOI: 10.1007/s13162-017-0100-0

Prahalad, C. K. (2012). Bottom of the pyramid as a source of breakthrough innovations. *Journal of Product Innovation Management*, *29*(1), 6–12. DOI: 10.1111/j.1540-5885.2011.00874.x

Radjou, N., Prabhu, J., & Ahuja, S. (2012). *Jugaad innovation: Think frugal, be flexible, generate breakthrough growth*. John Wiley & Sons.

Rana, N. (2024). The Environmental Impact of Fashion. In *Threaded Harmony: A Sustainable Approach to Fashion* (pp. 5–16). Emerald Publishing Limited. DOI: 10.1108/978-1-83608-152-420241004

Rao, B. C. (2013). How disruptive is frugal? *Technology in Society*, *35*(1), 65–73. DOI: 10.1016/j.techsoc.2013.03.003

Rao, B. C. (2018). Science is indispensable to frugal innovations. *Technology Innovation Management Review*, *8*(4).

Ray, P. K., & Ray, S. (2011). Product Innovation for the People's Car in an Emerging Economy. *Technovation*, *31*(5-6), 216–227. DOI: 10.1016/j.technovation.2011.01.004

Rosca, E., Arnold, M., & Bendul, J. C. (2017). Business models for sustainable innovation–an empirical analysis of frugal products and services. *Journal of Cleaner Production*, *162*, S133–S145. DOI: 10.1016/j.jclepro.2016.02.050

Rosca, E., Reedy, J., & Bendul, J. C. (2018). Does frugal innovation enable sustainable development? A systematic literature review. *European Journal of Development Research*, *30*(1), 136–157. DOI: 10.1057/s41287-017-0106-3

Scholderer, J., & Grunert, K. G. (2005). Consumers, food and convenience: The long way from resource constraints to actual consumption patterns. *Journal of Economic Psychology*, *26*(1), 105–128. DOI: 10.1016/j.joep.2002.08.001

Schulte, M., Balasubramanian, S., & Paris, C. M. (2021). Blood diamonds and ethical consumerism: An empirical investigation. *Sustainability (Basel), 13*(8), 4558. DOI: 10.3390/su13084558

Schwartz, M. S. (2016). Ethical decision-making theory: An integrated approach. *Journal of Business Ethics, 139*(4), 755–776. DOI: 10.1007/s10551-015-2886-8

Shahid, M. S., Hossain, M., Karami, M., & Anwar, T. (2023). Frugal entrepreneurship: A way to seize business opportunities for low-income customers. *Asia Pacific Journal of Management*, •••, 1–31.

Sharma, A., & Iyer, G. R. (2012). Resource-constrained product development: Implications for green marketing and green supply chains. *Industrial Marketing Management, 41*(4), 599–608. DOI: 10.1016/j.indmarman.2012.04.007

Shen, B., Wang, Y., Lo, C. K., & Shum, M. (2012). The impact of ethical fashion on consumer purchase behavior. *Journal of Fashion Marketing and Management, 16*(2), 234–245. DOI: 10.1108/13612021211222842

Soni, P., & Krishnan, R. T. (2014). Frugal Innovation: Aligning Theory, Practice, and Public Policy. *Journal of Indian Business Research, 6*(1), 29–47. DOI: 10.1108/JIBR-03-2013-0025

Soper, K. (2007). Re-thinking the Good Life: The Citizenship Dimension of Consumer Disaffection with Consumerism. *Journal of Consumer Culture, 7*(2), 205–229. DOI: 10.1177/1469540507077681

Strong, C. (1996). Features contributing to the growth of ethical consumerism-a preliminary investigation. *Marketing Intelligence & Planning, 14*(5), 5–13. DOI: 10.1108/02634509610127518

Tesfaye, L. A., & Fougère, M. (2022). Frugal innovation hijacked: The co-optive power of co-creation. *Journal of Business Ethics, 180*(2), 439–454. DOI: 10.1007/s10551-021-04883-4

Testa, F., Iraldo, F., & Frey, M. (2016). The effect of environmental regulation on firms' competitive performance: The case of the building & construction sector in some EU regions. *Journal of Environmental Management, 92*(9), 2136–2144. DOI: 10.1016/j.jenvman.2011.03.039 PMID: 21524840

Thφgersen, J. (1999). The ethical consumer. Moral norms and packaging choice. *Journal of Consumer Policy, 22*(4), 439–460. DOI: 10.1023/A:1006225711603

Uusitalo, O., & Oksanen, R. (2004). Ethical consumerism: A view from Finland. *International Journal of Consumer Studies*, *28*(3), 214–221. DOI: 10.1111/j.1470-6431.2003.00339.x

van Beers, C., Knorringa, P., & Leliveld, A. (2020). Can frugal innovations be responsible innovations? In *Responsible Innovation in Large Technological Systems* (pp. 80–95). Routledge. DOI: 10.4324/9781003019930-6

Varman, R., & Belk, R. W. (2009). Nationalism and ideology in an anticonsumption movement. *The Journal of Consumer Research*, *36*(4), 686–700. DOI: 10.1086/600486

Weyrauch, T., & Herstatt, C. (2017). What is frugal innovation? Three defining criteria. *Journal of Frugal Innovation*, *2*(1), 1–17. DOI: 10.1186/s40669-016-0005-y

Weyrauch, T., & Herstatt, C. (2019). What is frugal innovation? In *Frugal Innovation* (pp. 3–39). Routledge. DOI: 10.4324/9780429025679-1

White, K., MacDonnell, R., & Ellard, J. H. (2012). Belief in a just world: Consumer intentions and behaviors toward ethical products. *Journal of Marketing*, *76*(1), 103–118. DOI: 10.1509/jm.09.0581

Zeschky, M., Winterhalter, S., & Gassmann, O. (2014). From cost to frugal and reverse innovation: Mapping the field and implications for global competitiveness. *Research Technology Management*, *57*(4), 20–27.

KEY TERMS AND DEFINITIONS

Frugal Innovation: A method of innovation that focuses on developing affordable solutions by optimizing performance and reducing costs while using minimal resources. It is specially designed to meet the needs of the resource-constrained markets, promoting sustainability and accessibility.

Ethical Consumerism: The practice where consumers make purchasing decisions based on ethical considerations such as sustainability, social justice, and fairness. This behavior promotes responsible consumption by supporting businesses that prioritize environmental and social well-being.

Sustainability: A broad concept referring to the ability to meet present needs without compromising the ability of future generations to meet theirs. It involves practices that minimize environmental impact and promote long-term ecological balance.

Constraints-Based Thinking: An approach used in frugal innovation that leverages resource limitations to foster creativity and efficiency in product development. This involves identifying constraints, analyzing their causes, and developing solutions that maximize available resources.

Period Poverty: The lack of access to affordable menstrual hygiene products, education, and sanitation facilities, often leads to health issues and social stigma. Efforts to combat period poverty focus on providing accessible and affordable solutions to improve the well-being of women in disadvantaged communities.

Fair Labor Practices: Ethical labor standards ensure that workers are treated fairly, with safe working conditions and appropriate compensation. These practices are integral to ethical consumerism, promoting social justice, and protecting workers' rights.

Social Enterprise: A business model that seeks to address social issues through innovative and sustainable solutions, often focusing on community empowerment, environmental responsibility, and ethical practices. Social enterprises aim to create positive social impact alongside financial sustainability.

Resource Efficiency: The practice of using the Earth's limited resources in a sustainable manner while minimizing waste and environmental impact. Resource efficiency aims to create more value with fewer resources, a key concept in frugal innovation.

Sustainable Development: Development that meets the needs of the present without compromising the ability of future generations to meet their own needs, often achieved by balancing economic growth, environmental protection, and social equity.

Social Innovation: The process of developing and implementing new solutions to social challenges, often addressing issues such as poverty, education, health, and community development. Social innovation seeks to improve the well-being of individuals and communities through creative approaches.

Anti-Consumerism: A social movement opposing excessive consumption and materialism, promoting reduced consumption and sustainable living practices. Anti-consumerism advocates for minimizing environmental and social harm caused by overconsumption.

Circular Economy: An economic system aimed at eliminating waste and the continual use of resources by creating closed-loop systems where products, materials, and resources are reused, refurbished, or recycled rather than discarded.

Chapter 5
Thriving on Constraints: Harnessing Frugal Innovations for Entrepreneurial Growth

Radhika Sharma
IIS University (Deemed), Jaipur, India

ABSTRACT

In the dynamic landscape of entrepreneurship, resources are finite and challenges are omnipresent, the ability to innovate amidst constraints becomes paramount. This chapter presents an exploration of leveraging frugal innovations as catalysts for entrepreneurial success. The chapter delves into understanding frugal innovation, tracing historical evolution, and emphasizes the importance of embracing constraints for innovation. By shifting mindsets and adopting problem-solving techniques, entrepreneurs can reframe limitations as opportunities for growth. The chapter explores practical strategies for frugal innovation, the lean startup methodology and minimum viable product development, accompanied by case studies across various industries. It highlights best practices and lessons learned from successful frugal innovators, emphasizing scalability, sustainability, and importance of collaborative ecosystems. The chapter equips readers with knowledge and tools necessary to navigate resource-constrained environments and foster sustainable entrepreneurial growth through frugal innovations.

INTRODUCTION

In today's dynamic business landscape, entrepreneurs face multifaceted challenges, from limited resources to fierce competition and rapidly changing market dynamics. However, constraints need not stifle innovation; rather, they can serve as catalysts for creative problem-solving and entrepreneurial ingenuity (Adner, 2017; Govindarajan

DOI: 10.4018/979-8-3693-4050-9.ch005

& Ramamurti, 2015). This chapter explores the concept of frugal innovation as a potent strategy for thriving within constraints and driving entrepreneurial success. By harnessing frugal innovations, entrepreneurs can unlock new pathways to growth, resilience, and sustainable business development.

Understanding Frugal Innovation

Frugal innovation, born out of necessity, involves creating high-quality solutions using limited resources. It embodies the principles of simplicity, affordability, and efficiency, enabling entrepreneurs to achieve significant breakthroughs even with constrained resources (Zeschky, Widenmayer, & Gassmann, 2011). Frugal innovators leverage ingenuity and resourcefulness to deliver value to customers while keeping costs low. This section delves into the conceptual framework of frugal innovation, tracing its evolution and exploring its diverse manifestations across industries and regions. Whether it's the grassroots innovations in emerging markets or the lean startup methodologies in developed economies, frugal innovation offers a universal approach to doing more with less. Frugal innovation is a strategic approach to product development and business operations that emphasizes simplicity, affordability, and efficiency. It originated in resource-constrained environments, such as emerging markets and underserved communities, where entrepreneurs are compelled to do more with less (Zeschky, Widenmayer, & Gassmann, 2011). Frugal innovators leverage limited resources creatively to deliver high-quality solutions that meet the needs of their target customers while keeping costs low (Govindarajan & Ramamurti, 2015).

Frugal innovation is characterized by its focus on affordability and accessibility. By eliminating non-essential features and streamlining production processes, frugal innovators are able to offer products and services at price points that are affordable to a wide range of customers (Radjou, Prabhu, & Ahuja, 2012). This approach democratizes access to essential goods and services, empowering individuals and communities to improve their quality of life.

Moreover, frugal innovation embodies the principles of resourcefulness and resilience. Entrepreneurs in resource-constrained environments must constantly innovate to overcome challenges such as limited access to capital, unreliable infrastructure, and sparse distribution networks (Brem & Wolfram, 2014). Frugal innovators adopt a mindset of improvisation and adaptability, finding creative solutions to complex problems using the resources at their disposal.

Frugal innovation has implications beyond emerging markets; it is increasingly being embraced by entrepreneurs and businesses around the world as a means of driving sustainable growth and addressing pressing societal challenges (Govindarajan & Trimble, 2012). By adopting frugal innovation principles, businesses can develop products and services that are not only cost-effective but also environmentally sustainable and socially responsible.

Frugal innovation offers a powerful framework for addressing global challenges and driving entrepreneurial growth. By emphasizing affordability, accessibility, and resourcefulness, frugal innovators are able to create value for both customers and society as a whole.

HISTORICAL BACKGROUND OF HARNESSING FRUGAL INNOVATIONS FOR ENTREPRENEURIAL GROWTH

Frugal innovation, although gaining prominence in recent years, has its roots deeply embedded in historical contexts where resource constraints necessitated innovative solutions. This section delves into the historical background of frugal innovation, tracing its evolution from ancient civilizations to modern-day entrepreneurial endeavours, while highlighting key milestones, influential thinkers, and notable examples along the way.

1. Ancient Civilizations and Indigenous Knowledge

The concept of frugal innovation has ancient origins, with civilizations around the world demonstrating remarkable ingenuity in resource-constrained environments. Indigenous communities developed ingenious solutions to meet their needs using locally available materials and traditional knowledge (Brem & Wolfram, 2014). For example, the ancient Egyptians built the pyramids using rudimentary tools and techniques, demonstrating remarkable efficiency and resourcefulness in construction.

2. Industrial Revolution and Mass Production

The Industrial Revolution marked a significant shift in innovation paradigms, with the advent of mass production and mechanization. While this period saw remarkable technological advancements, it also led to a focus on efficiency and scale, often at the expense of sustainability and affordability (Zeschky, Widenmayer, & Gassmann, 2011). However, pockets of frugal innovation persisted, with small-scale artisans and craftsmen developing cost-effective solutions to meet local needs.

3. Post-War Era and Development Economics

The post-war era saw the emergence of development economics and a renewed focus on addressing poverty and inequality in the Global South. Scholars and practitioners began exploring alternative models of development that emphasized self-reliance, community empowerment, and appropriate technology (Govindarajan & Ramamurti, 2015). The concept of frugal innovation gained traction during this period, with initiatives such as the Intermediate Technology Development Group (now Practical Action) promoting simple, low-cost solutions for development challenges.

4. Jugaad and Grassroots Innovation

In recent decades, the concept of jugaad innovation has gained prominence in the context of emerging markets, particularly in India. Jugaad, a Hindi term meaning "making do with what you have," encapsulates the spirit of frugal innovation and improvisation (Radjou, Prabhu, & Ahuja, 2012). Grassroots innovators in India and other developing countries have developed low-cost, high-impact solutions to address a wide range of challenges, from healthcare and agriculture to energy and education.

5. Globalization and Reverse Innovation

The process of globalization has facilitated the spread of frugal innovation principles beyond traditional boundaries. Companies in developed economies are increasingly embracing frugal innovation as a means of driving growth and competitiveness in a rapidly changing world (Govindarajan & Trimble, 2012). This phenomenon, known as reverse innovation, involves leveraging insights and solutions from emerging markets to address challenges in developed economies.

6. Modern Entrepreneurship and Lean Startup Movement

In the realm of entrepreneurship, the lean startup movement has popularized frugal innovation principles, emphasizing rapid experimentation, customer feedback, and iterative development (Ries, 2011). Entrepreneurs are encouraged to start small, test assumptions, and pivot quickly based on market feedback, reducing the risk of failure and conserving resources in the process.

The historical background of harnessing frugal innovations for entrepreneurial growth reflects a long tradition of resourcefulness, creativity, and resilience in the face of constraints. From ancient civilizations to modern-day startups, the spirit of frugal innovation has persisted, driving progress and addressing societal challenges across diverse contexts. By understanding the historical roots of frugal innovation, entrepreneurs can draw inspiration from past successes and leverage proven strategies to drive sustainable growth and impact in the present and future.

EMBRACING CONSTRAINTS AS CATALYSTS FOR INNOVATION

Constraints, whether financial, technological, or environmental, can spark innovation when approached with the right mindset. This section emphasizes the importance of reframing constraints as opportunities for creativity and problem-solving. By embracing constraints, entrepreneurs can foster a culture of innovation within their ventures and drive meaningful change (Bhatti & Ventresca, 2019; Bhuyan & Bag, 2020). Strategies such as lean startup methodologies and agile development enable entrepreneurs to iterate quickly, validate assumptions, and adapt to evolving market conditions. Through real-world examples and case studies, we illustrate how entrepreneurs have transformed constraints into opportunities for innovation and growth. For instance, Aravind Eye Care System's frugal approach to healthcare delivery revolutionized cataract treatment, making it affordable and accessible to millions (Govindarajan & Ramamurti, 2015).

Constraints, whether they stem from financial limitations, technological barriers, or environmental challenges, are often viewed as impediments to innovation. However, astute entrepreneurs recognize that constraints can serve as powerful catalysts for creativity and innovation. By reframing limitations as opportunities for problem-solving and ingenuity, entrepreneurs can unlock new pathways to growth and drive meaningful change within their ventures (Bhatti & Ventresca, 2019; Bhuyan & Bag, 2020).

Frugal innovation thrives in resource-constrained environments, where entrepreneurs are compelled to develop solutions that are affordable, accessible, and impactful (Govindarajan & Ramamurti, 2015). For example, startups in developing countries face unique challenges such as limited access to capital and unreliable infrastructure. However, these constraints can inspire entrepreneurs to innovate by developing low-cost, high-impact solutions tailored to the needs of their target markets.

Agile development methodologies offer another avenue for embracing constraints as catalysts for innovation. By adopting an agile mindset, entrepreneurs can rapidly iterate, experiment, and adapt to changing market conditions (Ries, 2011). This iterative approach enables entrepreneurs to identify and address potential challenges early in the development process, reducing the risk of costly mistakes and accelerating time to market.

Collaborative problem-solving is yet another approach for leveraging constraints as catalysts for innovation. By engaging diverse stakeholders, including customers, suppliers, and partners, entrepreneurs can tap into a wealth of knowledge and expertise to develop novel solutions to complex challenges (Chesbrough, 2003). Co-creation enables entrepreneurs to develop products and services that are more aligned with the needs and preferences of their target audience, driving greater adoption and loyalty.

Therefore, embracing constraints as catalysts for innovation is essential for entrepreneurial success in today's dynamic business environment. By embracing limitations as opportunities for creativity and problem-solving, entrepreneurs can unlock new possibilities and drive sustainable growth within their ventures.

STRATEGIES FOR FRUGAL INNOVATION

Frugal innovation demands a systematic approach to value creation amidst constraints. This section outlines practical strategies and frameworks that empower entrepreneurs to drive frugal innovation within their ventures. Frugal innovation demands a systematic approach to value creation amidst constraints, requiring entrepreneurs to navigate resource limitations while delivering impactful solutions to their target markets. This section delineates practical strategies and frameworks that empower entrepreneurs to effectively drive frugal innovation within their ventures.

One key strategy for frugal innovation is the adoption of lean startup methodologies. Originating from Eric Ries' influential book "The Lean Startup," this approach advocates for rapid experimentation, iterative development, and customer-centricity (Ries, 2011). By starting with a minimum viable product (MVP) and gathering feedback from early adopters, entrepreneurs can validate assumptions, iterate quickly, and refine their offerings based on real-world insights. This iterative approach minimizes waste, reduces the risk of failure, and enables entrepreneurs to conserve resources while maximizing value creation.

Another essential strategy for frugal innovation is jugaad innovation, a concept rooted in Indian ingenuity and resourcefulness. Jugaad emphasizes flexibility, improvisation, and making do with limited resources to solve complex problems (Radjou, Prabhu, & Ahuja, 2012). Entrepreneurs practicing jugaad innovate under constraints, leveraging available resources creatively to develop simple yet effective solutions that address the needs of their customers. This approach fosters a culture of frugality and adaptability, enabling entrepreneurs to thrive in resource-constrained environments.

Furthermore, reverse innovation offers a strategic framework for driving frugal innovation by leveraging insights and solutions from emerging markets to address challenges in developed economies (Govindarajan & Trimble, 2012). By starting with the needs of customers in resource-constrained environments, entrepreneurs can develop cost-effective solutions that disrupt existing markets and create new growth opportunities.

By starting with the needs of customers in resource-constrained environments, entrepreneurs can tap into a wealth of untapped opportunities for innovation. These environments often present unique challenges that require innovative solutions tailored to the specific constraints faced by individuals and communities. By immersing themselves in the realities of these contexts, entrepreneurs can gain valuable insights into the unmet needs and pain points of their target customers.

Developing cost-effective solutions that address these needs not only meets immediate market demands but also has the potential to disrupt existing markets and create new growth opportunities. By innovating under constraints, entrepreneurs are forced to think creatively and find unconventional solutions to complex problems. This mindset of frugality and resourcefulness often leads to breakthrough innovations that challenge traditional business models and open up new market spaces.

Furthermore, addressing the needs of customers in resource-constrained environments can serve as a springboard for expansion into broader markets. The solutions developed in these contexts are often highly adaptable and scalable, making them attractive to a wider range of customers. As such, entrepreneurs can leverage their expertise in addressing resource constraints to enter new markets and gain a competitive advantage.

Considering the requirements of clients in resource-constrained environments not only enables entrepreneurs to develop cost-effective solutions but also positions them to disrupt existing markets and create new growth opportunities. By embracing constraints as opportunities for innovation, entrepreneurs can unlock new pathways to success and drive meaningful change in the world.

Overall, by adopting lean startup methodologies, embracing jugaad innovation principles, and leveraging insights from reverse innovation, entrepreneurs can navigate constraints effectively and drive frugal innovation within their ventures, unlocking new pathways to growth and value creation.

1. **Lean Startup Methodology:** The lean startup methodology advocates for rapid experimentation and iterative development to minimize waste and maximize learning (Ries, 2011). Entrepreneurs start by developing a minimum viable product (MVP) and gathering feedback from early adopters. This iterative approach enables entrepreneurs to validate assumptions, refine their offerings, and conserve resources (Blank, 2013).
2. **Jugaad Innovation:** Jugaad, a Hindi term meaning "frugal innovation," emphasizes resourcefulness and improvisation in solving complex problems (Govindarajan & Trimble, 2012). Jugaad innovators leverage limited resources to create simple yet effective solutions, exemplifying the spirit of frugal innovation.
3. **Reverse Innovation**: Reverse innovation involves innovating in emerging markets and then scaling those innovations back to developed markets (Govindarajan & Trimble, 2010). By starting with the needs of customers in emerging markets, entrepreneurs can develop cost-effective solutions that disrupt existing markets and create new growth opportunities.

4. **Open Innovation**: Open innovation fosters collaboration and knowledge sharing across organizational boundaries (Chesbrough, 2003). By engaging with external stakeholders, such as customers and partners, entrepreneurs can access a broader pool of resources, expertise, and ideas.
5. **Frugal Engineering**: Frugal engineering entails simplifying and redesigning products and processes to achieve cost savings without compromising quality (Brem & Wolfram, 2014). Entrepreneurs identify opportunities to streamline operations and optimize resource utilization, delivering value to customers at lower costs.
6. **User-Centric Design**: User-centric design prioritizes understanding the needs and preferences of end-users throughout the product development process (Norman & Draper, 1986). By incorporating user feedback and insights, entrepreneurs can create solutions that are intuitive and tailored to the needs of their target audience.
7. **Frugal Marketing**: Frugal marketing emphasizes low-cost, high-impact strategies to reach and engage customers (Radjou, Prabhu, & Ahuja, 2012). From guerrilla marketing tactics to leveraging social media, entrepreneurs can maximize visibility while minimizing costs.

Through these strategies, entrepreneurs can navigate constraints effectively and drive frugal innovation within their ventures.

Case Studies and Best Practices

Real-world case studies illustrate the transformative potential of frugal innovation in driving entrepreneurial growth and impact.

I. **Grameen Bank (Bangladesh):** Founded by Muhammad Yunus, Grameen Bank pioneered microfinance, providing small loans to impoverished individuals to start their own businesses. Through this frugal approach, Grameen Bank empowered millions to escape poverty and build sustainable livelihoods.

II. **SELCO India:** SELCO provides solar energy solutions to rural communities in India, making electricity accessible and affordable. By offering innovative financing options, SELCO has transformed lives and driven economic development.

III. **M-Pesa (Kenya):** M-Pesa revolutionized mobile payments in Kenya, enabling users to send and receive money via text messages. This frugal innovation has expanded financial inclusion, particularly among the unbanked population, and transformed the way people conduct transactions in emerging markets.

Through these case studies, entrepreneurs gain insights into the principles and practices of frugal innovation and its potential to drive meaningful change.

BUILDING SUSTAINABLE FRUGAL VENTURES

Sustainability is paramount for the long-term success of frugal ventures. This section explores strategies for building sustainable business models that can thrive over time. From scalability and market expansion to talent acquisition and organizational culture, entrepreneurs must consider various factors in building sustainable frugal ventures. Collaborative ecosystems and partnerships play a crucial role in supporting frugal innovation, enabling entrepreneurs to amplify their impact and drive systemic change.

Frugal innovation offers a compelling framework for entrepreneurial growth and impact in resource-constrained environments. By embracing constraints as opportunities for creativity and innovation, entrepreneurs can unlock new pathways to success and build sustainable ventures that make a difference. Through a combination of mindset shifts, strategic approaches, and practical insights, this chapter equips entrepreneurs with the knowledge and tools they need to thrive on constraints and harness the power of frugal innovations for entrepreneurial growth.

Embracing Constraints as Catalysts for Innovation

Constraints, whether they are financial, technological, or environmental, have long been perceived as barriers to innovation. However, astute entrepreneurs understand that constraints can spark creativity and drive innovative solutions. By embracing constraints as catalysts for innovation, entrepreneurs can foster a culture of creativity, resourcefulness, and resilience within their ventures (Bhatti & Ventresca, 2019; Bhuyan & Bag, 2020).

Frugal Innovation in Resource-Constrained Environments

Resource-constrained environments, such as emerging markets or underserved communities, provide fertile ground for frugal innovation. In these contexts, entrepreneurs are forced to rethink traditional business models and develop solutions that are affordable, accessible, and impactful (Govindarajan & Ramamurti, 2015). For example, startups in developing countries often face challenges such as limited access to capital, unreliable infrastructure, and sparse distribution networks. However, these constraints can drive entrepreneurs to innovate by developing low-cost, high-impact solutions tailored to the needs of their target markets.

Case Study: D.Light Design

D.Light Design, a social enterprise based in California, recognized the opportunity to address the energy needs of off-grid communities in developing countries. By embracing constraints as opportunities for innovation, D.Light developed affordable solar-powered lanterns and home systems tailored to the needs of rural customers. Through innovative financing models and distribution strategies, D.Light has transformed the lives of millions by providing access to clean, reliable energy (Brem & Wolfram, 2014).

Agile Development and Iterative Experimentation

Agile development methodologies emphasize rapid iteration, experimentation, and customer feedback. By adopting an agile mindset, entrepreneurs can quickly test assumptions, adapt to changing market conditions, and refine their offerings based on real-world feedback (Ries, 2011). This iterative approach enables entrepreneurs to identify and address potential challenges early in the development process, reducing the risk of costly mistakes and accelerating time to market.

Case Study: Zipline

Zipline, a drone delivery startup based in California, embraced constraints as opportunities for innovation by developing a scalable solution for delivering medical supplies to remote areas. Through iterative experimentation and agile development, Zipline refined its drone technology and operational processes to ensure safe and reliable delivery of blood and medical supplies to underserved communities in Rwanda and Ghana. By leveraging constraints as catalysts for innovation, Zipline has revolutionized healthcare logistics and saved countless lives (Adner, 2017).

Collaborative Problem-Solving and Co-Creation

Collaborative problem-solving involves engaging diverse stakeholders, including customers, suppliers, and partners, in the innovation process. By tapping into the collective wisdom and expertise of these stakeholders, entrepreneurs can identify novel solutions to complex challenges (Chesbrough, 2003). Co-creation enables entrepreneurs to develop products and services that are more aligned with the needs and preferences of their target audience, driving greater adoption and loyalty.

Case Study: Local Motors

Local Motors, an Arizona-based automotive company, embraced constraints as catalysts for innovation by adopting a collaborative approach to product development. Through its online platform, Local Motors engages a global community of designers, engineers, and enthusiasts in the co-creation of vehicles. By crowdsourcing ideas and feedback, Local Motors has developed innovative vehicles tailored to the needs of specific markets, from rugged off-road vehicles for the military to electric-powered shuttles for urban mobility (West & Bogers, 2014).

Embracing constraints as catalysts for innovation is essential for entrepreneurial success in today's dynamic business environment. By reframing limitations as opportunities for creativity and problem-solving, entrepreneurs can unlock new pathways to growth and drive meaningful change. Through a combination of frugal innovation, agile development, and collaborative problem-solving, entrepreneurs can navigate constraints effectively and create sustainable value for their stakeholders.

Through in-depth analysis and insights from these case studies, we extract key lessons and best practices that can be applied across industries and contexts. We examine the strategies and tactics employed by successful frugal innovators, from bootstrapping and lean operations to strategic partnerships and collaborative ecosystems. By learning from their experiences and challenges, entrepreneurs can gain valuable insights into the principles and practices of frugal innovation. Through a combination of inspiration and practical guidance, this section empowers entrepreneurs to apply frugal innovation principles to their own ventures and drive meaningful change.

HARNESSING FRUGAL INNOVATIONS FOR ENTREPRENEURSHIP IN THE INDIAN SCENARIO

India, with its diverse population, complex socio-economic challenges, and burgeoning entrepreneurial ecosystem, provides a fertile ground for the harnessing of frugal innovations. This section explores the Indian scenario of frugal innovation in entrepreneurship, examining key drivers, notable examples, and the impact of frugal innovations on economic growth and societal development.

1. Socio-Economic Context

India's vast population, coupled with significant socio-economic disparities, presents both challenges and opportunities for frugal innovation in entrepreneurship. The country is home to a large segment of the population living in rural and urban areas with limited access to basic services such as healthcare, education, and clean water (Govindarajan & Ramamurti, 2015). Frugal innovations have the potential to address these pressing needs by offering affordable, accessible, and scalable solutions tailored to the Indian context.

2. **Grassroots Innovation and Jugaad**

India has a rich tradition of grassroots innovation and jugaad, a Hindi term that conveys the concept of frugal innovation and improvisation. From jugaad vehicles made from recycled materials to low-cost medical devices developed by rural innovators, Indian entrepreneurs have demonstrated remarkable ingenuity in addressing local challenges with limited resources (Radjou, Prabhu, & Ahuja, 2012). These grassroots innovations often serve as inspiration for formal enterprises and policymakers seeking to harness frugal innovations for broader societal impact.

3. **Start-up Ecosystem and Tech Innovation**

India's vibrant start-up ecosystem, particularly in tech hubs such as Bengaluru, Mumbai, and Delhi-NCR, has emerged as a hotbed for frugal innovation in entrepreneurship. Start-ups are leveraging cutting-edge technologies such as artificial intelligence, machine learning, and blockchain to develop innovative solutions to a wide range of challenges, from financial inclusion and healthcare to agriculture and education (Bhatti & Ventresca, 2019). These tech-driven innovations are not only disrupting traditional industries but also creating new opportunities for inclusive growth and job creation.

4. **Policy Support and Government Initiatives**

The Indian government has recognized the importance of frugal innovation in driving entrepreneurship and economic development. Initiatives such as Start-up India, Make in India, and Atmanirbhar Bharat have been launched to support and promote entrepreneurship, innovation, and indigenous manufacturing (Bhuyan & Bag, 2020). Policy reforms aimed at simplifying regulations, improving access to finance, and fostering innovation ecosystems are creating an enabling environment for frugal innovators to thrive.

5. **Global Recognition and Market Expansion**

Indian frugal innovations have gained international recognition and are increasingly being adopted in global markets. From affordable healthcare solutions and renewable energy technologies to low-cost consumer products and mobile applications, Indian entrepreneurs are exporting frugal innovations to countries around the world (Govindarajan & Trimble, 2012). The global success of Indian frugal innovations not only generates revenue and creates jobs but also enhances India's reputation as a hub for innovation and entrepreneurship.

The Indian scenario of harnessing frugal innovations for entrepreneurship is characterized by a unique blend of grassroots innovation, tech-driven entrepreneurship, policy support, and global recognition. Indian entrepreneurs are leveraging frugal innovations to address pressing societal challenges, create economic opportunities, and drive inclusive growth. With continued support from policymakers, investors, and ecosystem stakeholders, frugal innovation has the potential to transform India's entrepreneurial landscape and contribute significantly to the country's journey towards sustainable development and prosperity.

THE ROLE OF THE INDIAN GOVERNMENT IN HARNESSING FRUGAL INNOVATIONS FOR ENTREPRENEURSHIP

The Indian government plays a pivotal role in fostering an environment conducive to harnessing frugal innovations for entrepreneurship. Recognizing the potential of frugal innovations to address pressing societal challenges, create economic opportunities, and drive inclusive growth, the government has implemented various policies, initiatives, and programs aimed at supporting and promoting frugal innovators and entrepreneurs. This section explores the key aspects of the Indian government's role in harnessing frugal innovations for entrepreneurship.

1. **Policy Support and Regulatory Reforms**

The Indian government has introduced policy frameworks and regulatory reforms to create an enabling environment for frugal innovators and entrepreneurs. Initiatives such as Start-up India, Make in India, and Atmanirbhar Bharat aim to streamline regulatory processes, reduce bureaucratic hurdles, and promote entrepreneurship and innovation across sectors (Bhuyan & Bag, 2020). These policies provide incentives, tax benefits, and easier access to funding for start-ups and innovators, encouraging them to develop and scale frugal innovations.

2. **Funding and Financial Support**

Access to finance is a critical factor in the success of frugal innovations and entrepreneurial ventures. The Indian government has launched several schemes and programs to provide funding and financial support to frugal innovators and entrepreneurs. For instance, schemes such as the Atal Innovation Mission (AIM), National Innovation Foundation (NIF), and Mudra Yojana offer grants, loans, and venture capital funding to innovative start-ups and MSMEs (Micro, Small, and Medium Enterprises) (Bhatti & Ventresca, 2019). These initiatives help bridge the funding gap and enable frugal innovators to commercialize their ideas and bring them to market.

The government has implemented various schemes, programs, and initiatives aimed at supporting innovators and entrepreneurs across different sectors such as:

I. **Start-up India Initiative**

The Start-up India initiative, launched in 2016, aims to create a conducive ecosystem for nurturing innovation and entrepreneurship in the country. Under this initiative, the government provides a range of benefits and incentives to start-ups, including tax exemptions, self-certification compliance, and easier access to funding (Bhuyan & Bag, 2020). Start-ups working on frugal innovations are eligible to apply for funding and support under this initiative, enabling them to accelerate their growth and scale their ventures.

II. **Atal Innovation Mission (AIM)**

The Atal Innovation Mission (AIM) is another flagship initiative of the Indian government aimed at promoting innovation and entrepreneurship among students, researchers, and entrepreneurs. AIM supports the establishment of Atal Incubation Centers (AICs) across the country to provide infrastructure, mentorship, and funding support to start-ups and innovators (Govindarajan & Ramamurti, 2015). These incubation centers play a crucial role in nurturing frugal innovations and helping entrepreneurs commercialize their ideas.

III. **Mudra Yojana**

The Mudra Yojana, launched in 2015, is a government scheme aimed at providing financial assistance to micro-enterprises and small businesses. Under this scheme, loans are offered to entrepreneurs to start or expand their businesses, with a focus on promoting self-employment and entrepreneurship (Brem & Wolfram, 2014). Frugal innovators and entrepreneurs can avail of loans under the Mudra Yojana to finance their ventures and bring their innovations to market.

IV. **National Innovation Foundation (NIF)**

The National Innovation Foundation (NIF) is an autonomous body under the Department of Science and Technology, Government of India, dedicated to promoting grassroots innovations and traditional knowledge systems. NIF provides financial support, mentorship, and incubation facilities to innovators and entrepreneurs working on frugal solutions to address local challenges (Radjou, Prabhu, & Ahuja, 2012). By nurturing grassroots innovations, NIF contributes to the development of a culture of innovation and entrepreneurship in the country.

V. **Research and Development Grants**

The Indian government provides research and development grants to support innovation and technology development across various sectors. These grants are offered by government agencies such as the Department of Science and Technology (DST), Department of Biotechnology (DBT), and Department of Electronics and Information Technology (DeitY) (Govindarajan & Trimble, 2012). Frugal innovators and entrepreneurs can access these grants to fund their research, prototype development, and technology commercialization efforts.

The Indian government plays a crucial role in providing funding and financial support to harness frugal innovations for entrepreneurship. Through initiatives such as Start-up India, Atal Innovation Mission, Mudra Yojana, National Innovation Foundation, and research and development grants, the government empowers innovators and entrepreneurs to develop, commercialize, and scale frugal solutions to address societal challenges and drive economic growth. By continuing to invest in frugal innovations and entrepreneurship, the Indian government can unlock the full potential of Indian innovators to create impact and foster inclusive development in the country.

3. **Innovation Ecosystem Development**

The Indian government has invested in building a robust innovation ecosystem that supports frugal innovation and entrepreneurship. Initiatives such as Technology Business Incubators (TBIs), Research Parks, and Entrepreneurship Development Cells (EDCs) provide infrastructure, mentorship, networking, and technical support to aspiring entrepreneurs and innovators (Govindarajan & Ramamurti, 2015). These ecosystem-building efforts foster collaboration, knowledge sharing, and resource mobilization, creating a conducive environment for frugal innovation to thrive.

4. Technology Transfer and Commercialization

The Indian government facilitates technology transfer and commercialization by promoting collaboration between academia, industry, and government research institutions. Initiatives such as the Technology Business Incubation (TBI) program, Technology Transfer Offices (TTOs), and Public-Private Partnerships (PPPs) facilitate the transfer of research findings and technologies from labs to market (Govindarajan & Trimble, 2012). By supporting technology transfer and commercialization, the government enables frugal innovators to access cutting-edge technologies and intellectual property, driving innovation and entrepreneurship.

5. Market Access and International Collaboration

The Indian government actively promotes market access and international collaboration for frugal innovators and entrepreneurs. Initiatives such as the National Intellectual Property Rights (IPR) Policy, Export Promotion Councils (EPCs), and International Cooperation Programs facilitate market entry, export promotion, and global partnerships (Radjou, Prabhu, & Ahuja, 2012). By facilitating market access and international collaboration, the government helps frugal innovators tap into global markets, expand their reach, and scale their ventures.

The Indian government plays a crucial role in harnessing frugal innovations for entrepreneurship by providing policy support, funding, ecosystem development, technology transfer, and market access. Through various initiatives and programs, the government creates an enabling environment for frugal innovators to thrive, driving economic growth, job creation, and societal development. By continuing to support and promote frugal innovation and entrepreneurship, the Indian government can unlock the full potential of frugal innovations to address India's socio-economic challenges and propel the country towards sustainable development and prosperity.

ADVANTAGES OF HARNESSING FRUGAL INNOVATIONS FOR ENTREPRENEURIAL GROWTH

Frugal innovation, characterized by its emphasis on simplicity, affordability, and efficiency, offers numerous advantages for entrepreneurial growth. Entrepreneurs who harness frugal innovations can unlock new opportunities, drive sustainable growth, and create significant value for both their businesses and society as a whole. This section explores some of the key advantages associated with leveraging frugal innovations for entrepreneurial growth.

1. Accessibility and Inclusivity

Frugal innovations are designed to be accessible to a wide range of consumers, including those in resource-constrained environments and underserved communities. By prioritizing affordability and simplicity, entrepreneurs can democratize access to essential goods and services, addressing unmet needs and improving quality of life for millions of people (Govindarajan & Ramamurti, 2015). Frugal innovations enable entrepreneurs to reach untapped markets and serve diverse customer segments that may have been previously overlooked.

2. Cost Efficiency and Affordability

One of the most significant advantages of frugal innovations is their cost efficiency. By focusing on minimizing costs and maximizing value, entrepreneurs can develop products and services that are significantly cheaper than traditional alternatives (Brem & Wolfram, 2014). This affordability not only expands market reach but also enhances customer value, as consumers are able to access essential goods and services at a fraction of the cost. Frugal innovations enable entrepreneurs to achieve higher profit margins and sustainable growth by operating within lean budgets and maximizing resource utilization.

3. Innovation Under Constraints

Frugal innovation thrives in resource-constrained environments, where entrepreneurs are forced to innovate under limitations such as limited access to capital, infrastructure, and skilled labor (Radjou, Prabhu, & Ahuja, 2012). These constraints drive creativity and ingenuity, inspiring entrepreneurs to develop novel solutions to complex problems using the resources at their disposal. By embracing constraints as opportunities for innovation, entrepreneurs can unlock new pathways to growth and drive meaningful change within their ventures.

4. Rapid Iteration and Adaptation

Frugal innovation encourages a culture of rapid iteration and adaptation, allowing entrepreneurs to respond quickly to changing market conditions and customer needs (Ries, 2011). By adopting agile development methodologies and lean startup principles, entrepreneurs can test assumptions, gather feedback, and refine their offerings in real-time (Govindarajan & Trimble, 2012). This iterative approach minimizes the risk of failure, reduces time to market, and enables entrepreneurs to stay ahead of the competition in dynamic business environments.

5. Environmental Sustainability

Frugal innovations often prioritize environmental sustainability by minimizing resource consumption, waste generation, and carbon emissions (Zeschky, Widenmayer, & Gassmann, 2011). By developing products and services that are eco-friendly and energy-efficient, entrepreneurs can reduce their environmental footprint and contribute to global efforts to combat climate change. Frugal innovations enable entrepreneurs to align their business objectives with environmental stewardship, creating value for both their businesses and the planet.

Harnessing frugal innovations offers a multitude of advantages for entrepreneurial growth, including accessibility, cost efficiency, innovation under constraints, rapid iteration, and environmental sustainability. By leveraging the principles of frugal innovation, entrepreneurs can unlock new opportunities, drive sustainable growth, and create meaningful impact in the world. Frugal innovations enable entrepreneurs to reach untapped markets, serve diverse customer segments, and address pressing societal challenges, positioning them for long-term success and resilience in today's competitive business landscape.

LIMITATIONS OF HARNESSING FRUGAL INNOVATIONS FOR ENTREPRENEURIAL GROWTH

While frugal innovation offers numerous benefits for entrepreneurial growth, it is essential to recognize and address its limitations. Understanding these limitations can help entrepreneurs navigate challenges effectively and maximize the potential of frugal innovations in driving sustainable growth. This section explores some of the key limitations associated with harnessing frugal innovations for entrepreneurial growth and discusses strategies for overcoming them.

1. Quality vs. Affordability Trade-off

One of the primary challenges of frugal innovation is balancing affordability with quality. In resource-constrained environments, entrepreneurs often face pressure to deliver low-cost solutions, leading to compromises in product quality or performance (Brem & Wolfram, 2014). While affordability is essential for reaching underserved markets, offering products or services that are perceived as low-quality may hinder long-term success and damage brand reputation.

2. Scalability Constraints

Frugal innovations developed for specific contexts may not always be easily scalable to broader markets or diverse customer segments. Scaling frugal solutions requires careful consideration of factors such as production capacity, distribution networks, and regulatory requirements (Govindarajan & Ramamurti, 2015). Entrepreneurs must invest in infrastructure and partnerships to scale their operations effectively while maintaining affordability and accessibility.

3. Limited Resources and Capacity

Resource constraints, including limited access to capital, talent, and infrastructure, can pose significant barriers to frugal innovation. Entrepreneurs in resource-constrained environments may struggle to access funding for research and development, technology acquisition, or market expansion (Bhatti & Ventresca, 2019). Additionally, a lack of skilled workforce or supportive ecosystems may hinder the execution of frugal innovation initiatives.

4. Market Acceptance and Cultural Factors

Frugal innovations developed for specific cultural or socio-economic contexts may face challenges in gaining acceptance in different markets or communities. Cultural differences, consumer preferences, and regulatory environments can vary significantly across regions, requiring entrepreneurs to adapt their offerings accordingly (Govindarajan & Trimble, 2012). Ensuring market fit and addressing cultural sensitivities are critical considerations for the success of frugal innovations in diverse settings.

5. Intellectual Property Concerns

Protecting intellectual property (IP) rights can be challenging in the context of frugal innovation, where open innovation and collaborative approaches are common (Chesbrough, 2003). Entrepreneurs must navigate the complexities of IP laws and regulations to safeguard their innovations while fostering collaboration and knowledge sharing within ecosystems (Bhuyan & Bag, 2020). Balancing the need for protection with the benefits of open innovation requires careful strategy and execution.

Strategies for Overcoming Limitations

While the limitations of harnessing frugal innovations for entrepreneurial growth are significant, there are several strategies that entrepreneurs can employ to mitigate these challenges and maximize the potential of frugal innovations:

1. **Focus on Value Proposition:** Emphasize the value proposition of frugal innovations by highlighting their affordability, accessibility, and impact. Clearly communicate the benefits of the innovation to customers, investors, and other stakeholders to overcome concerns about quality or performance trade-offs.
2. **Invest in Scalability:** Prioritize scalability in the design and development of frugal innovations. Invest in building scalable infrastructure, developing strategic partnerships, and leveraging technology to expand reach and impact while maintaining cost-effectiveness.
3. **Build Capacity and Resilience:** Invest in building organizational capacity and resilience to overcome resource constraints. Develop talent pipelines, foster innovation ecosystems, and diversify funding sources to strengthen the foundation for sustained growth and impact.
4. **Adapt to Market Dynamics:** Continuously monitor market dynamics and consumer preferences to adapt frugal innovations to changing needs and preferences. Tailor offerings to specific market segments, localize solutions as needed, and engage with communities to foster acceptance and adoption.
5. **Navigate IP Challenges**: Develop a comprehensive IP strategy that balances protection with collaboration. Explore alternative mechanisms for IP management, such as open-source licensing or strategic partnerships, to maximize the benefits of frugal innovation while minimizing risks.

While harnessing frugal innovations for entrepreneurial growth presents challenges, overcoming these limitations can unlock significant opportunities for value creation and social impact. By addressing concerns related to quality, scalability, resource constraints, market acceptance, and intellectual property, entrepreneurs can leverage the power of frugal innovation to drive sustainable growth and address pressing societal challenges.

CONCLUSION

Frugal innovation offers a powerful framework for driving entrepreneurial growth and impact within resource-constrained environments. By embracing constraints as opportunities for creativity and innovation, entrepreneurs can unlock new pathways to success and build sustainable ventures that make a difference in the world. Through a combination of mindset shifts, strategic approaches, and practical insights, this chapter equips entrepreneurs with the knowledge and tools they need to thrive on constraints and harness the power of frugal innovations for entrepreneurial growth.

REFERENCES

Adner, R. (2017). Ecosystem as structure: An actionable construct for strategy. *Journal of Management*, *43*(1), 39–58.

Bhatti, Y., & Ventresca, M. J. (2019). Beyond the IPR: Formalizing global knowledge networks through creative commoning. *Academy of Management Journal*, *62*(5), 1396–1431.

Bhuyan, A., & Bag, S. (2020). Effect of frugal innovation on sustainable development: A study in the Indian context. *Sustainable Development*, *28*(5), 1051–1064.

Blank, S. (2013). *The startup owner's manual: The step-by-step guide for building a great company*. John Wiley & Sons.

Brem, A., & Wolfram, P. (2014). Research and development from the bottom up—Introduction of terminologies for new product development in emerging markets. *Journal of Engineering and Technology Management*, *32*, 167–183.

Brown, T. (2009). *Change by design: How design thinking transforms organizations and inspires innovation*. HarperCollins Publishers.

Chesbrough, H. (2003). *Open innovation: The new imperative for creating and profiting from technology*. Harvard Business Press.

Govindarajan, V., & Ramamurti, R. (2015). Reverse innovation, emerging markets, and global strategy. *Global Strategy Journal*, *5*(1), 27–37.

Govindarajan, V., & Trimble, C. (2010). *The other side of innovation: Solving the execution challenge*. Harvard Business Press.

Govindarajan, V., & Trimble, C. (2012). *Reverse innovation: Create far from home, win everywhere*. Harvard Business Press. DOI: 10.5437/08956308X5506003

Nijssen, E. J., & Frambach, R. T. (2000). Creating customer value through strategic marketing planning: A management approach. *Journal of Market Focused Management*, *4*(1), 79–95.

Norman, D. A., & Draper, S. W. (1986). *User-centered system design: New perspectives on human-computer interaction*. Lawrence Erlbaum Associates, Inc. DOI: 10.1201/b15703

Radjou, N., Prabhu, J., & Ahuja, S. (2012). *Jugaad innovation: Think frugal, be flexible, generate breakthrough growth*. John Wiley & Sons.

Ries, E. (2011). *The lean startup: How today's entrepreneurs use continuous innovation to create radically successful businesses*. Crown Business.

West, J., & Bogers, M. (2014). Leveraging external sources of innovation: A review of research on open innovation. *Journal of Product Innovation Management*, *31*(4), 814–831.

Zeschky, M., Widenmayer, B., & Gassmann, O. (2011). Frugal innovation in emerging markets. *Research Technology Management*, *54*(4), 38–45.

Chapter 6
Small Business, Big Solutions:
Leveraging Frugal Innovation for MSME Digitalization

Jayasankar Prasad C.
https://orcid.org/0000-0001-9064-1386
A P J Abdul Kalam Technological University, Trivandrum, India

Lekshmi Krishna S.
A P J Abdul Kalam Technological University, Trivandrum, India

ABSTRACT

Frugal Digitalisation has proven to be a strategic approach which emphasizes on Cost effectiveness, simplicity, and optimized performance level. Harnessing Digitalisation frugally for MSMEs is an appropriative strategy for the firm's sustainability. Rapidly changing technologies and VUCA environment are emerging as the biggest business challenge and digitalisation of MSMEs has become essential these days. This chapter provides an overview of Frugal innovations that can digitalise MSMEs for their sustainability and, understanding ongoing digital transformations of MSMEs. It also explains the digitalization strategies tailored for MSMEs from adopting cloud computing and SaaS to building an online presence and leveraging e-commerce platforms also the key topics in the field. The chapter provide case studies of successful frugal digitalisation that illustrate real-world scenarios, offering lessons learned and best practices for MSMEs embarking on their digital adoption.

DOI: 10.4018/979-8-3693-4050-9.ch006

1. DIGITALISATION IN MSMES

1.1. Digitalisation

Digitalization is the use of digital technologies to change a business model and provide new revenue and value-producing opportunities; it is the process of moving to a digital business (Gartner). It is a powerful engine which contributes to the economic growth in the business (Ribeiro-Soriano, E. C.-M, 2023) Digitalization is the generic term for the movement of society and the economy by adopting technology. It describes the transition from an industrial age characterized by analogue technologies to an age of knowledge and creativity characterized by digital technologies and digital business innovation. Digitalization is technology-driven process of innovations and creations.

Social, Mobile, Analytics and Cloud (SMAC) technologies are driving digitalisation. It also refers to the interaction between digital technologies and both the social institutional process converting these technologies into infrastructural technologies and impacting on society and the economy and thereby advancing communication, mobility, speed, virtualization, the disappearance of frontiers, interconnections, market transparency, and competition (Teubner and Stockhinger,2020).

1.2 Digitalisation and ICT Adoption

1.2.1 ICT Definition

Information and communication technologies (ICT) is defined as a diverse set of technological tools and resources used to transmit, store, create, share, or exchange information. These technological tools and resources include computers, the Internet (websites, blogs and emails), live broadcasting technologies (radio, television and webcasting), recorded broadcasting technologies (podcasting, audio and video players, and storage devices) and telephony (fixed or mobile, satellite, vision /video-conferencing, etc.) (UNESCO Institute of Statistics, 2009)

ICT is seen as a vehicle for the empowerment of the socially and economically backward and enables development in underdeveloped regions of the world. Technology adoption refers to the integration of new technologies into the practices and routines of individuals or organizations. This process encompasses the learning and adjustment required to effectively utilize these innovations. As there is a slight difference in the concepts, we often fail to differentiate ICT and Digitalisation.

1.2.2 Difference Between ICT Adoption and Digitalisation

Though the words are used interchangeably in the common parlours there isa distinct difference between them. The difference between these terminologies is critical to note and are compared against various common parameters as under.

Table 1. Difference between digitalisation and ICT adoption

	Digitalization	**ICT Adoption**
Process	It is the process of transformation of services, and systems through digital technologies	It is the acceptance and utilization of specific information and communication technologies
Result	Transformation of operations and systems	Implementation and use of specific technologies
Focus	Broader impact on organizations and societies	Specific impacts on tasks, within organizations
Technological	Involves integration of multiple technologies and platforms	Focuses on the specific implementation of individual technologies
Implementation	Implementation of digital solutions to streamline operations, enhance customer experiences	Adoption of computers, software applications, internet services, communication devices

1.3 Factors Affecting ICT Adoption

1. ***Performance Expectancy*** - The perceived benefits or advantages that individuals or organizations expect to gain from adopting the technology that it will improve productivity, efficiency, or outcomes.
2. ***Effort Expectancy***: The perceived ease of use associated with the new technology such as the simplicity of the user interface, ease of learning, and the amount of effort required to operate the technology effectively.
3. ***Facilitating Condition:*** It facilitates the support systems and resources available to individuals or organizations to aid in the adoption and use of the technology which includes access to training, technical support, infrastructure, and compatibility with existing systems.
4. ***Social Influence***: The impact of interpersonal relationships, norms, and opinions on the adoption decision. It considers factors such as peer recommendations, expert opinions, and societal norms regarding the use of the technology.

1.4 Technology Systems and ICT Categorisations

Information Communication technologies are categorized based on their scope, domain, purpose, type of technology etc. ICT can be considered a critical facilitator for MSME sustainability. Entrepreneurs of MSMEs need to be trained and informed in uptaking the technologies for their capacity building, innovation process, and the development of sustainable business growth. ICT has proven to be the most effective tool for increasing development when compared to other options (Hafkin and Taggart, 2001). Like large companies, each MSME can adopt ICT for innovative practices and sustainable Growth. ICT adoption makes it much cheaper and easier to develop innovations. Firstly, ICT is a "general purpose technology" providing an "indispensable platform" upon which further productivity-enhancing changes, such as product and process innovations, can be based. Secondly, the spillover effects from ICT usage, such as network economies, can be sources of productivity gains. The following Table gives the listing of various systems under different categories of ICT technologies, commonly referred to.

Figure 1. ICT categories (Papasthathopoulos, Anastassopoulos, & Beneki, 2009)

Main ICT Categories	Technologies - Systems
Enterprise Systems	Enterprise Resource Planning – ERP & ERP II or XRP Customer Relationship Management - CRM Supply Chain Management - SCM
Information Systems	Transaction Processing Systems - TPS Management Information Systems - MIS Decision-Support Systems - DSS Executive Support Systems - ESS
Digital Technologies	E-Commerce (refers to electronic transactions such as procurement and sales over the Internet) – B2B, B2C, B2G E-Business (refers to automated business processes (both intra-and inter-firm) over computer mediated networks – Intranet, Extranet
Telecommunication Systems	Internet, e-mail, voice over IP Local Area Networks Wide Area Networks Virtual Private Networks
Identification and Data Capture Technologies & Telematics Technologies	Portable Data Collection, Hand Held Readers, Magnetic & Smart Card Readers, RFID and so forth.

1.5 Low Digitalisation

ICT (Information and Communication Technology) plays a crucial role in fostering digitalisation within businesses, including Micro, Small, and Medium Enterprises (MSMEs). The notable positive impacts of ICT suggest its ability to enhance digitisation and digitalisation across various facets, mainly in Informational, transactional, and transformational levels. It is imperative for companies to prioritize ICT integration, as it can significantly enhance efficiency, market focus, profitability, and organizational dynamics. Unfortunately, MSMEs are slow in embracing new ideas and in most times support initiatives from others are lacking; and there is limited time when considering adopting EICT (Sunday Chinedu Eze, Vera Chinwedu Chinedu-Eze, 2018).

Figure 2. Digital transformation

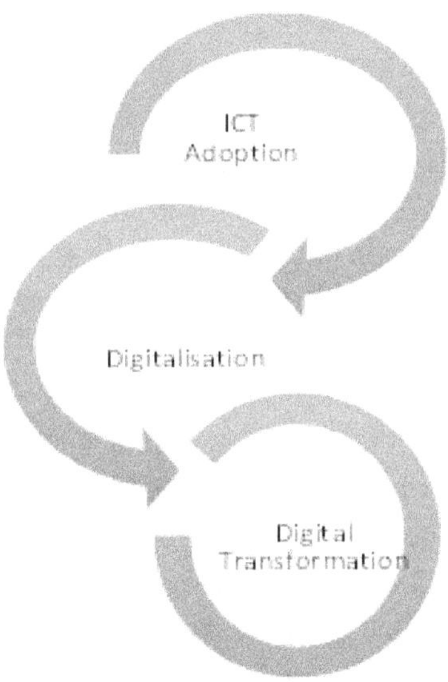

From the study we have conducted regarding the adoption of ICT by MSMEs, percentage adoption is still meagre due to various challenges and reasons.

Figure 3. Share of MSMEs selling through E-commerce platforms (Goyal T.M, 2022, ICRIER)

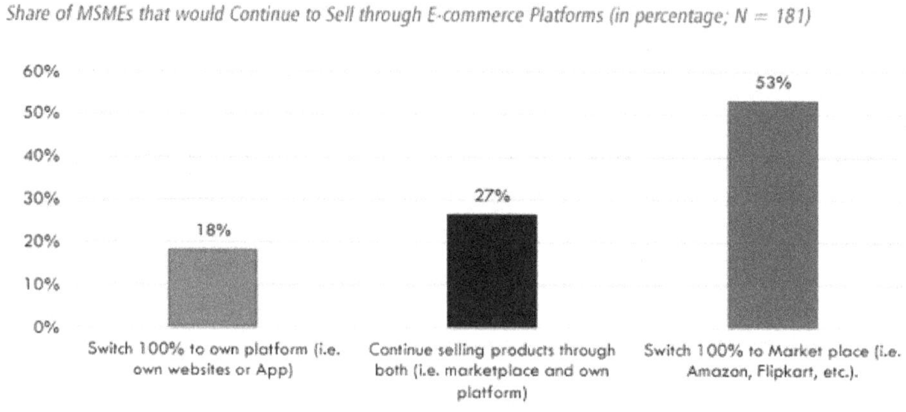

1.5.1 Reasons / Challenges

ICT adoption in MSMEs is facing certain challenges. Force Field Analysis (FFA) is a management tool designed to identify factors or forces that influence, drive, or impede change. Developed by Lewin in 1951, FFA helps to understand the dynamics of human behavior when change is introduced, or the status quo is disrupted. It was notably used to examine the ineffective transition from a paper to a paperless system in the MRO organizational process. According to Lewin's change theory and FFA principles, three key actions are necessary for change: identifying, determining, and developing. First, identify the factors or forces that influence behaviors, both positively and negatively. Second, determine which of these forces can be controlled or manipulated to drive change. Third, develop recommendations or action plans to facilitate positive change. In this exploratory case study, FFA is utilized as the main methodology to better understand the process of technology-enabled change. This involves identifying the factors influencing change and suggesting possible action steps to improve this process by addressing both driving and hindering factors. From various studies it can be analyzed that there are certain factors which drive and restrain adoption of ICT in MSMEs.

1.5.2 Data Collection

The data will be collected through in-depth interviews, focus group discussions, and questionnaire. The interviews will be conducted with the owners or managers of the MSMEs who have adopted ICT. The focus group discussions will be conducted with experts in the MSMEs sector especially those who have experience working with ICT implementation. The instrument developed will be used to understand the extent to which ICT is used in the day-to-day operations of the MSMEs.

1.5.3 Questionnaire

The questionnaire of 12 questions aims to evaluate the impact of Information and Communication Technology (ICT) usage on the sustainability of Micro, Small, and Medium Enterprises (MSMEs). It begins by collecting details about the nature and size of the respondents' businesses, categorizing them into sectors such as Manufacturing, Service, and Retail, and classifying them as Micro, Small, Medium, or Large enterprises. The survey then explores the specific ICT tools employed by these organizations, including websites, emails, social media, online payment systems, ERP software, Industry 4.0 technologies, and AI solutions, as well as the duration of ICT usage. It investigates how these tools are utilized in various business operations like communication with customers and suppliers, financial management, inventory and logistics, marketing, and human resources. The questionnaire also assesses the impact of ICT on company efficiency and productivity, the level of ICT training among the workforce, and identifies areas lacking training or awareness, such as cost-effective technologies and government support.

Furthermore, it examines the effects of ICT on social sustainability, including customer interaction, e-commerce, AI chatbots, market analysis, decision support systems, transaction cost reduction, operations optimization, energy efficiency, and environmental impact. Additionally, the survey identifies challenges in ICT adoption, like lack of awareness, trust issues, resource limitations, and fear of change, and explores opportunities, including cost-effectiveness, high-speed internet, mobile technology, and external support. The ultimate goal is to measure the effects of ICT on MSMEs' sustainability and pinpoint areas for improvement to enhance the sustainability impact of ICT adoption.

Analyzing the MSMEs through Lewins Force Field Analysis, we can find that the forces are:

Figure 4. Forces affecting ICT adoption

Framework revealing driving and restraining forces for ICT adoption by MSMEs	
Driving forces (positive for change)	Restraining forces (negative for change)
Technological	
Cost effective technology	Lack of awareness of ICT solutions
Availability of different affordable IT solutions	Lack of trust in reliable technologies
Increased and efficient use of smart phone	Increased cyber-attacks
Effectiveness of mobile technology	Difficulties in implementation
Access to high-speed internet	Lack of security implementation
Organizational	
Increasing number of skilled workforces	Lack of proper training programme
Flexibility in working conditions	Difficulty in harmonizing with change
ICT implementation as capital investment	High initial expense of implementation
Internal cohesion and collaboration	Lack of capabilities
External	
Ease of government norms	Lack of awareness about schemes
Competitors pressure favors adoption	Fear of change

1.5.3.1 Internal Driving Force (Positive for Change)

MSMEs are likely to adopt ICT if they find solutions that fit within their budget constraints, offering them cost savings and efficiency improvements. So, after the pandemic many of the MSMEs have adopted informational and transactional levels of ICT. E.g.: Website, UPI, Online Platforms, Social media etc. Therefore, cost effectiveness can be considered as one of the major driving forces for the adoption. There are a variety of affordable ICT options that allow MSMEs to choose solutions that best meet their specific needs and financial capabilities. The widespread use of smartphones enables MSMEs to access and utilize ICT tools and applications more conveniently and efficiently. Mobile technology offers flexibility and accessibility, allowing MSMEs to conduct business operations from anywhere at any time and the reliable high-speed internet connectivity is essential for MSMEs to leverage cloud-based services, communication tools, and online platforms effectively.

Access to skilled employees who are proficient in ICT can drive MSMEs to adopt technology to leverage their expertise and improve productivity. This is one of the other major aspects at organisational level. The flexibility level of MSMEs through technology intervention is high which enhances employee satisfaction and overall organizational agility. Viewing ICT as a strategic investment rather than just an operational expense can motivate MSMEs to prioritize technology adoption for long-term growth and competitiveness. In the area of internal cohesion and communication, ICT tools and platforms facilitate communication, collaboration, and knowledge sharing within MSMEs, fostering a more cohesive and efficient work environment.

Supportive government policies, incentives, or regulations can encourage and facilitate ICT adoption among MSMEs by reducing barriers and providing assistance. Competitors' pressure favors adoption: The competitive landscape and pressure from industry peers may incentivize MSMEs to adopt ICT to stay relevant, innovative, and competitive in the market while considering the external factors.

1.5.3.2 Restraining Forces (Negative for Change)

Lack of technology awareness is one of the major issues faced by MSMEs. MSMEs are not aware of the available ICT solutions or their potential benefits in which this lack of awareness hinders them from their adoption of technology. There are concerns about the reliability, security, effectiveness, and usage of ICT solutions may lead MSMEs to hesitate in adopting new technologies. Another crisis in the technology perspective is the fear of cyber threats and data breaches. This discourages MSMEs from embracing ICT, especially if they lack confidence in their ability to protect sensitive information.

There are also challenges in implementing and integrating ICT solutions into existing business processes and infrastructure can be daunting for MSMEs, slowing down adoption effort. Inadequate security measures and protocols may make MSMEs hesitant to adopt ICT, fearing potential vulnerabilities and risks to their business operations and data.

Another major restraining force is the lack of proper training programs. Insufficient training and skill development programs may impede MSMEs' ability to effectively utilize ICT solutions and maximize their benefits. This also causes difficulty in harmonizing with change which leads to the internal resistance to change within the organization, whether from employees or management, can slow down or disrupt the adoption of new ICT initiatives.

The upfront costs associated with acquiring and implementing ICT solutions may be prohibitive for MSMEs with limited financial resources. MSMEs may lack the internal capabilities, expertise, or resources required to successfully implement and manage ICT solutions, posing a barrier to adoption and utilization.

Awareness on govt schemes and its availability is scarce. The challenge arises when MSMEs are not informed or educated about the various government programs, initiatives, or support schemes designed to promote ICT adoption within their sector. These schemes often include financial incentives, subsidies, grants, or technical assistance aimed at helping businesses integrate and leverage ICT solutions effectively. The lack of awareness about such schemes can have several implications.

Therefore, MSMEs are missing such supporting initiatives and financial assistance or guidance that could facilitate their ICT adoption journey. Without knowledge of available schemes, they may struggle to access resources and support that could alleviate the financial burden or provide expertise necessary for successful implementation. This can result in suboptimal decision-making, inefficient resource allocation, and ultimately hinder business growth and competitiveness.

The lack of awareness about schemes may lead MSMEs to remain stagnant in their ICT adoption efforts, as they may perceive the process as too costly, risky, or complex without realizing the available avenues for support and assistance. Addressing this challenge requires proactive efforts from government agencies, industry associations, and other stakeholders to enhance awareness and education about existing schemes. This can involve outreach programs, workshops, online resources, and collaboration with local business communities to ensure that MSMEs are informed about the opportunities available to them. Resistance to change and uncertainty about the implications of adopting new technologies can significantly hinder MSMEs' willingness to embrace ICT initiatives. This fear of change can manifest in various ways.

Most of the MSMEs before the pandemic, may be accustomed to traditional methods of conducting business and may perceive ICT adoption as disruptive or unnecessary. They may resist change out of a sense of comfort or familiarity with existing processes, despite potential benefits offered by technological advancements. Adopting new technologies entails inherent risks, including financial investment, operational disruptions, and uncertainty about the outcomes. MSMEs may hesitate to embrace ICT initiatives due to concerns about potential failures, setbacks, or negative consequences for their business operations. Overcoming the fear of change requires proactive efforts to address concerns, mitigate risks, and foster a culture of innovation and adaptability within MSMEs. This involves effective communication, stakeholder engagement, training programs, and providing tangible evidence of the positive outcomes associated with ICT adoption. By addressing these underlying fears and uncertainties, MSMEs can become more receptive to embracing technological advancements and realizing the associated benefits for their business growth and competitiveness.

1.5.4 Correlation Analysis

The Pearson correlation matrix explains the relationships between business characteristics taken from the survey and technology adoption. There is a strong positive correlation between the period of business and rating (0.897), indicating that older businesses tend to have higher customer or performance ratings. Similarly, a strong positive correlation exists between employee strength and rating (0.813), suggesting that larger businesses also receive higher ratings. However, both period of business (-0.716) and employee strength (-0.354) are negatively correlated with technology adoption, implying that older and larger businesses are less likely to adopt new technologies. Usage and impact of technology show moderate positive correlations with each other (0.512), indicating that more frequent technology use is associated with a greater positive impact on the business. Overall, the matrix suggests that while established and larger businesses enjoy higher ratings, they tend to be slower in adopting new technologies, whereas younger and smaller businesses are more agile in technology adoption but might not have as high ratings.

2. GOI SCHEMES FOR SUPPORTING DIGITALISATION OF MSME

The Government of India has launched several schemes and initiatives to support the digitalization of Micro, Small, and Medium Enterprises (MSMEs). These initiatives aim to enhance the competitiveness, productivity, and sustainability of MSMEs by leveraging digital technologies. Here are some key schemes supporting MSME digitalization.

2.1 Digital India Programme

Digital India was an initiative taken by the Government of India for providing high-speed internet networks to rural areas. Digital India Mission was launched by PM Narendra Modi on 1st July 2015 as a beneficiary to other government schemes including Make in India, Bharatmala, Sagarmala, Startup India, BharatNet, and Standup India.

The nine pillars of Digital India are given below:

- **Broadband Highways**– This covers three subcomponents, namely Broadband for All – Rural, Broadband for All – Urban and National Information Infrastructure (NII).
- **Universal Access to Mobile Connectivity**- This initiative focuses on network penetration and filling the gaps in connectivity in the country.
- **Public Internet Access Programme**- The two subcomponents of Public Internet Access Programme are Common Services Centres (CSCs) and Post Offices as multi-service centres.
- **e-Governance**- Reforming Government through Technology-Government Process Re-engineering using IT to simplify and make the government processes more efficient is critical for transformation to make the delivery of government services more effective across various government domains and therefore needs to be implemented by all Ministries/ Departments.
- **e-Kranti** – Electronic Delivery of Services- To improve the delivery of public services and simplify the process of accessing them. In this regard, several e-governance initiatives have been undertaken by various State Governments and Central Ministries to usher in an era of e-Government. e-Governance in India has steadily evolved from the computerization of Government Departments to initiatives that encapsulate the finer points of Governance, such as citizen centricity, service orientation and transparency.
- **Information for All**- This pillar aims to ensure transparency and availability of reliable data generated by the line ministries for use, reuse and redistribution for the people of India.
- **Electronics Manufacturing**- This pillar focuses on promoting electronics manufacturing in the country.
- **IT for Jobs**- This pillar focuses on providing training to the youth in the skills required for availing employment opportunities in the IT/ITES sector.
- **Early Harvest Programmes**- This pillar consists of a group of different short-term projects which have immediate effect on the Indian digital ecosystem like IT platform for mass messaging, crowd Sourcing of eGreetings, biometric attendance in the government offices, WI-FI in all universities etc.

2.1.1 Important Initiatives

DigiLockers – This flagship initiative aims at 'Digital Empowerment' of the citizen by providing access to authentic digital documents to citizen's digital document wallet
https://www.digilocker.gov.in/
E-Hospitals – It is a Hospital Management Information System (HMIS) which is a one-stop solution in connecting patients, hospitals and doctors through a single digital platform. Till February 2021, as many as 420 e-Hospitals had been established under the Digital India campaign
https://ehospital.gov.in/
E-Pathshala – Developed by NCERT, e-Pathshala showcases and disseminates all educational e-resources including textbooks, audio, video, periodicals and a variety of other print and non-print materials through the website and mobile app
https://epathshala.nic.in/
BHIM – Bharat Interface for Money is an app that makes payment transactions simple, easy and quick using Unified Payments Interface (UPI)

2.2 MSME Sambandh Portal

The MSME Sambandh Portal serves as the Public Procurement Portal, aimed at overseeing the execution of Public Procurement from Micro and Small Enterprises (MSEs) by Central Public Sector Enterprises. On March 26, 2012, the Ministry of MSME introduced the Public Procurement Policy for Micro and Small Enterprises (MSE) Order. This policy mandated that each Central Ministry/Department/PSU establish an annual procurement objective for sourcing from the MSE sector, with the goal of achieving an overall procurement target of at least 20% of total annual purchases from products or services provided by MSEs. The MSME Sambandh portal holds significant importance due to its key features:

1. Modification of Procurement Target: The portal adjusts the procurement target from 20% to 25%, reflecting an increased emphasis on sourcing from MSEs.
2. Special Provision for Women-Owned Enterprises: Within the revised 25% procurement target, a specific provision is made for women-owned micro and small businesses. This provision ensures that 3% of the total annual purchases from Micro and Small Enterprises are allocated specifically for procurement from women-owned microenterprises.

2.3 Udyam Sakhi Portal

The Udyam Sakhi Portal serves as a network that promotes social entrepreneurship, focusing to encourage and assist women entrepreneurs in establishing, nurturing, and expanding their businesses. The Udyam Sakhi Portal contributes to the enhancement of women entrepreneurs by driving economic growth, fostering resilience, and ensuring competitiveness in the global marketplace.

Its range of services, which include:

- Assisting in the creation of business plans and providing entrepreneurial learning resources.
- Offering guidance on fundraising and connecting with investors.
- Providing mentorship opportunities for aspiring women entrepreneurs.
- Facilitating market surveys to aid in business decision-making

2.4 Udyam Registration

Launched on July 1st, 2020, the Udyam registration portal marks a significant milestone in the digital transformation of India's Micro, Small, and Medium Enterprises (MSMEs) sector by the Union MSME ministry. This online platform streamlines the registration process for MSMEs, eliminating the need for cumbersome documentation. Notably, it is intricately linked to the databases of the Central Board of Direct Taxes (CBDT) and the Goods and Services Tax Network (GSTN), enhancing efficiency and accuracy in data management. It establishes a seamless channel of communication between taxpayers, central and state governments, and other stakeholders. By leveraging this digital infrastructure, Udyam registration contributes to the Ease of Doing Business initiative, facilitating a smoother and more accessible environment for MSMEs. It also serves as a gateway for MSMEs to access a myriad of benefits and incentives offered by the Ministry of MSME. Moreover, it is a prerequisite for availing Priority Sector Lending from banks, further incentivizing MSMEs to register on the platform.

2.5 Technology Upgradation Fund Scheme (TUFS)

TUFS, administered by the Ministry of Textiles, provides financial assistance to MSMEs in the textile sector for upgrading their technology and machinery. The Technology Upgradation Fund Scheme (TUFS) was introduced by the Government of India in 1999 with the aim of supporting technological advancements in the textile industry. The primary objective was to enhance the competitiveness of the Indian textile sector on a global scale while also reducing operational costs. Initially launched, the scheme underwent revisions for its continuation during the 12th plan period. An allocation of Rs. 11,952 crore was made to attract investments totaling Rs. 1,51,000 crores between 2012 and 2017. This allocation included Rs. 9,290 crores for existing commitments and Rs. 2,662 crores for new investments. The modifications made to the scheme were geared towards enhancing the overall Ease of Doing Business environment.

2.6 Credit Guarantee Fund Trust for Micro and Small Enterprises (CGTMSE)

CGTMSE, a credit guarantee scheme launched by the Government of India and SIDBI, provides collateral-free credit facilities to MSMEs. CGTMSE is an initiative of the Government of India in collaboration with the Ministry of Micro, Small and Medium Enterprises (MSME) and the Small Industries Development Bank of India (SIDBI) launched on 30th August 2000. The CGTMSE full form is Credit Guarantee Fund Trust for Micro and Small Enterprises, and as is evident from the name, it is a Trust which provides the financial institutions with credit guarantee to provide loans to SMEs and MSMEs. The basic aim of CGTMSE is to encourage first-time entrepreneurs to establish SME and MSME, considered being the bulwark of the Indian economy by availing of collateral free loans from the eligible financial institutions. The guarantee covers default by the borrower to repay the advance. Thus, the CGTMSE scheme primarily envisages the provision of loans to first generation entrepreneurs so that they can flourish in the competitive environment without the burden of security or third-party guarantees. In turn the financial institutions are provided cover for the absence of security to fund SMEs and MSMEs promoted by small Indian businessmen up to a certain limit. MSMEs can use the funds availed under CGTMSE to invest in digital infrastructure, software, and technologies to improve their competitiveness and operational efficiency.

2.7 National Small Industries Corporation (NSIC) Schemes

NSIC offers various schemes and programs to support MSMEs, including the Raw Material Assistance Scheme (RMA), Marketing Assistance Scheme, and Performance and Credit Rating Scheme. MSMEs can avail of support under these schemes to procure digital tools, software solutions, and consultancy services to enhance their digital capabilities.

2.8 Technology Centre Systems Programme (TCSP)

TCSP, implemented by the Ministry of MSME, aims to establish and upgrade technology centers across India to provide technical support and consultancy services to MSMEs. MSMEs can access training, testing facilities, and technical assistance at these technology centers to adopt and implement digital technologies effectively.

2.9 Digital MSME Scheme

Launched by the Ministry of MSME, the Digital MSME Scheme aims to promote the adoption of Information and Communication Technology (ICT) tools and digital technologies by MSMEs. Key components

2.10 Objectives of the Digital MSME Scheme

1. Providing training and capacity-building programs to MSMEs to improve their digital literacy and skills.
2. Encouraging MSMEs to adopt digital technologies such as cloud computing, e-commerce platforms, digital marketing tools, and enterprise resource planning (ERP) systems.
3. Providing financial assistance or subsidies to MSMEs for the procurement of digital tools and technologies, including hardware, software, and digital services.
4. Facilitating access to digital marketplaces and platforms for MSMEs to promote their products and services online.
5. Formulating policies and regulations conducive to the digitalization of MSMEs, including measures to address cybersecurity, data privacy, digital payments, and regulatory barriers to digital innovation.
6. Establishing mechanisms for monitoring the progress and impact of the Digital MSME scheme, including tracking the adoption of digital technologies by MSMEs, measuring improvements in productivity and competitiveness, and assessing the overall effectiveness of the scheme in achieving its objectives.

3. FRUGAL DIGITALISATION

Frugal digitalization, also known as frugal innovation or jugaad innovation by the means of technology adoption and applications. This refers to the process of adopting and implementing digital technologies in a resource-constrained environment, typically characterized by limited financial resources, infrastructure, and expertise. It involves leveraging creative and cost-effective solutions to address complex challenges and achieve desired outcomes using digital tools and technologies. Frugal digitalization is often associated with emerging markets and sectors such as micro, small, and medium enterprises (MSMEs) where there is a need to maximize the impact of digital initiatives while minimizing costs and resources.

3.1. Defining Frugality

Frugality refers to the practice of using resources wisely and avoiding unnecessary waste or extravagance. It involves being economical, thrifty, and mindful of expenses, with the goal of maximizing value and minimizing unnecessary consumption. Frugality is often associated with living within one's means, making intentional choices about spending and saving, and prioritizing long-term financial stability over short-term gratification. It encompasses various behaviors and attitudes, such as budgeting, prioritizing needs over wants, seeking value for money, and finding creative solutions to achieve desired outcomes without overspending. Frugality can be applied to various aspects of life, including personal finances, consumption habits, lifestyle choices, and business practices, and it is often regarded as a virtue that promotes sustainability, resourcefulness, and resilience.

Features:

- **Simplicity**: Frugality prioritizes simplicity and ease of use, often employing straightforward designs and minimalistic features to ensure accessibility to a wide range of users.
- **Affordability:** Frugal innovations are designed to be cost-effective and affordable, making use of locally available materials and resources to keep production and maintenance costs low.
- **Adaptability:** Frugality is adaptable to diverse contexts and user needs, allowing for customization and flexibility in implementation. They can be easily modified or scaled to suit different environments and requirements.
- **Inclusive Design:** Frugal designs are inclusive and user-centric, taking into account the needs, preferences, and limitations of the target users, including those with limited access to resources or technology.
- **Resource Efficiency:** Frugal innovations emphasize resource efficiency and sustainability, minimizing waste and environmental impact throughout the product life cycle, from production to disposal.

3.2. Why Frugal Digitalisation?

Most of the MSME face Challenges, like Limited Resources, Lack of Expertise, Fear of Change can be overcome by frugal digitalisation.

3.2.1 Frugal Digitalization Strategies

Leveraging Open-Source Software: A vast array of free and open-source software (OSS) alternatives exist for various business functions like accounting, customer relationship management (CRM), and project management.

Using Cloud-based Solutions: Cloud computing offers scalable and cost-effective access to software and data storage, eliminating the need for expensive upfront investments in hardware and IT staff.

Freelancing and Outsourcing: MSMEs can leverage freelance marketplaces or outsource specific digital tasks like web development or social media marketing to skilled professionals at competitive rates.

Mobile-First Approach: In today's mobile-driven world, prioritizing a mobile-friendly website and utilizing free social media platforms for marketing can be highly effective.

Focus on Core Processes: Identify the most critical business processes that can benefit most from digitalization. Start by tackling one or two areas at a time to avoid overwhelming resource limitations.

Embrace Collaboration: Networking with other MSMEs and industry associations can provide valuable insights, shared learning opportunities, and potential collaboration on digital initiatives.

3.2.2 Advantages of Frugal Digitalization

Increased Efficiency: Streamlining operations through digital tools can save time and resources, allowing MSMEs to focus on core competencies.

Improved Customer Engagement: A strong online presence and effective digital marketing strategies can attract new customers and enhance brand visibility.

Enhanced Decision Making: Data-driven insights gleaned from digital tools can empower MSMEs to make informed business decisions.

Competitive Advantage: Even with limited resources, embracing digitalization can help MSMEs compete more effectively in an increasingly digital marketplace.

Figure 5. Framework for frugal digitalisation

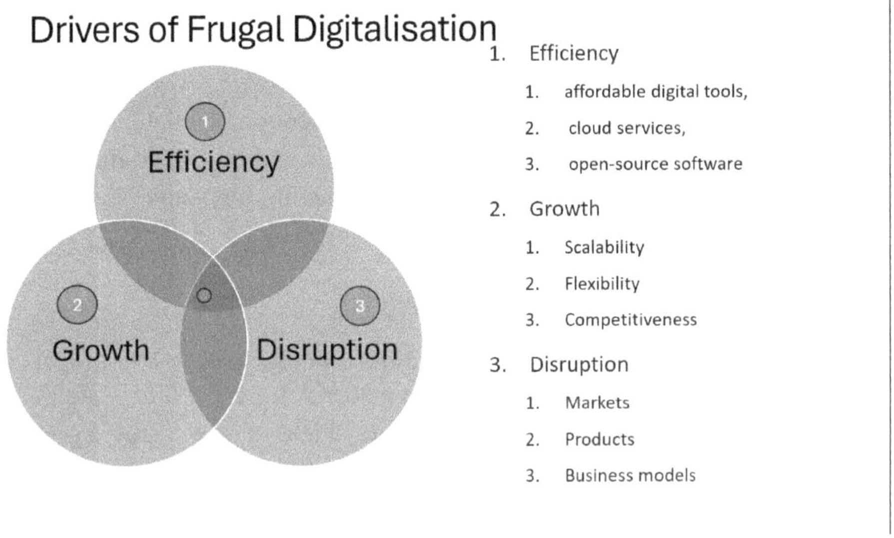

3.2.3 Drivers of Frugality

Frugality, once relegated to the realm of personal finance and thriftiness, has emerged as a strategic imperative for businesses and societies alike. In an era marked by resource constraints, environmental concerns, and economic uncertainties, the ability to do more with less has become a competitive advantage and a necessity. At the heart of this paradigm shift lie three fundamental **drivers: efficiency, growth, and disruption.**

3.2.3.1. Efficiency: The Engine of Frugality

Efficiency, the first cornerstone of frugality, embodies the ethos of optimization and resource maximization. Whether it's streamlining processes, minimizing waste, or enhancing productivity, efficiency lies at the core of frugal practices. By harnessing the power of efficiency, organizations can not only reduce costs but also improve performance, agility, and sustainability.

a. **Resource Optimization** - This involves maximizing the utilization of resources, be it raw materials, energy, or labor, to minimize waste and enhance productivity. Strategies such as lean manufacturing, just-in-time inventory management, and energy-efficient processes fall under this component.

b. **Cost Reduction** - Frugality often revolves around reducing costs without compromising quality or performance. This component focuses on identifying inefficiencies, streamlining operations, and implementing cost-saving measures across all aspects of the organization.
c. **Process Improvement** - Continuous improvement is essential for achieving efficiency gains over time. This component emphasizes the importance of refining processes, eliminating bottlenecks, and embracing innovative methodologies like Six Sigma or Kaizen to drive incremental efficiencies.

3.2.3.2 Growth: Fueling Frugal Innovation

Growth, the second pillar of frugality, represents the engine that propels innovation and prosperity. However, traditional notions of growth often entail a linear consumption of resources, leading to unsustainable outcomes. Frugal growth, on the other hand, emphasizes doing more with less, unlocking new opportunities, and expanding horizons within the confines of resource constraints.

a. **Sustainable Expansion** - Frugal growth prioritizes sustainable expansion that leverages existing resources and minimizes environmental impact. This component explores strategies for scaling operations, entering new markets, and diversifying product/service offerings while adhering to resource constraints.
b. **Innovation Ecosystem** - Growth in a frugal context thrives on an ecosystem of innovation that encourages experimentation, collaboration, and knowledge sharing. This component delves into fostering a culture of innovation, nurturing partnerships with startups and academia, and incentivizing creativity within the organization.
c. **Value Creation** - Frugal growth isn't just about increasing revenue; it's about creating value for all stakeholders. This component examines how organizations can align growth initiatives with social, environmental, and economic objectives, fostering inclusive and sustainable development.

3.2.3.3 Disruption: Rethinking Conventional Practices

Disruption, the final catalyst of frugality, challenges the status quo and fosters breakthrough innovation. By reimagining conventional practices, disrupting established industries, and introducing novel solutions, disruptive forces drive frugal transformation. Through disruptive technologies, business models, and mindsets, organizations can leapfrog barriers, unlock latent potential, and create value in unprecedented ways.

a. **Disruptive Technologies** - Technology plays a pivotal role in driving frugal disruption by enabling novel solutions and redefining industry norms. This component explores emerging technologies such as AI, blockchain, and 3D printing, and their potential to disrupt traditional business models and unlock new opportunities.
b. **Business Model Innovation** - Disruption often stems from reimagining business models to better serve evolving customer needs and market dynamics. This component delves into examples of disruptive business models, such as the sharing economy, subscription-based services, and platform-based ecosystems, and their implications for frugal transformation.
c. **Cultural Shift** - Frugal disruption requires a cultural shift within organizations, one that embraces risk-taking, agility, and adaptability. This component examines the importance of fostering an entrepreneurial mindset, empowering employees to challenge the status quo, and embracing failure as a learning opportunity in driving disruptive innovation.

3.3. Synergies and Interplay Among Drivers

A. **Efficiency-Growth Nexus** - Efficiency enables sustainable growth by optimizing resource allocation and enhancing productivity, while growth provides the impetus for investing in efficiency measures and expanding frugal practices.
B. **Growth-Disruption Intersection** -Frugal growth is often catalyzed by disruptive innovations that unlock new markets, drive operational efficiencies, and create value propositions that resonate with consumers.
C. **Efficiency-Disruption Integration** - Disruptive technologies and business models can significantly enhance efficiency by automating processes, reducing costs, and enabling new ways of working.

3.4 Value Chain Analysis

Let's conduct a value chain analysis incorporating the frugal drivers of efficiency, growth, and disruption:

Figure 6. Value chain analysis based on frugal digitalisation

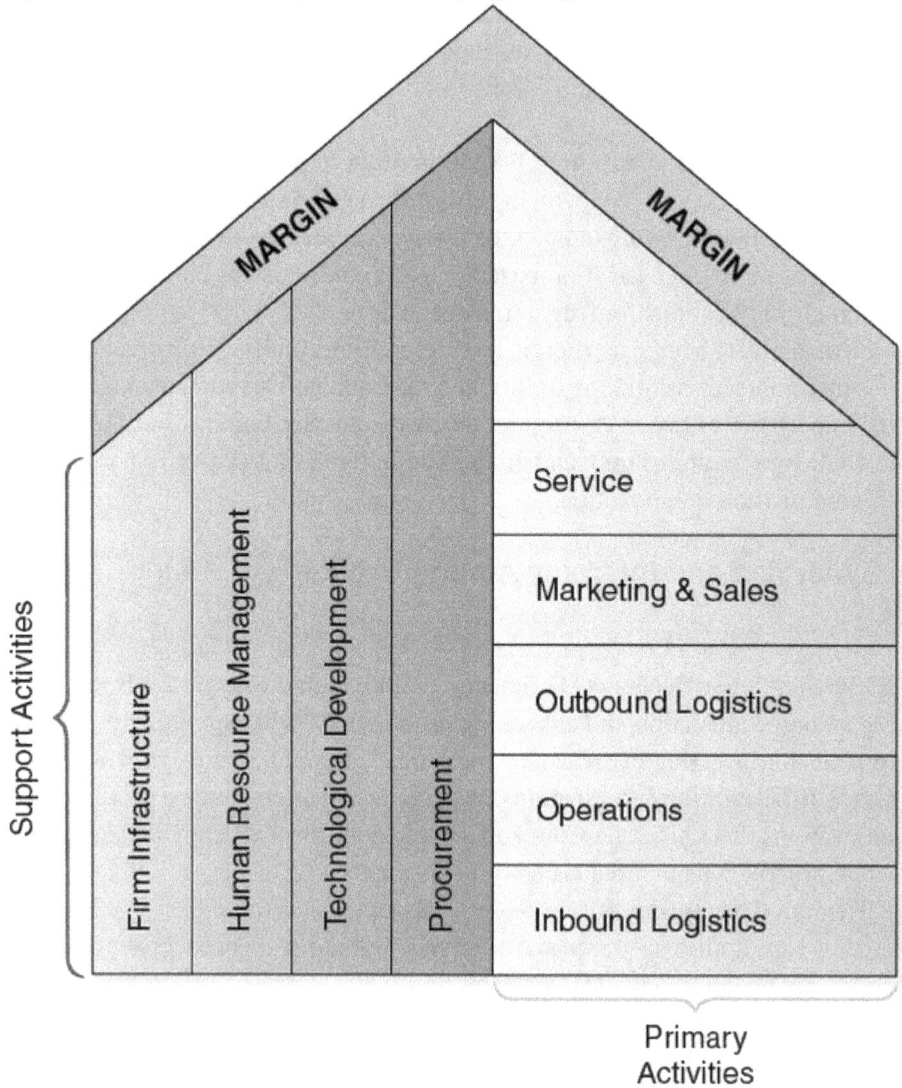

3.4.1 Primary Activities

3.4.1.1 Inbound Logistics

Efficiency - Implementing efficient procurement processes, optimizing transportation routes, and minimizing waste in the supply chain.

Growth - Seeking cost-effective sourcing options, scaling up procurement operations sustainably, and exploring new supplier partnerships.
Disruption - Embracing innovative technologies for supply chain optimization, such as blockchain for transparent and efficient transactions, and AI for demand forecasting.

3.4.1.2 Operations

Efficiency - Adopting lean manufacturing principles, optimizing production processes, and minimizing energy consumption.
Growth - Investing in scalable production technologies, expanding manufacturing capabilities, and diversifying product offerings.
Disruption - Leveraging 3D printing for on-demand manufacturing, implementing IoT-enabled smart factories for real-time monitoring and optimization, and exploring circular economy models for resource efficiency.

3.4.1.3 Outbound Logistics

Efficiency - Streamlining warehousing operations, optimizing inventory management, and reducing delivery lead times.
Growth - Expanding distribution networks, entering new markets, and enhancing customer reach.
Disruption - Introducing drone or autonomous vehicle delivery options, utilizing data analytics for route optimization, and partnering with third-party logistics providers for flexible and scalable solutions.

3.4.1.4 Marketing and Sales

Efficiency - Targeted marketing campaigns, digital marketing automation, and data-driven customer segmentation.
Growth - Market expansion strategies, product diversification, and strategic partnerships.
Disruption - Embracing e-commerce platforms and online marketplaces, leveraging social media influencers for brand promotion, and utilizing augmented reality for immersive shopping experiences.

3.4.1.5 Service

Efficiency - Implementing self-service customer support options, automated maintenance scheduling, and remote diagnostics.
Growth - Offering premium service packages, expanding service coverage globally, and enhancing after-sales support.

Disruption - Introducing predictive maintenance solutions using IoT sensors, implementing AI-driven chatbots for instant customer support, and exploring virtual reality for remote troubleshooting.

3.4.2. Support Activities

3.4.2.1 Procurement

Efficiency: Negotiating favorable contracts, optimizing procurement processes, and implementing supplier performance metrics.
Growth: Developing strategic supplier partnerships, exploring sustainable sourcing options, and investing in supplier development programs.
Disruption: Utilizing blockchain for transparent and secure procurement transactions, leveraging AI for predictive supplier analytics, and exploring alternative supply chain models like peer-to-peer sourcing platforms.

3.4.2.2 Technology Development

Efficiency: Investing in cost-effective R&D processes, prioritizing innovation projects with high ROI potential, and optimizing technology development cycles.
Growth: Expanding R&D capabilities, investing in breakthrough technologies, and fostering a culture of innovation.
Disruption: Collaborating with start-ups for disruptive innovation, leveraging open innovation platforms for idea generation, and exploring crowdsourcing for R&D solutions.

3.4.2.3 Human Resource Management

Efficiency: Implementing efficient recruitment processes, optimizing workforce scheduling, and investing in employee training programs.
Growth: Attracting top talent, fostering a culture of learning and development, and promoting career advancement opportunities.
Disruption: Embracing remote work arrangements, leveraging AI for talent acquisition and management, and implementing agile HR practices to adapt to changing workforce dynamics.

3.4.2.4 Firm Infrastructure

Efficiency - Optimizing organizational structures, streamlining decision-making processes, and reducing administrative overhead.
Growth - Investing in scalable IT infrastructure, expanding organizational capabilities, and enhancing strategic planning processes.

Disruption - Implementing digital transformation initiatives, adopting agile methodologies for project management, and exploring decentralized organizational models.

By integrating the frugal drivers of efficiency, growth, and disruption into each step of the value chain, the company can create a holistic approach to value creation that emphasizes resource optimization, sustainable expansion, and innovation leadership. This strategic alignment enables the organization to leverage its strengths, address weaknesses, and capitalize on emerging opportunities in a rapidly evolving market landscape.

3.5 ICT Adoption Vs Frugal Digitalisation

Table 2. ICT adoption vs frugal digitalisation

Aspect	ICT Adoption	Frugal Digitalization
Approach	Integration of established technology solutions	Innovative and cost-effective digital approaches
Objective	Enhance efficiency, productivity, and competitiveness	Achieve business goals while minimizing costs and resource consumption
Technology Utilization	Commercial off-the-shelf (COTS) solutions	Open-source, low-cost, and adaptable technologies
Investment	Significant upfront investment in technology	Minimized upfront investment with focus on cost-effectiveness
Focus	Functionality and performance	Cost-effectiveness and innovation
Complexity	May involve complex implementation processes	Embraces simplicity and adaptability
Agility and Flexibility	Less emphasis on agility and flexibility	Driven by agility and flexibility in adopting and adapting solutions
Target Organizations	Often larger enterprises with higher budgets	Particularly relevant for MSMEs and resource-constrained environments

When we observe these distinct approaches to incorporating technology into business operations, ICT Adoption typically involves integrating an established technology solution to enhance efficiency, productivity, and competitiveness. The approach is often relying on commercial off-the-shelf (COTS) solutions, necessitating a significant upfront investment in technology infrastructure. Its emphasis is mainly placed on functionality and performance, which sometimes resulting in complex implementation processes.

While ICT Adoption is common in larger enterprises with ample budgets, Frugal Digitalization takes a different route. Its innovative and cost-effective digital approaches focused at achieving business goals by minimizing costs and resource consumption.

Frugal Digitalization prefers open-source, low-cost, and adaptable technologies, leading to minimized upfront investment. It strikes a balance between functionality and cost-effectiveness with innovation, emphasizing simplicity and adaptability in implementation.

This can drive agility and flexibility in adopting and adapting solutions, making it particularly relevant for Micro, Small, and Medium Enterprises (MSMEs) and resource-constrained environments. ICT Adoption focuses on established solutions, where Frugal Digitalization champions innovation and efficiency, making it a promising strategy for businesses with limited resources seeking to leverage technology effectively.

4. FRUGAL DIGITALISATION AND MSMES

As we have already discussed the challenges and opportunities MSMEs have, frugality is the best strategy for the technology adoption. Technology adoption follows different levels of adoption based on its impact and application. Similarly, frugality delivers its competence in three levels for MSMEs. So, we can match the adoption level strategies to benefits frugality can offer. Thus, frugal digitalisation strategies can be implemented in MSMEs.

Table 3. Levels of adoption and benefits of frugality

Levels of adoption / frugality benefits	Cost efficiency	scalability	disruption
Informational	Application of open – source software for basic data collection and storage. Reducing software license costs	Implementing cloud-based solutions for data backup and retrieval Allowing flexible storage options	Adopting digital platforms for market research. Gaining insights into customer preferences and market trends
Transactional	Utilizing digital payment systems to reduce transaction costs associated with traditional banking methods	Implementing e-commerce platforms to reach a wider audience and handle increased sales volumes efficiently	Using blockchain technology for secure and transparent transactions, disrupting traditional financial processes
Transformational	Implementing AI-driven automation to optimize processes, reduce labour costs, and improve productivity	Adopting IoT solutions for real time monitoring and control of manufacturing processes, enabling scalable production	Using machine learning algorithms for predictive analytics, transforming decision making and business strategies.

4.1 Case

4.1.1 ONDC: Redefining Small Business Model Through Frugal Digitalisation

ONDC stands for the Open Network for Digital Commerce which is an initiative launched by the Government of India to digitize and streamline the country's commerce sector. ONDC aims to create a unified digital platform that connects buyers, sellers, and other stakeholders in the commerce ecosystem. This platform facilitates seamless transactions, enhances transparency, and promotes efficiency in various aspects of commerce, including e-commerce, supply chain management, and digital payments. ONDC also focuses on promoting fair competition and empowering small businesses by providing them with access to a wider market through digital channels. ONDC leverages Beckn protocol for decentralised commerce.

Figure 7. ONDC and Beckn protocol (Kalaari capital advisors Pvt. Ltd, 2023)

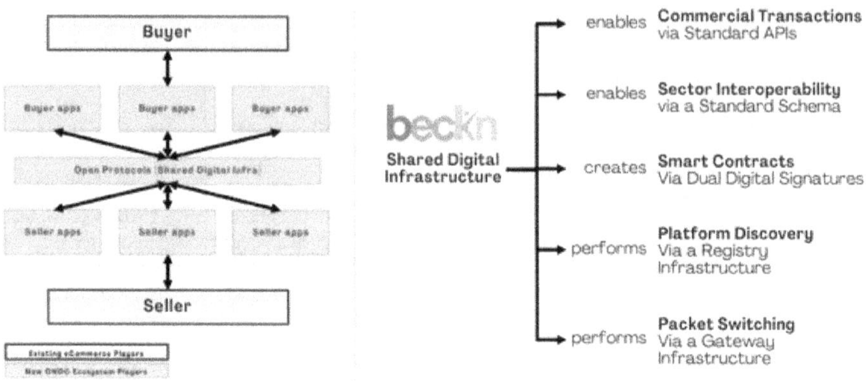

4.2 Why ONDC is Frugal?

4.2.1 Cost-Effective Solutions

ONDC aims to provide cost-effective solutions for various aspects of commerce, including e-commerce platforms, digital payments, and logistics. By leveraging ONDC's infrastructure, small businesses can access these solutions at a fraction of the cost compared to traditional methods, promoting frugality in their operations.

4.2.2 Efficiency and Optimization

Frugality often involves maximizing efficiency and optimizing resource utilization. ONDC facilitates streamlined processes and automation in commerce transactions, enabling businesses to operate more efficiently and minimize waste. This efficiency translates into cost savings and improved profitability for small businesses.

4.2.3 Access to Affordable Resources

Through ONDC, small businesses can access a wide range of affordable resources and services, such as digital marketing tools, cloud computing infrastructure, and online training programs. These resources empower businesses to achieve their goals while adhering to frugal principles and minimizing unnecessary expenses.

4.2.4 Innovation and Creativity

Frugality encourages innovation and creativity in finding cost-effective solutions to challenges. ONDC fosters a culture of innovation by providing a platform for businesses to experiment with new ideas, products, and business models in a low-risk environment. This encourages small businesses to think creatively about how they can deliver value to their customers while staying frugal.

4.2.5 Sustainable Practices

Frugality is often aligned with sustainable practices that minimize environmental impact and promote long-term viability. ONDC supports sustainable commerce by encouraging digital transactions, reducing the need for physical resources such as paper and transportation, and promoting eco-friendly practices among businesses and consumers.

Figure 8. Time frame of ONDC

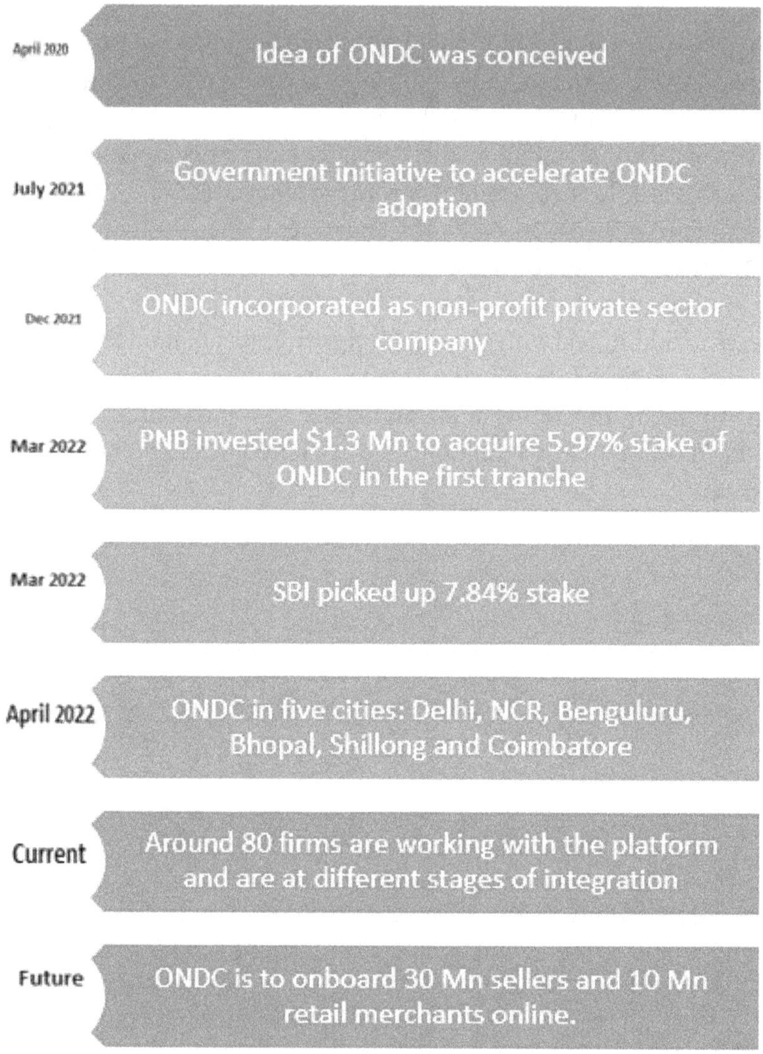

4.3 Advantages for MSMEs

4.3.1 Product Discoverability

ONDC provides a unified digital platform where sellers can list their products, making it easier for buyers to discover a wide range of offerings from different sellers. The platform may incorporate features such as search filters, categories, and recommendations based on user preferences to enhance discoverability and help users find the right sellers and products.

4.3.2 Execution of the Orders

ONDC facilitates the entire transaction process, from order placement to fulfilment, through its digital infrastructure. Thus, buyers can place orders directly through the platform, and sellers receive notifications to process and fulfil the orders promptly.

4.3.3 Delivery Time

ONDC can integrate with logistics providers to ensure timely delivery of orders to customers hence real-time tracking features allow buyers to monitor the status of their orders and receive updates on estimated delivery times.

4.3.4 Genuity

ONDC may implement verification processes to authenticate sellers and validate the authenticity of their products. Ratings, reviews, and feedback mechanisms help build trust by enabling buyers to assess the reputation and reliability of sellers and products.

4.3.5 Support and Resolutions

The platform offers mechanisms for dispute resolution and customer support to address issues such as order discrepancies, delivery delays, or product quality concerns therefore, buyers can escalate unresolved issues through the platform, and dedicated support teams work to resolve disputes in a fair and timely manner.

Figure 9. One-year ONDC journey (Economic Times, 2024)

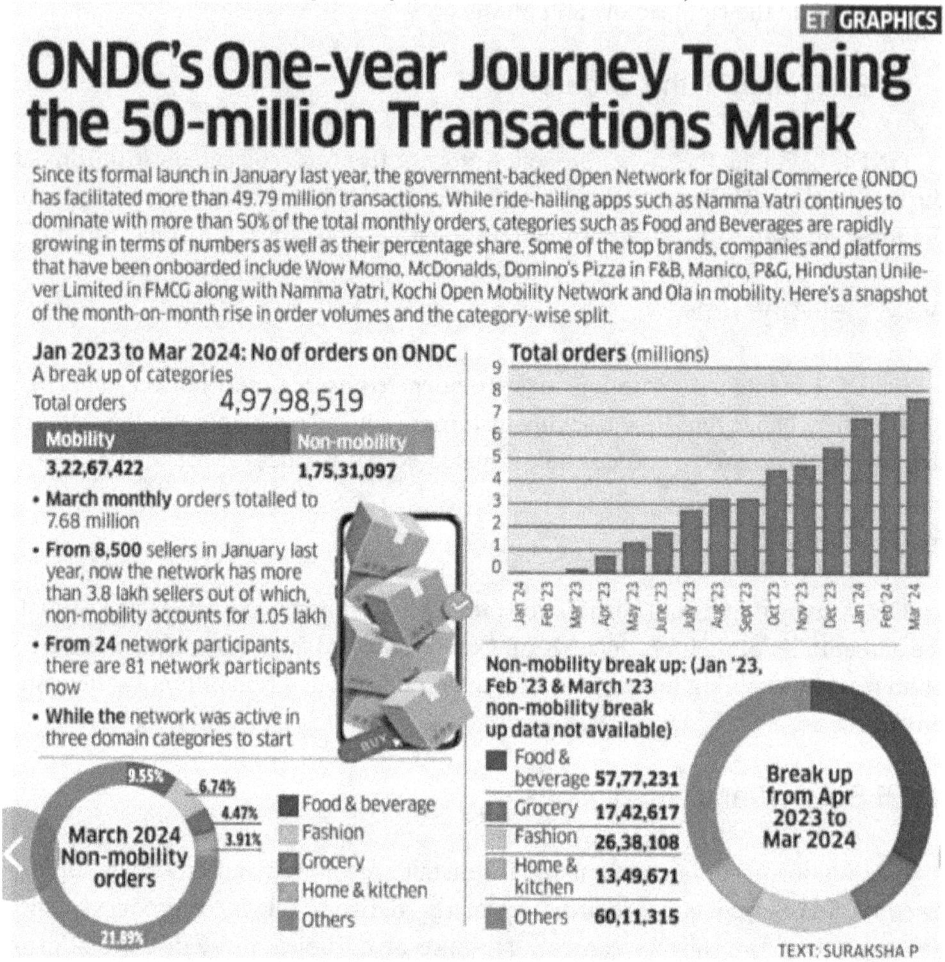

ONDC provides a streamlined onboarding process for MSME sellers, offering user-friendly interfaces and clear guidance to register and set up their accounts on the platform. Therefore, many challenges faced by MSMEs can be overcome with this solution. The platform may include self-service tools, tutorials, and documentation to assist sellers in uploading their catalog, setting up payment methods, and configuring shipping options efficiently. Once onboarded, sellers can easily upload their product catalogs to the ONDC platform, ensuring visibility to potential buyers. Its robust search and filtering capabilities, allowing buyers to discover products based on various criteria such as category, price range, brand, or seller ratings. Sellers' profiles and product catalogs are prominently displayed on the ONDC platform, providing buyers with comprehensive information about the sellers and their offerings.

Buyers can access detailed seller profiles, including seller ratings, reviews, and contact information, to make informed purchasing decisions. ONDC also facilitates the tracking and management of seller returns through integrated systems that allow sellers to process return requests and manage inventory adjustments. This platform can provide dashboards and reports for sellers to monitor return trends, track return shipments, and reconcile inventory levels according. One of major challenge faced by MSMEs are discrepancies during transactions through online. ONDCs payment reconciliation features to ensure transparency and accuracy in financial transactions between buyers, sellers, and payment service providers. Automated reconciliation processes reconcile payments with corresponding orders, facilitating accurate accounting and financial reporting for sellers. By addressing these aspects, ONDC streamlines the onboarding process for sellers, enhances catalog visibility, fosters transparency in seller-buyer interactions, facilitates returns management, and ensures accurate payments reconciliation, thereby contributing to a seamless and efficient digital commerce ecosystem.

REFERENCES

Goyal, T. M. (2022). *MSMEs Go Digital. India Council for Research on International Economic Relations*. ICRIER.

Hossain, M. (2020). Frugal innovation: Conception, development, diffusion, and outcome. *Journal of Cleaner Production*, *262*, 121456. DOI: 10.1016/j.jclepro.2020.121456

Hossain, M. (2021). Frugal innovation and sustainable business models. *Technology in Society*, *64*, 101508. DOI: 10.1016/j.techsoc.2020.101508

Kalaari Capital. (2024). Frictionless Digital Commerce.

Hafkin, N. J., & Taggart, N. (2001). *Gender, information technology, and developing countries: An analytic study. Office of Women in Development, Bureau for Global Programs, Field Support and Research*. United States Agency for International Development.

Reniati, R., Yusnita, M., & Purwasih, R. (2022, July). MSMEs Scale Up Model Post Next Normal through Frugal Innovation, Transformational Leadership, Blue Ocean Strategy and Government Policies. In ICSST 2021: Proceedings of the 1st International Conference on Social, Science, and Technology, ICSST 2021, 25 November 2021, Tangerang, Indonesia (Vol. 428). European Alliance for Innovation.

Calderon-Monge, E., & Ribeiro-Soriano, D. (2024). The role of digitalization in business and management: A systematic literature review. *Review of Managerial Science*, *18*(2), 449–491.

Eze, S. C., Chinedu-Eze, V. C., & Bello, A. O. (2018). The utilisation of e-learning facilities in the educational delivery system of Nigeria: A study of M-University. *International Journal of Educational Technology in Higher Education*, *15*(1), 1–20.

Suraksha, P. (2024). *ONDC's one-year journey touching the 50-million transactions mark*. Economic Times.

Teubner, R. A., & Stockhinger, J. (2020). Literature review: Understanding information systems strategy in the digital era. *The Journal of Strategic Information Systems*, *29*(4), 101642. DOI: 10.1016/j.jsis.2020.101642

UNESCO, I. (2009). Guide to measuring information and communication technologies (ICT) in education.

KEY TERMS AND DEFINITIONS

Frugal Innovation: Frugal innovation is the process of designing affordable, simple, and resource-efficient solutions to meet the needs of underserved or low-income populations, particularly in developing economies. It emphasizes affordability, simplicity, and the use of minimal resources by repurposing existing materials and focusing on essential functionalities. Frugal innovations are often scalable and adaptable to different contexts, addressing specific constraints such as limited financial resources and infrastructure. Examples include low-cost medical devices, affordable transportation options like the Tata Nano car, and locally made water filters, which demonstrate how innovation can thrive under constraints by delivering effective and sustainable solutions.

Digitalisation: Digitalization is the process of integrating digital technologies into various aspects of an organization, industry, or society to improve efficiency, enhance customer experiences, and create new opportunities. It involves transforming traditional processes, products, and services into digital formats, enabling more seamless data sharing, automation, and connectivity. Digitalization often leads to innovations in business models, the development of new digital services, and the creation of more data-driven decision-making processes, ultimately fostering greater agility and competitiveness in the digital age.

ICT Adoption: ICT adoption refers to the process by which individuals, organizations, or societies begin to use information and communication technologies (ICT) to improve operations, communication, and decision-making. This adoption involves integrating tools such as computers, software, the internet, and mobile technologies into everyday activities to enhance efficiency, productivity, and accessibility of information. Successful ICT adoption often requires changes in behavior, processes, and infrastructure, and it can lead to significant improvements in organizational performance, economic growth, and social development.

MSME: MSME stands for Micro, Small, and Medium Enterprises. These are businesses that are defined by their size, typically in terms of the number of employees, annual turnover, or investment in equipment and machinery. MSMEs are crucial for economic development as they contribute significantly to employment, innovation, and GDP in many countries. They are often more flexible and can adapt quickly to market changes, making them important drivers of economic growth and social development. The specific criteria for what constitute a micro, small, or medium enterprise can vary by country.

ONDC: ONDC, or the Open Network for Digital Commerce, is an initiative by the Government of India to create an open, interoperable, and decentralized network for e-commerce. The goal of ONDC is to democratize digital commerce by enabling small and medium enterprises, local stores, and consumers to connect and transact directly through an open digital platform, independent of large e-commerce marketplaces. By standardizing protocols and enabling interoperability between different digital platforms, ONDC aims to reduce the dominance of major e-commerce players, foster greater competition, enhance consumer choice, and support small businesses by giving them easier access to digital markets.

Frugal Digitalisation: Frugal digitalization refers to the adoption and implementation of digital technologies in a cost-effective, resource-efficient, and accessible manner, particularly in environments with limited resources or budgets. This approach focuses on using affordable, simple, and scalable digital solutions to meet specific needs without overcomplicating or over-investing in technology. Frugal digitalization aims to maximize impact by prioritizing essential functionalities, leveraging existing infrastructure, and minimizing costs, making digital transformation accessible to small businesses, startups, and organizations in developing regions. This concept aligns with the principles of frugal innovation, emphasizing practicality, affordability, and inclusivity in the digital era.

Digital Transformation: Digital transformation is the process of using digital technologies to fundamentally change how organizations operate, deliver value to customers, and adapt to market demands. It involves a strategic shift from traditional ways of doing business to more agile, data-driven, and technology-enabled approaches. Digital transformation can encompass various aspects, including automating processes, improving customer experiences, leveraging big data and analytics, enhancing digital communication, and developing new digital products and services. The goal is to increase efficiency, foster innovation, and create a more flexible and responsive organization that can thrive in an increasingly digital world.

Chapter 7
Driving Change:
Frugal Innovation in Rural Entrepreneurship in India

Siddharth Misra
XIM University, Harirajpur, India

Subhajit Bhattacharya
https://orcid.org/0000-0001-6460-0206
XIM University, Harirajpur, India

ABSTRACT

This chapter delves into frugal innovation in rural Indian entrepreneurship, tracing its roots, principles, and applications. Through qualitative research, it explores how frugal solutions, inspired by the Indian concept of jugaad, address social and economic challenges. Findings illustrate how these innovations improve access, productivity, and sustainability in sectors like healthcare, agriculture, and education. Collaboration among stakeholders is highlighted as vital for scaling these initiatives and promoting inclusive rural development.

FRUGAL INNOVATION: ORIGINS AND PRINCIPLES

Frugal innovation, firmly rooted in the Indian setting, stems from the frequent usage of jugaad, a Hindi phrase that implies "an innovative fix" or "an improvised solution" (Rao, 2023). Jugaad is profoundly embedded in Indian culture, where people have long depended on their ingenuity, innovation, and fast thinking to handle obstacles in their everyday life (Govindrajan & Trimble, 2012). Jugaad is a process that demonstrates the Indian idea of making the most of existing resourc-

DOI: 10.4018/979-8-3693-4050-9.ch007

es, whether it's via mending damaged equipment with homemade components or recycling abandoned materials.

India has always confronted issues with restricted funds and severe socio-economic inequality, forcing the creation of creative and cost-effective solutions to fulfill urgent needs. In remote places, residents may not always have availability of modern comforts. They have produced new solutions by using their existing resources and experience. These solutions are developed to satisfy the distinct needs of their communities. Countless new solutions have evolved in industries like as agriculture, healthcare, energy, and education because to this grassroots approach to development.

Principles of Frugal Innovation from an Indian Perspective

There are numerous essential qualities that play a role in the success of frugal innovation in India, determining its strategy and results:

Accessibility: Frugal innovation emphasizes the creation of solutions that can be conveniently accessible by a broad variety of consumers, especially those in resource-constrained contexts (Prahalad & Mashelkar, 2010). Experienced innovators ensure that their ideas may be readily accepted and executed by communities with varied socio-economic backgrounds by leveraging resources and methodologies that are locally available.

Simplicity: Emphasizing the value of simplicity in both design and execution is a major part of frugal innovation. It highlights the need of practical solutions that are straightforward to understand, employ, and maintain (Zeschky et al., 2011). Experienced innovators ensure that their solutions are easy and user-friendly, particularly in locations with limited resources and minimum training or infrastructure.

Affordability: Frugal innovation focuses making ideas inexpensive for the target community, guaranteeing that they are within their financial capabilities (Radjaou & Prabhu, 2015). Efficient innovators focus cost reduction while retaining high quality and performance, ensuring that their solutions are affordable to low-income families and underprivileged populations.

Sustainability: Sustainability is a vital feature of frugal innovation. Our key emphasis is to guarantee that the solutions we create have good benefits on both the environment and society in the long run (Bound & Thornton, 2012). Those that emphasize sustainability respect ecologically friendly behaviors and technology. They focus creating solutions that encourage equality in society and support economic progress.

The notion of frugal innovation in India is heavily impacted by the cultural philosophy of jugaad. The principles of this strategy stress accessibility, affordability, simplicity, and sustainability in tackling the socio-economic difficulties faced by the nation. India is adopting frugal innovation as a strategy for inclusive development. These ideals will continue to be vital in influencing the future of innovation in the nation.

Recent Trends

India has experienced a considerable growth in frugal invention, popularly referred to as jugaad innovation, in recent years. This form of innovation is spurred by the quest for cost-effective solutions in light of resource restrictions (McCormac et al., 2022). Frugal innovation is known for its potential to produce cost-effective solutions with minimal resources. It is typically driven by need and creativity (Yela Aranega et al., 2019). The strategy outlined in the article highlights the significance of producing something that is readily accessible, economical, easy, and sustainable. These ideas are generally regarded as the cornerstone, as mentioned by Wisniewska and Rocniewska (2017). India is now battling with a variety of socio-economic difficulties, and in response, the relevance of frugal innovation has expanded enormously. Frugal innovation facilitates the effective solutions of urgent issues by using current resources and harnessing global experience (Legood et al., 2022).

India is a country that offers a diverse tapestry of people and noticeable disparities in income and resource availability. This provides an atmosphere where inexpensive innovation may flourish. Recent studies have revealed that frugal innovation has led to great development in several areas in India.

Healthcare has undergone incredible improvements that are considerably assisting persons with limited availability of medical treatments. These offers comprise cost-effective medical gadgets, mobile health solutions, and telemedicine systems. These innovations have extended healthcare access for millions of persons who were previously underserved (McCormac et al., 2022). There have been amazing projects in agriculture that have considerably benefited small-scale farmers in boosting production and adjusting to climate change. For instance, the introduction of cost-effective drip irrigation systems, solar-powered agricultural equipment, and cutting-edge crop management approaches have showed considerable advantages (Yela Aranega et al., 2019).

The employment of cost-effective digital learning platforms, educational initiatives led by the community, and creative teaching techniques has expanded the ability of high-quality education in underprivileged and distant regions (Wisniewska & Roczniewska, 2017). Frugal technologies such as solar lamps, biogas digesters, and localized renewable energy systems have had a huge beneficial influence on rural electrification and have helped minimize our dependency on fossil fuels in sustainable energy (Legood et al., 2022).

This chapter shows the transformational effect of frugal innovation via a set of case stories from India. This chapter analyzes how frugal innovation is promoting sustainable development and tackling socio-economic concerns in India via real-world examples from diverse industries. The chapter extensively investigates these situations, giving in-depth analysis and debate to explain the progress, capacity building, and long-term development in India and abroad.

THEORY OF FRUGAL INNOVATION IN RURAL ENTREPRENEURSHIP

The notion of frugal innovation in rural entrepreneurship dives into the concept of creating cost-effective solutions to handle the requirements and obstacles experienced by entrepreneurs in rural regions.

The notion of frugal innovation in rural entrepreneurship highlights the significance of producing economical, adaptable, and eco-friendly solutions to solve the issues experienced in rural regions with limited resources. The philosophy of frugal innovation highlights the necessity of creative thinking and resourcefulness for organizations with limited resources. It underscores the necessity to make the most of what they have and successfully address the demands of their target market (Govindarajan & Trimble, 2012). This strategy combines technology and expertise from the local community and existing infrastructure to aid neglected groups.

The idea of frugal innovation theory is built on the belief that goods and services should be made to be accessible, inexpensive, and simple. Practical inventors prefer easy and cost-effective solutions over-elaborate and pricey ones. This method helps businesses to increase their reach to a bigger audience for their services (Zeschky et al., 2011).

The idea underlines the significance of customizing innovations to fit specific demands and limits of rural populations in India. This requires taking into consideration issues such as their low buying power, constrained access to infrastructure, and specific socio-economic dynamics (Prahalad & Meshelkar, 2010).

Furthermore, the idea of frugal innovation stresses the necessity of incorporating all personnel in the innovation process. As to Bhatti & Ventresca (2012), it is vital for entrepreneurs to include end consumers in the design and development process. This is vital because it allows the creation of solutions that properly fit the demands of the target market and communicate with them. When the community is involved in this process, it amplifies the relevance and efficacy of the invention. It further aids to developing a sense of empowerment and ownership among the persons engaged.

In addition, the notion of frugal innovation understands the need of sustainability and scalability in order to generate enduring effects. It is crucial for solutions to be accessible and cost-effective, as well as adaptable and sustainable in the long term (Govindranjan & Trimble, 2012). Entrepreneurs should evaluate numerous issues, such as the environmental effect, replicability, and adaptability of their ideas. This will assist guarantee that their goods are able for adjusting to evolving market circumstances and have a beneficial influence on society as a whole.

A modest approach to innovation in rural business requires developing an inclusive and practical perspective. It promotes cost efficiency, sustainability, and simplicity. Entrepreneurs has the skills to offer creative solutions that suit to the special needs of rural communities. They may do this by exploiting local resources, skills, and technology to make an important contribution to society and generate economic progress. Through active involvement with end users and an emphasis on scalability, professionals may have a big influence and support inclusive development in rural India and other locations.

SIGNIFICANCE OF FRUGAL INNOVATION IN RURAL ENTREPRENEURSHIP

To successfully foster rural entrepreneurship in India, it is vital to develop cost-effective solutions that directly satisfy the wants of the rural people. This needs cost-effective innovation (Basu & Roy, 2018). As stated by Moreno et al. (2022), it helps enterprises to navigate around resource limits and provide goods and services adapted to the local market. As to the study done by Mucci and Karau (2020), empowering people and giving them with opportunity to better their lives may result in holistic development with a focus on cost-effective innovation. Rural communities have the possibility to realize their full potential and move towards sustainable growth by actively engaging in frugal entrepreneurship (Vierikko et al., 2024).

Relevant Research and Innovation in the Field

There is a notion known as "jugaad innovation" that applies to creative and adaptable solutions that come from the local community (Rao, 2013). Jugaad invention is typically the outcome of need, creativity, and inventiveness, rather than being directed by conventional research and development. Jugaad innovations are highly recognized for their ability to deliver practical, cheap, and culturally relevant solutions by using existing connections and resources. These technologies have demonstrated their worth in different fields, including transportation, communication, energy, health, education, and agriculture. There have been noteworthy instances of revolutionary goods that have had a large beneficial influence. One such example is the Jaipur Foot, a prosthetic limb that is not only inexpensive but also gives those with disabilities with greater mobility and a feeling of pride. Another example is the MittoCool refrigerator, which employs unique clay-based cooling technology to successfully preserve food without depending on power. Finally, there is the ChotuKool, a portable refrigerator that functions on batteries and supports rural communities in keeping perishable food (Radjou et al., 2012).

Nevertheless, jugaad invention does have its limits. There are various crucial elements to consider, such as sustainability, scalability, quality, and dependability. Due to recent advances, there has been a trend towards a more systematic and purposeful approach in innovation. The emphasis is now on making items that are of excellent quality, inexpensive, and widely available. These items have the ability to stimulate development and bring about beneficial shifts in society and the environment. Several variables impact frugal innovation in India. These factors involve the changing requirements and preferences of individuals in rural and urban regions, technological advancements, and the availability of skilled workforce, government initiatives, and collaborations among various entities such as businesses, NGOs, communities, social entrepreneurs, and educational institutions (Bound & Thornton, 2012).

Frugal innovation is altering the way rural entrepreneurship functions in India, bringing innovative possibilities and value propositions for rural communities. Based on a research done by Ahmad et al. (2014), rural entrepreneurship entails the construction and management of firms that contribute to the social and economic development of rural areas. Rural businesses experience a number of hurdles, including poor infrastructure, restricted market access, financial limits, educational impediments, socio-cultural complications, and environmental limitations. Offering rural firms with cost-effective and adaptable solutions that are suited to their individual needs and conditions may aid them in surmounting problems. Through the development of their abilities, self-assurance, and competitiveness, rural entrepreneurs stand to gain significant influence from frugal innovation. Additionally, it aims to improve the community's social and environmental circumstances.

In this study, we'll look at actual cases of people and businesses in rural India that have created affordable solutions for a range of industries. India's rural entrepreneurship has greatly benefited from these solutions, and we'll explore how this innovative, low-cost idea is bringing about a revolutionary shift.

Healthcare: The healthcare industry is critical, particularly in underprivileged places like rural India. It poses particular difficulties that call for skill and close attention. The availability and demand of high-quality, reasonably priced healthcare goods and services differ significantly. Using frugal innovation to solve this issue is a great idea. It provides rural business owners with affordable, useful, and scalable solutions that improve the health and well-being of their communities. Dr. Govindappa Venkataswamy's social venture, Aravind Eye Care System, has revolutionized the provision of eye care in rural India. Millions of patients, especially those who are economically disadvantaged and visually handicapped, may get high-quality and reasonably priced eye procedures because of its economical business strategy, which takes advantage of economies of scale, cross-subsidization, and process innovation. Aravind Eye Care System has created a vision center network, which consists of independent rural business owners. Through telemedicine and mobile technologies, these centers provide basic eye care treatments and referrals to remote areas (Rangan, 2007). Another example is Embrace, a social company that has developed an inexpensive baby warmer that may save the lives of preterm and low-birth-weight newborns in rural areas by avoiding hypothermia. Infant warmers are sold and rented to families and rural health professionals by Embrace, which has educated and equipped these women entrepreneurs. They are called Embrace Nest Distributors. Concerning mother and child health concerns, they also provide education and awareness (Embrace, 2019).

Agriculture: For the majority of India's rural people, agriculture serves as their main source of income and way of life. Nevertheless, low productivity, high input prices, poor market linkages, climate change, and pest and disease outbreaks are only a few of the difficulties faced by India's rural agriculture. By providing rural entrepreneurs with effective and long-lasting solutions to increase the productivity, profitability, and resilience of agriculture in rural India, frugal innovation may aid in addressing these problems. As an example, Amrita Organic Farming Kit is a low-cost innovation made possible by Amrita SeRVe, a rural development program of Amrita Vishwa Vidyapeetham, a university located in Kerala. This package contains organic farming inputs that improve soil health, crop productivity, and agricultural produce quality in rural areas, such as bio-fertilizers, bio-pesticides, and bio-stimulants. A committed group of rural women business owners, Amrita has provided training and assistance to the Amrita Organic Farming Ambassadors. other farmers in their communities, but they also produce and sell organic farming supplies (Amrita SeRVe, 2019). Here's another example I'd like to share with you. It comes from Kheyti, a social company that created the reasonable Greenhouse-in-a-Box. Smallholder farmers in isolated regions can grow profitable crops all year round, thanks to this elegant and adaptable greenhouse, regardless of the weather. Kheyti has created a group of rural business owners called Kheyti Saathis. These individuals serve as local distributors and partners for the greenhouses. In addition, they offer farmers guidance and support in managing their crops, ensuring quality, and connecting them to markets. (Kheyti, 2019)

Energy: There are millions of people who face challenges in accessing clean cooking fuels and reliable, affordable power in rural India. Although energy is essential in many fields, its availability is limited. The energy demands of rural India may be satisfied by creative and reasonably priced technologies that provide decentralized, economical, and ecologically friendly ways to produce and distribute clean energy to rural homes and businesses. Harish Hande developed SELCO, which has become a major participant in the market for solar energy solutions in rural India. They provide a wide variety of services, such as customized designs, adaptable payment plans, on-site installation, and continuing assistance. In addition to giving communities access to energy, SELCO helps rural business owners launch and grow their own enterprises. These business owners include those who own solar stores, provide solar services, and are specialists in solar technology (SELCO, 2019). Here's another illustration: An innovative and efficient alternative known as the mini-grid has been created by Husk Power Systems, a social company. This power plant's goal is to effectively provide energy to isolated communities by fueling it with rice husk, a leftover from rice milling. Husk Power Operators are a group of rural company owners that Husk Power Systems has organized. In addition to owning and operating the mini-grids, the operators are also accountable for collecting money from customers who pay a small price for the electricity (Husk electricity Systems, 2019).

Education: India's rural populations place a great value on education, especially in areas where access to high-quality education is scarce. Through the provision of economical and effective solutions to rural entrepreneurs, frugal innovation may significantly enhance educational opportunities and results in rural India. These remedies might improve instruction and learning in schools and rural communities. For example, Pratham, a non-governmental organization committed to raising educational standards in India, created the novel teaching strategy known as Teaching at the Right Level (TaRL). Students are not categorized using this instructional technique according to their grade level or age. It groups people based on their educational backgrounds and offers them specialized, practical training based on their specific needs and skills. Pratham has provided education and support to community organizers, leaders in the area, and Pratham volunteers—many of whom are small-town business owners. These people play a crucial role in fostering a supportive learning environment by collaborating with educators and parents. They are also responsible for putting the TaRL approach into practice and making sure it is successfully implemented in isolated communities and educational institutions (Pratham, 2019). Peer Instruction is an inventive and reasonably priced solution created by Avanti, a social solutions firm. Under this learning technique, students' conceptual knowledge and problem-solving abilities are improved via peer participation and feedback. Rural entrepreneurs, such as the gifted young people from low-income families known as Avanti Fellows, have benefited from coaching and assistance provided by Avanti. These people work as mentors and tutors for pupils in remote villages and schools, according to Avanti (2019). They provide professional guidance and support in locating career opportunities and pursuing further education.

This initiative provides new chances and solutions for the rural people, demonstrating the significant impact of frugal innovation on rural entrepreneurship in India. Finding innovative ways to get around problems and optimize outcomes even in the face of little resources is a sign of resourcefulness. Rural areas might benefit economically and in terms of quality of life from efficient innovation. It gives business owners the ability to design and deliver high-quality, cost-effective solutions that are readily accessible. Furthermore, this helps India achieve its more general objectives of promoting development, sustainability, and inclusion.

Gaps

Even while frugal innovation and rural entrepreneurship are becoming more and more popular, there are still a lot of unanswered questions in the field. Investigating theoretical models that combine frugal innovation, inclusive entrepreneurship, sustainable development, and social innovation. This request makes reference to the study that Kaplinsky and Morris (2001) carried out. More study is needed to understand how ecosystem support, government policies, and institutions may promote frugal innovation and rural entrepreneurship (George et al., 2016). Research that facilitates cooperation between industry, government, and academia is becoming more and more in demand in order to advance knowledge sharing, professional growth, and interaction in the area of frugal innovation (Hargadon & Douglas, 2001).

METHODOLOGY

Through a thorough analysis of the literature, we will investigate the history, tenets, and most recent advancements of frugal innovation in the Indian setting in this chapter. The goal of this project is to provide a thorough compilation of academic journals, books, research papers, and reports on jugaad, inclusive development, and frugal innovation in India. Through a review of pertinent research, this chapter seeks to provide a thorough knowledge of frugal innovation and its potential to address social and economic issues. It offers conceptual information and a theoretical framework to help with this investigation.

The chapter evaluates case studies of frugal innovation in a number of Indian industries, such as renewable energy, healthcare, agriculture, and education, using a professional research methodology. We choose case studies with care, making sure they are relevant, noteworthy, and powerful in demonstrating how inexpensive innovation may lead to revolutionary change. We thoroughly examine every case study to get an in-depth understanding of the background, goals, tactics for execution, results, and lessons discovered.

> **Gathering of Data:** We gather information for the case studies from a variety of sources, such as scholarly journals, official documents from governments, publications from non-governmental organizations, business websites, and news stories. To get insightful firsthand information, one may also make use of primary data sources, such as speaking with important players participating in frugal innovation initiatives via interviews.

In order to analyze the material we have collected, we use qualitative analytical methods including content and theme analysis. A thorough examination of the many uses and outcomes of sensitive innovation in India is given in this chapter. To provide a comprehensive overview, it highlights reoccurring themes, patterns, and discoveries across the case studies.

The outcomes of the case study analysis and literature evaluation are combined and analyzed, and general findings and implications are made for both theory and practice. In-depth investigation and discussion of the critical elements that influence the success of frugal innovation projects in India are covered in this chapter. It also seeks to identify possible directions for further study and advancement.

Case Studies in India

According to Ahmad et al., (2014), entrepreneurship in rural regions entails starting and managing companies that promote the social and economic development of these communities. Based on information from secondary sources, below are some examples of innovative and entrepreneurial projects that have been implemented at a reasonable cost in rural areas around India.

Cases from the Eastern Part of India

Gramophone a social corporation, connects eastern Indian farmers to markets, information, and supplies online. Effective innovation and rural entrepreneurship are shown. Gramophone was created by four top graduates: Nishant Vats Mahatre, Tauseef Khan, Harshit Gupta, and Ashish Rajan Singh. Gramophone is a platform that offers support to over 700,000 farmers residing in 15,000 communities situated in Madhya Pradesh, Bihar, and Odisha. The platform provides farmers with personalized and timely advice related to crop management, disease and pest control, and market linkages, with the help of meteorological data, satellite imaging, and artificial intelligence. Additionally, Gramophone offers competitive pricing, various payment options, and high-quality supplies such as seeds, fertilizers, and insecticides to the farmers, which are delivered right to their doorstep. The platform works towards reducing the risks and costs associated with smallholder farming while increasing their productivity and income. Gramophone organises rural business entrepreneurs as Gramme Mitras. They are paid and rewarded for advocating and facilitating the platform locally.

Gramophone's technology innovation lies in its holistic approach to solving agricultural problems. By integrating real-time expert advisory, a digital marketplace for agricultural inputs, and essential agronomic information into a single platform, it empowers farmers to make informed decisions and enhance their productivity and profitability. This blend of technology and agriculture not only addresses the immediate needs of farmers but also sets a foundation for sustainable agricultural practices in the long run.

Problems and Difficulties Faced by Gramophone

- Farmers face challenges when using digital platforms because of their limited digital literacy.
- The use of the digital platform is being affected by connectivity issues in remote rural areas.
- The resistance from traditional agricultural middlemen to embrace digital platforms poses significant challenges.
- Making sure that smaller farmers can access top-notch inputs and services, regardless of changes in market prices.

Green Agrevolution is a social enterprise that works in eastern India. It offers agritech solutions to farmers and promotes rural entrepreneurship and frugal innovation. Green Agrevolution was established by Abhishek Agarwal, who is both an engineer and a businessman. Green Agrevolution supports over 100,000 farmers across 1,000 communities in the states of Bihar, Jharkhand, and Odisha. Green Agrevolution has facilitated the interaction between farmers and various services and stakeholders, including financial institutions, crop specialists, input suppliers, and market connections, via the creation of the inexpensive digital platform DeHaat. DeHaat is dedicated to reducing the risks and expenses faced by smallholder farmers, while simultaneously enhancing their revenue and productivity. The DeHaat Micro Entrepreneurs are a collective of rural entrepreneurs established by Green Agrevolution. These individuals, mostly young locals, serve as intermediaries and facilitators for the platform. They assist farmers in completing the last leg of their deliveries and provide assistance in return for commissions and other forms of compensation.

Green Agrevolution Private Limited, through its DeHaat platform, exemplifies the transformative potential of technology in agriculture. By integrating advanced data analytics, AI, e-commerce, and financial services, the company provides comprehensive support to farmers, enhancing their productivity and profitability. This innovation not only addresses the immediate challenges faced by farmers but also lays the groundwork for sustainable agricultural development in the future.

PROBLEMS AND DIFFICULTIES FACED BY GREEN AGREVOLUTION

- The low adoption rate of agritech solutions may be attributable to farmers' insufficient awareness of their advantages.
- Infrastructure deficiencies, such as inadequate energy and internet connectivity, are impeding the optimal functioning of digital markets like DeHaat.
- Ensuring the reliability and quality of the inputs provided via the platform, particularly in remote areas with little oversight.
- Establishing credibility and fostering confidence among farmers about the platform and the individuals associated with it.

Cases from the Western Part of India

Ecozen is a social enterprise located in western India that offers solar-powered cold storage and irrigation solutions to farmers. This exemplifies the concept of cost-effective innovation and entrepreneurial activities in rural areas. Ecozen was formed by Devendra Gupta, Prateek Singhal, and Vivek Pandey, all of whom are alumni of IIT Kharagpur. Ecozen provides services to around 25,000 farmers residing in 1,200 villages throughout several states, including Maharashtra, Gujarat, Karnataka, and Andhra Pradesh. Ecozen offers two innovative products: Ecofrost, a portable and customizable cold storage device capable of preserving food for a maximum of 21 days, and Ecotron, a solar-powered pump controller that enhances the performance and efficiency of irrigation pumps. Ecozen is dedicated to reducing agricultural losses, improving farmers' access to markets, and protecting energy and water resources. A network called Ecozeners was founded by entrepreneurs. The primary goals are to supervise the ownership and administration of commodities, provide other farmers with irrigation and cold storage services, and collect and evaluate data about the use and results of the products.

Ecozen's technological innovations, from solar-powered cold storage units to smart irrigation systems, exemplify the transformative potential of technology in agriculture. By focusing on sustainability, efficiency, and data-driven decision-making, Ecozen not only addresses immediate agricultural challenges but also contributes to the long-term resilience and sustainability of the sector.

ECOZEN HAS ENCOUNTERED SEVERAL DIFFICULTIES AND BARRIERS

- The upfront costs of driven irrigation and cold storage systems might make it difficult to expand on a larger scale.
- One of the problems we have is figuring out how to handle the intricate upkeep and repairs of solar-powered machinery in areas where there is a shortage of skilled specialists.
- It is important to make sure that small-scale farmers can use cold storage facilities, especially when they are not producing as much.
- The concerns about the potential damage or theft of solar equipment in remote areas.

Saral Designs is a western Indian firm that focuses in providing menstrual hygiene products to rural women. They are committed to making a constructive contribution to society. This demonstrates how creative and entrepreneurial activities may be implemented in rural regions with great success. Suhani Mohan and Kartik Mehta, both IIT Bombay alums, formed Saral Designs. Over 200,000 women in 2,000 villages in Maharashtra, Gujarat, and Rajasthan are the target audience for Saral Designs. Saral Designs has created a decentralized, very effective method for producing and distributing sanitary pads. To market and sell the items in their communities, they work together with local women. Furthermore, they use highly efficient gear to manufacture ecologically friendly and superior quality pads. Saral Designs is committed to raising awareness and dispelling myths about menstruation in society. Their commitment is on improving the general welfare and dignity of rural women. Saral Designs has provided empowerment and training to the Swachh

Shakti group, which is made up of female rural entrepreneurs. These women play a crucial role in managing the provision of menstrual hygiene supplies and education within their communities, as well as the maintenance of the equipment.

Saral Designs' innovative approach to menstrual hygiene combines advanced and automated production technology with a focus on accessibility, affordability, and sustainability. By providing high-quality, affordable sanitary pads and engaging in extensive outreach and education initiatives, the company addresses a critical need in menstrual health management. Saral Designs' efforts not only improve health outcomes but also contribute to the empowerment and economic development of women in underserved areas.

DIFFICULTIES AND PROBLEMS RELATED TO SARAL DESIGNS

- Promoting a more accepting and compassionate viewpoint on menstruation is essential. We may create a setting where people feel comfortable talking about and handling this innate occurrence by encouraging a more welcoming and tolerant environment. Consequently, this may encourage the use of sanitary pads and other menstrual hygiene supplies.
- One important goal is to make sure that menstrual hygiene products are easily accessible and affordable, especially in remote rural areas.
- We provide comprehensive education on menstrual health to women living in rural areas, with the aim of promoting proper disposal and usage practices.
- We managed to overcome the challenges of distributing the project and made sure that rural customers could easily access it.

Cases Related to Central India

Samagra is a renowned social organization based in Central India. The business highlights its dedication to offering urban slums sanitation solutions, with an emphasis on encouraging rural entrepreneurship and putting creative cost-cutting strategies into practice. Samagra was started by an extremely talented man with an engineering and business background named Swapnil Chaturvedi. Many people living in various slums in many states, including Madhya Pradesh, Chhattisgarh, and Maharashtra, get assistance from Samagra. Samagra is a master in building and maintaining hygienic, reliable, and accessible public bathrooms. As a result, cleanliness has been addressed thoroughly and effectively.

To attract customers to use their restrooms, they also offer additional services such as loyalty programs, Wi-Fi, and mobile phone charging. Samagra is committed to enhancing the physical well-being and hygiene of urban slum dwellers, while also promoting a circular economy and positive environmental outcomes. Samagra has provided training and assistance to Loo-Preneurs, who are individuals responsible for marketing in cities. These individuals are responsible for maintaining and managing the restrooms, as well as collecting input and data on restroom performance and usage.

Samagra Sanitation is at the forefront of technical innovation in the sanitation sector, driving significant improvements in waste management and hygiene practices. Through the integration of advanced technologies and a focus on community-centric solutions, the startup contributes to enhanced public health, environmental sustainability, and quality of life across India.

PROBLEMS AND DIFFICULTIES FACED BY SAMAGRA

- Financial problems with urban slum cleanliness programs, especially in places where the government is not very involved.
- Handling problems related to the local government or the opposition of the community to the use of cutting-edge sanitation methods and developments.
- Eventually, community bathrooms may be made more sustainable by addressing maintenance and cleaning issues.
- Focusing on addressing discrimination and economic inequality in relation to the availability of sanitary services to those living in urban slums.

Svadha is a social enterprise located in central India that offers sanitary solutions to rural households. This exemplifies the concept of cost-effective innovation and entrepreneurial activities in rural areas. Garima Sahai, a graduate of Harvard Management School, founded Svadha. Svadha provides services to over 300,000 families in 3,000 villages located in Chhattisgarh, Odisha, Jharkhand, and Bihar. Svadha's holistic strategy encompasses reuse, waste management, product design, installation, and a deep understanding of the sanitation value chain. Svadha advocates for the improvement of health and hygiene in rural areas, the adoption of circular economy practices, and the promotion of environmental sustainability. Svadha established Svadha Shreepreneurs, a network for rural businesses. These experts locally distribute sanitation products and provide installation and maintenance services for them. Recognition and remuneration are provided for their work.

Svadha is at the forefront of technical innovation in the sanitation sector, combining product innovation with digital tools and community engagement. By providing sustainable and scalable sanitation solutions, Svadha enhances public health, promotes economic development, and improves the quality of life in underserved communities across India.

PROBLEMS AND DIFFICULTIES FACED BY SVADHA

- Promoting knowledge and enthusiasm for sanitation solutions in rural families, particularly in culturally relevant areas, can be a challenging task.
- Surmounting logistical challenges in delivering sanitary products to rural areas with little infrastructure.
- Providing financial assistance or subsidies to guarantee that households with low incomes can get sanitation solutions.
- Tackling waste management and promoting environmental sustainability can be a challenging task, especially in rural regions.

Cases from the Northern Part of India

Frontier Markets exemplifies frugal innovation and rural enterprise in Northern India. As a social venture, it provides renewable energy to rural populations. Ajaita Shah, a Tufts graduate, founded Frontier Markets. Frontier Markets provides services to more than 500,000 families located in 7,000 villages in Rajasthan, Uttar Pradesh, and Bihar. Frontier Markets has meticulously curated a range of solar lights, TVs, fans, home systems, and cookstoves to meet the energy needs of rural clientele and decrease their reliance on kerosene and fossil fuels. Frontier Markets aims to enhance the economic well-being, living standards, and environmental sustainability of rural communities. Solar Sahelis is a network of rural entrepreneurs established by Frontier Markets. These women not only sell and fix sustainable energy equipment, but also teach others about the advantages of using them. They generate income for both their family and themselves via this scheme.

Frontier Markets is pioneering the use of technology and innovative business models to bridge the gap between urban and rural markets by an app called Meramaal and Saral Jeevan Sahelis. By empowering women entrepreneurs and providing access to essential products, the enterprise enhances rural livelihoods, promotes sustainable development, and improves the quality of life in India's underserved communities.

PROBLEMS AND DIFFICULTIES FACED BY FRONTIER MARKETS

- Tackling the issue of limited accessibility to renewable energy products among low-income rural communities.
- Building confidence among rural customers in the effectiveness and durability of renewable energy solutions.

- Tackling distribution obstacles in rural regions with restricted vehicular accessibility and insufficient road infrastructure.
- Providing maintenance and post-purchase assistance for sustainable energy items in remote regions.

Goonj exemplifies frugal innovation and rural entrepreneurship in northern India. This social company provides assistance to rural populations by offering clothes and food. Anshu Gupta, an Ashoka Fellow and social activist, initiated the establishment of Goonj. Goonj provides assistance to over 2 million individuals residing in 4,000 rural communities located in Uttar Pradesh, Uttarakhand, Himachal Pradesh, and Punjab. Goonj engages in the sustainable recycling, sorting, and collection of urban apparel that has been abandoned. Subsequently, the rural populations are provided with these garments to facilitate activities such as tree planting, well excavation, and road construction. Goonj promotes awareness and assistance for societal and ecological concerns while upholding the dignity of rural people. The Goonj Grassroots Fellows provided instruction and assistance to rural entrepreneurs. These community leaders coordinate and implement development initiatives, as well as supervise the distribution of clothing and assess the results.

Goonj exemplifies how technological innovation in recycling and upcycling can transform urban waste into valuable resources for rural communities. Their use of advanced upcycling techniques and digital logistics tools not only mitigates environmental issues but also fosters sustainable development and community empowerment. By bridging the gap between urban waste and rural need, Goonj provides a model for addressing resource scarcity and promoting a circular economy in India.

PROBLEMS AND DIFFICULTIES FACED BY GOONJ

- Ensuring the sustainability of the clothing swap model by addressing concerns related to logistics and supply chain management.
- Collaborating with local authorities and government organizations to support community development initiatives in return for clothing contributions.
- Exploring the challenges surrounding the distribution of recycled garments in rural areas and ensuring their durability and quality.
- Dealing with delicate issues and overcoming cultural obstacles in the distribution and donation of clothing in rural areas.

Cases from the North-Eastern India

Rang De is an incredible social enterprise that provides essential financial services to underserved rural areas in northeastern India. Rural enterprise and thrifty ingenuity are well shown. Ramakrishna NK and Smita, social entrepreneurs and engineers, formed Rang De. Rang De serves around 50,000 borrowers in 500 communities located in Assam, Meghalaya, Manipur, and Tripura. Rang De has created a digital platform that links people who need to borrow money from rural areas with people who are willing to lend money from metropolitan areas. At our company, we provide small loans for a variety of needs, including business, education, healthcare, and agriculture. Our interest rates are reasonable and designed to meet your financial requirements. Rang De's goal is to empower rural communities by making it easier to get loans and reducing the amount of money needed. Rang De Field Partners is a group of business owners who operate in rural areas. The partners, which can be community NGOs or cooperatives, have the responsibility of finding and assessing eligible borrowers. They also handle the process of granting and collecting loan payments. In addition, they offer help and support to borrowers.

Rang De harnesses technology to democratize access to finance, using a digital lending platform and mobile accessibility to connect underserved borrowers with social investors. This innovative approach not only facilitates financial inclusion and economic empowerment but also fosters community development and social impact. Through its technology-driven model, Rang De exemplifies how digital innovation can create a more inclusive and equitable financial system in India.

PROBLEMS AND DIFFICULTIES FACED BY RANG DE

- We aim to improve the financial knowledge of rural borrowers in order to promote responsible borrowing and repayment.
- Addressing the difficulties of repaying and distributing loans in rural areas that have limited access to banking services.
- Focus on enhancing the credibility and transparency of microfinance avnues in order to establish trust within rural communities.
- Striking a delicate balance between financial viability and social impact goals to ensure the sustainability of the microfinance model.

Zizira is dedicated to distributing organic northeastern Indian food as a social enterprise. It demonstrates the effectiveness of innovative rural business solutions. Ralph Budelman is the creator of Zizira, a successful venture born out of his entrepreneurial spirit and commitment to making a positive impact. Zizira proudly serves a diverse community of over 5,000 individuals, both locally and globally, from the beautiful region of Meghalaya. You can find a wide range of spices, herbs, honey, tea, and coffee sourced from the biodiverse soils of Meghalaya at Zizira. Our articles undergo minimal processing and packaging to guarantee top-notch quality. Zizira is committed to ensuring the well-being of consumers and safeguarding the natural and cultural heritage of the area. Zizira Farmers comprises a network of enterprising individuals from small towns. These producers specialise in cultivating and selling organic food. In order to guarantee fair and consistent payment for their crops, farmers are provided with instruction on organic and sustainable farming.

Zizira leverages technology through its e-commerce platform and advanced supply chain management tools to bridge the gap between farmers in the North East of India and broader markets. This technological innovation not only enhances market access and income for farmers but also promotes sustainable agriculture and the conservation of indigenous crops. Zizira's model exemplifies how digital solutions can transform agricultural supply chains, fostering economic empowerment and environmental sustainability.

PROBLEMS AND DIFFICULTIES FACED BY ZIZIRA

- Persistently advocating for the preservation of natural and organic agricultural methods in the face of environmental degradation and climate change can be a challenging task.
- Transporting organic food from rural to urban areas is a challenging task.
- Establishing customer confidence in the excellence and genuineness of natural and organic food products, while also increasing brand recognition.
- Focusing on the certification requirements and legal obstacles that impact the production and distribution of organic products.

Cases from the Southern India

Barefoot College is a remarkable social organization dedicated to educating and empowering women in rural areas of southern India. This exemplifies the concept of cost-effective innovation and entrepreneurial endeavors in rural areas. Barefoot College was founded by Bunker Roy, a passionate social activist and educator. Barefoot College provides assistance to nearly 2 million individuals in over 1,300 villages across various regions, such as Rajasthan, Andhra Pradesh, Karnataka, and Tamil Nadu. Barefoot College provides a cost-effective education that emphasises collaboration, volunteer work, and hands-on learning. Barefoot College is dedicated to creating self-sustaining and environmentally conscious rural communities, with the aim of combating poverty, gender inequality, and environmental degradation. Rural girls who have been trained and supported by Barefoot College are now successful commercial enterprise proprietors known as Barefoot Solar Engineers. These girls, who may not have had access to formal education, learn how to set up, operate, and repair solar lighting systems in their communities, providing affordable and clean energy.

Barefoot College exemplifies the transformative power of technology in rural development through its innovative use of solar energy and water management systems. By training rural women as solar engineers and community leaders, the organization not only brings sustainable solutions to energy and water challenges but also empowers communities and fosters gender equality. This technological innovation in renewable energy and water conservation highlights the potential for grassroots-level change and sustainable development in underserved areas.

PROBLEMS AND DIFFICULTIES FACED BY BAREFOOT COLLEGE

- Assist rural women who may face difficulties in understanding solar engineering due to illiteracy or lack of proper education.
- To encourage women to pursue careers in non-traditional industries such as sun engineering, if it is important to address cultural limitations.
- Securing a favorable price range and sufficient resources to expand Barefoot College's programs and provide education to additional girls from remote areas as Barefoot Solar Engineers.
- It's challenging to help Barefoot Solar Engineers gain access to local marketplaces to offer their solar lighting products and services while promoting sustainability and revenue growth.

S4S Technologies is a remarkable social enterprise from southern India that specializes in providing solar dehydration solutions to farmers and women. It exemplifies frugal innovation and rural entrepreneurship. S4S Technologies assists over 10,000 farmers and women residing in 500 villages across the states of Karnataka, Tamil Nadu, and Kerala. The Solar Conduction Dryer is a ground-breaking innovation by S4S Technologies. This device is highly efficient, reasonably priced, and requires minimal maintenance. Using the power of the sun, this innovative method preserves the freshness and nutritional benefits of fruits, vegetables, and herbs by removing their moisture. S4S Technologies is dedicated to minimizing harvest losses; increasing income for farmers, and women, and establishing a circular as well as a sustainable food system. S4S Technologies not only provides dehydrating services and commodities but also supports and empowers rural women entrepreneurs called Solar Sahelis. These women own and operate dryers, and play a crucial role in providing their communities with access to markets and finance.

S4S Technologies showcases the transformative potential of technological innovation in agriculture through its solar-powered dehydration units and digital platform for market access. By reducing food waste, enhancing food security, and empowering rural women, S4S Technologies provides a sustainable and scalable solution to some of the critical challenges faced by the agricultural sector. This innovative approach not only improves the livelihoods of farmers but also contributes to broader environmental and social goals.

PROBLEMS AND DIFFICULTIES FACED BY S4S TECHNOLOGIES

- It can be quite challenging to educate farmers and women about the potential of solar dehydration technology in reducing post-harvest losses and increasing earnings.
- It can be quite challenging to educate rural women entrepreneurs (Solar Sahelis) on the best practices for operating and maintaining Solar Conduction Dryers to ensure their long-lasting durability and optimal performance.
- Financial challenges faced by rural women business owners in acquiring and utilizing solar-conduction dryers, as well as accessing viable loans or micro-loans, can be quite daunting.
- Establishing robust business partnerships to expand Solar Sahelis' dehydrated food product market while simultaneously enhancing sustainability and income can be quite challenging.
- Tackling infrastructure challenges such as unreliable energy or limited storage facilities is essential for enhancing the efficiency of solar dehydration systems, which is no easy task.
- It can be quite a challenging task to ensure the safety and quality of solar-powered dryer-processed dehydrated food items in order to meet the needs of consumers and adhere to market standards.

ENTREPRENEURS OFTEN ENCOUNTER A RANGE OF CHALLENGES WHEN IT COMES TO EMPOWERING RURAL COMMUNITIES IN INDIA THROUGH FRUGAL INNOVATION

After analyzing the cases as we discussed earlier, it is clear that rural entrepreneurs are crucial in enhancing the existence of people living in rural areas and poorer neighborhoods in India, even though they face many challenges. The development and sustainability of the business model are hindered by these barriers, which in turn influence an opportunity for an enjoyable entrepreneurial journey and the aid supplied to rural areas. Here is a summary of the challenges and obstacles that rural entrepreneurs in India encounter.

There is a Lack of Resources and Infrastructure Available

The adoption and expansion of frugal innovation are often limited by a lack of resources, including raw materials, technology, and capital. Infrastructure issues like inconsistent electricity, limited mobility, and limited storage facilities make it difficult to provide successful service delivery.

i. One of the challenges is the lack of technical knowledge and skills development:

- We provide a wide range of training and skill-building opportunities to help rural entrepreneurs effectively manage new solutions and empower them in their businesses.
- We focus on enhancing literacy and education, with a special focus on empowering women. My goal is to promote a deeper understanding of technical skills and inspire entrepreneurship.

ii. Other challenges faced by rural communities is the lack of market access and awareness:

- It is important to inform these communities about cost-effective innovations that can be beneficial to them, in order to encourage greater adoption and utilization.
- Our goal is to create strong distribution and market connections that make it easier for people to access goods and services. By doing so, we aim to improve income and ensure the long-term success of our business.

iii. Overcoming Social and Cultural Barriers:

- Tackling cultural and gender norms that can limit women's choices in non-traditional or entrepreneurial careers.
- Overcome cultural barriers and societal misconceptions to promote the widespread acceptance and utilization of goods and services, including menstrual hygiene solutions.

iv. Financial Inclusion and Access to Finance:

- Providing rural company owners with access to affordable financing options or micro-loans to support their investments and business expansion.
- Tackling the financial obstacles that hinder consumers and businesses from accessing and acquiring cutting-edge solutions.
- Ensuring the safety and quality of goods and services in sectors such as healthcare, agriculture, and sanitation to meet consumer needs and market requirements is of utmost importance.
- Implementing certifications and quality control procedures to instill confidence and trust among stakeholders and customers.

v. Promoting Environmental Sustainability:

- Promote the use of sustainable methods such as solar-powered equipment and organic agriculture to minimize environmental impact and conserve natural resources.
- Managing recycling and waste for a circular economy and sustainable environment.
- Encouraging active involvement and participation of the community in creating, implementing, and maintaining low-cost innovations to ensure their value and long-term sustainability.
- Enabling local communities to become drivers of change and entrepreneurship, with a special emphasis on women and marginalized groups.

POLICY INTERVENTION, INFRASTRUCTURE SUPPORT, AND FUTURE OPPORTUNITIES

India encompasses several areas of frugal innovation and rural entrepreneurship, such as agricultural technology, renewable energy, sanitation, microfinance, and natural commodities. Legislative support, infrastructure development, sustainability, and collaboration are necessary to address the potential and problems in each subject area.

Gramophone and Green Agrevolution collaborate to enhance smallholder farmers' productivity and market reach by integrating Agritech solutions and digital platforms. In order to promote sustainability within this industry, it is crucial to prioritise community ownership and involvement, enabling farmers to actively engage in technology-driven solutions. The endorsement of such efforts is important from both federal and state governments. The Rashtriya Krishi Vikas Yojana (RKVY) and Pradhan Mantri Krishi Sinchayee Yojana (PMKSY) promote agricultural innovation and water management via financial support and specialised knowledge (Government of India, n.d.). Farmers are required to submit applications for these programmes to government organisations, which necessitates the provision of documents and evidence. To fully use the capabilities of agricultural technology, it is necessary to enhance the digital connectivity and logistical infrastructure in rural areas. Governmental entities, digital corporations, and agricultural cooperatives have the potential to work together in order to create and implement solutions that meet the specific needs of different regions, while also promoting the progress of rural development and the adoption of sustainable farming practices.

Barefoot College and Frontier Markets are using solar-powered solutions and clean energy products to tackle the issue of energy accessibility in rural areas within the renewable energy industry. To prioritise sustainability in this business, it is essential to adopt a community-centric strategy that involves the participation of local residents in the installation, upkeep, and functioning of solar systems. State and federal policy support is crucial for facilitating the transition to renewable energy sources. The Pradhan Mantri Sahaj Bijli Har Ghar Yojana, commonly known as the Saubhagya Scheme, is a programme that specifically targets solar energy to ensure that every rural household has access to electrical connections (Government of India, n.d.). In order to be eligible for these programmes, rural households must submit their applications via specific channels established by state electricity boards or implementing agencies. The long-term sustainability of renewable energy projects relies on enhancing the connection of the last stretch and allocating resources to decentralised energy systems to provide electricity to rural areas. Collaboration between energy corporations, financial institutions, and community organisations may enhance the availability of clean energy technologies and services, ultimately promoting rural development and sustainable energy access.

Samagra and Svadha are implementing new strategies in the sanitation sector to ensure that safe and hygienic sanitation facilities are accessible in both rural and urban areas. Achieving sustainability in this domain requires altering behaviour and engaging the community, with a focus on community-led sanitation initiatives and education on hygiene. Two methods in which the federal and state governments may provide assistance are by implementing regulations to encourage effective waste management and by facilitating funding for sanitation projects. Initiatives such as the Swachh Bharat Mission (SBM) provide monetary rewards for the building of toilets and encourage changes in behaviour to attain widespread access to sanitation and eliminate open defecation (Government of India, n.d.). In order to take part in such projects, it is sometimes necessary to submit applications via local government agencies or specific implementing organisations. Investments in water distribution systems, waste treatment facilities, and public bathrooms are crucial in order to address the lack of sanitary infrastructure. The collaboration of sanitation agencies, local governments, and social entrepreneurs offers a chance to combine resources and experience in providing sustainable sanitation solutions that are both environmentally friendly and beneficial to public health.

Within the microfinance industry, Microfinance programmes such as Rang De provide affordable and easily accessible funding to rural entrepreneurs and disadvantaged populations in the sector. Financial literacy and responsible borrowing habits are crucial for achieving sustainability in this field. These practices empower borrowers to effectively manage their finances. Microfinance firms may enhance their transparency and safeguard consumers by receiving support from both federal and state laws. The National Rural Livelihood Mission (NRLM), together with self-help organisations and microfinance institutions, strives to promote financial inclusion and offer livelihood support to rural households (Government of India, n.d.). In order to participate in these programmes, rural communities must make use of specific channels created by partner organisations or government agencies to access financial services. An effective digital payment and banking infrastructure is essential for enhancing financial inclusion. Government agencies, non-governmental organisations, and microfinance institutions may enhance the financial accessibility and entrepreneurial opportunities for rural communities, therefore empowering them economically and promoting sustainable livelihoods.

Within the realm of natural goods, Zizira supports sustainable agriculture and biodiversity conservation in the natural goods sector by engaging in organic food production and marketing. This firm prioritises regenerative farming and environmental stewardship to save ecosystems and natural resources. Government certification and incentives at the federal and state levels may encourage the use of organic farming. The Paramparagat Krishi Vikas Yojana (PKVY), implemented by the Government of India, encourages and supports organic agricultural practices and certification. These programmes need farmers to submit applications via government agricultural departments or officially recognised certification bodies. Investments in supply chain and market infrastructure are necessary to transport organic commodities to urban markets. Food processing enterprises, organic agricultural cooperatives, and merchants may contribute to the advancement of sustainable food systems and rural livelihoods in order to promote economic development and environmental sustainability.

CONCLUSION

Frugal innovation and rural entrepreneurship have become integral components of India's socio-economic landscape, catalyzing sustainable development across various sectors such as agricultural technology, renewable energy, sanitation, microfinance, and natural commodities. These initiatives are characterized by their ability to provide cost-effective solutions with minimal resources, driven by necessity, creativity, and community participation.

The frugal innovation and rural entrepreneurship in India are driving sustainable development by addressing pressing socio-economic challenges while maximizing resource efficiency and community participation. Legislative support, infrastructure development, sustainability, and collaboration are essential for scaling these initiatives and ensuring their long-term impact on rural livelihoods and environmental sustainability.

REFERENCES

Agarwal, N., & Brem, A. (2017). Frugal innovation-past, present, and future. *IEEE Engineering Management Review*, *45*(3), 37–41. DOI: 10.1109/EMR.2017.2734320

Ahmad, N.. (2014). Entrepreneurship in rural regions: Theoretical perspectives and practical insights. *Journal of Entrepreneurship and Innovation Management*, *1*(1), 4–20.

Ahmad, N., Chechi, A. A., & Khan, F. H. (2014). Entrepreneurship in Rural Areas: A Key to Rural Development. *International Journal of Innovation and Economic Development*, *1*(2), 47–54.

Avanti. (2019). Avanti Fellows Program. Retrieved from https://www.avantifellows .org/

Basu, S., & Roy, R. (2018). Frugal innovation: A strategic means for enabling universal healthcare in India. *Global Business and Organizational Excellence*, *37*(1), 6–16.

Bhatti, Y., & Ventresca, M. J. (2012). Practice, performance and materiality in entrepreneurship: The notion of entrepreneurship as performativity. *Organization Studies*, *33*(7), 979–1010.

Bound, K., & Thornton, J. (2012). Engineering innovation in global health: Ten Grand Challenges. *Proceedings of the Institution of Civil Engineers. Engineering Sustainability*, *165*(3), 181–186.

Embrace. (2019). About Us. Retrieved from https://www.embraceglobal.org/

Fredriksson, E., &Tömmervik, J. (2014). Frugal is the new innovative thinking: A qualitative study of frugal innovations and sustainable development in resource-poor environments.

Government of India. (n.d.). National Rural Livelihood Mission (NRLM). Ministry of Rural Development. Retrieved from https://nrlm.gov.in/

Government of India. (n.d.). Pradhan MantriKrishiSinchayeeYojana (PMKSY). Ministry of Agriculture & Farmers Welfare. Retrieved from https://pmksy.gov.in/

Government of India. (n.d.). Pradhan MantriSahajBijliHarGharYojana (Saubhagya Scheme). Ministry of Power. Retrieved from https://saubhagya.gov.in/

Government of India. (n.d.). RashtriyaKrishiVikasYojana (RKVY). Ministry of Agriculture & Farmers Welfare. Retrieved from http://rkvy.nic.in/

Government of India. (n.d.). Swachh Bharat Mission (SBM). Ministry of Housing and Urban Affairs. Retrieved from https://swachhbharaturban.gov.in/

Govindarajan, V., & Trimble, C. (2012). *Reverse innovation: Create far from home, win everywhere*. Harvard Business Press. DOI: 10.5437/08956308X5506003

Husk Power Systems. (2019). Our Impact. Retrieved from https://huskpowersystems .com/

Khan, R. (2016). How frugal innovation promotes social sustainability. *Sustainability (Basel)*, *8*(10), 1034. DOI: 10.3390/su8101034

Khan, W., Ali, T., & Dhamija, A. (2023). Perceived obstacles and performance of food and agribusiness enterprises: Implications for urban and rural entrepreneurship development. *Journal of Industrial Integration and Management*, *8*(01), 65–82. DOI: 10.1142/S2424862221500287

Kheyti. (2019). Our Solutions. Retrieved from https://www.kheyti.com/

Legood, A.. (2022). Sustainable Energy Solutions through Frugal Innovation: Insights from India. *Renewable & Sustainable Energy Reviews*, *150*, 111859.

Lim, C., & Fujimoto, T. (2019). Frugal innovation and design changes expanding the cost-performance frontier: A Schumpeterian approach. *Research Policy*, *48*(4), 1016–1029. DOI: 10.1016/j.respol.2018.10.014

McCormac, A.. (2022). Frugal Innovation in Healthcare: Case Studies from India. *Journal of Health Innovation*, *10*(2), 123–137.

Moreno, D. A.. (2022). Frugal innovation and rural development in India: Challenges and opportunities. *Sustainable Development*, *30*(2), 322–337.

Mucci, N., & Karau, S. J. (2020). Sustainable frugal innovation in rural India: Enabling village entrepreneurship. *Journal of Cleaner Production*, *244*, 118708.

ParamparagatKrishiVikasYojana (PKVY). (n.d.). Ministry of Agriculture & Farmers Welfare. Retrieved from https://pib.gov.in/

Prabhu, J. (2017). Frugal innovation: Doing more with less for more. *Philosophical Transactions. Series A, Mathematical, Physical, and Engineering Sciences*, *375*(2095), 20160372. DOI: 10.1098/rsta.2016.0372 PMID: 28461436

Prabhu, J., & Jain, S. (2015). Innovation and entrepreneurship in India: Understanding jugaad. *Asia Pacific Journal of Management*, *32*(4), 843–868. DOI: 10.1007/s10490-015-9445-9

Prahalad, C. K., & Mashelkar, R. A. (2010). Innovation's Holy Grail. *Harvard Business Review*, *88*(7/8), 132–141.

Pratham. (2019). What We Do. Retrieved from https://www.pratham.org/

Radjou, N.. (2012). *Jugaad innovation: Think frugal, be flexible, generate breakthrough growth*. John Wiley & Sons.

Radjou, N., & Prabhu, J. (2015). Frugal innovation: How to do more with less. The Economist.

Rangan, V. K. (2007). Aravind Eye Care System: Providing total eye care to the rural population. Harvard Business School Case, 9-505-075.

Rao, N. (2013). *Jugaad Innovation: Think Frugal, Be Flexible, Generate Breakthrough Growth*. Jossey-Bass.

SELCO. (2019). Impact. Retrieved from https://www.selco-india.com/

Vierikko, K.. (2024). Unlocking potential for sustainable development in rural India: Lessons from frugal entrepreneurship. *Journal of Rural Studies*, *87*, 100–112.

Wiśniewska, M., & Roczniewska, M. (2017). Frugal Innovation in Education: Lessons from India. *International Journal of Educational Development*, *53*, 128–136.

Yela Aránega, A.. (2019). Frugal Innovation in Agriculture: Empowering Small-Scale Farmers in India. *Agricultural Systems*, *172*, 42–50.

Yin, E., & Prabhu, J. C. (2018). Innovation in China and India. Handbook of research on new product development, 146-170. DOI: 10.4337/9781784718152.00016

Zeschky, M., Winterhalter, S., & Gassmann, O. (2011). From cost to frugal and reverse innovation: Mapping the field and implications for global competitiveness. [References]. *Research Technology Management*, *54*(4), 38–45. DOI: 10.5437/08956308X5404007

Zeschky, M. B., Widenmayer, B., & Gassmann, O. (2011). Frugal innovation in emerging markets. *Research Technology Management*, *54*(4), 38–45. DOI: 10.5437/08956308X5404007

Chapter 8
Empowering Rural Communities and Schools Towards Frugal Innovation and Entrepreneurship:
Lacking Information and Communication Technologies

Bongi G. Mahlangu
University of South Africa, South Africa

Leila Goosen
https://orcid.org/0000-0003-4948-2699
University of South Africa, Gauteng, South Africa

ABSTRACT

This chapter undertakes an examination of primary data sourced from interviews conducted with educators and principals from rural South African educational institutions. The purpose of this chapter is to investigate and comprehend the ramifications of Information and Communication Technologies (ICTs) within these scholastic settings, with a particular emphasis on the viewpoints and encounters of those directly engaged in such educational instruction. Against the background of frugal innovation in entrepreneurship and employing a qualitative analysis of the interview data, this chapter endeavors to unveil the salient themes encapsulated within the respondents' narratives. This, in turn, furnishes invaluable insights into the existent state of ICTs within rural educational establishments, the attendant

DOI: 10.4018/979-8-3693-4050-9.ch008

challenges encountered, and the prospective scope for subsequent integration and advancement.

INTRODUCTION

This section will describe the general perspective of the chapter and end by specifically stating the objective.

Frugal Innovation in Entrepreneurship

The ever-changing junction of frugal innovation and entrepreneurship is the subject of this edited book. The world is changing at a dizzying rate, and as part of this book, the chapter intends to provide a thorough overview of the innovative techniques and entrepreneurial ideas that drive constructive change. Entrepreneurs increasingly use frugal innovation as a strategic method to overcome obstacles and grab opportunities in an era characterized by uncertainty and resource constraints. The capacity to do more with less is the hallmark of frugal innovation, which has grown as a critical idea in entrepreneurship (Zeschky, Winterhalter, & Gassmann, 2014c).

"Product and service innovations aimed at resource-constrained customers in emerging markets have recently attracted much research and management attention" (Zeschky, et al., 2014c, p. 20). From cost to frugal and reverse innovation, the journal article on *research-technology management* by the latter authors was mapping the field and showing the implications for global competitiveness.

In their book on *jugaad innovation*, thinking frugally, being flexible and generating breakthrough growth, Radjou, Prabhu and Ahuja (2012, p. 4) delved into the intricacies of frugal innovation, the "flexible mindset of thousands of ingenious entrepreneurs" and the consequences of these for businesses that operate in contexts with limited resources. Frugal innovation is based on optimizing efficiency and attaining significant results with low resources. This statement questions conventional ideas about innovation, which commonly link it to expensive investments and advanced technologies

Instead, frugal innovation focuses on accessibility, affordability, and simplicity. As such, it is a valuable tactic for business owners dealing with "critical socioeconomic issues in their communities" like tight finances, inadequate infrastructure, and unstable markets. Researchers and practitioners must comprehend the applicability of frugal innovation in different entrepreneurial contexts as they explore its complexities. The chapters of the proposed book aim to offer a comprehensive understanding of how frugal innovation can promote entrepreneurship. This will be achieved by analyzing successful case studies, exploring empirical studies, conducting a meta-analysis of previous literature, and identifying theoretical foundations to evaluate the impact of frugal innovation on business sustainability and growth. The importance of frugal innovation in promoting entrepreneurship is emphasized by its ability to democratize innovation, making it available to a broader range of entrepreneurs, especially those in developing nations (George, McGahan, & Prabhu, 2012).

Inclusive Entrepreneurship and Social Equity

Inclusive innovation, which George, et al. (2012, p. 661) defined "as innovation that benefits the disenfranchised, is a process as well as a performance outcome." The journal article on management studies by the latter authors investigated innovation for inclusive growth towards a theoretical framework and research agenda.

Entrepreneurs may develop sustainable solutions that meet the requirements of various communities by using local expertise, adapting current technology, and adopting inventive business structures. The forthcoming book chapters will delve into the fundamental principles of frugal innovation, its utilization in entrepreneurship, and the obstacles and prospects it offers to well-established companies and emerging startups. The book aims to enhance the ongoing discussion on frugal innovation by thoroughly examining existing literature and empirical analysis. The implications of the book chapters will offer practical insights that can be utilized by entrepreneurs, policymakers, practitioners, and researchers for their future strategic formulation.

Effects Due to a Lack of Information and Communication Technologies at Rural Schools

This chapter undertakes an examination of primary data sourced from interviews conducted with educators and principals from rural South African educational institutions. The purpose of this chapter is to investigate and comprehend the ramifications of Information and Communication Technologies (ICTs) within these scholastic settings, with a particular emphasis on the viewpoints and encounters of those directly engaged in such educational instruction. Employing a qualitative analysis of the interview data, this chapter endeavors to unveil the salient themes encapsulated within the respondents' narratives. This, in turn, furnishes invaluable insights into the existent state of ICTs within rural educational establishments, the attendant challenges encountered, and the prospective scope for subsequent integration and advancement.

The ensuing analysis is organized around a constellation of pivotal themes discerned from the interviews:

- Positive Attitudes Towards ICTs
- Infrastructural Challenges
- Economic Constraints
- Professional Development Needs
- Security Concerns

The purpose of the most recent chapter by Mahlangu and Goosen (2024, p. 60) was "to present the methodology that" was "used to collect data for the study reported on. Against the background of enhancing education with intelligent systems" and ICTs, the latter chapter considered e.g., data-driven instruction and the context of rural schools.

Each theme is subjected to scrupulous scrutiny in tandem with the extant academic corpus, thereby affording a holistic comprehension of the multifarious factors exerting an influence upon the integration and efficacy of ICT within these scholastic environs. The discernments stemming from this analysis assume paramount significance in the formulation of strategies and interventions geared towards the augmentation of ICTs' role within rural educational institutions. Ultimately, this endeavor contributes substantially to the amelioration of educational outcomes and the attenuation of the digital divide inherent within South African society.

Recommended Topics

Due to the context of the study discussed in this chapter, it will especially focus on the following topic selected from those recommended for the book:

Empowering Rural Communities through Frugal Innovation

The authors will however, also make contributions related exploring the following:

1. Frugal Innovation for Social Entrepreneurs
2. Frugal and Sustainable Business Models and Entrepreneurship
    4. Inclusive Entrepreneurship and Social Equity
        9. Urban Sustainability through Frugal Innovation and Smart City Solutions

Target Audience

As part of the book Frugal Innovation in Entrepreneurship, this chapter is intended for readers interested in the convergence of frugal innovation and entrepreneurship. The target audience comprises:

- **Entrepreneurs and Business Leaders:** Owners of small and medium-sized companies, founders of startups, and seasoned businesspeople looking for real-world advice on applying frugal innovation ideas to build resource-efficient and sustainable businesses.
- **Managers and Strategists of Innovation:** Professionals in charge of innovation in companies that wish to know how to include frugal innovation into their plans to boost productivity and competitiveness.
- **Academics and Researchers:** Professionals with expertise in business studies, entrepreneurship, and innovation search for a thorough guide to frugal innovation's theoretical underpinnings and real-world applications.
- **Policy Makers:** Government officials and policymakers seeking to comprehend the potential economic benefits of frugal innovation, especially in developing nations.
- **Academics and Faculty Members:** Learners enrolled in courses on innovation management, business studies, and entrepreneurship, as well as instructors searching for a textbook or other resource that delves into the valuable applications of frugal innovation.
- **Non-Governmental Organizations (NGOs):** Groups that foster economic growth and entrepreneurship, particularly in settings with limited resources. They search for ideas for inclusive innovation and cost-effective **solutions**.
- **Corporate Social Responsibility (CSR):** Practitioners are professionals who engage in CSR activities to comprehend how frugal innovation may contribute to socially responsible and sustainable business operations.

As part of the book, this chapter will endeavor to serve as a helpful resource that connects theoretical principles with practical applications, providing actionable insights and direction for many players in the entrepreneurial ecosystem. This is achieved by catering to the requirements and interests of this varied audience.

Objective

The primary objective of the book Frugal Innovation in Entrepreneurship and this chapter is to offer a thorough examination of frugal innovation ideas and their use in promoting entrepreneurial endeavors. As part of this book, the chapter will attempt to explore, by using a wide range of successful case studies, empirical research, a meta-analysis of prior literature, and the identification of theoretical underpinnings, and assess the influence of frugal innovation.

- **Examine the Foundations of Frugal Innovation:** Learn about the basic ideas that drive frugal innovation and how business owners may maximize their limited resources to maximize productivity and produce significant results (Zeschky, et al., 2014c).

- **Analyze Frugal Innovation in Entrepreneurial Contexts:** Examine how frugal innovation is applied in entrepreneurial endeavors, considering how it affects product/service development, market entrance methods, and business models.
- **Investigate Frugal Innovation from a Global Perspective:** Explore the function of frugal innovation in various geographical and economic contexts, emphasizing its usefulness and efficiency in developing and developed nations (George, et al., 2012).
- **Provide Entrepreneurs with Useful Insights:** Emphasize adaptation and sustainable growth while providing entrepreneurs with strategic insights and actionable advice on incorporating frugal innovation ideas into their business endeavors.
- **Discuss Challenges and Opportunities:** Addressing questions like scalability, market acceptability, and the function of governmental frameworks in promoting frugal entrepreneurial endeavors, this discussion will delve into the prospects and constraints surrounding frugal innovation.

By fulfilling these goals, as part of the book, this chapter hopes to further the expanding field of study on frugal innovation and serve as a valuable tool for scholars, business owners, and legislators who want to comprehend and capitalize on the advantages of frugality in entrepreneurial environments.

The primary objective of this chapter is to investigate and comprehend the ramifications of ICTs within the scholastic settings as previously described, with a particular emphasis on the viewpoints and encounters of those directly engaged in such educational instruction.

BACKGROUND

This section of the chapter will provide broad definitions and discussions of the topic on Empowering Rural Communities and Schools Lacking ICTs Towards Frugal Innovation and Entrepreneurship and incorporate the views of others (in the form of a literature review) into the discussion to support, refute, or demonstrate the authors' position on the topic.

Frugal and Sustainable Business Models and Entrepreneurship

The study reported on by Winterhalter, Zeschky, Neumann and Gassmann (2017, p. 3) investigated "business models for frugal innovation" in emerging markets (i.e., "a specific form of resource-constrained innovation) in the medical device and laboratory equipment industry in the" case of the medical device and laboratory equipment industry.

Research on managing dual business models had "highlighted the challenge for firms when they compete with different business models in" emerging markets (Winterhalter, Zeschky, & Gassmann, 2016, p. 464). Drawing from ambidexterity literature, the latter authors provided an ambidexterity perspective against the background of Research and Development *(R&D) management.*

Frugal innovation "is an extreme case of innovation: radically new applications are innovated for an environment of extreme resource and cost constraints." The paper by Winterhalter, Zeschky, Gassmann and Weiblen (2014, p. 3) presented at a *R&D Management* conference looked at the role of resource-constraints in business models for frugal innovation.

Frugal Innovation for Social Entrepreneurs

Zeschky, Winterhalter and Gassmann (2014a) asked what frugal innovation was and provided a conceptualization and empirical evidence regarding.

A composition-based view in a journal article on social entrepreneurship by Ananthram, Luo and Peng (2022, p. 3) defined "frugal innovation as 'an attempt to maximize the ratio of value to resources'. "Known in the Indian context as jugaad in Hindi, frugal innovation requires frugality (low cost)".

In their Portland international conference on management of engineering and technology paper, Ma, Chai and Hang (2015, p. 986) defined "frugal entrepreneurship as the pursuit of hitherto unexploited" opportunities. "Based on the case analysis in" another section of their paper, the latter authors found that "frugal entrepreneurship is a more affordable way of value creation".

The theoretical contribution of an international business review incorporated "the determinants of frugal innovation and" how an entrepreneurship ecosystem influenced the development of frugal innovation and informal entrepreneurship (Igwe, Odunukan, Rahman, Rugara, & Ochinanwata, 2020, pp. 484-485).

At the 3rd international conference on reinventing business practices, start-ups and sustainability, Kumar (2024, p. 12) characterized frugal innovation and entrepreneurship, "distinguishing it from comparable concepts such as frugal innovation, social innovation, and entrepreneurship, as well as day-to-day change."

The study reported on by Agarwal, Bhatti and Levänen (2021) linked "frugal innovation, from the hitherto focus on ideation and development, to" frugal entrepreneurship through effectuation, causation, and bricolage.

"Entrepreneurial Orientation (EO) and firm performance have been extensively researched recently. Given the expanding and ever more diverse and dynamic business environment," Dixit and Manna (2023, p. 1) provided a bibliometric analysis in this regard.

"Start-ups are founded to develop some unique offerings to the market, which are crucial for any entrepreneurial economy" (Dixit & Acharya, 2023). These "are adept at bringing economic and social change". The latter authors therefore considered start-up ecosystems through the lens of action research.

Against the background of an international journal article on education and science, the study reported on by Manna and Singh (2021, p. 33) explored the personal characteristic and organizational environment as predictors of teachers' engagement with higher education. The teacher engagement included e.g., job engagement and organization.

"Today's global and heterogeneous markets increasingly require that firms master the entire range from simple low-cost innovations to advanced, high-end innovations. This is" particularly true in the case of resource-constrained innovation; thus requiring a classification of implications for multinational firms (Zeschky, Winterhalter, & Gassmann, 2014b, p. 1).

The study by Thangeni (2022, p. v) "aimed to explore the kind of digital leadership required for the development of an innovative technology-led culture of learning in" rural Limpopo schools.

The demonstration portion of their presentation highlighted lessons that had been developed by the "Preparing Tomorrow's Teachers to use Technology" (PT3) "staff for use in staff development sessions conducted in" partner schools (Phelps, Owens, & Jordan, 2002).

MAIN FOCUS OF THE CHAPTER

Issues, Problems, Challenges

This section of the chapter will present the authors' perspectives on the issues, problems, etc., as these relate to the main theme of the book on Frugal Innovation in Entrepreneurship, and arguments supporting the authors' position on Empowering Rural Communities and Schools Lacking ICTs Towards Frugal Innovation and Entrepreneurship. It will also compare and contrast with what had been, or is currently being, done as it relates to the specific topic of the chapter.

As part of a book on contemporary challenges in education: digitalization, methodology, and management, the purpose of the chapter by Mahlangu and Goosen (2023, p. 254) was "to present a literature review on issues related to the integration of information and communication technologies … in especially South African rural schools."

"In exploring the challenges and struggles of technology among students in rural areas," the research discovered factors that contributed to and determined the optimization of digital technologies in rural localities and schools (Omar, Dainal, Puad, & Zakaria, 2023, p. 1686).

Exploring the digital divide in educational technologies across Illinois school districts with a focus on business education in urban, suburban, and rural schools, the study by Kazmi (2023, p. 2) investigated "the disparities in access and usage of" such technologies "to identify the challenges and opportunities in order to promote equitable access to technology in" these schools.

Musingafi and Chaden'anga (2014, p. 77) presented a comparative study on the ICTs, as well as digital and "forms of projected media in use" in teaching and learning in classroom situations at six urban and rural secondary schools and areas in Masvingo "in Zimbabwe; to investigate the" utilization "in these schools; and to establish" the "challenges faced by these schools in their" endeavors.

Hawkins, et al. (2020) were reimagining human connections regarding technology and innovation in education at the World Bank.

Frugal and Sustainable Business Models and Entrepreneurship

Regarding entrepreneurship as such, Shahid, Hossain, Shahid and Anwar (2023, p. 1) investigated sustainable entrepreneurship, together with frugal innovation. The latter authors' results showed "that entrepreneurship based on frugal innovation" lead to several advantages, for "which frugal innovation can serve as a source of sustainable entrepreneurship to tackle social and environmental challenges."

In line with the theme of this book, the chapter by Ngugi and Goosen (2021) considered innovation, entrepreneurship, and sustainability for ICT students towards the post-COVID-19 era.

Frugal Innovation for Social Entrepreneurs

Towards reinvesting in European citizenship through entrepreneurship and frugal innovation, Hadjitchoneva, Pellat and Marasova (2023, p. 29) asked questions around the challenges to be addressed in their project proposed for the future? The latter authors studied "this axis through the concept of innovation and especially frugal innovation", while entrepreneurship was "understood in very different ways".

The study by Mashhour (2022, p. 1) aimed to explore the role of "frugal innovation and social entrepreneurship" in supporting socioeconomic life in emerging markets from the perspective of "nano, micro and small enterprises" (NMSEs). This journal article regarding research on business and social science was prompted by the "extreme context of institutional voids and resource scarcity."

Table 1 shows a summary of themes and corresponding codes identified during the data analysis.

Table 1. Themes and codes

Themes	Codes
Attitude Towards ICTs	Positive Perception, Essential for **Future** Success
Challenges Related to a Lack of ICTs	Electricity and Infrastructure, Load Shedding and Network **Issues**, Economic **Constraints**, Electricity and Theft **Issues**, Economic Background
Impact of ICT Availability	Enhanced Learning, Educational Improvement, Positive Change and Confidence, Enhanced Learning Methods
Infrastructure Readiness for ICTs	Inadequate Facilities, Partial Readiness, Designated ICT Room, Infrastructure Readiness

Table 2 provides a description of the respondents.

Table 2. Respondent keys

Respondent	Pseudonym	Respondent Type
Respondent 1	Michelle	Learner
Respondent 2	Molokele	Educator
Respondent 3	Dlomo	Principal
Respondent 4	Giyama	Educator
Respondent 5	Wright	Principal
Respondent 6	Prince	Learner
Respondent 7	Nkosinathi	Learner
Respondent 8	Lucy	Learner

Attitude Towards Information and Communication Technologies

The thematic exploration of 'Attitude Towards ICTs' within the environment of rural South African educational institutions unveils a prevailing affirmative disposition among educators and educational overseers. This positive perspective assumes a pivotal stance in the process of assimilating technological facets into the pedagogical paradigm, notwithstanding the concomitant challenges germane to these scholastic environs.

One educator, Ms. Molokele, an instructor at School A, exemplifies this stance, articulating: "'I hold a favorable view of ICT within the educational sphere. It augments pedagogic efficiency and engenders heightened student motivation." This pronouncement epitomizes the conviction that ICT serves as a metamorphic instrument within the educational domain, elevating both didactic methodologies and learner engagement.

In a similar vein, Mr. Wright, the principal of School A, accentuates the broader import of ICT in education, propounding "ICT assumes paramount significance as it embodies the future trajectory of our nation... If we aspire to fortify our nation's international competitiveness, we must commence this trajectory with the present cohort of learners". This declaration underscores the pivotal role of ICT in endowing learners with the acumen requisite for traversing a globalized terrain and underscores the putative long-term dividends of integrating ICT into the educational scaffold.

The prevailing affirmative stance towards ICT, as articulated by Ms. Molokele and Mr. Wright, resonated ubiquitously within the corpus of interviews, with other educators and principals espousing congruent sentiments. This unanimity underscores a collective cognizance of the transformative potential inherent to ICT within the ambit of education, particularly within the hinterlands where resources are constrained and the imperative for educational amelioration is pronounced.

Educators perceive ICT as a conduit to ameliorate the schism between rural and urban educational institutions, endowing access to informational reservoirs and didactic accoutrements capable of elevating the pedagogic sojourn for learners within underprivileged locales. This perspective is anchored in a discernment of the overarching ramifications of ICT proficiency vis-à-vis prospective labor markets and societal engagement, wherein digital competencies are progressively indispensable.

The enthusiasm for ICTs in the realm of education is moderated by a cognizance of the impediments concomitant with the incorporation of technology within rural educational establishments, encompassing limitations inherent to infrastructure and pecuniary exigencies. Nevertheless, the prevailing disposition remains one of unwavering resolve and sanguinity, with educators and overseers ardently poised to embrace the vistas promulgated by ICT. This positive outlook assumes pivotal significance in propelling efforts to surmount obstacles and amalgamate technology into the pedagogic environment, with the ultimate aspiration of augmenting educational outcomes for learners domiciled within the rural expanse of South Africa.

Findings in the study reported on by Kormos and Wisdom (2021, p. 35) in the journal article on theory and practice in rural education revealed that "rural schools utilized and perceived technology" in the learning experience to be effective. However, "a number of obstacles to successful integration exist. It is imperative teachers are" empowered to bridge the digital divide.

Challenges Related to a Lack of Information and Communication Technologies

The thematic exploration of 'Challenges of a Lack of ICTs' within rural South African educational institutions underscores formidable impediments that educators and overseers grapple with in the process of assimilating technology into the pedagogic environment. The interviews unveiled an array of challenges, spanning from infrastructural exigencies to pecuniary constraints, which substantially encumber the efficacious implementation of ICT within these precincts.

A conspicuous quandary manifests in the form of a dearth of dependable electricity, a sine qua non for the operation of any technological paraphernalia. This conundrum is succinctly encapsulated by Mrs. Dlomo, the principal of School B, who opined: "Lack of electricity is our core challenge. Yeah even though we have resources we also need money to substitute electricity parents in our area most of them are unemployed". This utterance underscores the multi-faceted complexity of the predicament, wherein not only does the corporeal infrastructure lacuna exist, but the fiscal circumstances of the community further convolute the scenario.

As Small and Medium Enterprises (SMEs) "increasingly internationalize their innovation activities," the study by Palmié, et al. (2016, p. 273) strived to improve an "understanding of the coordination mechanisms that SMEs can adopt", together with the effects on time-to-market and R&D task complexity as a moderator.

"In the growing corpus of education research about" the ethnography of technologies and digital tools "in schools, information about town and rural" elementary schools represent a gap in the literature in the book by Hamilton (2018, p. iv). Hamilton (2018, p. 15) further highlighted "the complexity of generalizing research conducted in rural schools."

Another salient facet of the predicament is the broader economic backdrop of the schools and their hinterlands. Mr. Wright, the principal of School A, brings this into focus, elucidating: "The school's rural setting and the economic background of the learners and their families contribute to the lack of ICT". This pronouncement alludes to the interconnectedness of educational resources and the comprehensive socio-political environment, illustrating how extraneous factors, such as the financial standing of families, can wield sway over the availability and efficacy of ICT within educational institutions.

These quotations from Mrs. Dlomo and Mr. Wright epitomized the overarching challenges confronted in the incorporation of ICT within rural South African schools, wherein infrastructural insufficiencies and fiscal constraints constitute formidable obstacles. Notwithstanding the enthusiasm for the potentiality of ICT in education, these adversities necessitate a judicious and all-encompassing approach to the integration of technology, one that takes cognizance of the idiosyncratic circumstances of each school and its environs.

The challenges stemming from the absence of ICT in rural educational institutions transcend infrastructure and economic challenges. Another pivotal concern pertains to the dearth of proficient educators capable of adeptly incorporating ICT into the academic syllabus. This apprehension is underscored by Mr. Giyama, an instructor at School A, who opined: "We also need teachers who are trained in ICT so that they can be able to teach these kids". This assertion accentuates the exigency of professional development to ensure that educators are endowed with the requisite competencies to proficiently harness ICT tools within the classroom environment.

Furthermore, apprehensions about security and the looming spectre of theft of technological contrivances constitute a noteworthy quandary, as articulated by Mr. Giyama in another segment of his interview. This mirrors the overarching issue of the preservation and safeguarding of ICT assets in environments wherein such resources are conspicuously susceptible especially to theft, abuse, misuse and damage.

The challenges arising from the lack of ICTs within rural South African scholastic establishments are varied, encompassing facets of infrastructure, finance, education, and security. The redressal of these challenges mandates an all-encompassing approach that takes into account the manifold factors that impinge upon the efficacious assimilation of ICT within these educational precincts.

Impact of Information and Communication Technologies' Availability

The theme 'Impact of ICT Availability' in rural South African schools underscores the potential transformative effects of technology in the education sector. Interviews with educators and principals demonstrate a firm belief in the positive influences of ICT on both teaching and learning processes.

The enhancement of the learning environment, making it more interactive and engaging for students, is identified as a key impact. Mrs. Dlomo, the principal of School B, articulates this impact, stating: "ICT makes teaching and learning more effective and learners pay more attention than textbooks since we know that they enjoy their phones, television, videos etc.". This viewpoint emphasizes the ability of ICT to engage students' attention more effectively than traditional methods.

Another significant influence of ICT availability is its role in modernizing the education system to meet the needs of a knowledge-based society. Ms Molokele, an educator at School A, highlights this, noting: "I like ICT in education. It improves learning efficiency and increases student motivation". This comment reflects the importance of ICT in updating education and preparing students for a future where digital literacy is essential.

These observations from Mrs. Dlomo and Ms. Molokele are indicative of a wider agreement among educators and administrators on the value of ICT in improving educational outcomes and preparing students for contemporary challenges. The presence of ICT in rural schools is viewed as essential in closing the digital divide and ensuring all students have access to necessary tools and skills for 21st-century success.

Moreover, the impact of ICT availability extends to preparing students for the challenges and opportunities of a digital world. Educators emphasize the necessity of equipping learners with ICT skills for their future academic and professional success. Mr. Giyama, an educator at School A, asserted: "If these kids are exposed to ICT, they will acquire significant knowledge, facilitating their proficiency in operating computers and other digital devices when they advance to higher grades". This statement underscores the role of ICT in establishing a foundation for lifelong learning and adaptability in an increasingly digitized society.

The interviews collectively emphasize the potential of ICT to revolutionize the educational experience in rural schools, providing novel opportunities for learning, engagement, and skill development. Despite the existing challenges, the presence of ICT is regarded as an indispensable step toward achieving educational equity and empowering students in rural areas. The focus lies in creating an environment conducive to student success in a globalized and technologically advanced world, with ICT serving as a pivotal enabler in this journey.

Infrastructure Readiness for Information and Communication Technologies

The theme 'Infrastructure Readiness for ICT' in rural South African schools emerges as a pivotal determinant in the seamless integration of technology within the educational landscape. The interviews conducted offer valuable insights into the prevailing state of infrastructure and the level of preparedness exhibited by these educational institutions concerning the adoption of ICT.

Central to the challenge of infrastructure readiness is the glaring absence of reliable electricity, an indispensable prerequisite for the operation and maintenance of ICT equipment. Mrs. Dlomo, the principal of School B, lucidly articulates this predicament, underscoring: "Lack of electricity is our core challenge... we also need money to substitute electricity". This underscores the imperative of exploring alternative power sources, such as generators or solar systems, to ensure uninterrupted functionality of ICT resources.

Furthermore, the dimension of infrastructure readiness extends to encompass considerations of physical space and security requisite for ICT implementation. Mr. Giyama, an educator at School A, acknowledges the significance of designating a dedicated room for ICT, indicative of the institution's proactive stance towards fostering an accommodating environment for the integration of technology. Nonetheless, the realization of such an endeavor frequently necessitates external support beyond the immediate resources available to the school.

These perceptions articulated by Mrs. Dlomo and Mr. Giyama encapsulated the broader spectrum of challenges entailed in infrastructure readiness confronting rural educational establishments. Effectively addressing these challenges assumes paramount significance in facilitating the successful incorporation of ICT in education, as it encompasses not solely the availability of technological resources but also the essential underpinning infrastructure conducive to its optimum utilization.

The preparedness of rural educational institutions for the integration of ICT infrastructure is contingent upon the provision of adequate internet connectivity, an indispensable factor exerting a profound impact on the efficacy of technology in the educational domain. Mr. Wright, the principal of School A, illuminates this concern, asserting: "The major challenge is the lack of internet... which limits what we can do with computers". This assertion unequivocally underscores the imperativeness of not only possessing ICT equipment but also ensuring their connectivity to the internet, thereby optimizing their utility.

Furthermore, the presence of proficient personnel capable of maintaining and rectifying **issues** pertaining to ICT equipment assumes a pivotal role in the landscape of infrastructure readiness. The dearth of such expertise can culminate in the underutilization of ICT resources, impeding their seamless integration into the educational environment. This predicament is exacerbated within the context of rural educational institutions, where accessibility to technical support may be constrained.

The ambit of infrastructure readiness for ICT within the rural South African educational framework encapsulates an array of facets, encompassing dependable access to electricity, allocation of physical space with due consideration to security, provision of internet connectivity, and the availability of technical support. Effectively addressing these multifaceted challenges constitutes the linchpin for unleashing the complete potential of ICT in augmenting educational outcomes and addressing the digital divide prevalent within these **communities**.

SOLUTIONS AND RECOMMENDATIONS

This section of the chapter will discuss **solutions and recommendations** in dealing with the **issues** or **problems** presented in the preceding section.

Urban Sustainability through Frugal Innovation and Smart City Solutions

Against a background of sustainability, agriculture, food and environmental research, a systematic literature review on the sustainable urban development of smart cities in India by Gupta and Gupta (2024, p. 8) indicated that the benchmark of what a 'smart city' is in India was well-explained. One of the routes towards a smart city is through the integration of ICTs with urban planning.

A case study of a water access solution and approach to sustainability were presented by López, Rohmer, Díaz-Pichardo and Reyes (2024). Under these considerations, the latter authors thought that exploring frugal innovation as an eco-design strategy can contribute to "the basic needs of people during the design and development of affordable solutions."

An environmental impact assessment review by Chen, Chen and Miao (2024, p. 1) asked whether a smart city pilot improved urban green economic efficiency as accelerator or inhibitor? The concept of a 'smart city' "plays a significant role in cities with high level of" urban expansion. The results in the latter article provided "the policy implications for the construction of smart" sustainable cities.

Towards Solutions Through Discussion of Empirical Findings in the Context of Literature

Attitude Towards Information and Communication Technologies

The theme '*Attitude Towards ICTs*' in rural South African schools, as reflected in the interviews, aligns with recent literature emphasizing the positive perception of ICT among educators and its potential impact on education. Researchers have noted that educators in developing countries, including South Africa, recognize the significance of ICT in enhancing teaching and learning processes (Mafini & Pooe, 2013). This recognition is based on the understanding that ICT can foster a more interactive and engaging learning environment, which is crucial for student motivation and participation (Kozma, 2011).

Moreover, the belief that ICT integration is vital for preparing students for a technology-driven world is supported by literature emphasizing the importance of ICT skills for future employment and societal participation (Van Dijk, 2012). This perspective is particularly relevant in rural areas, where the digital divide is more pronounced, and access to technology can significantly influence educational and career opportunities (Selwyn, 2014). Educators and administrators in rural schools understand the transformative potential of ICT, not just in terms of immediate educational outcomes but also in preparing students for the demands of the 21st-century globalized economy (Zhong, 2011).

However, the positive attitude towards ICT must be contextualized within the unique challenges faced by rural schools in implementing technology. Issues such as lack of infrastructure, unreliable electricity, and limited financial resources are significant barriers to ICT integration in these settings (Unwin, 2017). While educators and administrators are eager to embrace ICT, these challenges necessitate a pragmatic approach to technology adoption, focusing on achievable goals and incremental improvements (Hollow & Masperi, 2009). This aligns with the broader literature on ICT in education, which acknowledges the gap between the potential of technology and the practical realities of its implementation, particularly in under-resourced environments (Selwyn, 2014).

Furthermore, the enthusiasm for ICT in rural schools is also reflective of a global trend where educators increasingly recognize the importance of technology in education. This is evidenced by the growing investment in ICT infrastructure and training in schools worldwide, a trend that is seen as essential for equipping students with the skills needed to succeed in an increasingly digital world (Fraillon, Ainley, Schulz, Friedman, & Gebhardt, 2014). However, the literature also cautions against viewing technology as a panacea for educational challenges, emphasizing the need for a balanced approach that considers the pedagogical, social, and cultural contexts of technology use in education (Zhong, 2011; Selwyn, 2014).

Challenges Related to a Lack of Information and Communication Technologies

The challenges of ICT scarcity in rural schools, as revealed in interviews, are consistent with academic literature. Infrastructural issues, particularly reliable electricity, pose significant barriers to ICT integration, a common problem in developing countries (Unwin, 2017). This infrastructure deficit, especially in areas with unreliable electricity, hinders both the usage and maintenance of ICT resources.

Economic constraints in rural schools and communities also impede ICT access. Financial limitations affect the procurement and upkeep of ICT resources, which are often unaffordable for economically disadvantaged schools (Hollow & Masperi, 2009). Limited internet connectivity further exacerbates these challenges (Selwyn, 2014). Additionally, the economic background of learners' families' influences schools' capacity to garner community support.

Teacher training in ICT remains a crucial obstacle. The lack of educators skilled in ICT hinders effective technology implementation in the curriculum (Tondeur, Van Braak, Ertmer, & Ottenbreit-Leftwich, 2017, p. 570). Teachers require both technical and pedagogical skills for successful ICT integration. Security concerns, including the risk of theft or damage to ICT equipment, present additional challenges, necessitating investment in security measures (Trucano & Dykes, 2017). These challenges, comprising infrastructural, economic, educational, and security aspects, require a comprehensive approach, considering the unique contexts of rural schools and their socio-economic environments.

Impact of Information and Communication Technologies' Availability

The impact of ICT availability in South African rural schools, as evidenced in the interviews, aligns with the existing literature, highlighting its transformative role in education. Research underscores how ICT can enhance the learning environment, fostering greater student engagement and interactivity. This convergence aligns with the global shift towards student-centered learning approaches, with technology serving as a pivotal facilitator of diverse learning experiences (Kozma, 2011). Within the South African context, the presence of ICT in rural schools signifies a pathway to mitigating educational disparities and ensuring equitable access to quality education (Bozalek, et al., 2013).

Moreover, ICT assumes a vital role in aligning education with the demands of a knowledge-based economy. ICT integration in education extends beyond the realm of enhancing teaching and learning processes; it encompasses preparing students for the future workforce, where digital literacy holds increasing significance (Van Dijk, 2012). In South Africa, a nation grappling with the imperative to bridge the digital divide, ICT in education emerges as a conduit to equip students from diverse backgrounds with the essential skills required to partake in the digital economy (Chigona & Chigona, 2008).

Professional development for educators stands as a pivotal component in the effective integration of ICT into education. Research underscores the imperative of continual training and support for teachers, enabling them to adeptly incorporate technology into their pedagogical practices (Tondeur et al., 2017). In the South African context, this assumes heightened significance, given that many educators in rural areas may lack prior exposure to ICT or may possess limited confidence in utilizing technology in their instructional approaches (Herselman & Britton, 2002).

Furthermore, the impact of ICT availability extends beyond the confines of the classroom, encompassing broader societal advantages. The literature accentuates how ICT can nurture critical thinking, problem-solving, and collaborative skills, all of which are indispensable in today's interconnected world (Fraillon et al., 2014). In South Africa, where education is perceived as a fundamental catalyst for social and economic advancement, the role of ICT in equipping students with these proficiencies takes on particular prominence (Chigona & Chigona, 2008).

The impact of ICT availability in rural South African schools, as gleaned from the interviews, finds reinforcement in the existing literature. This includes its role in enhancing the learning environment, preparing students for a digital future, the imperative of teacher professional development, and the broader societal benefits of ICT in education. Addressing the challenges and capitalizing on the opportunities afforded by ICT assumes paramount importance in advancing educational equity and empowerment in the South African context.

Infrastructure Readiness for Information and Communication Technologies

The thematic focus on 'Infrastructure Readiness for ICT' within rural South African educational institutions, as underscored in the interview transcripts, represents a pivotal determinant in the efficacious execution of ICT integration into the pedagogical landscape. The extant scholarly discourse underscores that the purview of infrastructure readiness encompasses multifarious facets, encompassing the prerequisites of dependable electricity supply, internet accessibility, spatial allocation, and technical assistance (Hollow & Masperi, 2009). The dearth of steadfast electrical power within rural locales assumes the mantle of a formidable impediment to the seamless assimilation of ICT, given its sine qua non status in powering technological apparatus (Unwin, 2017). Mitigating this challenge mandates the exploration of alternative energy sources, with solar power emerging as a pragmatic solution in select contexts (Chigona & Chigona, 2008).

Internet connectivity surfaces as yet another indispensable dimension of infrastructure readiness vis-a-vis ICT. Scholarly accounts delineate that a multitude of rural schools grapple with the constraints of limited or non-existent internet access, a circumstance that considerably fetters the prospective advantages of ICT within the educational domain (Bozalek, et al., 2013). The provision of commensurate internet connectivity stands as a sine qua non for accessing pedagogic resources, facilitating collaborative learning efforts, and equipping learners for an interconnected digital milieu (Van Dijk, 2012).

Additionally, the considerations of spatial allocation and security vis-a-vis ICT equipment assume paramount significance. Educational institutions necessitate dedicated spaces to house computers and akin technological apparatus in a secure manner. This imperative encompasses the assurance that these facilities are adequately outfitted and fortified against potential pilferage or damage, a pertinence that acquires heightened salience within rural settings (Trucano & Dykes, 2017).

Technical support emerges as yet another pivotal facet within the ambit of infrastructure readiness. The scholarly panorama underscores the exigency of proficient personnel tasked with the maintenance and troubleshooting of ICT equipment within educational precincts. This assumes particularly pronounced significance within rural milieus, wherein the accessibility to technical acumen may be circumscribed, and educators may grapple with deficiencies in ICT resource management competencies (Tondeur et al., 2017).

The encompassing of infrastructure readiness vis-a-vis ICT within rural South African educational enclaves entails a concerted engagement with an array of exigencies, spanning steadfast electricity provision, internet accessibility, spatial allocation, security protocols, and technical support provisions. The surmounting of these impediments emerges as an imperative, resonant with the potential of ICT in augmenting pedagogical outcomes and addressing the digital chasm within these localities.

Recommendations

Infrastructure Enhancement

Rural educational institutions necessitate infrastructural enhancement, with a particular focus on bolstering electricity and internet connectivity. To ensure uninterrupted access to ICT, governments and non-governmental organizations should channel investments towards sustainable solutions, such as solar power and the establishment of community-centric internet hubs. Collaboration with private enterprises can expedite the deployment of these technologies, thereby enhancing the accessibility of ICT within rural locales.

Financial Support and Resource Allocation

The provision of financial assistance assumes paramount importance in the procurement and maintenance of ICT equipment. It is imperative that funding allocations from government budgets are supplemented by grants and contributions from NGOs and private enterprises to facilitate the acquisition of computers, tablets, and other essential hardware. Concurrently, schools must impart guidance on judicious resource management practices to optimize the utilization of these technological resources.

Community Engagement and Awareness

Engaging local communities in comprehending the pivotal role of ICT in education is a quintessential endeavor. Community backing can be galvanized through concerted awareness campaigns and active participation in school initiatives pertaining to ICT. This participatory approach holds the potential to engender community-driven efforts and garner support for the safeguarding and maintenance of ICT resources within educational institutions.

Policy Formulation and Advocacy

The formulation and advocacy of policies supportive of ICT integration within rural schools represent an exigent need. These policies should encompass a spectrum of concerns, including financing mechanisms, infrastructure augmentation, teacher capacity building, and curricular adaptations. Advocacy efforts can be further enriched through collaborative liaisons with stakeholders, culminating in a collective influence on policy determinations at both regional and national echelons.

Establishment of Monitoring and Evaluation Mechanisms

The establishment of monitoring and evaluation mechanisms is a prerequisite for gauging the efficacy of ICT initiatives. Data gleaned from these assessments serves as a lodestar for shaping future strategies and effecting refinements. Persistent evaluation engenders a culture of accountability and serves as a crucible for the distillation of best practices in the realm of ICT assimilation within the context of rural education.

Educator Training and Professional Advancement

Investments should be directed towards comprehensive training initiatives tailored for educators in rural schools, with a profound emphasis on the development of their ICT competencies. These training programs should encompass not only technical proficiencies but also pedagogical methodologies conducive to the seamless integration of technology within the curriculum. Ongoing opportunities for professional growth are indispensable in ensuring that educators remain abreast of the latest **emerging trends** with regard to educational technologies.

FUTURE RESEARCH DIRECTIONS

This section of the chapter will discuss future and, as well as provide insights about the future of the theme of the book on Frugal Innovation in Entrepreneurship from the perspective of the chapter focus on Empowering Rural Communities and Schools Lacking ICTs Towards Frugal Innovation and Entrepreneurship. The viability of a paradigm, model, implementation issues of proposed programs, etc., may be included in this section. If appropriate, this section will suggest future research directions within the domain of the topic.

In an analysis of emerging trends regarding the adoption of Human Resource (HR) analytics for enhancing business performance by Bankar and Manna (2023, p. 234), the article initially overviewed "the HR software and technologies used to implement HR analytics", while the second half discussed the implementation of three multinational companies (MNCs).

Assessing the Impact of Information and Communication Technology Interventions in Rural Educational Settings

Prospective research efforts should concentrate on the meticulous evaluation of ICT interventions within rural schools. Such investigations would scrutinize the influence of diverse ICT implementations, encompassing computer laboratories, internet connectivity provisions, and digital literacy initiatives, on diverse facets of educational dynamics. These facets would encompass student learning outcomes, the efficacy of educators, and the comprehensive performance of educational institutions. Employing longitudinal studies would facilitate the tracking of temporal transformations, endowing the research with the capacity to elucidate the preeminent strategies and tools conducive to the seamless integration of ICT within rural scholastic environments.

Investigating Community Engagement in Information and Communication Technologies Education

Another prospective domain for research inquiry pertains to the intricate interplay between community involvement and the triumph of ICT programs in rural educational precincts. This investigative endeavor could delve into the mechanisms through which community engagement, consciousness-raising initiatives, and supportive measures contribute to the perennial viability and efficacy of ICT undertakings. By juxtaposing diverse models of community participation, the research could proffer recommendations germane to the optimization of the integration of local communities in the entire gamut of ICT efforts, spanning planning, execution, and the perpetuation thereof within rural educational settings.

"It is now widely accepted that the transmission of disciplinary knowledge is insufficient to prepare students leaving higher education for the workplace. Authentic learning has been suggested as a way to bring the necessary complexity into learning to deal with challenges in professional practice after graduation."

A British journal article on educational technologies by Bozalek, et al. (2013, p. 629) discussed a South African study in higher education on the use of emerging trends regarding technologies for such authentic learning.

The international computer and information literacy (CIL) study international report by Fraillon, et al. (2014, p. 27) looked at preparing for life in a digital age, "in which young people develop" CIL "to support their capacity to ... participate effectively at home, at school," etc.

Analyzing the role of ICTs in bridging the digital divide amongst learners, the South African journal article on education by Herselman and Britton (2002, p. 270) indicated that "ICTs are changing every facet of" life. "It is changing the way" business is done "and, more importantly, the way" everything is learnt. "In this new Golden Age of" technologies, "more and more an increasing rift between those who have access to" ICTs "and those who do not" is seen.

CONCLUSION

This section of the chapter will provide a discussion of the overall coverage of the chapter and concluding remarks.

Key Insights from the Data

Positive Attitude Towards Information and Communication Technologies

The primary data derived from the interviews manifests a robust affirmative disposition towards ICT within the cohort of educators and principals. Their cognizance extends to the pivotal role of ICT in contemporary education, particularly in the augmentation of pedagogical processes, amplification of student involvement, and preparation of learners for an era characterized by digitalization. This perspective concurs with the scholarly corpus, which posits that the assimilation of ICT into the educational environment engenders enhanced educational outcomes, encompassing heightened student engagement and heightened comprehension of intricate concepts (Fraillon et al., 2014). Educators envisage ICT as a catalyst for instilling innovation into the classroom ethos and as a means to bridge the chasm between conventional pedagogical paradigms and the evolving requisites of the digital epoch (Tondeur et al., 2017). This affirmative disposition constitutes a pivotal determinant for the efficacious instantiation of ICT in education, wielding influence over the proclivity of educators to interweave technology into their didactic methodologies.

Infrastructure Challenges

The interviews exhibit a consistent accentuation of infrastructural impediments as substantial impediments to the integration of ICT in rural educational institutions. The recurring motifs encompass the paucity of dependable electricity and the dearth of internet accessibility, which obstruct the efficacious utilization of ICTs. These challenges resonate in the erudition, wherein scholars have identified infrastructure as a linchpin in the fruition of ICT ventures in the sphere of education (Hollow & Masperi, 2009). The nonattendance of steadfast electrical supply and internet connectivity not only circumscribes the utilization of technological contrivances but also exerts an influence on the viability of ICT initiatives (Unwin, 2017). The rectification of these infrastructural conundrums assumes paramount significance for the efficacious infusion of ICT within rural scholastic establishments, for it serves as the underpinning upon which technology-mediated education can be edified.

Economic Constraints

The economic constrictions confronting rural schools and their respective communities exert a substantial influence on their ability to access and implement ICT resources. The empirical data elucidates that numerous educational institutions grapple with financial constraints, thereby impinging upon their capacity to procure indispensable technological apparatus and infrastructure. This predicament finds consonance within the academic literature, which accentuates the pivotal role of the economic status of schools and their surrounding environs in shaping the feasibility of ICT integration (Herselman & Britton, 2002). Educational establishments situated in economically disadvantaged locales frequently encounter financial exigencies that encompass the initial investments in ICT and recurring expenses such as maintenance and subscriptions to internet services. Furthermore, the socio-economic environment of students and their familial backgrounds can circumscribe the school's ability to amass supplementary funds, thereby compounding the quandary associated with the infusion of ICT into the educational environment.

Professional Development Needs

The interviews underscore the imperativeness of professional development in ICT for educators. Educators acknowledge the significance of being adequately trained to adroitly amalgamate technology into their pedagogical methodologies and curricular paradigms. This revelation aligns with the exegesis proffered by extant scholarship, which accentuates that the preparedness and proficiency of educators in the utilization of ICT are pivotal for the efficacious realization of technological interventions within the classroom precinct (Tondeur et al., 2017). Programs dedicated to professional development assume paramount significance in endowing educators with the requisite acumen and self-assurance to harness ICT resources, thereby accentuating the erudition experience for students. The absence of such pedagogical training can precipitate the underutilization of extant ICT resources and abate the prospective educational dividends.

Security Concerns

The primary data elucidates security concerns entailing the specter of pilferage or detriment to ICT equipment. This concern assumes heightened salience within rural scholastic enclaves, where ICT assets are a rarity and are endowed with exalted value. The imperative for impregnable storage and maintenance facilities is underscored as a bulwark against the peril to these invaluable possessions. The scholarly oeuvre buttresses this apprehension, underscoring that the assurance of the security of ICT equipment represents a pivotal facet of technology integration within educational institutions (Trucano & Dykes, 2017). Secure repositories not only serve as custodians for the equipment but also ensure their durability and sustained utilization within the purview of the educational continuum. Thus, the amelioration of security concerns constitutes an elemental constituent of ICT preparedness within educational establishments.

This chapter undertook an examination of primary data sourced from interviews conducted with educators and principals within rural South African educational institutions. The primary objective of this chapter is to investigate and comprehend the ramifications of ICTs within these scholastic settings, with a particular emphasis on the viewpoints and encounters of those directly engaged in the educational instruction. Employing a qualitative analysis of the interview data, this chapter efforts to unveil the salient themes encapsulated within the respondents' narratives. This, in turn, furnishes invaluable insights into the extant state of ICT within rural educational establishments, the attendant impediments encountered, and the prospective scope for subsequent integration and advancement.

The ensuing analysis was organized around a constellation of pivotal themes discerned from the interviews:

- Positive Attitude Towards ICT
- Infrastructural Challenges
- Economic Constraints
- Professional Development Needs
- Security Concerns

Each theme is subjected to scrupulous scrutiny in tandem with the extant academic corpus, thereby affording a holistic comprehension of the multifarious factors exerting an influence upon the integration and efficacy of ICT within these scholastic environs. The discernments stemming from this analysis assume paramount significance in the formulation of strategies and interventions geared towards the augmentation of ICT's role within rural educational institutions. Ultimately, this endeavor contributes substantially to the amelioration of educational outcomes and the attenuation of the digital divide inherent within South African society.

REFERENCES

Agarwal, N., Bhatti, Y. A., & Levänen, J. (2021). *Linking Frugal Innovation to Frugal Entrepreneurship through Effectuation, Causation, and Bricolage. Proceedings.* Academy of Management., Retrieved from https://journals.aom.org/doi/abs/10.5465/AMBPP.2021.11386abstract DOI: 10.5465/AMBPP.2021.11386abstract

Ananthram, S., Luo, Y., & Peng, M. W. (2022). Social entrepreneurship and frugal innovation: A composition-based view. *Journal of Social Entrepreneurship*, •••, 1–22. DOI: 10.1080/19420676.2022.2091643

Bankar, S., & Manna, R. (2023). Adoption of HR Analytics for Enhancing Business Performance: Trend Analysis. *Journal of Xidian University*, *17*(3), 234–247. DOI: 10.37896/jxu17.3/024

Bozalek, V., Gachago, D., Alexander, L., Watters, K., Wood, D., Ivala, E., & Herrington, J. (2013). The use of emerging technologies for authentic learning: A South African study in higher education. *British Journal of Educational Technology*, *44*(4), 629–638. DOI: 10.1111/bjet.12046

Chen, Y., Chen, S., & Miao, J. (2024). Does smart city pilot improve urban green economic efficiency: Accelerator or inhibitor. *Environmental Impact Assessment Review*, *104*, 107328. Advance online publication. DOI: 10.1016/j.eiar.2023.107328

Chigona, A., & Chigona, W. (2008). MXit it up in the media: Media discourse analysis on a Mobile instant messaging system. *The Southern African Journal of Information and Communication*, (9), 42–57.

Dixit, K., & Acharya, S. R. (2023). Start-up Ecosystem through the Lens of Action Research. *15th Biennial Conference on Entrepreneurship.* Delhi: Bookwell. Retrieved from http://library.ediindia.ac.in:8181/xmlui//handle/123456789/13886

Dixit, K., & Manna, R. (2023). Bibliometric Analysis of Entrepreneurial Orientation and Firm Performance. *Korea Review of International Studies, 16*(49). doi:https://doie.org/client/index.php?tag=generatedoi

Fraillon, J., Ainley, J., Schulz, W., Friedman, T., & Gebhardt, E. (2014). *Preparing for life in a digital age: The IEA International Computer and Information Literacy Study international report.* Springer Nature. DOI: 10.1007/978-3-319-14222-7

George, G., McGahan, A. M., & Prabhu, J. (2012). Innovation for inclusive growth: Towards a theoretical framework and a research agenda. *Journal of Management Studies*, *49*(4), 661–683. DOI: 10.1111/j.1467-6486.2012.01048.x

Gupta, M., & Gupta, H. (2024). Sustainable urban development of smart cities in India-a systematic literature review. *Sustainability, Agri. Food and Environmental Research, 12*. Advance online publication. DOI: 10.7770/safer-V12N1-art2578

Hadjitchoneva, J., Pellat, G., & Marasova, J. (2023). Reinvesting in European Citizenship Through Entrepreneurship and Frugal Innovation. In *Cooperation and Enlargement: Two Challenges to be Addressed in the European Projects - 2022* (pp. 29–49). Springer.

Hamilton, B. (2018). *Digital Tools in Schools: Ethnography of Technology in Town and Rural Elementary Schools*. Denver: (PhD dissertation). University of Colorado.

Hawkins, R., Trucano, M., Cobo, C., Juan, T., Alex, S., & Inaki, A. (2020). *Re-imagining Human Connections: Technology and Innovation in Education at the World Bank*. World Bank Group. Retrieved from http://documents. worldbank. org/curated/en/829491606860379513/Reimagining-Human-Connections-Technology-and-Innovation-in-Education-at-the-World-Bank

Herselman, M., & Britton, K. G. (2002). Analysing the role of ICT in bridging the digital divide amongst learners. *South African Journal of Education, 22*(4), 270–274.

Hollow, D., & Masperi, P. (2009, April). An evaluation of the use of ICT within primary education in Malawi. *International Conference on Information and Communication Technologies and Development (ICTD)* (pp. 27-34). IEEE. DOI: 10.1109/ICTD.2009.5426707

Igwe, P. A., Odunukan, K., Rahman, M., Rugara, D. G., & Ochinanwata, C. (2020). How entrepreneurship ecosystem influences the development of frugal innovation and informal entrepreneurship. *Thunderbird International Business Review, 62*(5), 475–488. DOI: 10.1002/tie.22157

Kazmi, Z. S. (2023). *Exploring the Digital Divide in Educational Technology across Illinois School Districts: a Focus on Business Education in Urban, Suburban, and Rural Schools*. (MSc thesis). Illinois State University.

Kormos, E., & Wisdom, K. (2021). Rural schools and the digital divide: Technology in the learning experience. *Theory and Practice in Rural Education, 11*(1), 25–39. DOI: 10.3776/tpre.2021.v11n1p25-39

Kozma, R. B. (2011). The technological, economic, and social contexts for educational ICT policy. In *Transforming Education: the Power of ICT Policies* (pp. 3–18). United Nations Educational, Scientific and Cultural Organisation., Retrieved from https://policycommons.net/artifacts/8224447/the-technological-economic-and-social-contexts-for-educational-ict-policy/9139858/

Kumar, C. (2024, February). Frugal Innovation and Entrepreneurship. *3rd International Conference on Reinventing Business Practices, Start-ups and Sustainability (ICRBSS 2023)* (pp. 4-15). Atlantis Press. DOI: 10.2991/978-94-6463-374-0_2

López, S. L., Rohmer, S., Díaz-Pichardo, R., & Reyes, T. (2024). Exploring Frugal Innovation as an Ecodesign Strategy: A Case Study of a Water Access Solution at the BoP. In *EcoDesign for Sustainable Products, Services and Social Systems* (pp. 89-102). Springer Nature Singapore. Retrieved from https://link.springer.com/chapter/10.1007/978-981-99-3818-6_7

Ma, R., Chai, K. H., & Hang, C. C. (2015, August). Disruptive innovation and latecomer's catching-up dilemma: Toward a demand-side perspective of frugal entrepreneurship. *Portland International Conference on Management of Engineering and Technology (PICMET)* (pp. 978-987). IEEE. DOI: 10.1109/PICMET.2015.7273202

Mafini, C., & Pooe, D. R. (2013). The relationship between employee satisfaction and organisational performance: Evidence from a South African government department. *SA Journal of Industrial Psychology*, *39*(1), 1–9. DOI: 10.4102/sajip.v39i1.1090

Mahlangu, B. G., & Goosen, L. (2023). The Impact of a Lack of Information and Communication Technologies at Rural Schools: Digitalization in a Changing Education Environment. In Arinushkina, A., Morozov, A., & Robert, I. (Eds.), *Contemporary Challenges in Education: Digitalization, Methodology, and Management* (pp. 254–275). IGI Global., DOI: 10.4018/979-8-3693-1826-3.ch019

Mahlangu, B. G., & Goosen, L. (2024). Enhancing Education With Information and Communication Technologies: Data-Driven Instruction in Rural Schools. In Bhatia, M., & Mushtaq, M. (Eds.), *Enhancing Education With Intelligent Systems and Data-Driven Instruction* (pp. 60–79). IGI Global., DOI: 10.4018/979-8-3693-2169-0.ch004

Manna, R., & Singh, A. (2021). Predictors of Teacher's Engagement of Higher Education: An Exploratory Study. *International Journal of Educational Sciences*, *4*(3-4), 33–39. DOI: 10.26697/ijes

Mashhour, Q. M. (2022). The Role of Frugal Innovation and Social Entrepreneurship in Supporting Socioeconomic Life in Emerging Markets. *Journal for Research on Business and Social Science*, *5*(5). www.jrbssonline.com

Musingafi, M. C., & Chaden'anga, C. (2014). Information and communication technology in classroom situations in rural and urban areas in Zimbabwe: A comparative study on the use of digital and projected media in teaching and learning at six secondary schools in Masvingo. *Review of Information Engineering and Applications*, *1*(4), 77–92. DOI: 10.18488/journal.79/2014.1.2/79.2.77.92

Ngugi, J. K., & Goosen, L. (2021). Innovation, Entrepreneurship, and Sustainability for ICT Students Towards the Post-COVID-19 Era. In Carvalho, L. C., Reis, L., & Silveira, C. (Eds.), *Handbook of Research on Entrepreneurship, Innovation, Sustainability, and ICTs in the Post-COVID-19 Era* (pp. 110–131). IGI Global., DOI: 10.4018/978-1-7998-6776-0.ch006

Omar, M. K., Dainal, E., Puad, M. H., & Zakaria, A. (2023). Factors Determining the Optimization of Digital Technology in Rural Schools. *International Journal of Academic Research in Progressive Education and Development*, *12*(1), 1685–1704. DOI: 10.6007/IJARPED/v12-i1/16559

Palmié, M., Zeschky, M., Winterhalter, S., Sauter, P. W., Haefner, N., & Gassmann, O. (2016). Coordination mechanisms for international innovation in SMEs: Effects on time-to-market and R&D task complexity as a moderator. *Small Business Economics*, *46*(2), 273–294. DOI: 10.1007/s11187-015-9683-8

Phelps, M., Owens, C., & Jordan, P. (2002). Technology delivery using a flex cam to cross the digital divide in rural Tennessee schools. *Society for Information Technology & Teacher Education International Conference* (pp. 1648-1649). Association for the Advancement of Computing in Education (AACE). Retrieved from https://www.learntechlib.org/p/6826/

Radjou, N., Prabhu, J., & Ahuja, S. (2012). *Jugaad innovation: Think frugal, be flexible, generate breakthrough growth.* Jossey-Bass.

Selwyn, N. (2014). *Digital technology and the contemporary university: Degrees of digitization.* Routledge. DOI: 10.4324/9781315768656

Shahid, M. S., Hossain, M., Shahid, S., & Anwar, T. (2023). Frugal innovation as a source of sustainable entrepreneurship to tackle social and environmental challenges. *Journal of Cleaner Production*, *406*, 137050. Advance online publication. DOI: 10.1016/j.jclepro.2023.137050

Thangeni, F. (2022). *Digital leadership: towards developing an innovative technology-led culture of learning in rural Limpopo schools.* (MEd dissertation). University of Johannesburg. Retrieved from http://hdl.handle.net/102000/0002

Tondeur, J., Van Braak, J., Ertmer, P. A., & Ottenbreit-Leftwich, A. (2017). Understanding the relationship between teachers' pedagogical beliefs and technology use in education: A systematic review of qualitative evidence. *Educational Technology Research and Development*, *65*(3), 555–575. DOI: 10.1007/s11423-016-9481-2

Trucano, M., & Dykes, G. (2017). *Building and Sustaining National Educational Technology Agencies*. World Bank. Retrieved from https://openknowledge.worldbank.org/bitstream/10986/26507/1/114271-WP-PUBLIC-ADD-SABER-ICT-technical-paper-series.pdf

Unwin, T. (2017). *Reclaiming information and communication technologies for development*. Oxford University Press. DOI: 10.1093/oso/9780198795292.001.0001

Van Dijk, J. A. (2012). The evolution of the digital divide-the digital divide turns to inequality of skills and usage. In *Digital enlightenment yearbook* (pp. 57–75). IOS Press.

Winterhalter, S., Zeschky, M., Gassmann, O., & Weiblen, T. (2014, June). Business models for frugal innovation: the role of resource-constraints. *R&D Management Conference*, (pp. 3-6).

Winterhalter, S., Zeschky, M. B., & Gassmann, O. (2016). Managing dual business models in emerging markets: An ambidexterity perspective. *R & D Management, 46*(3), 464–479. DOI: 10.1111/radm.12151

Winterhalter, S., Zeschky, M. B., Neumann, L., & Gassmann, O. (2017). Business models for frugal innovation in emerging markets: The case of the medical device and laboratory equipment industry. *Technovation, 66*, 3–13. DOI: 10.1016/j.technovation.2017.07.002

Zeschky, M., Winterhalter, S., & Gassmann, O. (2014a, June 3). What is frugal innovation?: Conceptualization and empirical evidence. Retrieved from https://www.alexandria.unisg.ch/handle/20.500.14171/86840

Zeschky, M. B., Winterhalter, S., & Gassmann, O. (2014b, June 8-11). "Resource-constrained innovation": Classification and implications for multinational firms. *XXV ISPIM Conference Proceedings* (pp. 1-19). Dublin: The International Society for Professional Innovation Management. Retrieved from https://www.alexandria.unisg.ch/handle/20.500.14171/86806

Zeschky, M. B., Winterhalter, S., & Gassmann, O. (2014c, July). From cost to frugal and reverse innovation: Mapping the field and implications for global competitiveness. *Research Technology Management, 57*(4), 20–27. DOI: 10.5437/08956308X5704221

Zhong, Z.-J. (2011). From access to usage: The divide of self-reported digital skills among adolescents. *Computers & Education, 56*(3), 736–746. DOI: 10.1016/j.compedu.2010.10.016

KEY TERMS AND DEFINITIONS

Fourth Industrial Revolution: This is an emerging environment in which innovative industries are no longer determined by the capital they can access or the physical resources at their disposal. Rather, the new revolution is based on the knowledge economy where creative and innovative ideas can be instantly leveraged into business models.

Information and Communication Technologies (ICTs): This is an umbrella term for a range of technologies, which include both the software and hardware that are necessary for providing internet technologies to rural schools.

Microsoft Teams: Microsoft Teams is another platform owned by Microsoft, which provides both audio and video communication between multiple people. Microsoft Teams was designed with business communication in mind and as a result, it has added functions, which can facilitate a meeting or conference online.

Quintile: A system to classify schools according to lower-, middle- and higher-income levels.

Resource Constrained Environment: These environments, which lack the necessary resources both physical and human to achieve the kind of development that is needed. For the purposes of this study, rural schools constitute an example of a resource constrained environment.

Skype: This is another communications platform, which is owned by Microsoft. Skype has been around much longer than most of the other platforms like WhatsApp and Zoom. Skype offers the same functionality as WhatsApp and it has the added advantage of being available on multiple platforms and devices including computers, smartphones, tablets and gaming consoles.

WhatsApp: WhatsApp is the largest instant messaging platform in the world with an estimated 2 billion active users. The platform provides both audio and video conferencing facilities, as well as group conversations that can be used by learners.

Zoom: This is an internet-based audio and video communication platform which has since been the de-facto platform for communicating between and within organizations since the outbreak of COVID 19.

Chapter 9
Tech for Good:
Frugal Innovations in Social Technologies

Ravi Shankar Saripalle
GITAM University, Vishakhapatnam, India

Jayasri Sai Venkata Angara
GITAM University, Visakhapatnam, India

ABSTRACT

In a world confronted with multifaceted challenges in healthcare, agriculture, and education, frugal innovation emerges as a beacon of hope, offering affordable and accessible solutions to address pressing societal needs. This chapter explores the principles and applications of frugal innovation in social technological domains, emphasizing its transformative potential in bridging the gap between technology and underserved communities. Through an in-depth examination of case studies, including Cropin's revolutionary impact on agriculture, Karkinos Distributed Cancer Care Model in healthcare, and a few others, the chapter showcases how frugal innovation leverages low-cost resources, creative problem-solving to empower communities and drive positive social change. The analysis underscores the importance of stakeholder engagement, capacity building, and continuous evaluation in the successful implementation of frugal innovation initiatives. Furthermore, it highlights the scalability and replicability of frugal innovation models in addressing similar challenges across diverse contexts.

DOI: 10.4018/979-8-3693-4050-9.ch009

1. INTRODUCTION

1.1 Definition, Importance, and Historical Context of Frugal Innovation

In a world grappling with complex challenges like poverty, healthcare access, and environmental degradation, technology has emerged as a potential game-changer. From AI-powered diagnostics to AI-Powered Metaverse driven digital teachers/ educational apps reaching remote villages, advancements are rapidly evolving and offer a glimmer of hope. However, the high cost and complex nature of technology often leave underserved communities behind. Here's where frugal innovation in the tech sector steps in, offering a unique path towards positive social impact.

Frugal innovation, rooted in finding affordable and accessible solutions, has gained traction in the tech sector as a means to harness technology for the greater good. Also known as “jugaad” or “resourceful innovation,” frugal innovation refers to developing affordable and accessible solutions that cater to the needs and constraints of resource-limited communities (Prabhu, 2017).

Frugal innovation challenges the notion that effective solutions require hefty budgets and intricate designs. Instead, it celebrates affordability, accessibility, and simplicity, leveraging low-cost resources and creative problem-solving to address pressing needs. Imagine a portable diagnostic tool built with readily available materials, enabling rural communities to access basic healthcare. Or picture an educational app, stripped of unnecessary features, running on low-bandwidth internet, bringing vital knowledge to children in areas with limited connectivity. These are just glimpses of the immense potential frugal innovation holds.

Frugal innovation is also referred as reverse innovation, Jugaad innovation, bottom of the pyramid, Gandhian innovation, empathetic innovation, long tail and long tailoring innovation, below-the-radar innovation, inclusive innovation, propoor innovation by various authors in different contexts (Parwez and Shekar, 2019).

Frugal innovation is a hybrid approach tuned to environments with extreme resource constraints and voids. It promotes the idea that technology should not only be accessible and affordable but also relevant and impactful in addressing the needs of underserved communities (Bhatti et al., 2018).

Frugal Innovations are low cost but many a times outperform the alternatives and available in large scale. Frugal innovation is a distinctive approach to innovation both in its means and its ends. Sometimes factors like lacklustre growth, developed economies, environmental constraints (frugal models for production and consumption), rapidly aging societies, fastest growing markets and new technology platforms (in reducing the costs and new opportunities for frugal innovators), etc drive the frugal innovations. Having said that it is not always related to cheap and low-tech products. On contrary, it encourages and enforces four different features- 1. “Making better things, not just cheaper things” 2. “Extends to services, not just products” 3. “Remodelling, not just de–featuring” 4. “Low cost is not low–tech”. These four features drive the definition to new dimension (Bound and Thornton, 2012).

Grassroots innovation and frugal innovation both prioritize local needs and resource constraints, fostering solutions that are community-driven and cost-effective, respectively, while aiming for broad societal impact. while both types of innovation share a focus on resourcefulness and societal impact, they differ in their origins, scopes, drivers, and approaches to scaling and implementation. Studying grassroots innovation, as championed by the Honey Bee Network, offers valuable insights into local problem-solving and transferable knowledge for fostering social inclusion technologies across diverse settings (Gupta et al., 2003). Grassroots innovations thrive at individual, group, and societal levels, making them powerful sources of new ideas when nurtured (Grabs et al., 2016).

Grassroots innovation thrives on a culture of collaboration (negotiation, social learning, democracy) and thrives under conditions that value openness, diversity, and empowering local learning structures (Ornetzeder and Rohracher, 2013). Grassroots innovation, driven by marginalized communities and those living in poverty, leverages unique insights to address challenges like climate change, social inequality, and economic development (Rani and Srivastava, 2023). Grassroots innovations, driven by local values, encompass sectors like community energy and organic food, contributing uniquely to sustainable development despite facing challenges in funding and policy support (Hossain, 2018). Both types of innovation (frugal/grassroots) demonstrate how creative solutions can arise from diverse contexts and constraints, emphasizing the importance of context-specific approaches to innovation.

Exploring how technology can be harnessed for the greater good, not just the privileged few, is no longer an option, but an imperative. By embracing cost-effective and accessible solutions, we can unlock technology's true potential to empower communities, bridge the digital divide, and create a more equitable world. Imagine the ripple effect of scaling up these frugal innovations – improved health outcomes, expanded educational opportunities, and communities empowered to solve their own problems.

This vision drives this chapter to delve deeper, explore inspiring case studies, and unlock the potential for a future where technology truly serves humanity. It presents how social technological frugal innovations can transform the communities, ensuring that technological advancements leave no one behind and pave the way for a brighter, more inclusive future. It highlights the importance of exploring cost-effective and accessible solutions to address societal challenges.

2. CASE STUDIES

This section presents real-world examples to illustrate the principles and concepts discussed earlier. Two meticulously crafted case studies have been developed through direct interviews with key stakeholders, while several others draw on secondary survey data. Together, these examples provide insights into the application of theoretical frameworks in practical settings, highlighting the complexities and nuances of Frugal Innovation in the Modern and Digital context. Valuable lessons and best practices are extracted to inform future research and practice in the field.

Case Study 1: Title: Transforming Agriculture: A Case Study on Cropin (https://www.cropin.com/)

Method: Primary Survey (Interviews)

Introduction

In the ever-evolving landscape of agriculture, technological advancements play a pivotal role in addressing the challenges faced by farmers and stakeholders across the agri-food ecosystem. Cropin, a global B2B agtech company, has emerged as a leader in this domain, revolutionizing the industry with its innovative solutions. This case study delves into Cropin's journey, highlighting its impact on agriculture and the transformative role played by its flagship product, Cropin Cloud. In the contemporary times, Frugal Innovation, also known as frugal engineering is an approach to product development and problem-solving that focuses on creating simple, affordable, and effective solutions. A specific study affirmed that IoT and AI both are valid predictors of frugal innovation. Enterprises should incorporate both capabilities to achieve frugal innovation and compete in the market (Qin, 2024). Cropin's mature AI and ML models offer actionable predictive insights, including crop and yield health, pest and disease prediction, yield estimation, prescriptive recommendations, operational optimization, and climate and risk advisory. With 22 AI models covering various aspects of agriculture, Cropin ensures data-driven decision-making for over 250 enterprises worldwide. It aptly uses data analytics, earth observation, and weather intelligence with agronomy sciences to solve complex agricultural problems. Cropin has digitized 30 million acres of farmland, improving the livelihoods of more than 7 million farmers. The company is shaping the global 'Ag-intelligence' movement with Cropin Cloud, powered by the most comprehensive crop knowledge graph built on analysing trillions of data points from 500+ crops and 10000+ crop varieties across 103 countries. Cropin Cloud's Intelligence platform has already enabled 200 million acres of farmlands worldwide. Google, Bill and Melinda Gates Foundation, JSR Corporation and ABC Impact among others invested in this company at a tune of USD $47 Million.

Background

Founded in 2010, Cropin embarked on a mission to leverage digital transformation to empower the agricultural sector. Recognizing the need for a comprehensive solution to address the complexities of large-scale farming operations, Cropin developed Cropin Cloud, the world's first industry cloud for agriculture. This platform integrates cutting-edge technologies such as artificial intelligence, machine learning, data analytics, and earth observation, along with agronomy sciences, to provide actionable insights throughout the farming lifecycle. Cropin Cloud enables various stakeholders in the agricultural ecosystem to make informed decisions to improve the efficiency and productivity of large-scale global farming operations. It also helps manage and mitigate risks impacting food security and climate change, and build a sustainable agri value chain by leveraging digital technologies and predictive intelligence that are easy to adopt and deploy at the grassroots level. Cropin helps build a connected and sustainable agricultural ecosystem that can benefit farmers, farming companies, agri-input providers, food processing companies, retailers, financial service providers, governments, and development agencies. The company has been instrumental in building the global Agtech category as part of its mission to eliminate the uncertainties associated with agriculture and make it predictable, traceable, and sustainable.

Challenges Faced by Agriculture

The agriculture industry faces multifaceted challenges ranging from ensuring food security and mitigating climate change risks to improving productivity and sustainability. Traditional farming practices often lack the technological infrastructure and knowhow to effectively manage these emerging challenges, leading to inefficiencies and uncertainties.

Cropin's Solution

Cropin Cloud serves as a catalyst for transformation within the agricultural ecosystem. By digitizing farmland and leveraging predictive intelligence, Cropin enables stakeholders to make informed decisions, optimize resource utilization, and mitigate risks effectively. The platform facilitates real-time monitoring and management of farming operations, from cultivation to harvesting and beyond, thereby enhancing efficiency and productivity.

Impact and Results

Cropin's impact on agriculture has been profound. With over 250 B2B customers and 30 million acres of farmland digitized, Cropin has improved the livelihoods of more than 7 million farmers worldwide. By harnessing the power of data analytics and AI, Cropin Cloud has enabled the optimization of agricultural practices, leading to increased yields, reduced environmental footprint, and enhanced food traceability (Cropin, 2024).

Furthermore, Cropin's collaboration with various stakeholders across the agricultural value chain has fostered a connected and sustainable ecosystem. From farming companies to agri-input providers, food processing companies, retailers, and governments, Cropin's solutions cater to diverse needs, driving positive change and innovation in the industry.

Cropin Technology Solutions

Cropin Cloud combines a suite of agriculture digitization applications, access to powerful, ready-to-use data sources, and AI-powered agri-intelligence into an integrated, easy-to-use platform. Cropin Cloud will help accelerate digital transformation across the agri-ecosystem. It will deliver a scalable agri-stack that comprises a powerful triad of capabilities, including Cropin Apps, Cropin Data Hub, and Cropin Intelligence:

Cropin Apps - Enables digital transformation at scale across agriculture and allied industries, including forestry, commodity, banking and insurance: They enable a range of use cases such as global farming operations management, food safety measures, supply chain visibility, predictability and risk management, farm-to-fork traceability, farmer enablement and engagement, advance Seed R&D, trialling, production management and multi-generational seed traceability. Cropin Apps also enables the adoption of Climate Smart and Regenerative Agriculture, crop protection and nutrition management on/off the field, and monitoring and managing deforestation and carbon emissions.

As part of Cropin Apps, the company offers

1. Farm Monitoring and Management Solution:

   Cropin's comprehensive farm monitoring and management solution (Cropin Grow) offer a range of capabilities, including geotagging farm plots, implementing Package of Practices, crop health management advisory, yield predictability, and real-time alerts for pest and disease control. This solution has been successfully deployed by hundreds of customers globally, ensuring efficient farm operations and verifiable adherence to best practices.

2. Communication Solution for Seamless Connectivity:

   The easy-to-use communication solution by Cropin (Cropin Connect) connects growers, agri-businesses, and field officers, facilitating digitized grower activities. Features like plot monitoring, task progress recording, instant advice, farmer feedback, and multi-language support contribute to improved communication and streamlined operations.

3. QR Code-Enabled Traceability Solution:

   Cropin's QR code-enabled farm-to-fork traceability solution (Cropin Trace) ensures end-to-end traceability with patented labelling technology. This solution helps eliminate counterfeiting, rewards everyone involved in the food supply chain, and maintains quality benchmarks.

   Cropin Data Hub - Delivers the power of unified data: The Data Hub enables interfacing with multiple agri-data sources - on-field farm management apps, IoT devices, drones, mechanization data from farming resources, remote sensing satellite and weather data. Businesses can access structured and contextualized data from various sources for correlation and data analysis at scale. Cropin Data Hub also has pre-built advanced data frameworks to solve the most challenging problems, such as cloud-free satellite imagery, boundary detection of farm plots, and segmentation of land use.

   Cropin Intelligence - As part of the Intelligence platform, Cropin's 22 contextual deep-learning AI models will help agribusinesses with intelligence around crop detection, crop stage identification, yield estimation, irrigation scheduling, pest and disease prediction, nitrogen uptake, water stress detection, harvest date estimation, change detection, among others. Built using the world's largest crop knowledge graph, these field-tested models are fine-tuned for specific crop varieties, conditions, and locations.

Cropin's Impactful Case Studies

1. Case Study: Maximizing Yield through Predictive Intelligence & Remote Sensing Solutions

   Client Overview: North America's largest food and beverage processing company faced challenges in maintaining a consistent supply of high-quality potatoes due to the complex and unpredictable nature of potato cultivation. With varying conditions and disease risks, ensuring optimal crop output and quality was a daunting task.

   Challenges Faced:

- Intricate and uncertain processes in potato cultivation.
- Varying conditions affecting crop output and quality.
- Risk of diseases impacting yield.

Cropin's Solution: Cropin provided the client with Plot-level Intelligence, a digital solution enabling real-time monitoring and management of potato crops across multiple farms and regions in Asia. This tool offered valuable data on yield, crop health, and irrigation-related issues, empowering the client to make informed decisions.

Key Features of Plot-level Intelligence:

- Detailed insights at the plot level.
- Optimization of farm operations and profitability.
- Yield estimation, crop stage monitoring, and harvest date prediction.
- Weather condition updates.
- Utilization of AI/ML models including Canopy Greenness Index, Canopy Water Stress, Crop Progression Index, and Disease Early Warning System.

Results Achieved: By implementing Cropin's solutions, the client achieved remarkable outcomes:

- 90% Weather prediction accuracy.
- 87% Disease early warning system accuracy.
- 87% Crop stage progression accuracy.
- 84% Canopy greenness accuracy.
- 80% Nitrogen uptake accuracy.
- 80% Water stress identification accuracy.

Impact:

- Enhanced operational efficiency.
- Increased yield and improved crop quality.
- Proactive disease management.
- Optimized resource utilization.
- Real-time insights driving decision-making.

2. Global Brewing Company: Streamlining Procurement for Seamless Production

Challenges: Manual intervention in crop yield estimation, inconsistent yield forecasting, intentional data manipulation.

Cropin's Solution: AI-led predictive mapping of sorghum growing areas in Nigeria, accurate yield prediction with 84% accuracy.

Impact: Analysed over 25 million hectares, 84% accuracy in sorghum yield prediction, streamlined procurement strategy.

3. Major Sugarcane Producer in Zambia: Digitization for Improved Operational Management

    Challenges: Cumbersome manual data capture, lack of transparency, absence of irrigation insights.

    Cropin's Solution: End-to-end farm management solution for 15,00 hectares, real-time insights, proactive pest and disease alerts.

    Impact: 100% digitization, daily task scheduling, efficient irrigation management.

4. Tea Plantations in Tamil Nadu: Redefining the Tea Value Chain

    Challenges: Cumbersome manual data capturing, lack of real-time information on crop health.

    Cropin's Solution: Unique dashboard for monitoring 50 plantations, AI/ML, satellite imagery, and big data for accurate yield estimates.

    Impact: 2500 hectares covered, alerts for pest infestations, and weather-based advisories.

5. Gebana: Enhancing Transparency for Global Banana Trade

    Challenges: Need for digitization, centralized operations, transparency in global trade.

    Cropin's Solution: End-to-end farm management in Togo and Burkina Faso, 100% digitization, improved visibility.

    Impact: Managed 1700+ hectares in Togo, 21,000 hectares in Burkina Faso, 100% digitization.

6. AWBA Myanmar: Empowering Rural Farming Communities

    Objectives: Sustainable solutions, providing plot-level information, satellite- and weather-based advisories.

    Cropin's Solution: Digitization for marketing, dealer management, farmer engagement, and loyalty.

    Impact: Efficient management of sales and farm teams, visibility of sales points, customer loyalty.

7. **East-West Seed:** East-West Seed is one of the world's largest vegetable seed companies. The key challenges include, Cost-inefficient and cumbersome data collection process, inherent inaccuracy associated with manual data collection, Challenge in monitoring the quantity of agrochemicals, and Inconsistent metrics. Cropin Grow has enabled a remarkable 96% real-time

data capture. Cropin's centralized management and operations dashboards proved to be a game-changer for East-West Seed, improving monitoring and aiding better decision-making. End-to-end visibility for business transformation across six countries, impacting audited area of 21,624+ hectares, farmers 14,200+, crop varieties covered 400+, Field staff empowered 272, and Crops recorded 35+.

8. **Loacker: Digitizing the hazelnut value chain:** Loacker, an Italian company based in South Tyrol (Italy), produces wafers, chocolates, and derivative products with the promise of wholesome natural goodness, highest quality standards and absolute deliciousness.

Challenges:

- ✓ The inability to provide technical advice to farmers and monitor farms
- ✓ Poor visibility into farmers' cultivation processes and demarcation of their plots
- ✓ Inherent quality issues of the hazelnut crop

How Cropin helped: Deployed Cropin's farm digitization and traceability apps - Cropin Grow (SmartFarm) and Cropin Trace (RootTrace) to ensure its objectives of quality and sustainability in hazelnut production.

Impact:

- ✓ Total Number of Farmers: 85+
- ✓ Total Number of Plots: 95+
- ✓ Acres of audited Area: 225+
- ✓ Tonnes of harvest: 2000+

9. **Cropin partnered with Government of Bihar, Madhya Pradesh & World Bank for Project Jeevika** across 244 villages, covering 77 crop varieties.

Benefits:

- ✓ Improved water management
- ✓ Pest and disease forecast
- ✓ Monitor input usage
- ✓ Improved soil fertility
- ✓ More than 90% of farmers were satisfied with the solution

10. Cropin also involved in Pradhan Mantri Fasal Bima Yojana (PMFBY), the world's largest crop insurance program implemented in 250k panchayats across India.

Benefits:

- ✓ Accurate smart sampling
- ✓ Crop detection
- ✓ Yield benchmarking
- ✓ Scale: 50+ districts
- ✓ Accuracy - 92%
- ✓ Crops - paddy, maize, chickpea, wheat, cotton.

Cropin Future Plans:

As Cropin continues to expand its global footprint and innovate within the agtech space, the company remains committed to its mission of eliminating uncertainties in agriculture and fostering a predictable, traceable, and sustainable future. With its unparalleled expertise and technological prowess, Cropin is poised to shape the future of agriculture through data-driven insights and transformative solutions.

Case Conclusion:

Cropin exemplifies the transformative potential of technology in agriculture. By harnessing the power of data and digital innovation, Cropin has not only addressed the challenges faced by the industry but has also paved the way for a more sustainable and resilient future. As the agricultural landscape continues to evolve, Cropin stands as a beacon of innovation, driving positive change and empowerment across the agri-food ecosystem.

Case Study 2: Empowering Cancer Care: The Distributed Cancer Care Model (DCCM) Transforming Rural Healthcare (www.karkinos.in)

Method: Primary Survey (Interviews)

Introduction

The healthcare industry in India has been grappling with challenges related to cancer care, including limited access to screening and treatment services in rural areas. The rising incidence of cancer cases in regions like Kerala has underscored the need for innovative solutions to bridge these gaps. Technology-enabled models, such as the Distributed Cancer Care Model (DCCM) developed by Karkinos Healthcare, have emerged as promising approaches to address these issues by leveraging frugal technology and strategic partnerships with private health centers.

Objectives

The primary objective of this case study is to examine the impact of the DCCM in Kerala in a hub-and-spoke hierarchy, focusing on how technology can drive social impact in healthcare communities.

Methodology

Data for this case study was collected through a combination of interviews with key stakeholders involved in the implementation of the DCCM, document analysis of program reports and outcomes, and on-site observations of the model in action at various healthcare facilities in Kerala.

Case Presentation

Between July to December 2021, a total of 2,459 individuals were screened for cancer across various hospitals within the Distributed Cancer Care Model (DCCM). Out of the 2,459 individuals screened for cancer at the spoke centers identified 299 individuals with positive results. 145 patients underwent further diagnostic tests at spoke centres for confirmatory diagnosis.

Existing patients who would have otherwise travelled to cities inside or outside Kerala, received care at the spoke hospitals nearer to their homes. A total of 189 chemotherapy sessions and 17 surgeries were performed at the spokes for cancer patients. 70 patients were referred to the hub. Seamless transitions within the DCCM network with the help of the digital command center ensured coordinated care and navigation.

By aligning with the hub and spoke centers within the DCCN framework, it becomes evident how the hierarchical model optimizes cancer care delivery by distributing services based on the complexity of care required.

Solution

Frugal technologies such as mobile applications for patient engagement and teleconsultations were key components of the solution, enabling efficient delivery of care in remote areas. The command center leveraged technology and centralized data management to provide essential support in patient navigation, care coordination, appointment scheduling, data management, teleconsultations, and the network as a whole.

Results

Enhance access to cancer diagnosis and treatment

The DCCN model significantly enhanced access to cancer diagnosis and treatment, particularly for individuals residing in rural areas where tertiary cancer care centers are limited.

Enable Early Diagnosis

By decentralizing cancer care services and establishing a network of hub and spoke centers, the DCCN addressed accessibility challenges and improved outcomes through early detection and timely intervention.

Improved Patient Experience

The command center of Karkinos Healthcare ensured efficient patient navigation and visit management, which has helped accelerate the overall workflow of healthcare delivery.

Challenges Faced

During the implementation of the DCCM, challenges were encountered in terms of integrating the technology platforms across different healthcare facilities, ensuring consistent quality of care, and addressing logistical barriers in remote areas. External challenges such as limited infrastructure and awareness about cancer care also posed obstacles to the successful implementation of the model.

Lessons Learned

The case study reflects on the importance of stakeholder engagement, capacity building, and continuous monitoring and evaluation in the successful implementation of technology-enabled healthcare models like the DCCM. Insights gained from the case study underscore the need for ongoing training, infrastructure development, and community outreach to sustain and scale such initiatives.

Scalability and Replicability

The DCCM model demonstrates potential for scalability and replicability in other contexts and regions facing similar challenges in cancer care delivery. By adapting the model to local needs, building partnerships with existing healthcare providers, and leveraging frugal technologies, the solution can be effectively implemented in diverse settings with appropriate adjustments.

Case Conclusion

By addressing key challenges in cancer care delivery through innovative solutions, the DCCM serves as a promising model for enhancing access to quality care and reducing disparities in cancer treatment.

Secondary Survey Based Case Studies

A. M-Pesa: A Case Study in Financial Inclusion

M-Pesa, a mobile phone-based money transfer service in Kenya and Tanzania. It is a testimonial for technology-driven frugal innovation with social impact, reducing cash-driven crime. This service has directly or indirectly promoted six SDGs and has the potential to enable long-term social sustainability by empowering communities, improving livelihoods, and fostering inclusive development (Rosca et al., 2017; Centre for Public Impact [CPI], 2016). M-Pesa, launched in Kenya in 2007 by Safaricom, is a pioneering mobile money transfer service that revolutionized financial access for millions.

Problem:

- ✓ Lack of access to formal financial services for a large portion of the Kenyan population, particularly in rural areas.
- ✓ Reliance on cash, leading to security risks and inefficiency.

Solution:

- ✓ M-Pesa allows users to send, receive, and store money using their mobile phones.
- ✓ Network of agents (shops) facilitates cash deposits and withdrawals.
- ✓ User-friendly interface through SMS menus.

Impact:

- ✓ **Financial Inclusion**: From the launch, M-Pesa had become the leading money transfer method in the country. In 2009, over 50 percent of people sending money via M-Pesa and over 65 percent receiving funds through the system. By 2015 there were 19.9 million active M-Pesa users. By that time, more than 43 percent of Kenya's GDP flowed through M-Pesa, with over 237 million person-to-person transactions.

- ✓ **Economic Growth**: Facilitated easier and faster money transfers, boosting small businesses and trade.
- ✓ **Security**: Reduced reliance on cash, minimizing theft and loss.
- ✓ **Convenience**: Simplified bill payments, shopping, and sending remittances.

Challenges:

- ✓ **Security Concerns:** Mitigating fraud and cyber threats.
- ✓ **Regulation:** Adapting to evolving regulations in the mobile money space.
- ✓ **Competition:** Maintaining market share with emergence of similar services.

Future:

- ✓ M-Pesa continues to expand its services, offering bill payments, micro-loans, and savings products.
- ✓ Integration with other fintech solutions is fostering a broader financial ecosystem.
- ✓ M-Pesa serves as a model for mobile money services in developing countries worldwide.

B. Aravind Eye Care System: A Case Study in Frugal Healthcare

Aravind Eye Care is an apt testimonial for frugal innovation, addressing various aspects of social sustainability, including human well-being, quality of life, social justice, poverty alleviation, building social infrastructure and capital, employment, and education (Khan, 2016).

Aravind Eye Care System, established in 1976 with humble beginnings as an 11-bed hospital, has evolved into a network encompassing six tertiary care centers, six secondary care centers, six outpatient examination clinics, and 63 primary eye care centers. The network centers perform about 12,500 outpatient visits and 1500 surgeries daily. Annually, it handles over 1.2 million outpatient appointments.

Founded on principles of never turning away patients, delivering high-quality care, and promoting self-reliance, Aravind Eye Care System emphasizes continuous improvement and innovation in meeting patient needs. The organization's founder, Dr. Govindappa Venkataswamy, instilled a culture of efficiency and resourcefulness to maximize patient care despite resource constraints.

Aravind Eye Care System integrates sustainability practices, including low carbon dioxide emissions per surgery and extensive recycling efforts. Since its inception, Aravind Eye Care System has conducted over 48 million outpatient visits, 5.5 million surgeries, and trained 8,300 eye care professionals globally. The organization's manufacturing arm, Aurolab, exports intraocular lenses worldwide, further enhancing its impact on global eye care accessibility. (Powell, 2017; Virmani and Lépineux, 2016)

C. Khan Academy: A Case Study in Secondary Education

Introduction

Khan Academy (KA) has emerged as a prominent online platform offering educational resources across various subjects, including mathematics. This case study explores the effectiveness of Khan Academy in conjunction with traditional learning methods among secondary students, focusing on their perceptions and outcomes.

Implementation of Khan Academy

The study by Vidergor and Ben-Amram (2020) investigates the effectiveness of Khan Academy (KA) in conjunction with traditional learning, examining secondary students' perceptions. Findings highlight students' increased perception of independence, commitment to math, and positive views on KA's role in encouraging independence and making learning more motivating. The study underscores the importance of teacher-student relationships in conjunction with KA to promote personalized and innovative teaching-learning processes.

Impact:

- ✓ **Increased Access to Education:** Khan Academy removes geographical and financial barriers, making quality education accessible to anyone with an internet connection.
- ✓ **Mastery Learning:** Students can practice and master concepts before moving on, promoting deeper understanding.
- ✓ **Teacher Support:** Khan Academy offers tools and data to help teachers personalize instruction and track student progress.
- ✓ **Flipped Classroom Model:** Teachers can use Khan Academy videos as pre-work, allowing them to dedicate classroom time to deeper exploration and activities.

D. MeraPashu360 (Dairy)

MeraPashu360 is a technology-cum-physical platform aimed at improving the lives of dairy farmers by providing access to quality cattle, nutrition, veterinary services, and health advisory. According to their website, they have served over

27,000 farmers, delivered 75,000 orders, sold 650+ buffaloes and cows, and provided 11,000+ tons of feed (MeraPashu360, 2024)

E. DeHaat (Agriculture)

DeHaat Farmer App provides multiple services to farmers on crop reminders, voice calls in regional languages, crop advisories, weather reports, local mandi rates, etc. to over 1.4 million farmers in 12 major agri-based states in India. They have 8000+ OneStop DeHaat centers, providing advisory for sustainable agriculture about 300+hrs/month, available in 6 regional languages, impacted 80,000+ hectares (DeHaat, 2024).

F. Ninjacart (B2C Delivery Service)

Ninjacart was founded in 2015, working as hyperlocal B2C delivery service, having products like Ninjacart (Delivering farm-fresh produce daily to retailers), Ninjamandi (for agri commodity traders), Ninjakisan (smart solutions for farmers), Ninjakirana (credit opportunities for kirana owners), Ninjaglobal (for global trade) (Ninjacart, 2024).

G. PhysicsWallah (Education)

Alakh Pandey, an unconventional physics teacher, started PhysicsWallah as a free YouTube channel in 2016. Today, he has huge social following with 31 million subscribers, 61 YouTube channels, and 5.3 billion views. PhysicWallah revenue jumped to Rs751 crore in FY23. It stayed bootstrapped for 6 years, and then raised $100 million in 2022, and now it is part of Unicorn. This is classic frugal innovation in EduTech domain (Singh, 2023).

H. Embrace Incubator (Neonatal Care)

Jane Chen, co-founder of Embrace, witnessed the dire consequences of neonatal hypothermia during a trip to India, inspiring the development of the Embrace Incubator. This portable solution, utilizing phase-change material technology, has saved over 350,000 newborns to date. Recognized for its impact, Embrace continues to strive towards its goal of impacting 1 million babies by 2025, epitomizing the power of frugal innovation in healthcare. Through strategic partnerships and ongoing innovation, Embrace remains at the forefront of transforming neonatal care worldwide (Embrace Incubator, 2024).

I. MomConnect (Child Health Services)

MomConnect is a South African National Department of Health initiative which aims to support maternal health through the use of cell phone-based technologies integrated into maternal and child health services. The services are free to the user, and messages are available in all our 11 official languages. The women were consistently positive about MomConnect, attaching high value to the content of the messages and the medium in which they were delivered. (Skinner, 2018).

J. Digital Green (Agriculture)

Digital Green is a pioneering research initiative in India focused on delivering tailored agricultural knowledge to small and marginal farmers through digital video technology. Its distinctive features include a participatory content creation process, a locally curated digital video repository, human-mediated dissemination, and strategic community engagement. Unlike approaches relying solely on technology, Digital Green synergizes with existing extension systems and harnesses social dynamics to enhance effectiveness. Through leveraging local social networks and the allure of being showcased on video, it fosters farmer-expert connections and minimizes the distance between learners and educators. Digital Green has had a significant impact on agriculture, achieving cost reductions, tech-assisted solutions, increased income, production, and partnerships. They reduced the cost per farmer for adopting safer farming practices from $35 to $3.50, making their methods 10 times more cost-effective than traditional approaches. They provided assistance to over 5.6 million farmers, with 60% being women, increasing farmer incomes by up to 24% and crop yields by up to 12%. They partnered with Ministries of Agriculture in Ethiopia, India, and Kenya and participated in World Bank programs. Additionally, they helped 100,000 government extension agents facilitate video-training screenings and gather farmer feedback and data. Digital Green facilitated the production of 7,000+ location-specific, climate-smart videos in 50 languages, garnering over 82 million YouTube views (Digital Green, 2024).

K. Project Loon (Internet Access)

In fact, the projects like Project Loon, initiated by Alphabet Inc., aimed at providing internet access to rural and remote areas using high-altitude balloons, is a mission towards Frugal Innovations in the social technology context. The project involved deploying a network of these balloons into the Earth's stratosphere, where they could float and navigate through winds to provide internet coverage to underserved regions (Alphabet Inc., 2024).

L. SELCO (Sustainable Energy)

SELCO India exemplifies frugal innovation by providing sustainable energy solutions tailored to the needs of underserved communities. Through strategic partnerships and visionary leadership, SELCO has thrived for three decades, demonstrating the viability of inclusive business models in addressing pressing societal challenges (SELCO, 2024).

M. Miscellaneous (Multiple Domains)

There are similar impactful examples like Jaipur foot, Kerala's Palliative Care, Narayana Hrudayalaya, and Vortex Engineering (Solar Powered ATMs), etc., exhibit the principles of frugal innovation (Khan, 2016).

Anirudh Sharma, an innovator and entrepreneur, has developed a revolutionary technology aimed at enhancing mobility and independence for the visually impaired. The Haptic Shoe represents a significant advancement in assistive technology, offering tactile feedback to users through their footwear (Pareek, 2014)

The Mitticool refrigerator is an innovative and eco-friendly product developed by Mansukhbhai Prajapati, a traditional clay craftsman from Gujarat, India. This refrigerator does not require electricity to function, making it a sustainable solution for food preservation, especially in rural areas. Mitticool is a natural refrigerator made entirely from clay that stores vegetables, fruits, and cools water without requiring electricity. It can keep fruits, vegetables, and milk fresh for 2 to 3 days, utilizing the evaporation principle for cooling. For optimal performance, it should be placed in a well-ventilated area and its outer body should be cleaned every two to three days. Capacity: 20 litre of water, 5 kg fruit/vegetable & 5 litre of milk/any other liquid can be stored, Temperature: 5-8 °C less than the outside Temperature, Weight: 23 kg, Dimensions: 27"×15"×12", Material: Clay (National Innovation Foundation - India, n.d.).

Dr. Rajagopalan Vasudevan, a 73-year-old chemistry professor from Madurai, India, has pioneered the use of waste plastic in road construction. His innovative method, which combines molten plastic with bitumen and gravel, has improved road durability and reduced the environmental impact of plastic waste. This technique has been widely adopted across India, significantly contributing to sustainable infrastructure development (Thiagarajan, 2018).

Arunachalam Muruganantham, an innovator from Coimbatore, Tamil Nadu, developed a low-cost, semi-automatic machine to produce affordable sanitary napkins. This invention has significantly improved access to hygiene products for women, especially in lower-income groups, by reducing the cost of sanitary pads (Economic Times, 2017).

3. COMPARATIVE ANALYSIS

Frugal innovation has emerged as a transformative approach to addressing complex challenges in various sectors by focusing on cost-effectiveness, accessibility, and sustainability.

Agricultural innovations are primarily driven by the need to increase productivity and sustainability while ensuring accessibility to small-scale and resource-poor farmers. Examples include low-cost drip irrigation systems that enhance water use efficiency, mobile apps providing real-time farming information, and drought-resistant seed varieties. These innovations often employ user-centered design, utilize local resources to minimize costs, and are designed for scalability to benefit a large number of farmers.

In healthcare, frugal innovation focuses on reducing the cost of medical services and devices, thereby improving access to healthcare in remote and underserved areas. Key examples include low-cost diagnostic tools like handheld ECG machines and portable ultrasound devices, telemedicine platforms enabling remote consultations, and the production of affordable generic medicines. Approaches in healthcare often involve the simplification of technology, task shifting to train non-specialist health workers, and partnerships with non-profits and governments to expand reach.

Both sectors prioritize affordability and accessibility, yet they face distinct challenges and adopt sector-specific methodologies. Agriculture innovations address variable climatic conditions and market access, while healthcare innovations combat high equipment costs and infrastructural constraints. Technological adoption is typically slower in agriculture due to traditional practices, whereas healthcare sees faster adoption driven by the urgent need for improved solutions.

Extending the analysis to other sectors such as energy and education highlights further contrasts and parallels. In the energy sector, frugal innovations aim to provide sustainable and affordable solutions through renewable energy sources and decentralized systems, often requiring significant initial investments. In education, innovations focus on improving access to quality education via digital platforms and low-cost materials, emphasizing content delivery and pedagogical methods. Both energy and education share the frugal innovation principles of cost reduction and accessibility but differ in their specific implementations and challenges.

The comparative analysis underscores the versatility of frugal innovation in addressing diverse challenges across different sectors. While the fundamental principles remain consistent, the application and impact vary significantly based on sector-specific needs and constraints.

4. CHALLENGES AND LIMITATIONS

One of the primary challenges faced in frugal innovation is overcoming financial constraints. Innovators often work with limited budgets, restricting their ability to invest in research, development, and scaling up of their solutions. Lack of access to funding sources and high upfront costs for prototyping and testing can hinder the progress of innovative ideas, especially in resource-constrained settings. In the case of Grassroots initiatives, though powerful for tackling local problems, struggle with development hurdles and lack effective tools to assess success. This highlights the need for better methods to identify potential pitfalls and emphasizes the importance of community involvement for stronger grassroots movements (Dana et al., 2021).

Navigating regulatory frameworks presents another significant challenge. In sectors like healthcare and agriculture, stringent regulations may require extensive certifications and approvals for new products or technologies. These processes can be time-consuming, costly, and complex, particularly for innovations originating from developing countries where regulatory systems may not be streamlined or supportive of novel approaches.

Cultural resistance poses a substantial barrier to the adoption of frugal innovations. Societal norms, beliefs, and traditions can influence acceptance and uptake of new technologies or practices. Innovators must navigate cultural sensitivities and preferences, often requiring tailored approaches to ensure that innovations align with local customs and are perceived as beneficial and relevant by the community.

Achieving scalability is a critical challenge for frugal innovations aiming to reach large populations. Scaling requires efficient production processes, distribution networks, and sustainable business models. Innovators must address logistical challenges, supply chain complexities, and operational scalability while maintaining affordability and accessibility across diverse geographical and demographic contexts.

Addressing financial constraints, regulatory hurdles, cultural resistance, and scalability issues are critical for the success and impact of frugal innovations. By learning from diverse case studies across sectors, innovators can develop strategies to navigate these challenges effectively, ensuring that their innovations are sustainable, scalable, and beneficial to communities worldwide.

5. FUTURE DIRECTIONS AND RECOMMENDATIONS

A. Frugal Innovations Landscape Matrix

To advance frugal innovations, it is crucial to create an ecosystem that supports and nurtures such initiatives. Governments, non-profits, and private sector entities should collaborate to provide funding, resources, and mentorship programs specifically tailored for frugal innovators. Establishing dedicated innovation hubs and incubators can offer a conducive environment for idea generation, prototyping, and scaling.

The following Figure 1 "Frugal Innovations Landscape Matrix", presents the landscape of frugal innovations, that can effectively illustrate how different innovations and ecosystems interact based on their innovation ability, efficiency, and the level of ecosystem support they receive. Using this matrix, agencies can evaluate the innovation's potential and provide necessary support.

Figure 1. Frugal innovations landscape matrix

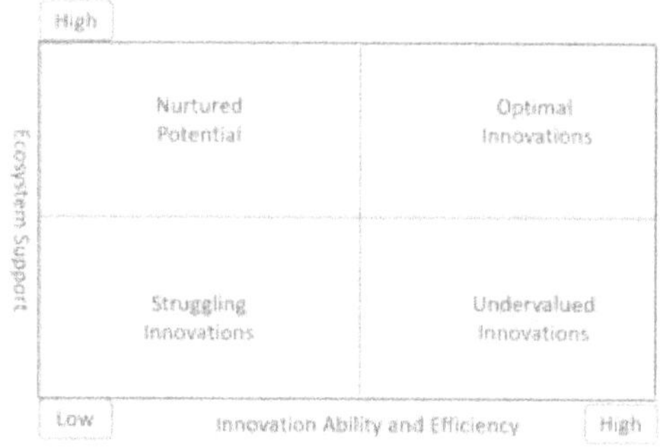

Nurtured Potential (Top-Left Quadrant)

Description: These innovations receive significant support from the ecosystem (government policies, funding, infrastructure, etc.) but currently have lower innovation ability and efficiency. They have the potential to grow and improve due to the high support.
Example: A startup with an innovative idea but still in the early stages of development, heavily supported by incubation centres and grants.

Optimal Frugal Innovations (Top-Right Quadrant)

Description: Innovations in this quadrant are highly efficient and innovative, receiving strong ecosystem support. They are examples of successful frugal innovations that leverage both their internal capabilities and external support effectively.

Example: Well-established frugal innovations with proven impact, such as low-cost medical devices widely adopted and supported by healthcare policies.

Struggling Innovations (Bottom-Left Quadrant)

Description: Innovations here have low efficiency and innovation ability and receive little to no ecosystem support. These are often initiatives that face significant challenges and may struggle to survive or scale.
Example: Small grassroots innovations with minimal resources and support, struggling to make an impact.

Undervalued Innovations (Bottom-Right Quadrant)

Description: These innovations are highly efficient and innovative but lack adequate ecosystem support. They have significant potential but are undervalued and underutilized due to the lack of external backing.
Example: Highly effective, low-cost agricultural tools developed by local innovators that are not widely adopted due to lack of policy support or market access.

B. Strengthening Technology Support for Frugal Innovations

Technological advancements play a pivotal role in driving frugal innovations. Strengthening technology support involves several key actions: enhancing access to affordable and advanced tools, fostering collaboration between technology developers and frugal innovators, and ensuring that technological solutions are adaptable to local contexts. Encouraging open-source platforms and shared technology resources can significantly reduce costs and promote widespread adoption.

The world's largest Video hosting website, YouTube has created Social Impact in many fields. YouTube has become de facto search engine after Google. It gives prime opportunity to businesses to showcase their brands to the billions (Lawson, 2022). YouTube has become an important visual journalism platform. YouTube has more than 2.7 billion monthly active users as of 2024 (33% of world population) which is 51% of all internet users access the video sharing platform every month. India tops in terms of active users with 467 million. It generated $29.24 billion revenue as of 2022. Users spent over $35 million using YouTube in-app purchases. Users consume 1 billion hours worth every day. Among users, 53.9% male and 46.1% female. Among users, 25-34 age group accounts 20.2%. MrBeast channel in YouTube earns $54 million (2024) with 237M subscribers & 775 videos (Feb 07, 2024), which is highest among all channels. 2.98 million businesses out of the 33.2 million use YouTube for their video marketing strategy in USA. 66% of respondents in a Statista survey said that their YouTube usage will increase in the future (Shewale, 2024).

These statistics signifies the importance of digital penetration and how frugal innovations can leverage these mediums. YouTube has become digital frugal platform to reach out to more audience with less marketing cost. Yashoda alias Dehati Madam, an ordinary household lady from Uttar Pradesh state (India) reached out to large number of subscribers (3,09,000 as of 07-02-2024) with her simple English communication videos. This platform is providing empowerment and truly presents the "doing more with less for more" philosophy (Dogra, 2023).

C. Need to Create Foundations in Social Space (Alignment with SDGs):

Recognizing that traditional models of innovation may not be feasible in environments with extreme resource constraints, frugal innovation seeks to find creative, low-cost solutions that can be scaled up to address societal challenges on a larger scale. Frugal innovations are philosophically connected to social sustainability themes however it is necessary to align with UN Sustainable Development Goals (SDGs). They not only offer a cost-effective approach to developing solutions that can address pressing challenges faced by marginalized communities, such as poverty, healthcare access, and environmental sustainability, etc but also bring long term sustainability in the planet.

6. CONCLUSION

In conclusion, the exploration of frugal innovation in the social and technological spheres unveils a promising path towards addressing pressing societal challenges. Frugal innovation challenges the conventional notion that effective solutions require hefty budgets and intricate designs, instead advocating for affordability, accessibility, and simplicity. By leveraging low-cost resources and creative problem-solving, frugal innovation endeavours to bridge the gap between technology and underserved communities. The case studies presented in this chapter illustrate the practical application of frugal innovation principles in diverse contexts, from healthcare and education to agriculture and energy.

REFERENCES

Alphabet Inc. (2024, March 26). Project Loon. Retrieved from https://x.company/loon/

Bound, K., & Thornton, I. (2012). *Our Frugal Future: Lesson from India's Innovation System*. NESTA.

Centre for Public Impact (CPI). (2016). Mobile Currency in Kenya: the M-Pesa. Retrieved from https://www.centreforpublicimpact.org/case-study/m-currency-in-kenya

CropIn. (2024, March 12). Agriculture Technology Company. Retrieved from https://www.cropin.com/

Dana, L. P., Gurău, C., Hoy, F., Ramadani, V., & Alexander, T. (2021). Success factors and challenges of grassroots innovations: Learning from failure. *Technological Forecasting and Social Change*, *164*, 119600.

DeHaat. (2024, March 22). Solutions for Farmers. Retrieved from https://agrevolution.in/solution-for-farmers

Dogra, P. K. (2023, December 27). With viral English lessons, 'Dehati Madam' from small UP village takes YouTube by storm. The Indian Express. Retrieved from https://indianexpress.com/article/india/dehati-madam-youtuber-up-village-viral-english-lessons-9049997/

Economic Times. (2017, April 24). Meet Arunachalam Muruganantham, the man who wore a sanitary pad to break a taboo. Retrieved from https://economictimes.indiatimes.com/news/politics-and-nation/meet-arunachalam-muruganantham-the-man-who-wore-a-sanitary-pad-to-break-a-taboo/padman-is-here/slideshow/58340285.cms

Grabs, J., Langen, N., Maschkowski, G., Schäpke, N. (2016) Understanding role models for change: A multilevel analysis of success factors of grassroots initiatives for sustainable consumption. Journal of Cleaner Production (134. A): 98-111.

Green, D. (2024, March 26). Global Impact. Retrieved from https://digitalgreen.org/global-impact/

Gupta, A. K., Sinha, R., Koradia, D. K., Patel, R. K., Parmar, M., Rohit, P. E., Patel, H. V., Patel, K., Chand, V. S., James, T. J., Chandan, A., Patel, M. M., Prakash, T., & Vivekanandan, P. (2003). Mobilizing grassroots' technological innovations and traditional knowledge, values and institutions: Articulating social and ethical Capital, futures. *Futures*, *35*(9), 975–987. DOI: 10.1016/S0016-3287(03)00053-3

Hossain, M. (2018). Grassroots innovation: The state of the art and future perspectives. *Technology in Society*, *55*, 63–69. DOI: 10.1016/j.techsoc.2018.06.008

Incubator, E. (2024, March 22). Revolutionizing Neonatal Care. Retrieved from Embrace Global website: https://www.embraceglobal.org/

Khan, R. (2016). How Frugal Innovation Promotes Social Sustainability. *Sustainability (Basel)*, *8*(10), 1034. DOI: 10.3390/su8101034

Lawson, C. (2022). Intro to Social Media. Oklahoma State University Libraries. Retrieved from https://shareok.org/bitstream/handle/11244/335899/oksd_lawson_introtosocialmedia_2022.pdf

MeraPashu360. (23-02-2024). About Us. Retrieved from https://merapashu360.com/about-us

National Innovation Foundation (NIF) - India. (n.d.). Mitticool: The Natural Refrigerator. Retrieved from https://nif.org.in/innovation/mitti-cool-refrigerator/751

Ninjacart (2024, March 22). Sowing Innovation, Harvesting trust. Retrieved from https://www.ninjacart.com

Ornetzeder, M., & Rohracher, H. (2013). Of solar collectors, wind power, and car sharing: Comparing and understanding successful cases of grassroots innovations. *Global Environmental Change*, *23*(5), 856–867. DOI: 10.1016/j.gloenvcha.2012.12.007

Pareek, S. (2014, September 22). He designed a shoe for the visually impaired that vibrates to show them the right path. The Better India. Retrieved from https://thebetterindia.com/12631/man-designed-shoe-blind-will-let-navigate-without-help/

Parwez, S., & Shekar, K. C. (2019). Understanding of grassroots innovations in India: evidence from the countryside. Society and Business Review., 10.1108, SBR-07-2018-0081.

Powell, S. (2017, November 7). An open door: OT finds out how the Aravind Eye Hospital in Tamil Nadu operates. Optometry Today. Retrieved from https://www.aop.org.uk/ot/professional-support/health-services/2017/11/07/an-open-door

Prabhu, J. (2017). Frugal innovation: Doing more with less for more. *Philosophical Transactions. Series A, Mathematical, Physical, and Engineering Sciences*, *375*(2109), 20160372. DOI: 10.1098/rsta.2016.0372 PMID: 28461436

Qin, W. (2024). How to unleash frugal innovation through internet of things and artificial intelligence: Moderating role of entrepreneurial knowledge and future challenges. *Technological Forecasting and Social Change*, *202*, 123286. DOI: 10.1016/j.techfore.2024.123286

Rani, R., & Srivastava, S. (2023). Grassroots innovation: A state of art literature review. Innovation The Research Concept, 8(2). ISSN: 2456-5474. Retrieved from http://www.socialresearchfoundation.com/innovation.php#8

Rosca, E., Reedy, J., & Bendul, J. C. (2018). Does Frugal Innovation Enable Sustainable Development? A Systematic Literature Review. *European Journal of Development Research*, *30*(1), 136–157. DOI: 10.1057/s41287-017-0106-3

SELCO. (2024, March 26.). SELCO India. Retrieved from https://selco-india.com/

Shewale, R. (2024, January 10). YouTube Statistics For 2024 (Users, Facts & More). Demand Sage. Retrieved from https://www.demandsage.com/youtube-stats/

Singh, R. (2023, July 24). How PhysicsWallah solved the profitability equation. Forbes India. Retrieved from https://www.forbesindia.com/article/take-one-big-story-of-the-day/how-physicswallah-solved-the-profitability-equation/86915/1

Skinner, D., Delobelle, P., Pappin, M., Pieterse, D., Esterhuizen, T. M., Barron, P., & Dudley, L. (2018). User assessments and the use of information from MomConnect, a mobile phone text-based information service, by pregnant women and new mothers in South Africa. *BMJ Global Health*, *3*(Suppl 2), e000561. DOI: 10.1136/bmjgh-2017-000561 PMID: 29713504

Thiagarajan, K. (2018, July 9). The man who paves India's roads with old plastic. The Guardian. https://www.theguardian.com/world/2018/jul/09/the-man-who-paves-indias-roads-with-old-plastic

Vidergor, H. E., & Ben-Amram, P. (2020). Khan academy effectiveness: The case of math secondary students' perceptions. *Computers & Education*, *157*, 103985. DOI: 10.1016/j.compedu.2020.103985

Virmani, A., & Lépineux, F. (2016). Aravind Eye Care System as Transformational Entrepreneurship: Spiritual Roots, Multi-Dimensional Impact. *Philosophy of Management*, *15*(1), 83–94. DOI: 10.1007/s40926-016-0032-z

KEY TERMS AND DEFINITIONS

Frugal Innovation: The creation of simple, cost-effective solutions that meet essential needs with limited resources, emphasizing practicality and value.

Social Impact: The significant, often transformative effect of frugal innovations on improving the lives of individuals and communities, particularly in underserved regions.

Affordability: The ability of frugal innovations to be priced within reach of low-income populations, ensuring broad accessibility.

Accessibility: The ease with which frugal innovations can be used or obtained by people of diverse abilities and socio-economic backgrounds.

Social Technologies: Low-cost tools and platforms designed to enhance social interaction and address societal challenges, often central to the success of frugal innovations.

Case Studies: In-depth analyses of frugal innovation projects that illustrate their impact, challenges, and potential for scalability.

Stakeholder Engagement: The inclusive process of collaborating with all parties affected by or interested in frugal innovation, ensuring solutions are relevant and widely accepted.

Chapter 10
Digital Transformative Trajectories:
Exploring the Drivers, Barriers, and Technologies for a Frugal Overhaul in the Pipeline Construction

Vinay Simoga Baburao
CRC Evans, Houston, USA

Premasish Roy
Bharati Vidyapeeth Deemed University, Navi Mumbai, India

ABSTRACT

Several industries have seen improvements in their business processes, revenues, and stock performance by adopting new digital technology and undergoing a digital transformation. Industries range from technological conglomerates to toy producers, sports apparel manufacturers, and home improvement merchants. The pipelines construction can also enable the exact effects observed in other industry sectors. Pipelines are used for a variety of things, including moving gas and oil from the field to refineries and customers, delivering water to towns, controlling sewage, and even the hyper-loop. Pipeline construction is highly traditional. Adopting digital technologies at least in some applicable processes for frugal benefits, including building information modeling, virtual reality, prefabrication, 3D printing, digital twins, IoT, and asset monitoring, has recently made little progress. This study examines some of the technologies, the forces behind them, and the obstacles that stand in the way of digital transformation for a frugal overhaul in the pipeline construction sector.

DOI: 10.4018/979-8-3693-4050-9.ch010

INTRODUCTION

Several industries have seen improvements in their business processes, revenues, and stock performance by adopting new digital technology and undergoing a digital transformation. Industries range from technological conglomerates to toy producers, sports apparel manufacturers, and home improvement merchants (Morgan, 2019). The pipelines construction can also enable the exact effects observed in other industry sectors. Pipelines are used for a variety of things, including moving gas and oil from the field to refineries and customers, delivering water to towns, controlling sewage, and even the hyper-loop. Most of the nations around the world rely very much on pipelines and their ongoing operations. Construction is a crucial stage in getting the pipeline operational. Pipeline construction is highly traditional, much like any other construction company. However, the construction sector and its subsectors continue to be quite traditional and have resisted implementing any new technologies for several years (Olanipekun & Sutrisna, 2021). Adopting digital technologies at least in some applicable processes for frugal benefits, including building information modeling, virtual reality, prefabrication, 3D printing, digital twins, IoT, and asset monitoring, has recently made little progress. A detailed literature review reveals that there isn't much research on digital transformation for pipeline construction. Understanding digital technologies used across industries and how to apply them in pipeline construction requires an organized approach. From the literature review, it was deduced that the technologies, drivers, and challenges are crucial to comprehend and chart an actionable plan for a digital transformation in pipeline construction. This study examines some of the technologies, the forces behind them, and the obstacles that stand in the way of digital transformation for a frugal overhaul in the pipeline construction sector.

Although it may seem like a tired buzzword, digital transformation is far but passé. Businesses that invest in digital transformation reap substantial business benefits (Gurumurthy, et al. 2020). A thorough attempt to embrace digital transformation can have various real-world positive effects on a business, from enhanced customer satisfaction and product quality to more effective operations and higher profits (Reis et al., 2018). Disruptive technologies are used in digital transformation to create value for stakeholders and to boost productivity and performance across the board, assisting markets and businesses in becoming long-term lucrative and sustainable (Gurumurthy, et al. 2020).

Customers are constantly expanding and changing in this connected age (Reis et al., 2018). To address client expectations, IT leaders are updating services and user experiences. Based on a survey by the independent marketing research firm Rabin Research Company, a report was released in 2021 by BDO, also known as Binder Dijker Otte. The Rabin Research business conducted the survey, which spoke with 100 C-level executives at technology companies with annual sales between $100 million and $3 billion. Chief technology officer, chief executive officer, chief financial officer, chief operating officer, chief marketing officer, line of business executives, and chief information or security officer are among the positions held by C-level executives. The technology sector is accelerating its preparations for digital transformation as the need for digital grows across industries. 92% of tech companies have a digital transformation strategy in place. Nearly every business has to become a tech corporation in order to survive due to the events of 2020 and pandemics. Tech businesses are crucial to a number of important processes and industries, both for growth and resilience. (2021, BDO USA, LLP).

Unfortunately, there are many examples of businesses today failing to adapt to the new digital era: the failure of the movie rental company Blockbuster, the companies' inability to contemplate being disrupted as they swiftly create and deploy new business models based on digital technology (Reis, et al., 2018).

The organizations that have implemented digital technology have witnessed a remarkable transformation. Corporations' departments and divisions collaboratively reinvent how businesses run, link people, enhance procedures, boost productivity, and cut costs. Can the pipeline sector profit from implementing digital technologies and digital business transformation? This study gives a broad overview of how digital transformation may impact pipeline construction.

According to Deloitte's 2019 study on oil and gas, the oil and gas business has the least digital maturity, with a score of 1.3. Since the pipeline is essential to the transportation of oil and gas, the pipeline and its construction industry require a similar level of digital maturity. It is due to infrastructure, geopolitical concerns, environmental limitations, right-of-way, and rugged terrain, the construction of the pipeline is becoming more complicated.

As pipeline building uses traditional business practices, such as paper-based reporting (Webb, 2018), timely insight extraction and data-driven decision-making may not occur, resulting in a catastrophe like oil leaks. Digital infrastructure may help prevent such tragedies. The Colonial Pipeline cybersecurity incident resulted in long queues of drivers, and attacks on the power system or gas pipeline turned out to be war-like. Fuel billing was challenged by the malware that had corrupted the back office (Sanger & Perlroth, 2021). According to the CEO of Colonial Pipeline, hackers only need to obtain one password to access the pipeline system (Kelly and Resnick-ault 2002).

In the last six to eight years, there has been a lot of research on digital transformation and how it affects different businesses. Both quantitative and qualitative research are conducted. However, more must be done in the pipeline construction sector to confirm the findings. The construction of pipelines is similar to other types of construction. A literature review of related industries has been conducted as part of this study to gain a deeper understanding of the effects of digital transformation on the construction sector and related sectors like manufacturing and transportation. Real-time and transparent communication between all parties involved ensures that the construction stays on budget and schedule and is of high quality. Adopting modern technologies and taking a data-driven strategy can help the building-project reach its goals and turn a profit. This study aims to comprehend the effects of digital transformation on various industries, the technologies that have helped companies become more digitally mature, and the best ways to support pipeline construction companies in becoming productive and profitable.

This study aims to list pipeline construction methods and their use scenarios. According to a preliminary examination of the literature, there isn't much research on digital transformation for a frugal overhaul in the pipeline construction sector.

2. METHODS

A structured literature review of published journals, articles, reports, conference proceedings, and websites was carried out to achieve the research objective. The Boolean search technique was used. The following steps were initiated:

- Step 1: Sourcing the literature
- Step 2: Selecting the relevant literature
- Step 3: Understanding & Analyzing the literature
- Step 4: Visual Representation
- Step 5: Pipeline construction areas where digitalization is possible

Step 1: Sourcing of the literature: Research firms, news organizations, business pieces, and journals for business trends were among the sources used to survey the literature. Other reputable sources were Google Scholar, Research Gate, Science Direct, Web of Science, and Scopus-indexed journals for scholarly literature. Conference proceedings, news stories, industry reports, research papers, and book excerpts are all included in the literature review.

Step 2: Selecting the relevant literature: In Google Scholar, searches for "digital transformation" or "Industry 4.0" returned more than three million items. More than 500,000 results are produced when the date range from 2017 onwards is used to filter this result further. To review all 500,000 findings and undertake research would be nearly impossible. The literature selection process began with industry studies released by reputable research organizations like Mckinsey, PWC, Deloitte, and BDO to avoid the aforementioned issue; moreover, only some publications give the information needed for this research. The most recent articles and publications with pertinent material were chosen from three keyword searches (Digital Transformation in Construction, Digital Transformation in Oil and Gas, and Digital Transformation of Pipeline Construction) to improve the literature review.

Step 3: Understanding & Analyzing the Literature: Three input factors were considered for analysis. Potential technologies for digital transformation are listed first, followed by motivations behind it, and third, obstacles to it. The industry reports were used to manually compile a list of pertinent digital transformation technologies, motivators for digital transformation, and hurdles to digital transformation. The software application is designed to read the manual list as input in the chosen literature and report the frequency of each word in the manual list. The weighted frequency of the terms in the list was normalized to evaluate under the same scale.

Step 4: Visual Representation: A word cloud was used as the research's visual representation. Word frequency in the list determines the size of the word in a word cloud. The more significant a term is to pipeline construction, the larger it must be. Three-word clouds would be a part of this stage, one for each parameter chosen in step 3. A list of word frequencies was also included.

Step 5: Pipeline construction areas: This process identified pipeline construction areas that would benefit from digital transformation.

3. LITERATURE REVIEW

This section reviews the literature investigating the impacts of digital transformation on the pipeline construction industry. For the review to encompass the most recent trends and technology, journals, papers, and reports published after 2015 were considered in this study. To ascertain the current state of the digital transition, literature research was conducted using four different perspectives: (1) Digital Transformation, (2) Pipeline Construction, (3) Digital Transformation Technologies, and (4) Transformational Barriers.

Digital Transformation

The term "digital transformation" has generated a lot of publicity in recent years (Bloomberg, 2018); terms like "digitalization" and "digitization" have contributed to the confusion.

The three phases of digital transformation are, according to (Verhoef, et al., 2021), phase one digitization, phase two digitalization, and phase three digital transformation. Each phase exerts specific demands on an organization's structure, growth tactics, and key performance indicators. Companies looking to undergo a digital transformation must have digital resources and assets as well as develop or add to their digital agility, networking, and data analytics skills.

The following is a definition of digitization, digitalization, and digital transformation from the Gartner Glossary (Gartner, 2021):

- Digitization converts an analog process into a digital one while making no other changes to the process itself.
- Digitalization uses digital technologies to change a business model and provide new revenue and value-producing opportunities.
- Digital transformation can refer to anything from I.T. modernization (for instance, cloud computing) to digital optimization to the invention of new digital business models.

Digital Transformation is a challenging process of developing a broad range of competencies that depends on the needs and commercial environment of the organization (Reis, et al., 2018). The goal of the process of "digital transformation," which is endogenous, is to benefit from the potential offered by digital technologies (José António Porfírio, et al., 2021).

Almost all quality standards, including performance, safety, usability, cybersecurity, and adaptability, are present in the critical sector, such as the automotive industry. Any of those standards not being met results in expensive callbacks and legal action. These problems will soon affect various industries (Ebert, Christof & Duarte, Carlos Henrique, 2018). Digital transformation can assist businesses in establishing the adaptability to thrive in the future in a market that is continuously changing due to evolving stakeholder and customer expectations (Gurumurthy, et al., 2020).

Even if digital transformation is a complex project, its benefits are now more clear than ever. All ships are raised by rising tides. Our economy is the ships; technology is the tide (BDO USA, LLP, 2021).

In its research, PWC presents a clear picture of the digital product development ecosystem and the five interwoven layers that make up the digital transformation process (PWC, 2018) (Refer: Figure 1) and showcases the blueprint of how to go about digital product development in Figure 2.

Figure 1. Digital product development ecosystem

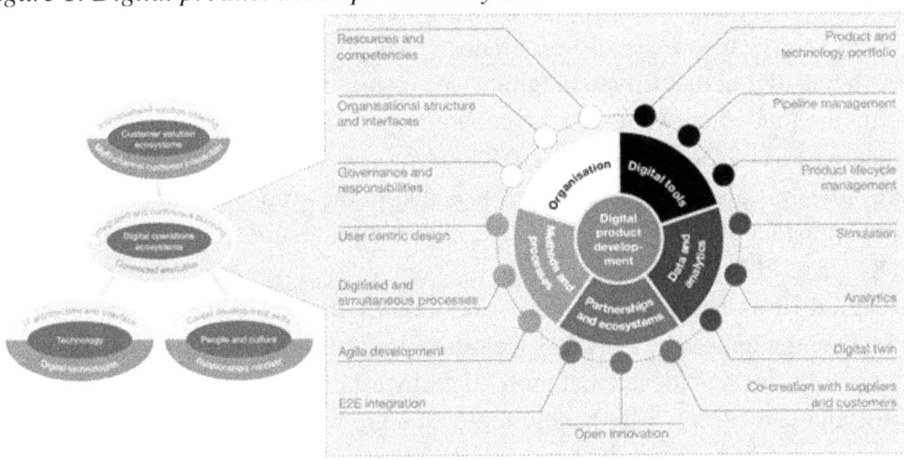

Sources: Digital Product Development Study 2025 – Agile, Collaborative, AI Driven and Customer Centric, PwC's Strategy& *Global Digital Operations Study 2018*, PwC analysis.

Figure 2. Blueprint for digital product development

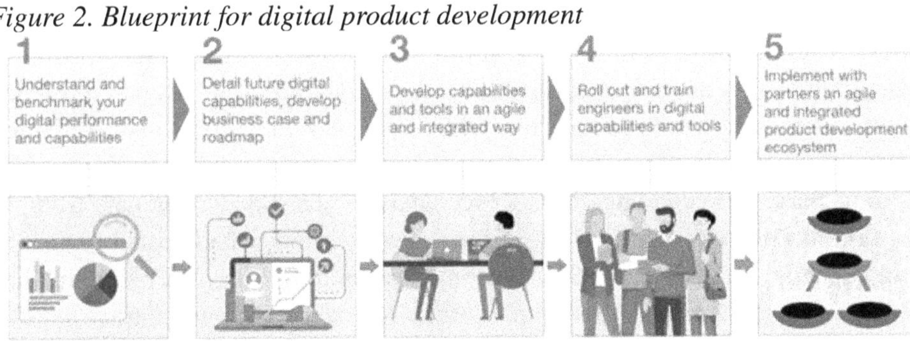

Digital Transformation Impact

Due to digital transformation, businesses' operational efficiency has improved top and bottom lines. The BDO's most recent report stated that the return increases with risk. 20% of executives said that the biggest digital threat is lousy customer experience. 87% said that their business would be greatly impacted by customer experience digitization (BDO USA, LLP, 2021).

The American fast-casual restaurant brand Chipotle is seeing strong revenue growth and digital maturity. Its digital sales increased by more than 100% year on year in the following two quarters, accounting for 18.3% of total sales in Q3 2019 compared to 11.2 percent in Q3 2018, and progress in total revenue and similar store sales was also augmented. This was due to the company's introduction of a mobile app that allowed customers to easily customize orders to their preferences (BDO USA, LLP, 2021).

Digital firms have an advantage over less digitally advanced competitors in thriving under upheaval. The 2021 Deloitte Digital Transformation Executive Survey provides fresh evidence that more digitally established organizations are more robust and can successfully handle rapid change, which improves their financial performance. Higher-maturity businesses could report considerable increases in net profit margins, yearly revenue growth and outperform industry norms, according to the 2021 Survey (Gurumurthy et al., 2021).

According to (TEKSYSTEMS, 2021), leaders in digital transformation anticipate a top-line growth of 30% compared to 11% for digital laggards. Similar to this, according to the BDO Industry 4.0 research (BDO, 2021), 50% of manufacturers believe that top-line growth from digital investments will occur in the upcoming year. Additionally, according to the BDO Report (BDO, 2021), natively digital manufacturers have a 96% success rate with digital activities, compared to 47% for legacy manufacturers.

To increase fuel economy, Rolls-Royce analyses sensing element data from its jet engines. Rolls-Royce can assure airline clients of lower fuel costs because to these capabilities (Elizalde, 2021). Customers seem to be charmed by the model: A major Asian airline recently awarded Rolls-Royce a five-year contract for 130 aircraft powered by these engines. Rolls-Royce can charge the customer for the use of the engine, parts, and repair facilities by real-time analyzing the sensing element data. By assessing engine safety in real-time and anticipating repairs, it may also increase safety (Gurumurthy, et al., 2021).

According to Daniel's article, the Internet of Things (a key component of digital transformation) focuses on gaining and producing differentiated value for the customer with the help of IoT products' constant connectivity. Daniel highlights the following top business models: (1) Subscription, (2) Outcome-based, (3)

Asset-Sharing, (4) Razer Blade, (5) Monetize Data, (6) Pay-per-Use, and (7) offer a Service. According to Daniel, businesses and customers who use these models can benefit (Elizalde, 2021).

Successful digital transformation may increase the efficiency of oil and gas enterprises, improve workplace safety, benefit society by reducing emissions and water use, and pass savings on to customers (World Economic Forum, 2017).

Another example of using industrial 4.0 and digital transformation is provided by John Deere (Intel Corporation, 2021), which collaborated with Intel to integrate the hardware and software capabilities to produce real-time insights using edge computing and artificial intelligence on John Deere Gas Metal Arc Welding in John Deere's 52 factories around the world. John Deere is utilizing artificial intelligence to try and solve the age-old issue with welding. By using artificial intelligence, John Deere is automating previously manual processes that required highly skilled labor and identifying problems like porosity in real-time. Porosity issues must be discovered later in the manufacturing process, requiring costly and disruptive rework.

The following particular pipeline construction cases highlight the possibility of digital transformation:

Case 1: Optimizing pipeline routing

Organization: Shell

Project: Niger Delta Pipeline Project

Technology: Remote sensing and Geographic Information System (GIS)

Advantages: Enhanced efficiency, less environmental impact, and better pipeline routing. Shell minimized environmental harm and optimized pipeline routing in the Niger Delta region by utilizing GIS and remote sensing technologies (Ogbimi, P. O., & Ugbomeh, G. 2020).

Case 2: -Analyzing sensor data and prediction

Organization: Chevron

Initiative: Tengizchevroil Pipeline Project

Technology: Machine Learning (ML) and Artificial Intelligence (AI)

Advantages: Better safety, less downtime, and predictive maintenance. Chevron reduced downtime and increased safety by using AI and ML algorithms to evaluate sensor data and forecast probable pipeline faults (Kulkarni, S. S., & Gupta, S. 2020).

Digital Transformation Investment

As the demand for technology products and services increases the pressure to deliver, digital transformation involves more than just investing in new solutions. It also entails taking stock of the current situation and identifying improvement opportunities. Technology organizations are looking inward and identifying potential operational weak points in order to make sure they satisfy the criteria. Inefficiency results in missed opportunities and lost money. Interoperability with legacy systems and procedures is one of the primary causes of the underperformance of digital projects, according to 36% of executives (BDO USA, LLP, 2021).

Corporations are reportedly pouring millions of dollars into "digital transformation" programs, according to a 2019 HBR article published in the Change management section (Tabrizi, et al., 2019). Despite this, a sizable portion of these initiatives fail to produce the desired results. These failures result from concentrating on a certain technology instead of altering the whole business strategy.

Developing a skilled, educated, and adaptable staff is one of CEOs' top concerns, according to PWC's 24th global CEO survey study. The efficacy of CEOs' organizations is also being increased through digital investments in the workforce; 36% of CEOs plan to concentrate on efficiency through automation and technology, a 124% rise from 2016. CEOs in a number of different industries reportedly have plans to introduce or expand automation (PWC, 2021).

Three times as much money is invested in digital transformation as spent overall on information technology. In the early phases of the life cycle, digital transformation efforts can produce efficiency, productivity, and savings that can support investments in innovation, new operating models, and enhanced growth. This gives digital transformation the potential to be self-sufficient (Gurumurthy, et al., 2020).

In a similar vein, BDO Report (BDO, 2021) asserts that the financial sector is intensifying its digital investments and undergoing a digital revolution due to changes in consumer behavior following the Covid-19 epidemic. Some investments in digital are made to improve organizational agility, become cloud-native, and acquire businesses with digital skills.

Security and Data Privacy

Technology companies prioritize security and data privacy to protect consumer and proprietary information. During the COVID-19 interruptions, trust has become crucial and challenging to achieve. Tech businesses are cautious due to a paradigm shift in workplace culture and the rise in digital transactions and cloud usage. The number one digital threat is cyber-attacks or breaches, and 33% of executives say that has been their most challenging difficulty (BDO USA, LLP, 2021).

PricewaterhouseCoopers (PWC, 2021) found heightened worry about cyber threats and false information overlaps with the acceleration of digitalization transformation during the pandemic in its poll of CEOs from 5,050 organizations across 100 countries and territories in early 2021. Conglomerate Sime Darby Berhad's group CEO, Jeffri Salim Davidson, emphasized the need to be agile while releasing digital goods. It is about going to market quickly and making adjustments as you go, only after everything is perfect. According to the report, low-touch services have become popular, and businesses are adjusting their offerings to meet these demands using digital technologies, including noncash payment services, e-money, and reservation services. According to a different PWC (2018) survey, 78% of organizations lack an established cybersecurity process. (BDO, 2021).

Here are certain scenarios involving cybersecurity issues in pipeline construction: Cybersecurity Scenarios (Kumar, K., Singh, S. K., & Zong, W. 2020):

1. Ransomware Incident: A pipeline construction firm's project management application becomes infected with ransomware, jeopardizing essential project information and causing construction delays.
2. SCADA System Intrusion: Cyber intruders gain unauthorized entry into a pipeline's Supervisory Control and Data Acquisition (SCADA) system, altering valve operations and hindering workflows.
3. Phishing Scam: Employees within a pipeline construction firm are targeted by deceptive emails, risking the exposure of confidential information and possibly granting hackers access to vital systems.
4. Data Manipulation: Unauthorized individuals alter pipeline design or construction data, which could endanger safety and structural integrity.
5. Denial-of-Service (DoS) Attack: A pipeline construction company's website and communication platforms are inundated by a DoS attack, disrupting interaction with stakeholders.

Pipeline construction companies can improve cybersecurity concerns by recognizing these scenarios and putting mitigation strategies into place.

Leadership, Culture, Agility, and Strategy

In order to link different stakeholders in an organization's digital transformation, leadership is essential (José António Porfírio, et al., 2021). New C-suite leadership positions have arisen in recent years as Digital Transformation has gained momentum, and businesses are working to establish these positions in their organizational structures. One of those positions is that of chief digital officer. The CDO takes on three key roles: A businessperson; a digital evangelist; and a coordinator (Singh, Anna & Hess, Thomas, 2017). The CDO's entrepreneurial function supports the adoption of cutting-edge technology in novel business models. People of all levels are motivated by the digital evangelist position. To follow the digital "journey," it cultivates a culture of open communication inside its digital transformation plan. Finally, the coordinator's responsibilities are more varied. It aids in planning the initial structural change and encouraging cross-functional collaboration in order to advance the long-term strategic development of its I.T. and I.S. system (Singh, Anna & Hess, Thomas, 2017).

When faced with uncertainty and inevitability, Amit Zavery, VP/GM and head of the platform at Google Cloud, advised businesses to "consider digital transformation not as a technology project to be completed but as a state of continuous agility, at all times prepared to evolve for customers next need " (Gurumurthy, et al., 2021).

To effectively accomplish a digital transformation, a cultural shift is necessary. A cultural transformation in collaboration, leadership, and communication is necessary to adapt to the digital shift. The term "digital transformation" describes how communities and organizations must deal with the possibility of a digital divide (Papadonikolaki, et al., 2020). The report also emphasizes building soft skills like collaboration, flexibility, and integration to function seamlessly across diverse platforms and teams. This method aids businesses in producing resilient, adaptive people and cultural shifts.

Here are some situations of workforce adaptability (Lee, J. 2020):

1. Aging Workforce: When seasoned pipeline construction workers retire, they leave behind important knowledge, which leads to a skills gap.
2. Skills Gap: Although workforce training and upskilling initiatives lag, new technologies demand specialized skills.
3. Diversity and Inclusion: Innovative viewpoints are limited by pipeline construction companies' inability to draw in diverse talent.
4. Challenges of Remote Work: In distributed or remote work settings, pipeline construction teams encounter challenges in effectively collaborating and communicating.
5. Change Management: Businesses that build pipelines find it difficult to adjust to new procedures, technologies, or legal requirements.

By recognizing these situations and putting mitigation plans in place, pipeline construction firms can improve workforce flexibility and resilience in general.

According to IDC's assessment (International Data Corporation, 2020), 58% of businesses reportedly implement digital efforts haphazardly and need a clear focus on their customers. IDC contends that the construction sector is prepared for digital transformation at the same time. According to IDC, higher performance and efficiency, cloud-based software, and mobile apps can help construction companies collaborate better and save money.

Digital Transformation Technology

Electronic Transformation Impact and investment literature demonstrates that technology is not the main factor in digital transformation. It does, however, have a significant impact. According to the (TEKSYSTEMS, 2021) research, companies with a developed plan for digital transformation with established attitudes and procedures in the organization's DNA are considered digital leaders. Their study reveals that the firm can support transformation by utilizing technology. Data analytics, cloud computing, the Internet of Things, mobile devices, and artificial intelligence are a few of the technologies mentioned.

Drones could help the construction industry cut down on the US$160 billion in waste materials disposed of in landfills yearly, accounting for 25 to 40% of the solid waste produced in the USA (Gurumurthy, et al., 2020).

Tesco uses artificial intelligence (AI) analytics to measure its environmental effect and meet ambitious carbon emission reduction goals (Gurumurthy, et al., 2020). Digital technologies are being used by even less mature organizations to address environmental sustainability by lowering carbon emissions and resource usage (Papadonikolaki, et al., 2020). The construction sector makes substantial use of several digital technologies, including 3D BIM, cloud computing, augmented reality, virtual reality, and the Internet of Things. These technologies will develop conceptually and practically in the future (Papadonikolaki et al., 2020).

The use of technologies like the Internet of Things, building information modeling, RFID, augmented reality, cloud computing and storage, geo-fencing, sensor data monitoring, harmonizing communication between various machinery, 4G or 5G communication, using data lakes, using APIs, using digital twins, and using mobile apps are discussed in a conference paper about the digital transformation of the construction industry (Zhou, et al., 2020).

The journal released by (Christ of Ebert & Carlos Henrique Duarte, 2018) cites the following technologies as disruptive: (1) drones, (2) robots, (3) additive manufacturing, (4) 3D printing, (5) Internet of Things, (6) agile development, (7) blockchain, (8) API, and (9) artificial intelligence (Jose António Porfrio et al., 2021).

The rush to embrace advanced analytics and artificial intelligence for learned decision-making is hinted at in PWC's 24th global CEO survey report (PWC 2021).

Techment (Techment, 2021) recommends using blockchain for patient health records, augmented reality, virtual reality, IT platforms, cloud services, remote care technologies, and data analytics in the healthcare sector.

The most recent research from IoT Analytics (Lueth, 2021) indicates that IoT's growth is generally accelerating. Additionally, the research explains the technologies that consumers are willing to pay for, including (1) Cloud Services, (2) Low-Code/

No-Code, (3) Cybersecurity, (4) API, (5) Connected and Intelligent Solutions, (6) Services that are environmentally friendly, and (7) artificial intelligence.

There is a list of technologies that would help with the digital transformation provided by (World Economic Forum, 2017). (1) Internet of Things, (2) Big Data/ Analytics (3) Portable, (4) Cloud, robotics (5) (6) Drone, Artificial intelligence (AI), (Eight) Wearable technology (9) Social and Collaboration Tools. Here are some examples of organizations which reaped the benefits of the emerging technologies:

Case 3: - Organization: TransCanada

Project: Keystone XL Pipeline Project -Technology: Digital Twins and Building Information Modeling (BIM)

Advantages: Better project management, lower expenses, and security by building a virtual model of the pipeline using BIM and digital twins, TransCanada was able to collaborate in real time and enhance project results (Fazal, S., & Khan, S. 2019).

Case 4: Organization: Saudi Aramco- Initiative: Extension of the Master Gas System

Technology: Sensor networks and the Internet of Things (IoT) Benefits include less leakage, increased efficiency, and real-time monitoring. IoT sensors were used by Saudi Aramco to track pipeline conditions, find leaks, and improve maintenance, which increased productivity and decreased expenses (Al-Turki, K. M., & Obeid, A. M. 2020).

The following are some real-time and IoT detection scenarios that are unique to pipeline construction:

IoT Situations (Alam, S., & Shakil, K. A. 2020):

1. Leak Detection: By identifying abnormalities in pipeline temperature, pressure, or flow rates, Internet of Things sensors notify operators of possible leaks.
2. Predictive repair: IoT sensors track the state of pipelines, forecasting possible malfunctions and planning repair.
3. Pipeline Monitoring: IoT sensors monitor the integrity of pipelines, identifying issues such as rust or cracks.
4. Real-time Tracking: IoT-enabled GPS tracking tracks the movement of materials, equipment locations, and pipeline construction progress.
5. Environmental Monitoring: To guarantee pipeline integrity, IoT sensors keep an eye on temperature, humidity, and vibration.

Real-time Detection Scenarios (Khan, S., & Lee, S. C. 2020):

1. Anomaly Detection: Machine learning algorithms analyze sensor data to detect unusual patterns indicating potential issues.

2. Pipeline Breach Detection: Acoustic sensors detect changes in pipeline noise, indicating potential breaches.
3. Gas Detection: IoT sensors detect hazardous gases, alerting operators to potential safety risks.
4. Vibration Analysis: IoT sensors monitor pipeline vibration, detecting potential issues before they become critical.
5. Geographic Information System (GIS) Integration: Real-time mapping and spatial analysis enable swift response to pipeline incidents.

These examples show how real-time detection and the Internet of Things can improve pipeline construction's safety, effectiveness, and dependability.

Digital Transformation Drivers

Secure, Flexible infrastructure, Data Mastery, Ecosystem, Intelligent workflow, Unified Customer Experience, Adaptable Business Model, Digitally Savvy, and Open Talent Network are some of the digital pivots that drive a company toward digital maturity (Gurumurthy et al., 2020).

In a study published in 2021, Olanipekun and Sutrisna identified enablers that can propel digital transformation. These enablers include innovation, digital attraction, research, champions, culture, support, and legitimacy. The implementation of digital technologies, with data, automation, connectivity, and access as the constituent parts, was acknowledged in this study as having increased the likelihood of a digital transformation in construction.

The center of digital transformation is the customer. 60% of respondents believe their main objective is improving the client experience ((TEKSYSTEMS, 2021).

According to the BDO analysis, customer experience was emphasized among the CEOs questioned for the survey. Tech leaders focus on improving the experience to keep current consumers and fend off the ever-expanding competition. This is done to meet and exceed the constantly changing customer needs and expand expectations for speed, dependability, and consistency. This frequently entails integrating services like cloud computing, teamwork, contactless alternatives, and more (BDO USA, LLP, 2021).

According to BDO, most tech businesses place a high priority on digital innovation. Tech companies went back to the drawing board to rewrite their pre-pandemic plans since they needed to consider the market's needs. According to the report, 67% of businesses updated their long-term strategic goal, 57% introduced fresh digital initiatives, and 41% sped up plans. In the upcoming 12 months, 80% of organizations are expected to boost their digital spending (BDO USA, LLP, 2021). Digitalization aids in setting short-term emissions goals, using uniform and reliable reporting, tracking responsibility across the pyramid, enabling remote operations, and guiding human-machine partnerships (Dickson, 2020).

Digital Transformation Barriers

Barriers to digital transformation exist both internally and externally. Internal barriers include (1) a lack of a digital transformation strategy, (2) a lack of insight into return on investment, (3) a heterogeneous company culture, (4) the expense of digital technologies, (5) a sense of cannibalization of an existing business, and (6) the cost of adopting new technology (7). The presence of skilled labor, a lack of infrastructure, a lack of regulations, and an ineffective value recognition system are examples of external impediments (Ebert, Christof & Duarte, Carlos Henrique, 2018).

The financial ramifications and regulatory limitations of digital transformation in pipeline construction are as follows:

Regulation Restrictions: Rules set forth by the Pipeline and Hazardous Materials Safety Administration (PHMSA); The rules of the Occupational Safety and Health Administration (OSHA); Rules set forth by the Environmental Protection Agency (EPA); Guidelines issued by the Federal Energy; Regulatory Commission (FERC); Local and state laws; International norms (such as API and ISO); Cybersecurity and data privacy laws; Adherence to industry norms (such as AGA and API) (Kim, J., & Lee, S. C. 2020).

And eventually these regulations affect the Digital Revolution for instances: Delays the uptake of innovative technology; Costs rise as a result of compliance obligations; Requires large investments in security measures; Restricts collaboration and data sharing; Prevents exploration and creativity; Makes integrating with current systems more difficult; Requires specific knowledge and instruction; Raises the possibility of non-compliance fines

And furthermore it impacts the Digital Transformation on Costs like: The cost of hardware and software (such as sensors and Internet of Things devices); Costs of integration and implementation; Expenses for change management and training; Cybersecurity protocols; Tools for data analytics and visualization (Alam, S., & Khan, S. 2020).

According to a recent study (Olanipekun & Sutrisna, 2021), the construction industry has many obstacles, strategic considerations, and enablers for digital transformation. According to the study, some of the hurdles include system integration, data processing complexity, ROI uncertainty, outdated business models, process standardization, digital divide, data access, data ownership, buy-in, experience and senior worker displacement, and system attacks. The study identified collaboration, process, data, lifecycle, choice of digital, value, and learning as strategic factors that need to be considered.

Similar barriers are also present in the healthcare sector (Techment, 2021); some of these include (1) Slow adoption; only 7% of companies have adopted digital; (2) Complex regulations and strict policy stance; (3) Interoperability; (4) Privacy concerns of connected devices; (5) Not ready for Data Analytics; and (6) Customer playing second fiddle.

Pipeline Construction

The effectiveness, timeliness, and quality of building projects are directly impacted by the need for interoperability between the numerous actors involved in construction sites. Consequently, there is a critical need to digitize building sites using digital technologies. The current construction process will be enhanced by a data-driven method where real-time data is collected and analyzed (Zhou, et al., 2020).

The use of Inspection Robots as a concept of digital technology to inspect the tapping of crude oil, pipeline vandalism, and the leak detection technology tapping of the pipeline is difficult to identify as it does not reduce the pressure in the pipeline as suggested in a paper presented at the SPE Nigeria Annual International Conference and Exhibition (Idachaba, 2018). With video feedback, a battery-operated, self-actuated robot was used to examine the pipeline (World Economic Forum, 2017).

A case study using intelligent pipeline technology, which combines data from various sources to analyze risk risks and offer data-driven solutions, was published by the World Economic Forum in 2017. Unexpected incidents will be reduced thanks to our sophisticated pipeline technology. Geographical, call center, outside sources, atmospheric, and job management systems are a few examples of sources.

According to the Osha Report, there are 252,000 construction sites in the USA where 6,500,000 people work daily. On average, 18 fatalities are reported for every 100,000 construction workers each year (Vasquez, 2019). The use of digital technologies and change can help to address these regrettable occurrences. Crane is one of the modern technologies.

According to the research (Bo, et al., 2020), pipeline operations and management are plagued by numerous bottlenecks, which technology aids in removing. Digital Twin, Cloud Computing, Artificial Intelligence, Internet of Things, 5G, Blockchain, and Virtual Reality are a few of the technologies they have named.

Unmanned aerial vehicles with photogrammetry technologies are suggested by (Yan Yan, et al., 2021) as a way to identify potential threats to the security of oil and gas pipelines.

(Vladova, 2021) proposes adopting digitalization for soil condition monitoring to research the impact of frozen soil surrounding pipelines and the thermal stability of permafrost.

4. DISCUSSION & CONCLUSION

From the literature review, it was deduced that the technologies, drivers, and challenges have a significant impact on the digital transformation of pipeline construction. This section examines some of these technologies, the forces behind them, and the obstacles that stand in the way of digital transformation. Furthermore, it examines how incorporating certain frugality elements, pipeline construction companies can achieve significant cost savings, improve efficiency, and reduce environmental impact.

Result Visualization

Visualizing words as clouds of text helps visually represent the research's findings. The importance of a word is determined by its size.

The significance of each parameter in the compiled list is shown in Figures 3, 4, and 5

Figure 3. Technology occurrence visualization (Authors' Analysis)

Figure 4. Drivers' occurrence visualization (Authors' Analysis)

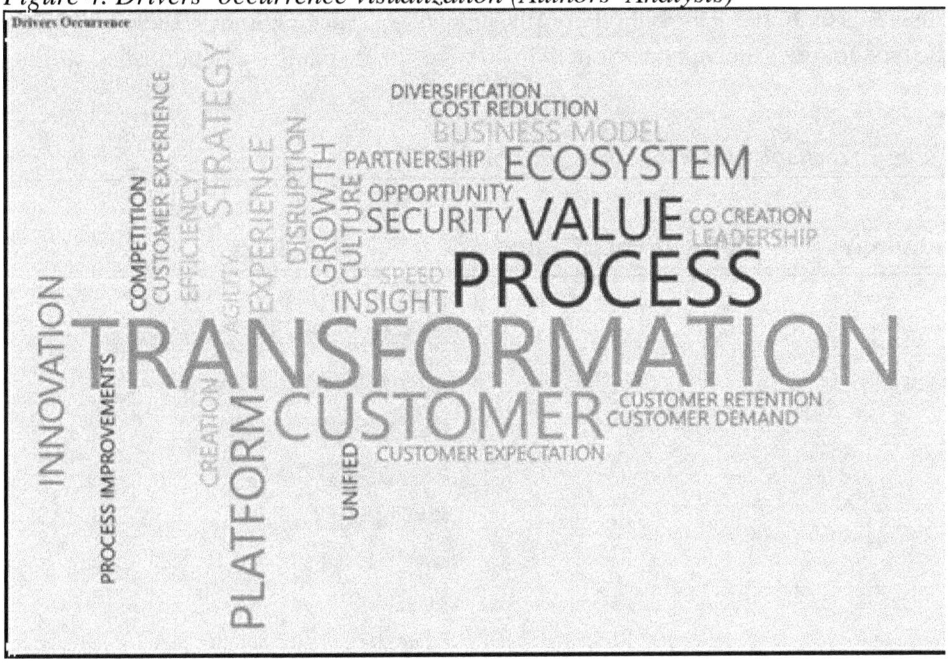

Figure 5. Barrier's occurrence visualization (Authors' Analysis)

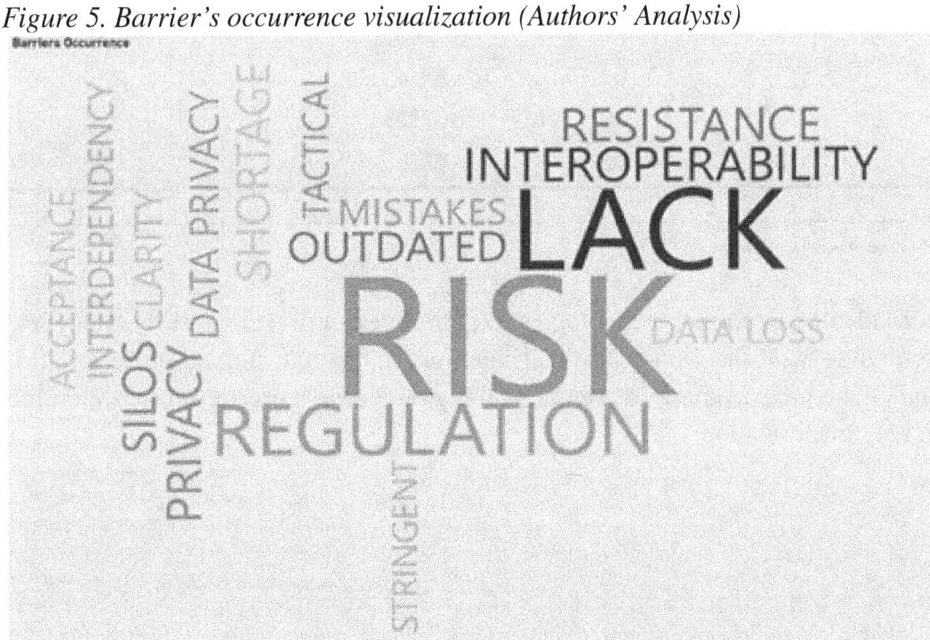

The research produced a substantially shorter list of the most potent technologies impacting digital transformation from the input list of 29 technologies. Table 1 includes the technologies that appear more than 50 times in the database of published works.

Table 1. Technologies list with occurrence ≥ 50

Technology	Occurrence Count	Chart
IoT	534	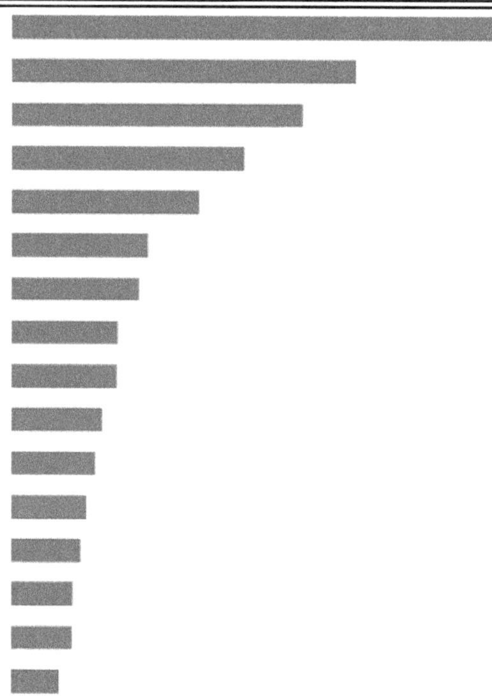
Analytics	376	
Digital Twin	317	
Cloud	254	
AI	204	
Drone	149	
Mobile	139	
BIM	116	
API	115	
Big Data	99	
Cyber Security	92	
Robots	82	
Blockchain	76	
3D Printing	67	
Autonomous	66	
Robotics	52	

Source: Authors' Analysis

Evidently, important technologies like the Internet of Things (IoT), analytics, the digital twin, the cloud, artificial intelligence, drones, mobile devices, BIM, application programming interfaces, and big data have a greater influence on the digital transformation.

Drivers

Table 02 includes a list of factors that can have a more significant impact on the digital transformation. Transformation, Process, Customer, Value, Platform, Ecosystem, Strategy, Innovation, and Leadership are a few of the major factors found in the study.

Table 2. Drivers list with occurrence ≥ 50

Drivers	Occurrence Count	Chart
Transformation	1427	
Process	1072	
Customer	852	
Value	723	
Platform	532	
Ecosystem	502	
Strategy	360	
Innovation	296	
Security	272	
Growth	271	
Experience	242	
Insight	214	
Business Model	184	
Culture	141	
Disruption	128	
Efficiency	103	
Creation	83	
Leadership	74	
Agility	72	
Speed	69	
Partnership	67	
Opportunity	54	

Source: Authors' Analysis

Barriers

Table 03 lists potential roadblocks to the adoption of digital transformation. Risk aversion, regulation, interoperability, privacy, and silos are some of the major obstacles that prevent or impede the successful adoption of digital transformation. According to research, there might not be many obstacles to digital transformation, however, the one's in the way, might offer major resistance.

Table 3. Barriers list with occurrence ≥ 10

Barriers	Occurrence Count	Chart
Risk	265	
Lack	158	
Regulation	77	
Interoperability	28	
Privacy	27	
Resistance	26	
Shortage	24	
Silos	23	
Outdated	18	
Data Privacy	11	

Source: Authors' Analysis

Frameworks

The role of technologies, the motivating factors of drivers, and the challenging presence of barriers are all critical components of digital transformation. These factors interact with each other, and these interactions are convoluted and multi-dimensional. These factors can be thematically grouped to represent the unique aspects of the transformation.

Group 1: Innovation and Technology advancement

By utilizing cutting-edge technologies such as AI, Machine learning, and 3D printing along with the driving forces such as innovation and growth, Pipeline construction industries can push the boundaries in technological applications, However, barriers like acceptance and data privacy challenges persist, requiring strategic approaches to encourage adoption and ensure security.

Group 2: Connectivity and Efficiency

In this group, IoT and 5G technologies streamline processes, driven by the need for efficiency and agility. However, challenges like interoperability and data loss present significant hurdles. Overcoming these barriers is crucial to leverage the connectivity benefits these technologies offer fully.

Group 3: Customer-Centric Transformation

Focusing on the end-user, technologies like Augmented Reality enhance customer experience. Drivers like customer demand and insight guide development, but clarity in customer needs and regulatory compliance are barriers that must be navigated carefully to align technology with user expectations.

Group 4: Security and Data Management

Here, the focus is on cybersecurity and blockchain, driven by the need for secure and innovative business models. While these technologies offer robust solutions, risk and regulatory compliance pose significant challenges, emphasizing the need to balance innovation and security.

Group 5: Automation and Operational Excellence

In this domain, robotics and automation are propelled by drivers like cost reduction. However, organizational silos and skill shortages pose barriers, necessitating a focus on training and strategic planning to harness the benefits of automation fully.

Further exploring the interconnections with these Five Groups reveals a complex network of effects and dependencies where advancements, challenges, and goals in one area significantly impact others.

Figure 6. Interconnections between the groups (Authors' Analysis)

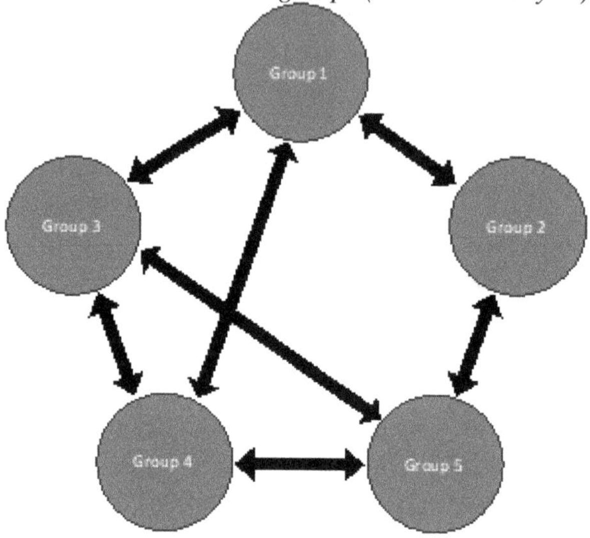

Frugality

The frugality components on digital transformation in pipeline construction are (J. Lee, S. C. Lee, and K. S. Park, 2020):

1. Cost Reduction: By using digital technologies, pipeline construction, maintenance, and operation costs can be decreased.
2. Resource Optimization: Using data analytics, AI, and IoT to maximize resource use, reduce waste, and boost productivity.
3. Simplified Procedures: To cut down on complexity and boost efficiency, automate manual procedures and remove pointless steps.
4. Minimal Infrastructure: To cut down on infrastructure expenditures, software-as-a-service (SaaS) models and cloud-based solutions are used.
5. Low-Code or No-Code Solutions: Using low-code or no-code platforms can lower development costs and hasten the digital transformation process.
6. Open-Source Technologies: Making use of open-source technologies to lower licensing fees and encourage cooperation.
7. Energy Efficiency: Reducing energy consumption and environmental impact by putting energy-efficient solutions into practice.
8. Remote Monitoring: By using digital technologies, pipelines can be monitored remotely, eliminating the need for in-person inspections and cutting down on travel expenses.

9. Predictive Maintenance: Predictive maintenance can be used to lower maintenance costs, increase equipment lifespan, and decrease downtime.
10. Skills Optimization: Retraining and upskilling current employees to reduce training expenses and optimize resource use.

Strategies for Frugal Innovation

1. Incremental Innovation: concentrating on making small, gradual enhancements to current procedures and technological systems.
2. Resource-Constrained Innovation: Promoting innovation while keeping resources limited in order to boost efficiency and creativity.
3. Collaborative Innovation: Joining forces with academic institutions, startups, and stakeholders to pool resources and leverage expertise.

Companies that build pipelines can save a lot of money, increase productivity, and lessen their environmental effect by implementing these frugal practices:

ROI, or return on investment; Ownership Total Cost (TCO); Financial Savings; Increase in Productivity; Efficiency in Energy Use; Reduction of Downtime; MTTR, or Mean Time To Repair MTBF, or Mean Time Between Failures.

Pipeline Construction

Surveying, preparation, pipe manufacturing, welding, inspection, coating, burying, and replacement are a few of the critical tasks performed in the pipeline construction industry.The construction and upkeep of pipelines is an expensive endeavor. Oil and gas businesses always seek ways to save costs and improve pipeline construction efficiency. Surveying is one of the more expensive parts of the total construction. Drones and other unmanned aerial vehicles can assist make surveying more efficient, safe, and precise with comprehensive data collection (Souter & Saksa, 2020).

IoT Business demonstrates how IoT may increase the overall effectiveness of the welding process by collecting and monitoring data. Artificial intelligence (AI)-assisted automated welding, according to IoT Business, can decrease waste and increase output. AI may make it possible for welding businesses to recruit less skilled welders while saving money (IoT Business, 2021). Similarly, John Deere uses AI to enhance the welding process. John Deere uses gear and software for computer vision to find weld flaws automatically.

Yuqian & Xun's research in connected manufacturing has made it possible for cloud-based manufacturing equipment to monitor manufacturing equipment in real-time and assess its health using data gathered from the equipment and analytics on the data acquired. The authors use a steel manufacturing use case to show how

IoT, cloud, data analytics, and big data can be used to provide real-time reporting of equipment condition and health, project status, production report, invoicing, and logical data visualization. The use of a service business model with these technologies is also covered in research. Numerous heavy and light pieces of equipment are used during pipeline building, and numerous parties are involved in the process overall. Similar outcomes to those found in the research by (Yuqian & Xun, 2019) can be achieved by using digital technology.

The pipeline construction sector is only just beginning to embrace the digital revolution. While this was happening, other sectors like the automobile, e-commerce, and healthcare successfully embraced digital transformation and saw improvements in profitability, business efficiency, cost optimization, and new business methods. It is clear from the prior study that change cannot be realized by concentrating solely on technologies.

To achieve the desired state of transformation, a 360-degree focus is necessary, including sponsorship and accountability from Top Leaders within the organization, building a talent pool, creating a data-driven strategy, creating a cultural shift to get everyone on board with digital, constantly innovating, creating value for the customer and getting value for the organization, being agile and lean to transform the process and governance. The most important is setting up a clear road map and commitment to achieving transformation.

Is it conceivable for the pipeline construction industry to shift digitally? The pipeline construction industry can shift digitally, according to research. There is no reason why pipeline construction cannot undergo the same type of evolution as other businesses that share characteristics with it, such as manufacturing and construction, which have done so with the aid of digital transformation.

The goal of this research was to determine the digital technologies needed for the digital transformation, their impact, and the drivers and hurdles that would hamper it. Digital twins, IoT, Big Data, Analytics, drones, mobile devices, and the cloud are a few technologies that have the potential to alter the way pipeline construction is done online significantly. A fully integrated ecosystem that collects and analyses data would greatly speed up the transformation. The pipeline construction industry can realize the benefits of the digital revolution by embracing new technology and building a data-driven ecosystem.

One of the study's main conclusions is that technology alone cannot bring about a transformation. The cornerstone or enabler of the transformation shall be technology. There were many motivating reasons found that would fuel the change process. A few identified factors are leadership, the customer, culture, strategy, innovation, business model, and agility. As was previously indicated, a 360-degree approach is necessary to get the desired outcome. Technologies and drivers work together to help pipeline companies overcome any obstacles they may encounter while changing. Risk aversion, a lack of skill, legacy system interoperability, operating in silos, cultural reluctance, and privacy are significant challenges. Deploying technology and drivers in concert is crucial to overcoming and breaking down the barriers. Digital transformation is progressively embraced by pipeline construction, but due to the rapidly evolving technological landscape, the transformation process is forced to speed up.

Given the amount of literature considered, it might not be possible to determine the precise impact of each technology, driver, and barrier. This study may serve as a springboard for further investigations in this field. This study uncovered a lot of convincing supporting data regarding the advantages of digital transformation for pipeline construction. The research can be used to investigate further each of the variables given in the technology, drivers, and barriers to determine each impact. Recent technological advancements have been more rapid than ever, and this has resulted in a significant shift in the difficulties facing business. Continuously assessing the need for transformation and how to achieve it is advised to overcome the issue.

REFERENCES

Al-Turki, K. M., & Obeid, A. M. (2020). IoT-Based Monitoring System for Pipeline Integrity Management: A Case Study of Saudi Aramco's Master Gas System Expansion. *Journal of Pipeline Systems Engineering and Practice*, *11*(3). Advance online publication. DOI: 10.1061/JPEODS.PEENG-05020003

Alam, S., & Khan, S. (2020). Cost-Benefit Analysis of Digital Transformation in Pipeline Construction. *Journal of Construction Engineering and Management*, *146*(8).

Alam, S., & Shakil, K. A. (2020). IoT-Based Leak Detection System for Pipelines. *Journal of Pipeline Systems Engineering and Practice*, *11*(2).

BDO. 2021. *2021 Financial Services Digital,* NA: BDO.

BDO. 2021. *2021 Industry 4.0 Survey,* NA: BDO.

BDO USA, LLP. (2021). *2021 Technology Digital Transformation Survey*. BDO.

Bo, L., Jiannan, G., & Xiangdong, X. (2020). The Digital Twin of Oil and Gas Pipeline System. *IFAC-PapersOnLine*, *53*(5), 710–714. DOI: 10.1016/j.ifacol.2021.04.162

Deloitte. 2021. *Using ecosystems to accelerate smart manufacturing*. [Online] Available at: https://www2.deloitte.com/global/en/pages/energy-and-resources/articles/accelerating-smart-manufacturing-the-value-of-an-ecosystem-approach.html [Accessed 21 November 2021].

Dickson, D. 2020. *2021 oil and gas industry outlook.* [Online] Available at: https://www2.deloitte.com/us/en/pages/energy-and-resources/articles/oil-and-gas-industry-outlook.htm....html [Accessed 03 October 2021].

Christof, E., & Henrique, D. C. (2018). Digital transformation. *IEEE Software*, *35*(4), 16–21.

Elizalde, D. 2021. *7 IoT Business Models That Are Transforming Industries.* [Online] Available at: https://danielelizalde.com/monetize-your-iot-product/ [Accessed 07 October 2021].

Fazal, S., & Khan, S. (2019). Digital Twin Application in Oil and Gas Pipeline Projects: Keystone XL Pipeline Case Study. *Proceedings of the 2019 International Conference on Construction Engineering and Management*, pp. 345-354.

Gartner. (2021). *Gartner Glossary.* [Online] Available at: https://www.gartner.com/en/informationtechnology/glossary?startsWith=D&pageSize=all&nPage=1&showLocalizedContent=false&languageCode=en&glossaryTypeTag=emt:page/function/it [Accessed 04 October 2021].

Geissbauer, R., Schrauf, S., Schneider, J., & Hermans, M. (2020). Connected and autonomous supply chain ecosystems 2025. PricewaterhouseCoopers (PwC).

Gurumurthy, R., Nanda, R., & Schatsky, D. (2021). *Putting digital at the heart of strategy*. Deloitte Insights.

Gurumurthy, R., Schatsky, D., & Camhi, J. 2020. *Uncovering the connection between digital maturity and financial performance.* [Online] Available at: https://www2.deloitte.com/us/en/insights/topics/digital-transformation/digital-transformation-survey.html [Accessed 10 September 2021].

Hartigan, M., Mussomeli, A., Laaper, S. & Gish, D. (2017). *The smart factory Responsive, adaptive, connected manufacturing,* s.l.: Deloitte.

Hovnanian, G., Kroll, K., & Sjödin, E. (2019). *How analytics can drive smarter engineering and construction decisions.* [Online] Available at: https://www.mckinsey.com/business-functions/operations/our-insights/how-analytics-can-drive-smarter-engineering-and-construction-decisions [Accessed 15 July 2023].

Idachaba, F. E. (2018). *Design of a Pipeline Pre-Activation Inspection Robot for Pipeline Tap Detection*. OnePetro. DOI: 10.2118/193384-MS

Insights, D. 2020. *Digital lean manufacturing.* [Online] Available at: https://www2.deloitte.com/us/en/insights/focus/industry-4-0/digital-lean-manufacturing.html [Accessed 05 October 2021].

Intel Corporation. (2021). *At John Deere, 'Hard Iron Meets Artificial Intelligence'.* [Online] Available at: https://www.intel.com/content/www/us/en/newsroom/news/john-deere-hard-iron-meets-artificial-intelligence.html#gs.cvlwoq [Accessed 10 October 2021].

Internation Data Corporation. (2020). *Digital Transformation: The Future of Connected Construction,* s.l.: Autodesk.

International Data Corporation. (2020). *Digital Transformation: The Future of connected construction, NA*. International Data Corporation.

IoT Business. (2021). *How IoT Is Helping To Benefit The Welding Industry.* [Online] Available at: https://iotbusinessnews.com/2021/11/12/58255-how-iot-is-helping-to-benefit-the-welding-industry/ [Accessed 24 November 2021].

Porfírio, J. A., Carrilho, T., Felício, J. A., & Jardim, J. (2021). Leadership characteristics and digital transformation. *Journal of Business Research, 124*, 610–619.

Kelly, S., & Resnick-ault, J. 2021. *One password allowed hackers to disrupt Colonial Pipeline, CEO tells senators,* NA: Reuters.

Khan, S., & Lee, S. C. (2020). Machine Learning-Based Anomaly Detection for Pipeline Monitoring. *Journal of Pipeline Systems Engineering and Practice, 11*(2).

Kim, J., & Lee, S. C. (2020). Regulatory Framework for Digital Transformation in Pipeline Construction. *Journal of Pipeline Systems Engineering and Practice, 11*(2). Advance online publication. DOI: 10.1061/JPEODS.PEENG

Kulkarni, S. S., & Gupta, S. (2020). Application of Artificial Intelligence and Machine Learning in Predictive Maintenance of Pipelines: A Case Study of Chevron's Tengizchevroil Pipeline Project. *Journal of Pipeline Systems Engineering and Practice, 11*(3).

Kumar, K., Singh, S. K., & Zong, W. (2020). Ransomware Attack on Pipeline Construction Project Management Software. *Journal of Pipeline Systems Engineering and Practice, 11*(2), 05020002. DOI: 10.1061/JPEODS.PEENG

Lapper, S. & Kiefer, B., 2020. *Digital lean manufacturing Industry 4.0 technologies transform lean processes to advance the enterprise,* s.l.: Deloitte.

Lee, J. (2020). *Workforce Adaptability in Pipeline Construction.* Springer., DOI: 10.1007/978-3-030-45671-5

Lueth, K. L. (2021). *IoT technology market attractiveness: Where to invest going into 2022.* [Online] Available at: https://iot-analytics.com/iot-technology-market-attractiveness-where-to-invest-going-into-2022/ [Accessed 04 October 2021].

Lueth, L. K. (2020). *State of the IoT 2020: 12 billion IoT connections, surpassing non-IoT for the first time.* [Online] Available at: https://iot-analytics.com/state-of-the-iot-2020-12-billion-iot-connections-surpassing-non-iot-for-the-first-time/ [Accessed 21 November 2021].

Ogbimi, P. O., & Ugbomeh, G. (2020). Application of GIS and Remote Sensing in Pipeline Routing Optimization: A Case Study of Shell's Niger Delta Pipeline Project. *Journal of Pipeline Systems Engineering and Practice, 11*(2). Advance online publication. DOI: 10.1061/JPEODS.PEENG-05020002

Papadonikolaki, E., Krystallis, I., & Morgan, B. (2020). *Digital transformation in construction-Systematic literature review of evolving concepts.* London, Engineering Project Organization Conference (EPOC) 2020.

PWC, (2018). *Digital Product Development 2025,* Na: PWC.

PWC. (2021). *A leadership agenda to take on tomorrow*. PWC.

Reis, J., Amorim, M., Melao, N., & Matos, P. (2018). Digital Transformation: A Literature Review and Guidelines for Future Research. In: Á. Rocha, H. Adeli, L. Paulo Reis & S. Costanzo, eds. *Trends and Advances in Information Systems and Technologies*. NA: Springer International Publishing, p. 1518. DOI: 10.1007/978-3-319-77703-0_41

Sanger, D. E., & Perlroth, N. (2021). *Colonial Pipeline Hack Reveals Weaknesses in US Cybersecurity*. [Online] Available at: https://www.nytimes.com/2021/05/14/us/politics/pipeline-hack.html [Accessed 21 November 2021].

Sanger, D. E., & Perlroth, N. (2021). *Pipeline Attack Yields Urgent Lessons About U.S. Cybersecurity*. NewYork Times.

Singh, A., & Hess, T. (2017). How Chief Digital Officers Promote the Digital Transformation of their Companies. *MIS Quarterly Executive*, *16*(1), 5.

Tabrizi, B., Lam, E., Girard, K., & Irvin, V. 2019. *Digital Transformation Is Not About Technology*. [Online] Available at: https://hbr.org/2019/03/digital-transformation-is-not-about-technology [Accessed 02 October 2021].

Techment. (2021). *The Rising Heat On Digital Transformation In Healthcare And What Lies Ahead In 2021*. [Online] Available at: https://www.techment.com/the-rising-heat-on-digital-transformation-in-healthcare-and-what-lies-ahead-in-2021/ [Accessed 05 October 2021].

TEKSYSTEMS. (2021). *State of Digital Transformation (Building a Framework for Digital Success)*. TEKSYSTEMS.

Vasquez, A. V. (2019). *Increase Construction Safety With Digital Transformation*. [Online] Available at: http://constructionexec.com/article/increase-construction-safety-with-digital-transformation [Accessed 10 October 2023].

Verhoef, P. C., Broekhuizen, T., Bart, Y., Bhattacharya, A., Qi Dong, J., Fabian, N., & Haenlein, M. (2021). Digital transformation: A multidisciplinary reflection and research agenda. *Journal of Business Research*, *122*(1), 889–901. DOI: 10.1016/j.jbusres.2019.09.022

Vladova, A. Y. (2021). Regional Specifics of Digitalization the Oil Midstream Soil Monitoring. NA, Springer. DOI: 10.1007/978-3-030-73261-5_23

Webb, S. P. (2018). *Digitalization for Pipeline Construction.* [Online] Available at: https://metegrity.com/media/articles/digitalization-for-pipeline-construction [Accessed 10 October 2021].

Wightman, A.. (2021). *A leadership agenda*. PWC.

World Economic Forum. (2017). *Digital Transformation Initiative Oil and Gas Industry,* Geneva: World Economic Forum.

World Economic Forum. (2018). *Taking expectations of on-demand and quick services to healthcare.* [Online] Available at: https://reports.weforum.org/digital-transformation/pager/ [Accessed 24 November 2021].

Y. Y. et al. (2021). Detection and Numerical Simulation of Potential Hazard in Oil Pipeline Areas Based on UAV Surveys. *Frontiers of Earth Science*, *9*(1), 272.

Yuqian, L. & Xun, X., (2019). Cloud-based manufacturing equipment and big data analytics to enable on-demand manufacturing services, *Science Direct,* June, Volume 57, pp. 92-102.

Zhou,. H. A. et al., (2020). Towards a Digital Process Platform for Future Construction Sites. *2020 ITU Kaleidoscope: Industry-Driven Digital Transformation*

KEY TERM AND DEFINITION

Digital Transformation: can include everything from cloud computing and information technology modernization to digital optimization and the creation of new digital business models.

Trajectory: is a way to describe and predict the journey of any institution or concept or point over time, taking into account the external and internal forces and constraints acting upon it.

Frugal Overhaul: the process of carefully reviewing and enhancing a system, procedure, or product in an economical and effective way without sacrificing its functionality or quality is known as a frugal overhaul.

Pipeline Construction: Surveying, preparation, pipe manufacturing, welding, inspection, coating, burying, and replacement are a few of the critical tasks performed in the pipeline construction industry. The construction and upkeep of pipelines is an expensive endeavor.

Digital Transformation Drivers: enablers that can propel digital transformation which includes innovation, digital attraction, research, culture, support, and legitimacy.

Digital Transformation Barriers: An ineffective value recognition system, a lack of infrastructure, a lack of regulations, a heterogeneous company culture, the expense of digital technologies, a sense of cannibalization of an existing business, the cost of adopting new technology, the presence of skilled labour, and a lack of digital transformation strategy are just a few of the internal and external obstacles that stand in the way of digital transformation.

Customer-Centric Transformation: clarity in customer needs and regulatory compliance are navigated carefully to align technology with user expectations.

Visual Representation: Visualizing words as clouds of text helps visually represent the research's findings. The importance of a word is determined by its size.

Compilation of References

Adner, R. (2017). Ecosystem as structure: An actionable construct for strategy. *Journal of Management, 43*(1), 39–58.

Agarwal, N., Bhatti, Y. A., & Levänen, J. (2021). *Linking Frugal Innovation to Frugal Entrepreneurship through Effectuation, Causation, and Bricolage. Proceedings.* Academy of Management., Retrieved from https://journals.aom.org/doi/abs/10.5465/AMBPP.2021.11386abstract DOI: 10.5465/AMBPP.2021.11386abstract

Agarwal, N., & Brem, A. (2017). Frugal innovation-past, present, and future. *IEEE Engineering Management Review, 45*(3), 37–41. DOI: 10.1109/EMR.2017.2734320

Agarwal, N., Grottke, M., Mishra, S., & Brem, A. (2017). A systematic literature review of constraint- based innovations: State of the art and future perspectives. *IEEE Transactions on Engineering Management, 64*(1), 3–15. DOI: 10.1109/TEM.2016.2620562

Agarwal, N., Oehler, J., & Brem, A. (2021). Constraint-based thinking: A structured approach for developing frugal innovations. *IEEE Transactions on Engineering Management, 68*(3), 739–751. DOI: 10.1109/TEM.2020.3042929

Ahmad, N.. (2014). Entrepreneurship in rural regions: Theoretical perspectives and practical insights. *Journal of Entrepreneurship and Innovation Management, 1*(1), 4–20.

Ahmad, N., Chechi, A. A., & Khan, F. H. (2014). Entrepreneurship in Rural Areas: A Key to Rural Development. *International Journal of Innovation and Economic Development, 1*(2), 47–54.

Alam, S., & Khan, S. (2020). Cost-Benefit Analysis of Digital Transformation in Pipeline Construction. *Journal of Construction Engineering and Management, 146*(8).

Alam, S., & Shakil, K. A. (2020). IoT-Based Leak Detection System for Pipelines. *Journal of Pipeline Systems Engineering and Practice, 11*(2).

Albert, M. (2019). Sustainable frugal innovation-The connection between frugal innovation and sustainability. *Journal of Cleaner Production*, *237*, 117747. DOI: 10.1016/j.jclepro.2019.117747

Albert, M. (2022). Assessing the sustainability impacts of frugal innovation–A literature review. *Journal of Cleaner Production*, *365*, 132754. DOI: 10.1016/j.jclepro.2022.132754

Alphabet Inc. (2024, March 26). Project Loon. Retrieved from https://x.company/loon/

Altmann, P., & Engberg, R. (2016). Frugal innovation and knowledge transferability. *Research Technology Management*, *59*(1), 48–55. DOI: 10.1080/08956308.2016.1117323

Al-Turki, K. M., & Obeid, A. M. (2020). IoT-Based Monitoring System for Pipeline Integrity Management: A Case Study of Saudi Aramco's Master Gas System Expansion. *Journal of Pipeline Systems Engineering and Practice*, *11*(3). Advance online publication. DOI: 10.1061/JPEODS.PEENG-05020003

Ananthram, S., Luo, Y., & Peng, M. W. (2022). Social entrepreneurship and frugal innovation: A composition-based view. *Journal of Social Entrepreneurship*, •••, 1–22. DOI: 10.1080/19420676.2022.2091643

Annala, L., Sarin, A., & Green, J. L. (2018). Co-production of frugal innovation: Case of low cost reverse osmosis water filters in India. *Journal of Cleaner Production*, *171*, S110–S118. DOI: 10.1016/j.jclepro.2016.07.065

Antolin-Lopez, R., & Montiel, I. (2018, July). Entrepreneurial collective responses to sustainability-related grand challenges. In Academy of Management Proceedings (Vol. 2018, No. 1, p. 11471). Briarcliff Manor, NY 10510: Academy of Management. DOI: 10.5465/AMBPP.2018.83

An, W., Zhao, X., Cao, Z., Zhang, J., & Liu, H. (2018). How bricolage drives corporate entrepreneurship: The roles of opportunity identification and learning orientation. *Journal of Product Innovation Management*, *35*(1), 49–65. DOI: 10.1111/jpim.12377

Audretsch, D. (2014). From the entrepreneurial university to the university for the entrepreneurial society. *The Journal of Technology Transfer*, *39*(3), 313–321. DOI: 10.1007/s10961-012-9288-1

Avanti. (2019). Avanti Fellows Program. Retrieved from https://www.avantifellows.org/

Baird, L., & Peterson, M. (2024). Introduction to community asset mapping. https://www.innovatingjustice.org/sites/default/files/documents/asset_mapping.pdf

Bankar, S., & Manna, R. (2023). Adoption of HR Analytics for Enhancing Business Performance: Trend Analysis. *Journal of Xidian University*, *17*(3), 234–247. DOI: 10.37896/jxu17.3/024

Basu, S., & Roy, R. (2018). Frugal innovation: A strategic means for enabling universal healthcare in India. *Global Business and Organizational Excellence*, *37*(1), 6–16.

Baud, I. (2016). Moving towards inclusive development? Recent views on inequalities, frugal innovations, urban geo-technologies, gender and hybrid governance. *European Journal of Development Research*, *28*(2), 119–129. DOI: 10.1057/ejdr.2016.1

Baxter, W. H., & Sagart, L. (2014). *Old Chinese: A new reconstruction*. Oxford University Press., DOI: 10.1093/acprof:oso/9780199945375.001.0001

Bayuo, B., Chaminade, C., & Go¨ransson, B. (2020). Unpacking the role of universities in the emergence, development and impact of social innovations – a systematic review of the literature. *Technological Forecasting and Social Change*, *155*, 1–11. DOI: 10.1016/j.techfore.2020.120030

BDO USA, LLP. (2021). *2021 Technology Digital Transformation Survey*. BDO.

BDO. 2021. *2021 Financial Services Digital,* NA: BDO.

BDO. 2021. *2021 Industry 4.0 Survey,* NA: BDO.

Belbağ, A. G., Üner, M. M., Cavusgil, E., & Cavusgil, S. T. (2019). The new middle class in emerging markets: How values and demographics influence discretionary consumption. *Thunderbird International Business Review*, *61*(2), 325–337. DOI: 10.1002/tie.21980

Benneworth, P., & Cunha, J. (2015). Universities' contributions to social innovation: Reflections in theory & practice. *European Journal of Innovation Management*, *18*(4), 508–527. DOI: 10.1108/EJIM-10-2013-0099

Benneworth, P., Pinheiro, R., & Sanchez-Barrioluengo, M. (2016). One size does not fit all! New perspectives on the university in the social knowledge economy. *Science & Public Policy*, *43*(6), 731–735. DOI: 10.1093/scipol/scw018

Berkey, B. (2021). Ethical consumerism, democratic values, and justice. *Philosophy & Public Affairs*, *49*(3), 237–274. DOI: 10.1111/papa.12191

Bhatti, Y. A. (2012). What is frugal, What is innovation? Towards a theory of frugal innovation. DOI: . https://www.researchgate.net/publication/228121294_What_is_Frugal_What_is_Innovation_Towards_a_Theory_of_Frugal_Innovation#:~:text=The%20theory%20of%20frugal%20innovation,%2C%20affordable%20and%20appropriate%20products%22%2CDOI: 10.2139/ssrn.2005910

Bhatti, Y. (2012). Frugal innovation: An accessible innovation concept for Africa's social and economic development. *International Journal of Engineering and Science Invention, 1*(2), 18–27.

Bhatti, Y. A. (2012). *What is Frugal, What is Innovation? Towards a Theory of Frugal Innovation*. University of Oxford.

Bhatti, Y. A., Basu, R., Barron, D., & Ventresca, M. J. (2018). *Frugal Innovation: Models, Means, Methods*. Cambridge University Press. DOI: 10.1017/9781316986783

Bhatti, Y. A., & Ventresca, M. (2013). How Can 'Frugal Innovation' Be Conceptualized? (January 19, 2013). Available at *SSRN*: https://ssrn.com/abstract=2203552 or http://dx.doi.org/DOI: 10.2139/ssrn.2203552

Bhatti, Y. A., & Ventresca, M. (2013). How can 'frugal innovation' be conceptualized? *Available atSSRN* 2203552.

Bhatti, Y., Khilji, S. E., & Basu, R. (2013). Frugal innovation. In *Globalization, change and learning in South Asia* (pp. 123–145). Chandos Publishing. DOI: 10.1016/B978-0-85709-464-3.50007-6

Bhatti, Y., & Prabhu, J. (2019). Frugal Innovation and Social Innovation: Linked Paths to Achieving Inclusion Sustainably. In George, G., Baker, T., Tracey, P., & Joshi, H. (Eds.), *Handbook of Inclusive Innovation: The Role of Organizations, Markets and Communities in Social Innovation*. Edward Elgar. DOI: 10.4337/9781786436016.00031

Bhatti, Y., & Ventresca, M. J. (2012). Practice, performance and materiality in entrepreneurship: The notion of entrepreneurship as performativity. *Organization Studies, 33*(7), 979–1010.

Bhatti, Y., & Ventresca, M. J. (2019). Beyond the IPR: Formalizing global knowledge networks through creative commoning. *Academy of Management Journal, 62*(5), 1396–1431.

Bhuyan, A., & Bag, S. (2020). Effect of frugal innovation on sustainable development: A study in the Indian context. *Sustainable Development, 28*(5), 1051–1064.

Blank, S. (2013). *The startup owner's manual: The step-by-step guide for building a great company*. John Wiley & Sons.

Bohach, A. (1997). Fundamental principles of asset-based community development. *The Journal of Volunteer Administration, 15*(4), 22–29.

Bo, L., Jiannan, G., & Xiangdong, X. (2020). The Digital Twin of Oil and Gas Pipeline System. *IFAC-PapersOnLine, 53*(5), 710–714. DOI: 10.1016/j.ifacol.2021.04.162

Bonnici, F., Klijn, V., & Nowack, D. (2024). The state of social enterprise: A review of global data from 2013-2023.https://www3.weforum.org/docs/WEF_The_State_of_Social_Enterprise_2024.pdf

Borchardt, M., Pereira, G., Viegas, C., Reolon, D., Xavier, Y. and Battaglia, D. (2018). Providing goods to the base of the pyramid: opportunities for micro, small and medium-sized local producers, *Journal of Small Business Strategy*, Vol. 28 No. 2.

Bound, K., Thornton, I.W., 2012. Our Frugal Future: Lessons from India's Innovation System.

Bound, K., & Thornton, I. (2012). *Our Frugal Future: Lesson from India's Innovation System*. NESTA.

Bound, K., & Thornton, I. (2012). *Our Frugal Future: Lessons from India's Innovation System*. Nesta.

Bound, K., & Thornton, J. (2012). Engineering innovation in global health: Ten Grand Challenges. *Proceedings of the Institution of Civil Engineers. Engineering Sustainability*, *165*(3), 181–186.

Boyatzis, C. J. (2024). Spiritual development during childhood and adolescence. In Miller, L. J. (Ed.), *The Oxford handbook of psychology and spirituality* (2nd ed., pp. 100–124). Oxford University Press., DOI: 10.1093/oxfordhb/9780190905538.013.5

Bozalek, V., Gachago, D., Alexander, L., Watters, K., Wood, D., Ivala, E., & Herrington, J. (2013). The use of emerging technologies for authentic learning: A South African study in higher education. *British Journal of Educational Technology*, *44*(4), 629–638. DOI: 10.1111/bjet.12046

Bray, J., Johns, N., & Kilburn, D. (2011). An exploratory study into the factors impeding ethical consumption. *Journal of Business Ethics*, *98*(4), 597–608. DOI: 10.1007/s10551-010-0640-9

Brem, A., & Wolfram, P. (2014). Research and development from the bottom up - Introduction of terminologies for new product development in emerging markets. *Journal of Innovation and Entrepreneurship*, *3*(1), 9. DOI: 10.1186/2192-5372-3-9

Brem, A., & Wolfram, P. (2014). Research and development from the bottom up—Introduction of terminologies for new product development in emerging markets. *Journal of Engineering and Technology Management*, *32*, 167–183.

Brown, T. (2009). *Change by design: How design thinking transforms organizations and inspires innovation*. HarperCollins Publishers.

Cai, Q., Ying, Y., Liu, Y., & Wu, W. (2019). Innovating with limited resources: The antecedents and consequences of frugal innovation. *Sustainability (Basel), 11*(20), 5789. DOI: 10.3390/su11205789

Calderon-Monge, E., & Ribeiro-Soriano, D. (2024). The role of digitalization in business and management: A systematic literature review. *Review of Managerial Science, 18*(2), 449–491.

Calo, F., Sancino, A., & Scognamiglio, F. (2024). Social enterprise and social entrepreneurship in the Public Administration (PA) a scholar field bibliometric analysis and some conceptual considerations. *Public Management Review, 26*(10), 3013–3039. Advance online publication. DOI: 10.1080/14719037.2024.2311181

Cambridge Centre for social Innovation (2024). The rise of social extrapreneurship. https://socialinnovation.blog.jbs.cam.ac.uk/2015/12/04/the-rise-of-social-extraprenuership/The rise of social extrapreneurship

Carrington, M. J., Neville, B. A., & Whitwell, G. J. (2014). Lost in translation: Exploring the ethical consumer intention–behavior gap. *Journal of Business Research, 67*(1), 2759–2767. DOI: 10.1016/j.jbusres.2012.09.022

Carrington, M., Chatzidakis, A., Goworek, H., & Shaw, D. (2021). Consumption Ethics: A Review and Analysis of Future Directions for Interdisciplinary Research. *Journal of Business Ethics, 168*(2), 215–238. DOI: 10.1007/s10551-020-04425-4

Centre for Public Impact (CPI). (2016). Mobile Currency in Kenya: the M-Pesa. Retrieved from https://www.centreforpublicimpact.org/case-study/m-currency-in-kenya

CFTE. (2024). What is extrapreneurship. https://courses.cfte.education/extrapreneurship-programmes/#:~:text=We%20define%20Extrapreneurship%20as%20the,managers%2C%20transformation%20leaders%20or%20investors.

Chan, R. Y. K., Sharma, P., Alqahtani, A., Leung, T. Y., & Malik, A. (2024). Mediating role of cultural values in the impact of ethical ideologies on Chinese consumers' ethical judgments. *Journal of Business Ethics, 191*(4), 865–884. Advance online publication. DOI: 10.1007/s10551-024-05669-0

Chataway, J., Hanlin, R., & Kaplinsky, R. (2014). Inclusive innovation: An architecture for policy development. *Innovation and Development, 4*(1), 33–54. DOI: 10.1080/2157930X.2013.876800

Chen, Y., Chen, S., & Miao, J. (2024). Does smart city pilot improve urban green economic efficiency: Accelerator or inhibitor. *Environmental Impact Assessment Review, 104*, 107328. Advance online publication. DOI: 10.1016/j.eiar.2023.107328

Chesbrough, H. (2003). *Open innovation: The new imperative for creating and profiting from technology*. Harvard Business Press.

Chibuike, C. U., & Ovharhe, O. H. (2022). Emergence of risk culture and lean culture in Nigeria during pandemic and crisis era: Using confirmatory analysis. *International Journal of Multidisciplinary Research and Growth Evaluation*, *3*(1), 263–271. DOI: 10.54660/anfo.2021.3.1.14

Chibuike, C. U., Ovharhe, O. H., & Abada, A. M. (2022). Synchronization of lean accounting alert and entrepreneurial sustainability among micro firms in Nigeria during pandemic and catastrophe: Using confirmatory factor analysis. *International Journal of Business and Management*, *10*(1), 1–13. DOI: 10.54660/anfo.2021.2.6.15

Chigona, A., & Chigona, W. (2008). MXit it up in the media: Media discourse analysis on a Mobile instant messaging system. *The Southern African Journal of Information and Communication*, (9), 42–57.

Choe, K. A., & Roberts, B. H. (2011). *Competitive cities in the 21st century: Cluster-based local economic development*. Asian Development Bank.

Christof, E., & Henrique, D. C. (2018). Digital transformation. *IEEE Software*, *35*(4), 16–21.

Cıftcı, D. (2020). Political Consumerism: Discussion on the Motivation of Boycotting and Buycotts. *Dördüncü Kuvvet Uluslararası Hakemli Dergi*, *3*(1), 39–55.

Cohen, B., & Winn, M. I. (2007). Market imperfections, opportunity, and sustainable entrepreneurship. *Journal of Business Venturing*, *22*(1), 29–49. DOI: 10.1016/j.jbusvent.2004.12.001

Conrad, A., & Schreiber, A. (2022). Circular Entrepreneurship: A pathway to circular entrepreneurship: An empirical study on how governmental institutions can improve the external environment of entrepreneurs.

Cope, A. P., Barnes, M., Belson, A., Binks, M., Brockbank, S., Bonachela-Capdevila, F., Carini, C., Fisher, B. A., Goodyear, C. S., Emery, P., Ehrenstein, M. R., Gozzard, N., Harris, R., Hollis, S., Keidel, S., Levesque, M., Lindholm, C., McDermott, M. F., McInnes, I. B., & Isaacs, J. D. (2018). The RA-MAP consortium: A working model for academia – industry collaboration. *Nature Reviews. Rheumatology*, *14*(1), 53–61. DOI: 10.1038/nrrheum.2017.200 PMID: 29213124

Corsini, L., Dammicco, V., & Moultrie, J. (2021). Frugal innovation in a crisis: The digital fabrication maker response to COVID-19. *R & D Management*, *51*(2), 195–210. DOI: 10.1111/radm.12446

Crisp, L. (2014). Mutual learning and reverse innovation: Where next? *Globalization and Health*, *10*(1), 1–4. DOI: 10.1186/1744-8603-10-14 PMID: 24673828

CropIn. (2024, March 12). Agriculture Technology Company. Retrieved from https://www.cropin.com/

Cuhadar, S., & Rudnák, I. (2022). Literature review. *Sustain. Leadership*, *9*(3), 55–65. DOI: 10.18531/Studia.Mundi.2022.09.03.55-65

Cunha, M. P., Rego, A., Oliveira, P., Rosado, P., & Habib, N. (2014). Product Innovation in Resource-Poor Environments: Three Research Streams. *Journal of Product Innovation Management*, *31*(2), 202–210. DOI: 10.1111/jpim.12090

D'Angelo, V., & Magnusson, M. (2020). A bibliometric map of intellectual communities in frugal innovation literature. *IEEE Transactions on Engineering Management*, *66*, 653–666.

Dabić, M., Obradović, T., Vlačić, B., Sahasranamam, S., & Paul, J. (2022). Frugal innovations: A multidisciplinary review & agenda for future research. *Journal of Business Research*, *142*, 914–929. DOI: 10.1016/j.jbusres.2022.01.032

Dana, L. P., Gurău, C., Hoy, F., Ramadani, V., & Alexander, T. (2021). Success factors and challenges of grassroots innovations: Learning from failure. *Technological Forecasting and Social Change*, *164*, 119600.

Darley, L. (2022). Red light in entrepreneurship. https://www.grin.com › document

Dawa, S., & Marks, J. (2023) An effectuation approach to sustainable entrepreneurship. *Journal of Entrepreneurship in Emerging Economies*, (ahead-of-print).

Dawood, M. A. (2023). What is the frugal innovation model, and how does it work? https://growenterprise.co.uk/2023/02/09/what-is-the-frugal-innovation-model-and-how-does-it-work/#:~:text=Frugal%20innovation%20is%20reducing%20the,developing%20countries%20using%20affordable%20prices

Dean, T. J., & McMullen, J. S. (2007). Toward a theory of sustainable entrepreneurship: Reducing environmental degradation through entrepreneurial action. *Journal of Business Venturing*, *22*(1), 50–76. DOI: 10.1016/j.jbusvent.2005.09.003

Dee, E. (2024). MGE303 Social entrepreneurship 2024. https://www.scribd.com/document/719869450/MGE303-Social-Entrepreneurship-2024

Degli Antoni, G., & Faillo, M. (2022). Ethical consumerism and wage levels: Evidence from an experimental market. *Business Ethics, the Environment & Responsibility*, *31*(3), 875–887. DOI: 10.1111/beer.12447

DeHaat. (2024, March 22). Solutions for Farmers. Retrieved from https://agrevolution.in/solution-for-farmers

Delfa, B. (2020). *Innovación frugal: más con menos para un mundomejor*. The Conversation.

Delmas, M. A., & Toffel, M. W. (2004). Stakeholders and environmental management practices: An institutional framework. *Business Strategy and the Environment, 13*(4), 209–222. DOI: 10.1002/bse.409

Deloitte. 2021. *Using ecosystems to accelerate smart manufacturing*. [Online] Available at: https://www2.deloitte.com/global/en/pages/energy-and-resources/articles/accelerating-smart-manufacturing-the-value-of-an-ecosystem-approach.html [Accessed 21 November 2021].

Desrochers, P. (2004). Industrial symbiosis: The case for market coordination. *Journal of Cleaner Production, 12*(8-10), 1099–1110. DOI: 10.1016/j.jclepro.2004.02.008

Dickson, D. 2020. *2021 oil and gas industry outlook*. [Online] Available at: https://www2.deloitte.com/us/en/pages/energy-and-resources/articles/oil-and-gas-industry-outlook.htm....html [Accessed 03 October 2021].

Dictionary, C. (2024). Light. https://www.collinsdictionary.com/dictionary/english/light

Dima, A., Bugheanu, A. M., Dinulescu, R., Potcovaru, A. M., Stefanescu, C. A., & Marin, I. (2022). Exploring the research regarding frugal innovation and business sustainability through bibliometric analysis. *Sustainability (Basel), 14*(3), 1326. DOI: 10.3390/su14031326

Dixit, K., & Acharya, S. R. (2023). Start-up Ecosystem through the Lens of Action Research. *15th Biennial Conference on Entrepreneurship*. Delhi: Bookwell. Retrieved from http://library.ediindia.ac.in:8181/xmlui//handle/123456789/13886

Dixit, K., & Manna, R. (2023). Bibliometric Analysis of Entrepreneurial Orientation and Firm Performance. *Korea Review of International Studies, 16*(49). doi:https://doie.org/client/index.php?tag=generatedoi

Dogra, P. K. (2023, December 27). With viral English lessons, 'Dehati Madam' from small UP village takes YouTube by storm. The Indian Express. Retrieved from https://indianexpress.com/article/india/dehati-madam-youtuber-up-village-viral-english-lessons-9049997/

EADI. (2024). Frugal innovation and development. https://www.eadi.org/network/eadi-working-groups/frugal-innovation-and-development

Economic Times. (2017, April 24). Meet Arunachalam Muruganantham, the man who wore a sanitary pad to break a taboo. Retrieved from https://economictimes.indiatimes.com/news/politics-and-nation/meet-arunachalam-muruganantham-the-man-who-wore-a-sanitary-pad-to-break-a-taboo/padman-is-here/slideshow/58340285.cms

Effa, G. A., Ovharhe, O. H., Ezirim, A. C., & Igwe, S. (2023b). Strategic procurement initiatives and logistics performance in Nigeria. International Journal of Marketing and Communication Studies (IJMCS), 7(1), 38-55. DOI: . Erika, S., & Jo, N. (2024). What is Strenght–based approach. https://positivepsychology.com/strengths-based-interventions/DOI: 10.56201/ijmcs.v7.no1.2023.pg38.55

Effa, G. A., Ovharhe, O. H., Ezirim, A. C., & Igwe, S. (2023a). Procurement sustainability policy and logistics performance in Nigeria. [IJMCS]. *International Journal of Marketing and Communication Studies*, *7*(1), 56–72. DOI: 10.56201/ijmcs.v7.no1.2023.pg56.72

Egharevba, M. E., Eguavoen, A., Azuh, D., Iruonagbe, T. C., & Chiazor, I. A. (2016). Microfinance and poverty reduction strategy for promoting national development: The challenge of social/financial inclusion. *Social Sciences*, *11*(22), 5373–5386.

Elbeshbishi, A. N., & Al A'ali, E. A. (2020). Fair trade and ethical consumerism: A complementary perspective. In *Ethical consumerism and comparative studies across different cultures: Emerging research and opportunities* (pp. 101–125). IGI Global. DOI: 10.4018/978-1-7998-0272-3.ch007

Eleni, P., Paparoidamis, N. G., & Chumpitaz, R. (2015, October 21). Modelling Ethicality in Consumption: Bridging the Literature on Ethics. *Thriving in a New World Economy*. Springer International Publishing. DOI: 10.1007/978-3-319-24148-7_65

Elizalde, D. 2021. *7 IoT Business Models That Are Transforming Industries.* [Online] Available at: https://danielelizalde.com/monetize-your-iot-product/ [Accessed 07 October 2021].

Embrace. (2019). About Us. Retrieved from https://www.embraceglobal.org/

Endres, M., Bican, P. M., & Wollner, ¨. T. (2022). Frugal innovation with Scrum: How can Scrum be used to develop resource-efficient innovations in developed world companies? *Journal of Cleaner Production*, •••, 130871. DOI: 10.1016/j.jclepro.2022.130871

Eze, S. C., Chinedu-Eze, V. C., & Bello, A. O. (2018). The utilisation of e-learning facilities in the educational delivery system of Nigeria: A study of M-University. *International Journal of Educational Technology in Higher Education*, *15*(1), 1–20.

Ezeudu, O. B., Agunwamba, J. C., Ugochukwu, U. C., & Oraelosi, T. C. (2022). Circular economy and frugal innovation: A conceptual nexus. *Environmental Science and Pollution Research International*, *29*(20), 1–16. DOI: 10.1007/s11356-022-18522-6 PMID: 34997516

Farooq, R. (2017). A conceptual model of frugal innovation: Is environmental munificence a missing link? *International Journal of Innovation Science*, *9*(4), 320–334. DOI: 10.1108/IJIS-08-2017-0076

Fazal, S., & Khan, S. (2019). Digital Twin Application in Oil and Gas Pipeline Projects: Keystone XL Pipeline Case Study. *Proceedings of the 2019 International Conference on Construction Engineering and Management*, pp. 345-354.

Fischer, B., & Guerrero, M., Guimoń, J., Schaeffer, P.R. (2020). Knowledge transfer for frugal innovation: Where do entrepreneurial universities stand? *Journal of Knowledge Management*, *25*, 60–379.

Fischer, B., Guerrero, M., Guimón, J., & Schaeffer, P. R. (2021). Knowledge transfer for frugal innovation: Where do entrepreneurial universities stand. *Journal of Knowledge Management*, *25*(2), 360–379. DOI: 10.1108/JKM-01-2020-0040

Fonrouge, C. (2024). How to Change Entrepreneurs' Attitudes toward a Circular Economy: An Exploratory Framework to Reduce the Gap between Circular Intentions and Circular Actions. *Sustainability (Basel)*, *16*(5), 2048. DOI: 10.3390/su16052048

Fraillon, J., Ainley, J., Schulz, W., Friedman, T., & Gebhardt, E. (2014). *Preparing for life in a digital age: The IEA International Computer and Information Literacy Study international report*. Springer Nature. DOI: 10.1007/978-3-319-14222-7

Fredriksson, E., &Tömmervik, J. (2014). Frugal is the new innovative thinking: A qualitative study of frugal innovations and sustainable development in resource-poor environments.

Freeman, M. A. (2020). Are entrepreneurs touched with fire. https://econa.net/wp-content/uploads/2020/08/Are-Entrepreneurs-Touched-with-Fire.pdf.https://www.linkedin.com/pulse/entrepreneurs-touched-fire-michael-a-freeman-m-d

Freestone, O. M., & McGoldrick, P. J. (2008). Motivations of the ethical consumer. *Journal of Business Ethics*, *79*(4), 445–467. DOI: 10.1007/s10551-007-9409-1

Friedman, M. (1962). *Capitalism and Freedom*. The University of Chicago Press., DOI: 10.1016/j.jclepro.2020.121456

Ganapati, L. S. (2024). What's the difference between an ultrapreneur and an entrepreneur? https://www.quora.com/What-s-the-difference-between-an-ultrapreneur-and-an-entrepreneur#:~:text=Ultrapreneurs%20can%20be%20seen%20as,entrepreneur%20who%20is%20comparatively%20restless

Gartner. (2021). *Gartner Glossary.* [Online] Available at: https://www.gartner.com/en/informationtechnology/glossary?startsWith=D&pageSize=all&nPage=1&showLocalizedContent=false&languageCode=en&glossaryTypeTag=emt:page/function/it [Accessed 04 October 2021].

Gbolarumi, F. T., Wong, K. Y., & Olohunde, S. T. (2021, February). Sustainability assessment in the textile and apparel industry: A review of recent studies. [). IOP Publishing.]. *IOP Conference Series. Materials Science and Engineering*, *1051*(1), 012099. DOI: 10.1088/1757-899X/1051/1/012099

Geissbauer, R., Schrauf, S., Schneider, J., & Hermans, M. (2020). Connected and autonomous supply chain ecosystems 2025. PricewaterhouseCoopers (PwC).

Geissdoerfer, M., Savaget, P., Bocken, N. M., & Hultink, E. J. (2017). The Circular Economy–A New Sustainability Paradigm? *Journal of Cleaner Production*, *143*, 757–768. DOI: 10.1016/j.jclepro.2016.12.048

George, G., Howard-Grenville, J., Joshi, A., & Tihanyi, L. (2016). Understanding and tackling societal grand challenges through management research. *Academy of Management Journal*, *59*(6), 1880–1895. DOI: 10.5465/amj.2016.4007

George, G., McGahan, A. M., & Prabhu, J. (2012). Innovation for inclusive growth: Towards a theoretical framework and a research agenda. *Journal of Management Studies*, *49*(4), 661–683. DOI: 10.1111/j.1467-6486.2012.01048.x

Ghisellini, P., Cialani, C., & Ulgiati, S. (2016). A review on circular economy: The expected transition to a balanced interplay of environmental and economic systems. *Journal of Cleaner Production*, *114*, 11–32. DOI: 10.1016/j.jclepro.2015.09.007

Gillani, A., & Kutaula, S. (2018). An introduction to special issue: Sustainability and ethical consumerism. *Management Decision*, *56*(3), 511–514. DOI: 10.1108/MD-03-2018-949

Giuggioli, G., & Pellegrini, M. M. (2023). Artificial intelligence as an enabler for entrepreneurs: A systematic literature review and an agenda for future research. *International Journal of Entrepreneurial Behaviour & Research*, *29*(4), 816–837. DOI: 10.1108/IJEBR-05-2021-0426

Glasbeek, L., Wickert, C., & Schad, J. (2024). Evaluating definitions of social entrepreneurship: A rulebook from the philosophy of science. *International Journal of Management Reviews*, *26*(3), 1–26. DOI: 10.1111/ijmr.12359

Government of India. (n.d.). National Rural Livelihood Mission (NRLM). Ministry of Rural Development. Retrieved from https://nrlm.gov.in/

Government of India. (n.d.). Pradhan MantriKrishiSinchayeeYojana (PMKSY). Ministry of Agriculture & Farmers Welfare. Retrieved from https://pmksy.gov.in/

Government of India. (n.d.). Pradhan MantriSahajBijliHarGharYojana (Saubhagya Scheme). Ministry of Power. Retrieved from https://saubhagya.gov.in/

Government of India. (n.d.). RashtriyaKrishiVikasYojana (RKVY). Ministry of Agriculture & Farmers Welfare. Retrieved from http://rkvy.nic.in/

Government of India. (n.d.). Swachh Bharat Mission (SBM). Ministry of Housing and Urban Affairs. Retrieved from https://swachhbharaturban.gov.in/

Govindan, K. (2022). How artificial intelligence drives sustainable frugal innovation: A multitheoretical perspective. *IEEE Transactions on Engineering Management*, *71*(1), 638–655.

Govindarajan, V., & Ramamurti, R. (2015). Reverse innovation, emerging markets, and global strategy. *Global Strategy Journal*, *5*(1), 27–37.

Govindarajan, V., & Trimble, C. (2010). *The other side of innovation: Solving the execution challenge*. Harvard Business Press.

Govindarajan, V., & Trimble, C. (2012). *Reverse Innovation: Create Far From Home, Win Everywhere*. Harvard Business Review Press. DOI: 10.5437/08956308X5506003

Govind, R., Singh, J. J., Garg, N., & D'Silva, S. (2019). Not walking the walk: How dual attitudes influence behavioral outcomes in ethical consumption. *Journal of Business Ethics*, *155*(4), 1195–1214. DOI: 10.1007/s10551-017-3545-z

Goyal, T. M. (2022). *MSMEs Go Digital. India Council for Research on International Economic Relations*. ICRIER.

Grabs, J., Langen, N., Maschkowski, G., Schäpke, N. (2016) Understanding role models for change: A multilevel analysis of success factors of grassroots initiatives for sustainable consumption. Journal of Cleaner Production (134. A): 98-111.

Greco, M., Savage, L., & Souza, S. (2024). Asset mapping in a rural context: Asset based community development in collaboration with Cairo, Georgia. https://coss.fsu.edu/durp/wp-content/uploads/sites/9/2024/03/January-Final-Draft-1-1-compressed.pdf

Green, D. (2024, March 26). Global Impact. Retrieved from https://digitalgreen.org/global-impact/

Guerrero, M., & Urbano, D. (2016b). The transformative role of universities: determinants, impacts, and challenges, in Leita˜o, J. and Alves, H. (Eds), Entrepreneurial and Innovative Practices in Public Institutions, *Springer*, Cham, pp. 1-17.

Guerrero, M., & Urbano, D. (2016a). The impact of triple helix agents on entrepreneurial innovations' performance: An inside look at enterprises located in an emerging economy. *Technological Forecasting and Social Change*, *119*, 294–309. DOI: 10.1016/j.techfore.2016.06.015

Gupta, A. K., Sinha, R., Koradia, D. K., Patel, R. K., Parmar, M., Rohit, P. E., Patel, H. V., Patel, K., Chand, V. S., James, T. J., Chandan, A., Patel, M. M., Prakash, T., & Vivekanandan, P. (2003). Mobilizing grassroots' technological innovations and traditional knowledge, values and institutions: Articulating social and ethical Capital, futures. *Futures*, *35*(9), 975–987. DOI: 10.1016/S0016-3287(03)00053-3

Gupta, A. K., & Wang, H. (2008). Global Enterprise 2020: Five factors that will give you the edge in the race to access the world's most rapidly developing markets. *Chief Executive-New York*, *234*, 32.

Gupta, A., & Wang, H. (2009). *Getting China and India Right: Strategies for leveraging the world's fastest-growing economies for global advantage*. Wiley.

Gupta, A., & Wang, H. (2009). *Getting China and India Right: Strategies for Leveraging the World's Fastest-Growing Economies for Global Advantage*. Wiley.

Gupta, M., & Gupta, H. (2024). Sustainable urban development of smart cities in India-a systematic literature review. *Sustainability, Agri. Food and Environmental Research*, *12*. Advance online publication. DOI: 10.7770/safer-V12N1-art2578

Gupta, R., Chandrasekaran, D., Sen, S., & Gupta, T. (2024). Marketing to bottom-of-the-pyramid consumers in an emerging market: The responses of mainstream consumers. *Journal of Business Ethics*, *191*(4), 739–755. Advance online publication. DOI: 10.1007/s10551-024-05664-5

Gurumurthy, R., Schatsky, D., & Camhi, J. 2020. *Uncovering the connection between digital maturity and financial performance.* [Online] Available at: https://www2.deloitte.com/us/en/insights/topics/digital-transformation/digital-transformation-survey.html [Accessed 10 September 2021].

Gurumurthy, R., Nanda, R., & Schatsky, D. (2021). *Putting digital at the heart of strategy*. Deloitte Insights.

Hadjitchoneva, J., Pellat, G., & Marasova, J. (2023). Reinvesting in European Citizenship Through Entrepreneurship and Frugal Innovation. In *Cooperation and Enlargement: Two Challenges to be Addressed in the European Projects - 2022* (pp. 29–49). Springer.

Hafkin, N. J., & Taggart, N. (2001). *Gender, information technology, and developing countries: An analytic study. Office of Women in Development, Bureau for Global Programs, Field Support and Research.* United States Agency for International Development.

Hamilton, B. (2018). *Digital Tools in Schools: Ethnography of Technology in Town and Rural Elementary Schools.* Denver: (PhD dissertation). University of Colorado.

Harris, M., Bhatti, Y., Buckley, J., & Sharma, D. (2020). Fast and frugal innovations in response to the COVID-19 pandemic. *Nature Medicine*, *26*(6), 814–817. DOI: 10.1038/s41591-020-0889-1 PMID: 32393803

Hartigan, M., Mussomeli, A., Laaper, S. & Gish, D. (2017). *The smart factory Responsive, adaptive, connected manufacturing,* s.l.: Deloitte.

Hawkins, R., Trucano, M., Cobo, C., Juan, T., Alex, S., & Inaki, A. (2020). *Re-imagining Human Connections: Technology and Innovation in Education at the World Bank.* World Bank Group. Retrieved from http://documents. worldbank. org/curated/en/829491606860379513/Reimagining-Human-Connections-Technology-and-Innovation-in-Education-at-the-World-Bank

Heaton, S., Siegel, D. S., & Teece, D. J. (2019). Universities and innovation ecosystems: A dynamic capabilities perspective. *Industrial and Corporate Change*, *28*(4), 921–939. DOI: 10.1093/icc/dtz038

Herselman, M., & Britton, K. G. (2002). Analysing the role of ICT in bridging the digital divide amongst learners. *South African Journal of Education*, *22*(4), 270–274.

Hindawi (2024). Implementation of Frugal Innovation Approach in Moroccan Industry through the Development of a New Frugal System. https://www.hindawi.com/journals/je/2024/3971088/fig10

Hindocha, C. N., Antonacci, G., Barlow, J., & Harris, M. (2021). Defining frugal innovation: A critical review. *BMJ Innovations*, *7*(4), 647–656. DOI: 10.1136/bmjinnov-2021-000830

Hockerts, K., & Wüstenhagen, R. (2010). Greening Goliaths versus emerging Davids—Theorizing about the role of incumbents and new entrants in sustainable entrepreneurship. *Journal of Business Venturing*, *25*(5), 481–492. DOI: 10.1016/j.jbusvent.2009.07.005

Hollow, D., & Masperi, P. (2009, April). An evaluation of the use of ICT within primary education in Malawi. *International Conference on Information and Communication Technologies and Development (ICTD)* (pp. 27-34). IEEE. DOI: 10.1109/ICTD.2009.5426707

Hossain, M. (2020). Frugal innovation: Conception, development, diffusion, and outcome. Journal of Cleaner Production, Volume 262, 2020, 121456, ISSN 0959-6526.

Hossain, M. T., & Rakib, M. D. (2024). Evaluating the effectiveness of the social marketing mix: a study of social marketing dynamics in Godrej Bangladesh. https://urn.fi/URN:NBN:fi:amk-2024052918106

Hossain, M., Levänen, J., & Wierenga, M. (2021). Pursuing frugal innovation for sustainability at the grassroots level. 2021;(May):374– 381

Hossain, M., Park, S., & Shahid, S. (2023). Frugal innovation for sustainable rural development. Technol. Forecast. Soc. Chang., 193, Article 122662

Hossain, M. (2018). Frugal innovation: A review and research agenda. *Journal of Cleaner Production*, *182*, 926–936. DOI: 10.1016/j.jclepro.2018.02.091

Hossain, M. (2018). Grassroots innovation: The state of the art and future perspectives. *Technology in Society*, *55*, 63–69. DOI: 10.1016/j.techsoc.2018.06.008

Hossain, M. (2021). Frugal innovation and sustainable business models. *Technology in Society*, *64*, 101508. DOI: 10.1016/j.techsoc.2020.101508

Hossain, M. (2022). Frugal entrepreneurship: Resource mobilization in resource-constrained environments. *Creativity and Innovation Management*, *31*(3), 509–520. DOI: 10.1111/caim.12502

Hossain, M., Agarwal, N., Bhatti, Y., & Levänen, J. (2022). Frugal innovation: Antecedents, mediators, and consequences. *Creativity and Innovation Management*, *31*(3), 521–540. DOI: 10.1111/caim.12511

Hossain, M., Park, S., & Shahid, S. (2023). Frugal innovation for sustainable rural development. *Technological Forecasting and Social Change*, *193*, 122662. DOI: 10.1016/j.techfore.2023.122662

Hossain, M., & Sarkar, S. (2021). Frugal entrepreneurship: Profiting with inclusive growth. *IEEE Transactions on Engineering Management*, *70*(11), 3812–3825.

Hossain, M., Shahid, M. S., & Park, S. (2024). The business models of frugal enterprises for sustainable development in a constrained environment. *IEEE Transactions on Engineering Management*, *71*, 3448–3463. DOI: 10.1109/TEM.2023.3342440

Hossain, M., Simula, H., & Halme, M. (2016). Can frugal go global? Diffusion patterns of frugal innovations. *Technology in Society*, *46*, 132–139. DOI: 10.1016/j.techsoc.2016.04.005

Hosta, M., & Zabkar, V. (2021). Antecedents of environmentally and socially responsible sustainable consumer behavior. *Journal of Business Ethics*, *171*(2), 273–293. DOI: 10.1007/s10551-019-04416-0

Hovnanian, G., Kroll, K., & Sjödin, E. (2019). *How analytics can drive smarter engineering and construction decisions*. [Online] Available at: https://www.mckinsey.com/business-functions/operations/our-insights/how-analytics-can-drive-smarter-engineering-and-construction-decisions [Accessed 15 July 2023].

Howard-Grenville, J., Buckle, S. J., Hoskins, B. J., & George, G. (2014). Climate change and Management. *Academy of Management Journal*, *57*(3), 615–623. DOI: 10.5465/amj.2014.4003

Husk Power Systems. (2019). Our Impact. Retrieved from https://huskpowersystems.com/

Idachaba, F. E. (2018). *Design of a Pipeline Pre-Activation Inspection Robot for Pipeline Tap Detection*. OnePetro. DOI: 10.2118/193384-MS

Igwe, P. A., Odunukan, K., Rahman, M., Rugara, D. G., & Ochinanwata, C. (2020). How entrepreneurship ecosystem influences the development of frugal innovation and informal entrepreneurship. *Thunderbird International Business Review*, *62*(5), 475–488. DOI: 10.1002/tie.22157

Incubator, E. (2024, March 22). Revolutionizing Neonatal Care. Retrieved from Embrace Global website: https://www.embraceglobal.org/

Insights, D. 2020. *Digital lean manufacturing*. [Online] Available at: https://www2.deloitte.com/us/en/insights/focus/industry-4-0/digital-lean-manufacturing.html [Accessed 05 October 2021].

Intel Corporation. (2021). *At John Deere, 'Hard Iron Meets Artificial Intelligence'.* [Online] Available at: https://www.intel.com/content/www/us/en/newsroom/news/john-deere-hard-iron-meets-artificial-intelligence.html#gs.cvlwoq [Accessed 10 October 2021].

Internation Data Corporation. (2020). *Digital Transformation: The Future of Connected Construction,* s.l.: Autodesk.

International Centre for frugal Innovation (2024). Student challenges 2023-2024 – LDE minor frugal innovation for sustainable global development. https://www.icfi.nl/news/student-challenges-2023-2024-lde-minor-frugal-innovation-for-sustainable-global-development

International Data Corporation. (2020). *Digital Transformation: The Future of connected construction, NA*. International Data Corporation.

IoT Business. (2021). *How IoT Is Helping To Benefit The Welding Industry.* [Online] Available at: https://iotbusinessnews.com/2021/11/12/58255-how-iot-is-helping-to-benefit-the-welding-industry/ [Accessed 24 November 2021].

Isaak, R. (2002). The making of the ecopreneur. *Greener Management International, 2002*(38), 81–91. DOI: 10.9774/GLEAF.3062.2002.su.00009

Johnstone, M. L., & Tan, L. P. (2015). Exploring the gap between consumers' green rhetoric and purchasing behaviour. *Journal of Business Ethics, 132*(2), 311–328. DOI: 10.1007/s10551-014-2316-3

Jones, J. (2017). The two problems with the strengths-based approach. Dr. Jason Jones. Retrieved from https://drjasonjones.com/characterstrengthsapproach/

Joshi, Y., & Rahman, Z. (2015). Factors affecting green purchase behaviour and future research directions. *International Strategic Management Review, 3*(1-2), 128–143. DOI: 10.1016/j.ism.2015.04.001

Joung, H. M., & Park-Poaps, H. (2013). Factors motivating and influencing clothing disposal behaviours. *International Journal of Consumer Studies, 37*(1), 105–111. DOI: 10.1111/j.1470-6431.2011.01048.x

Kalaari Capital. (2024). Frictionless Digital Commerce.

Kang, J., & Hustvedt, G. (2014). Building trust between consumers and corporations: The role of consumer perceptions of transparency and social responsibility. *Journal of Business Ethics, 125*(2), 253–265. DOI: 10.1007/s10551-013-1916-7

Karnani, A. (2007). The mirage of marketing to the bottom of the pyramid: How the private sector can help alleviate poverty. *California Management Review*, *49*(4), 90–111. DOI: 10.2307/41166407

Kasser, T. (2002). *The High Price of Materialism*. MIT Press. DOI: 10.7551/mitpress/3501.001.0001

Kazmi, Z. S. (2023). *Exploring the Digital Divide in Educational Technology across Illinois School Districts: a Focus on Business Education in Urban, Suburban, and Rural Schools.* (MSc thesis). Illinois State University.

Kelly, S., & Resnick-ault, J. 2021. *One password allowed hackers to disrupt Colonial Pipeline, CEO tells senators,* NA: Reuters.

Kelvin, H. (2020). *Introduction to the theory of Yin-Yang*. Independent.

Khan, R. (2016). How frugal innovation promotes social sustainability [Sustainability]. *Sustainability (Basel)*, *8*(10), 1–29. DOI: 10.3390/su8101034

Khan, S., & Lee, S. C. (2020). Machine Learning-Based Anomaly Detection for Pipeline Monitoring. *Journal of Pipeline Systems Engineering and Practice*, *11*(2).

Khan, W., Ali, T., & Dhamija, A. (2023). Perceived obstacles and performance of food and agribusiness enterprises: Implications for urban and rural entrepreneurship development. *Journal of Industrial Integration and Management*, *8*(01), 65–82. DOI: 10.1142/S2424862221500287

Khare, P., Ghura, A. S., & Agrawal, A. (2024). A process model of social enterprise scaling using the legitimacy lens. https://doi.org/. Journal of Social Entrepreneurship, 15(1)DOI: 10.1080/19420676.2024.2315933

Kheyti. (2019). Our Solutions. Retrieved from https://www.kheyti.com/

Kim, J., & Lee, S. C. (2020). Regulatory Framework for Digital Transformation in Pipeline Construction. *Journal of Pipeline Systems Engineering and Practice*, *11*(2). Advance online publication. DOI: 10.1061/JPEODS.PEENG

Kitzmueller, M., & Shimshack, J. (2012). Economic perspectives on corporate social responsibility. *Journal of Economic Literature*, *50*(1), 51–84. DOI: 10.1257/jel.50.1.51

Klofsten, M., Fayolle, A., Guerrero, M., Mian, S., Urbano, D., & Wright, M. (2019). The entrepreneurial university as driver for economic growth and social change-key strategic challenges. *Technological Forecasting and Social Change*, *141*, 149–158. DOI: 10.1016/j.techfore.2018.12.004

Knizkov, S., & Arlinghaus, J. C. (2020). Frugal processes: An empirical investigation into the operations of resource-constrained firms. *IEEE Transactions on Engineering Management*, *683*, 667–684.

Knorringa, P., Peša, I., Leliveld, A., & van Beers, C. (2016). Frugal innovation and development: Aides or adversaries? *European Journal of Development Research*, *28*(2), 143–153. DOI: 10.1057/ejdr.2016.3

Koerich, G. V., & Cancellier, E. L. P. D. L. (2020). Frugal Innovation: Origins, evolution and future perspectives. *Cadernos EBAPE.BR*, *17*, 1079–1093.

Korhonen, J., Honkasalo, A., & Seppälä, J. (2018). Circular economy: The concept and its limitations. *Ecological Economics*, *143*, 37–46. DOI: 10.1016/j.ecolecon.2017.06.041

Kormos, E., & Wisdom, K. (2021). Rural schools and the digital divide: Technology in the learning experience. *Theory and Practice in Rural Education*, *11*(1), 25–39. DOI: 10.3776/tpre.2021.v11n1p25-39

Kozma, R. B. (2011). The technological, economic, and social contexts for educational ICT policy. In *Transforming Education: the Power of ICT Policies* (pp. 3–18). United Nations Educational, Scientific and Cultural Organisation., Retrieved from https://policycommons.net/artifacts/8224447/the-technological-economic-and-social-contexts-for-educational-ict-policy/9139858/

Kretzmann, J. P., & McKnight, J. L. (1993). *Building communities from the inside: A path toward finding a community's assets*. Center for Urban Affairs and Policy Research, Northwestern University.

Kulkarni, S. S., & Gupta, S. (2020). Application of Artificial Intelligence and Machine Learning in Predictive Maintenance of Pipelines: A Case Study of Chevron's Tengizchevroil Pipeline Project. *Journal of Pipeline Systems Engineering and Practice*, *11*(3).

Kumar, C. (2024, February). Frugal Innovation and Entrepreneurship. *3rd International Conference on Reinventing Business Practices, Start-ups and Sustainability (ICRBSS 2023)* (pp. 4-15). Atlantis Press. DOI: 10.2991/978-94-6463-374-0_2

Kuruvilla, S. J. (2017). Theory of Constraints and the Thinking Process. *International Journal of Business Insights & Transformation*, *11*(1).

Kutaula, S., Gillani, A., Gregory-Smith, D., & Bartikowski, B. (2024). Ethical Consumerism in Emerging Markets: Opportunities and Challenges. *Journal of Business Ethics*, *191*(4), 651–673. DOI: 10.1007/s10551-024-05657-4

Laker, B. (2023, May 28). *How frugal entrepreneurship can be a competitive advantage*. Forbes.https://www.forbes.com/sites/benjaminlaker/2022/05/05/how-frugal-entrepreneurship-can-be-a-competitive-advantage/

Lapper, S. & Kiefer, B., 2020. *Digital lean manufacturing Industry 4.0 technologies transform lean processes to advance the enterprise,* s.l.: Deloitte.

Lawson, C. (2022). Intro to Social Media. Oklahoma State University Libraries. Retrieved from https://shareok.org/bitstream/handle/11244/335899/oksd_lawson_introtosocialmedia_2022.pdf

Le Bas, C., & Czyżewska-Misztal, D. (2022). The economics of frugal Innovation: An integrative literature review. *Revue d'Economie Industrielle*, (4), 87–102. DOI: 10.4000/rei.11959

Lee, M. S., Seifert, M., & Cherrier, H. (2017). Anti-consumption and governance in the global fashion industry: Transparency is key. *Governing corporate social responsibility in the apparel industry after Rana Plaza*, 147-174.

Lee, J. (2020). *Workforce Adaptability in Pipeline Construction*. Springer., DOI: 10.1007/978-3-030-45671-5

Legood, A.. (2022). Sustainable Energy Solutions through Frugal Innovation: Insights from India. *Renewable & Sustainable Energy Reviews*, *150*, 111859.

Lehner, A. C., & Gausemeier, J. (2016). A pattern-based approach to the development of frugal innovations. *Technology Innovation Management Review*, *6*(3), 13–21. DOI: 10.22215/timreview/971

Lehner, M., Mont, O., & Heiskanen, E. (2016). Nudging–A promising tool for sustainable consumption behaviour? *Journal of Cleaner Production*, *134*, 166–177. DOI: 10.1016/j.jclepro.2015.11.086

Leih, S. and Teece, D. (2016). Campus leadership and the entrepreneurial university: a dynamic capabilities perspective, *Academy of Management Perspectives*, Vol. 30No. 2, pp. 182-210.

Leliveld, A., & Knorringa, P. (2017). Frugal Innovation and Development Research. *European Journal of Development Research*. Advance online publication. DOI: 10.1057/s41287-017-0121-4

Lenox, M., & York, J. G. (2011). Environmental entrepreneurship.

León, E. M., Pichardo, R. D., Tatiana Reyes-Carrillo, T. R., & Santiago, M. R. R. (2024). What is unique about sustainable business models for the base of the pyramid? *Business Strategy and the Environment*, *3*(33), 2345–2366. DOI: 10.1002/bse.3609

Le, P. B., Tran, D. T., Phung, T. M. T., & Vu, K. D. (2022). *Leadership and knowledge management practices for frugal innovation of firms in the emerging market: moderating role of collaborative culture*. Asia-Pacific J. Bus. Admin., DOI: 10.1108/APJBA-03-2021-0130

Lev¨anen, J., Hossain, M., Lyytinen, T., Hyv¨arinen, A., Numminen, S., & Halme, M., 2016.

Leva¨nen, J., Hossain, M., Lyytinen, T., Hyva¨rinen, A., Numminen, S., & Halme, M. (2015). Implications of frugal innovations on sustainable development: Evaluating water and energy innovations. *Sustainability (Basel)*, *8*(1), 4. DOI: 10.3390/su8010004

Levänen, J., & Lindemann, S. (2016, June). Frugal innovations in circular economy: exploring possibilities and challenges in emerging markets. In *The International Society for Ecological Economics 2016 conference, transforming the economy: sustaining Food, water, energy, and justice. Washington DC, USA*.

Levänen, J., Hossain, M., & Wierenga, M. (2022). Frugal innovation in the midst of societal and operational pressures. *Journal of Cleaner Production*, *347*, 131308. DOI: 10.1016/j.jclepro.2022.131308

Lewis, T. (2019). Ethical Consumption: Practices and Perspectives. *Journal of Consumer Ethics*, *3*(1), 45–62.

Lim, C., & Fujimoto, T. (2019). Frugal innovation and design changes expanding the cost-performance frontier: A schumpeterian approach. *Research Policy*, *48*(4), 1016–1029. DOI: 10.1016/j.respol.2018.10.014

Lim, C., Lee, J. H., Sonthikorn, P., & Vongbunyong, S. (2021). Frugal innovation and leapfrogging innovation approach to the Industry 4.0 challenge for a developing country. *Asian Journal of Technology Innovation*, *291*(1), 87–108. DOI: 10.1080/19761597.2020.1786707

Long, M. A., & Murray, D. L. (2013). Ethical consumption, values convergence/divergence and community development. *Journal of Agricultural & Environmental Ethics*, *26*(2), 351–375. DOI: 10.1007/s10806-012-9384-0

López, S. L., Rohmer, S., Díaz-Pichardo, R., & Reyes, T. (2024). Exploring Frugal Innovation as an Ecodesign Strategy: A Case Study of a Water Access Solution at the BoP. In *EcoDesign for Sustainable Products, Services and Social Systems* (pp. 89-102). Springer Nature Singapore. Retrieved from https://link.springer.com/chapter/10.1007/978-981-99-3818-6_7

López-Sánchez, J. Á., & Santos-Vijande, M. L. (2022). Key capabilities for frugal innovation in developed economies: Insights into the current transition towards sustainability. *Sustainability Science*, *17*(1), 191–207. DOI: 10.1007/s11625-021-01071-1 PMID: 35035587

Lorentzen, J. (2010). Low-income countries and innovation studies: A review of recent literature. *African Journal of Science, Technology, Innovation and Development*, *2*(3), 46–81.

Lubowiecki-Vikuk, A., Dąbrowska, A., & Machnik, A. (2021). Responsible consumer and lifestyle: Sustainability insights. *Sustainable Production and Consumption*, *25*, 91–101. DOI: 10.1016/j.spc.2020.08.007 PMID: 32864405

Lueth, K. L. (2021). *IoT technology market attractiveness: Where to invest going into 2022*. [Online] Available at: https://iot-analytics.com/iot-technology-market-attractiveness-where-to-invest-going-into-2022/ [Accessed 04 October 2021].

Lueth, L. K. (2020). *State of the IoT 2020: 12 billion IoT connections, surpassing non-IoT for the first time*. [Online] Available at: https://iot-analytics.com/state-of-the-iot-2020-12-billion-iot-connections-surpassing-non-iot-for-the-first-time/ [Accessed 21 November 2021].

Mafini, C., & Pooe, D. R. (2013). The relationship between employee satisfaction and organisational performance: Evidence from a South African government department. *SA Journal of Industrial Psychology*, *39*(1), 1–9. DOI: 10.4102/sajip.v39i1.1090

Mahlangu, B. G., & Goosen, L. (2023). The Impact of a Lack of Information and Communication Technologies at Rural Schools: Digitalization in a Changing Education Environment. In Arinushkina, A., Morozov, A., & Robert, I. (Eds.), *Contemporary Challenges in Education: Digitalization, Methodology, and Management* (pp. 254–275). IGI Global., DOI: 10.4018/979-8-3693-1826-3.ch019

Mahlangu, B. G., & Goosen, L. (2024). Enhancing Education With Information and Communication Technologies: Data-Driven Instruction in Rural Schools. In Bhatia, M., & Mushtaq, M. (Eds.), *Enhancing Education With Intelligent Systems and Data-Driven Instruction* (pp. 60–79). IGI Global., DOI: 10.4018/979-8-3693-2169-0.ch004

Mair, J., & Marti, I. (2009). Entrepreneurship in and around institutional voids: A case study from Bangladesh. *Journal of Business Venturing*, *24*(5), 419–435. DOI: 10.1016/j.jbusvent.2008.04.006

Mair, J., Marti, I., & Ventresca, M. J. (2012). Building Inclusive Markets in Rural Bangladesh: How Intermediaries Work Institutional Voids. *Academy of Management Journal*, *55*(4), 819–850. DOI: 10.5465/amj.2010.0627

Manna, R., & Singh, A. (2021). Predictors of Teacher's Engagement of Higher Education: An Exploratory Study. *International Journal of Educational Sciences*, *4*(3-4), 33–39. DOI: 10.26697/ijes

Ma, R., Chai, K. H., & Hang, C. C. (2015, August). Disruptive innovation and late-comer's catching-up dilemma: Toward a demand-side perspective of frugal entrepreneurship. *Portland International Conference on Management of Engineering and Technology (PICMET)* (pp. 978-987). IEEE. DOI: 10.1109/PICMET.2015.7273202

Mariano, E. B., Mariano, E. B., & Silva, H. M. R. (2021). Pro-poor innovations to promote instrumental freedoms: A systematic literature review. *Sustainability (Basel)*, *13*(24), 13587. DOI: 10.3390/su132413587

Martínez, N., Dutrénit, G., Gras, N., & Tecuanhuey, E. (2018). Actores, relaciones estructurales y causalidad en la innovación inclusiva: Un caso de telemedicina en México. [Actors, structural relationships, and causality in inclusive innovation: A case of telemedicine in Mexico]. *Innovar (Universidad Nacional de Colombia)*, *28*(70), 23–38.

Mashhour, Q. M. (2022). The Role of Frugal Innovation and Social Entrepreneurship in Supporting Socioeconomic Life in Emerging Markets. *Journal for Research on Business and Social Science*, *5*(5). www.jrbssonline.com

McCashen, W. (2016, December 1). What is "the strengths approach"? Innovative Resources. Retrieved from https://innovativeresources.org/what-is-the-strengths-approach/

McCormac, A.. (2022). Frugal Innovation in Healthcare: Case Studies from India. *Journal of Health Innovation*, *10*(2), 123–137.

McDonald, S., & Oates, C. J. (2006). Sustainability: Consumer perceptions and marketing strategies. *Business Strategy and the Environment*, *15*(3), 157–170. DOI: 10.1002/bse.524

McKelvey, M., & Zaring, O. (2018). Co-delivery of social innovations: Exploring the university's role in academic engagement with society. *Industry and Innovation*, *25*(6), 594–611. DOI: 10.1080/13662716.2017.1295364

McKnight, J. L., & Kretzmann, J. P. (1996). *Mapping community capacity* (rev. ed.). Institute for Policy Research, Northwestern University., Retrieved from http://www.northwestern.edu /ipr/publications/papers/mcc.pdf

McPhee, C., Schillo, R. S., Earl, L., & Kinder, J. (2018). Inclusive Innovation in Developed Countries. *Technology Innovation Management Review*, *8*(2), 3–6. DOI: 10.22215/timreview/1134

Medium (2024). Ultrapreneur.https://theultrapreneur.medium.com/the-meaning-of-the-word-ultrapreneur-de4036e1a4c4

Melkas, H., Oikarinen, T., & Pekkarinen, S. (2019). Understanding frugal innovation: A case study of university professionals in developed countries. *Innovation and Development*, *9*(1), 25–40. DOI: 10.1080/2157930X.2018.1437687

Mendoza, R. U., & Thelen, N. (2008). Innovations to make markets more inclusive for the poor. *Development Policy Review*, *26*(4), 427–458. DOI: 10.1111/j.1467-7679.2008.00417.x

MeraPashu360. (23-02-2024). About Us. Retrieved from https://merapashu360.com/about-us

Merriam-Webster. (2016). Frugal. EnDiccionario online Merriam-Webster. (11e ed.).

Michaelis, T. L., Carr, J. C., Scheaf, D. J., & Pollack, J. M. (2020). The frugal entrepreneur: A self-regulatory perspective of resourceful entrepreneurial behavior. *Journal ofBusiness Venturing*, *35*(4), 105969. DOI: 10.1016/j.jbusvent.2019.105969

Micheletti, M., & Stolle, D. (2007). Mobilizing Consumers to Take Responsibility for Global Social Justice. *The Annals of the American Academy of Political and Social Science*, *611*(1), 157–175. DOI: 10.1177/0002716206298712

Miller, J. (2024). Frugal innovation: Doing more with less in resource-constrained environments. https://www.linkedin.com/pulse/frugal-innovation-doing-more-less-environments-jason-miller-rdqgc/

Milthon, L. M. (2024).Frugal innovation: definition, principles, characteristics, and examples. https://innovaromorir.com/en/frugal-innovation-definition-principles-examples/

Ministry of Environment. Forest and Climate Change (MoEFCC). (2016). Extended Producer Responsibility. Retrieved from https://pib.gov.in/PressReleaseIframePage.aspx?PRID=1579741

Mishra, O. (2021a). Principles of frugal innovation and its application by social entrepreneurs in times of adversity: An inductive single-case approach. *Journal of Entrepreneurship in Emerging Economies*, *13*(4), 547–574. DOI: 10.1108/JEEE-07-2020-0247

Mishra, O. (2021b). Design thinking and bricolage for frugal innovations during crisis. *Journal of Innovation Management, 9*(3), 1–26. DOI: 10.24840/2183-0606_009.003_0002

Mishra, O., Sharma, R., & Agrawal, B. (2020). Facilitating women prosperity with higher purpose at Vyomini. *South Asian Journal of Business and Management Cases, 9*(2), 198–207. DOI: 10.1177/2277977920905820

Molina-Maturano, J., Bucher, J., & Speelman, S. (2020). Understanding and evaluating the sustainability of frugal water innovations in M'exico: An exploratory case study. *Journal of Cleaner Production, 274*, 122692. DOI: 10.1016/j.jclepro.2020.122692

Moorhouse, D., & Moorhouse, D. (2018). Sustainability in the fashion industry. *Clothing Cultures, 5*(1), 3–5. DOI: 10.1386/cc.5.1.3_1

Moreno, D. A.. (2022). Frugal innovation and rural development in India: Challenges and opportunities. *Sustainable Development, 30*(2), 322–337.

Mucci, N., & Karau, S. J. (2020). Sustainable frugal innovation in rural India: Enabling village entrepreneurship. *Journal of Cleaner Production, 244*, 118708.

Mukherjee, S. (2018). Frugal innovation: Aligning theory, practice, and public policy. *Journal of Management Science, 10*(1), 15–31.

Murphy, K. P. (2024). On distillation of guided diffusion models. search/index_htm_files/On_Distillation_Of_Guided_Diffusion_Models.pdf.https://interactive.cornish.edu › index_htm_files Murphy, K. P. (2024).

Murray, R., Caulier-Grice, J., & Mulgan, G. (2010). *The Open Book of Social Innovation*. NESTA and The Young Foundation.

Musingafi, M. C., & Chaden'anga, C. (2014). Information and communication technology in classroom situations in rural and urban areas in Zimbabwe: A comparative study on the use of digital and projected media in teaching and learning at six secondary schools in Masvingo. *Review of Information Engineering and Applications, 1*(4), 77–92. DOI: 10.18488/journal.79/2014.1.2/79.2.77.92

Nahi, T. (2016). Cocreation at the base of the pyramid: Reviewing and organizing the diverse conceptualizations. *Organization & Environment, 29*(4), 416–437. DOI: 10.1177/1086026616652666

Nakahara, H. (2017). *International Trends in Ethical Consumerism. Material Cycles and Waste Management Research*. Japan Society of Waste Management Experts., DOI: 10.3985/mcwmr.28.261

Nambisan, S., & Nambisan, P. (2008). How to profit from a better 'virtual customer environment'. *MIT Sloan Management Review*, *49*(3), 53–61.

Nangia, P., Bansal, S., & Thaichon, P. (2023). Doing more with less: An integrative literature review on responsible consumption behaviour. *Journal of Consumer Behaviour*, *23*(1), 141–155. DOI: 10.1002/cb.2163

Nassani, A. A., Sinisi, C., Mihai, D., Paunescu, L., Yousaf, Z., & Haffar, M. (2022). Towards the achievement of frugal innovation: Exploring major antecedents among SMEs. *Sustainability (Basel)*, *14*(7), 4120. DOI: 10.3390/su14074120

Natalicchio, A., Ardito, L., Petruzzelli, A. M., & Giudice, M. D. (2018). The origins of external knowledge inflows and the impact of university technologies. *R & D Management*, *49*(4), 639–651. DOI: 10.1111/radm.12354

National Innovation Foundation (NIF) - India. (n.d.). Mitticool: The Natural Refrigerator. Retrieved from https://nif.org.in/innovation/mitti-cool-refrigerator/751

Nature. (2023). Why the world needs to foster frugal innovation. *Nature, 620*(7970), 312-313. DOI: 10.1038/d41586-023-03816-7

Needham, J. (1956). *Science and civilization in China: History of scientific thought*. Cambridge University Press.

Neumann, T. (2021). The impact of entrepreneurship on economic, social, and environmental welfare and its determinants: A systematic review. *Management Review Quarterly*, *71*(3), 553–584. DOI: 10.1007/s11301-020-00193-7

Ngugi, J. K., & Goosen, L. (2021). Innovation, Entrepreneurship, and Sustainability for ICT Students Towards the Post-COVID-19 Era. In Carvalho, L. C., Reis, L., & Silveira, C. (Eds.), *Handbook of Research on Entrepreneurship, Innovation, Sustainability, and ICTs in the Post-COVID-19 Era* (pp. 110–131). IGI Global., DOI: 10.4018/978-1-7998-6776-0.ch006

Nielsen, M. S. (2023). What is light. https://chromaviso.com/en/knowledge-about-light/what-is-light

Nigel, C. (2024). Five element of ultrapreneur. https://ultrapreneursuccess.com/what-is-an-ultrapreneur/elements/

Nijssen, E. J., & Frambach, R. T. (2000). Creating customer value through strategic marketing planning: A management approach. *Journal of Market Focused Management*, *4*(1), 79–95.

Nimmagadda, R. (2024). Frugal Innovation and Entrepreneurship. Proceedings of the 3rd International Conference on Reinventing Business Practices, Start-ups and Sustainability (ICRBSS 2023), Advances in Economics, Business and Management Research, 277.

Ninjacart (2024, March 22). Sowing Innovation, Harvesting trust. Retrieved from https://www.ninjacart.com

Norman, D. A., & Draper, S. W. (1986). *User-centered system design: New perspectives on human-computer interaction*. Lawrence Erlbaum Associates, Inc. DOI: 10.1201/b15703

Numminen, S., & Lund, P. D. (2017). Frugal energy innovations for developing countries–a framework. *Global Challenges (Hoboken, NJ)*, *1*(1), 9–19. DOI: 10.1002/gch2.1012 PMID: 31565251

Nussholz, J., Assmann, I. R., Kelly, P., & Bocken, N. (2024). Circular Business Models for Digital Technologies in the Built Environment. A Circular Built Environment in the Digital Age, 245.

Ogbimi, P. O., & Ugbomeh, G. (2020). Application of GIS and Remote Sensing in Pipeline Routing Optimization: A Case Study of Shell's Niger Delta Pipeline Project. *Journal of Pipeline Systems Engineering and Practice*, *11*(2). Advance online publication. DOI: 10.1061/JPEODS.PEENG-05020002

Olsen, A.Ø., Sofka, W. and Grimpe, C. (2016). Coordinated exploration for grand challenges: the role of advocacy groups in search consortia, *Academy of Management Journal*, Vol. 59No. 6, pp. 2232-2255.

Omar, M. K., Dainal, E., Puad, M. H., & Zakaria, A. (2023). Factors Determining the Optimization of Digital Technology in Rural Schools. *International Journal of Academic Research in Progressive Education and Development*, *12*(1), 1685–1704. DOI: 10.6007/IJARPED/v12-i1/16559

Onsongo, E. K., Knorringa, P., & Beers, C. V. (2023). Frugal business model innovation in the base of the pyramid: The case of Philips Community Life Centres in Africa. *Technovation*, *121*, 102675. https://www.sciencedirect.com/science/article/abs/pii/S0166497222002267 DOI: 10.1016/j.technovation.2022.102675

Ornetzeder, M., & Rohracher, H. (2013). Of solar collectors, wind power, and car sharing: Comparing and understanding successful cases of grassroots innovations. *Global Environmental Change*, *23*(5), 856–867. DOI: 10.1016/j.gloenvcha.2012.12.007

Ottosson, E., & Oweini, R. (2023). Developing a closed-loop supply chain to eliminate Single Use Plastic products: Implementing Circular Economy practices driven by EU commission directives.

Ovharhe, O. H. & Woko, B. E. (2024b). Environmental pollution and infant mortality on entrepreneurial opportunities: A champiopreneurship approach. International Journal of Geography & Environmental Management (IJGEM), 10 (3), 144-171. D.O.I: DOI: 10.56201/ijgem.v10.no3.2024.pg144.171

Ovharhe, O. H. (2024). Business intelligence and innovation moderating roles on entrepreneurship and management using champiopreneurship approach. In K. Kankaew, P. Nakpathom, A. Chnitphattana, K. Pitchayadejanant, & S. Kunnapapdeelert (Eds.). Applying business intelligence and innovation to entrepreneurship advances in business strategy and competitive advantage (p. 171-223). IGI Global.com. DOI: 10.4018/979-8-3693-1846-1.ch009

Ovharhe, O. H., & Okolo, B. S. (2022). Sustainable development goals: Lean entrepreneurship and Green entrepreneurship. International Journal of Research and Scientific Innovation, 9(10), 59-71. ISSN: 2321-2705

Ovharhe, O. H. (2022a). Sustainable development goals: Multicollinearity between therapeutic entrepreneurship and rehabilitation therapy among African nations. *International Journal of Small Business and Entrepreneurship Research, 10*(3), 1–59. DOI: 10.37745/ijsber.2013/vol10n3157

Ovharhe, O. H. (2022b). Sustainable development goals: Therapeutic entrepreneurship and entrepreneurship Injelititis among West Africa Countries. [WJEDS]. *World Journal of Entrepreneurial Development Studies, 7*(1), 87–113. DOI: 10.56201/wjeds.v7.no1.2022.pg87.113

Ovharhe, O. H., & Abada, A. M. (2023). *IFRS adoptions on entrepreneurship entry and entrepreneurship exit: The Nigeria experience from 2006-2017. 2(2).* American Journal of Social Development and Entrepreneurship., DOI: 10.54536/ajsde.v2i2

Ovharhe, O. H., & Abada, A. M. (2023). IFRS: Entrepreneurial exit and Entrepreneurial entre. *American Journal of Social Development and Entrepreneurship, 2*(2), 1–8. DOI: 10.54536/ajsde.v2i2.1578

Ovharhe, O. H., Ahunanya, V., & Woko, E. B. (2022). Consignment inventory system and entrepreneurial survival in Lagos State. *International Journal of Social Science & Management Research, 8*(5), 29–42. DOI: 10.56201/ijssmr.v8.no5.2022.pg29.42

Ovharhe, O. H., & Akandu, C. J. (2024). Innovation accounting and innovation entrepreneurship. [WJIMT]. *World Journal of Innovation and Modern Technology*, *8*(2), 31–49. DOI: 10.56201/wjimt.v8.no2.2024.pg31.49

Ovharhe, O. H., & Chibuike, C. U. (2024a). Creative accounting and creative entrepreneurship. [JAFM]. *Journal of Accounting and Financial Management*, *10*(7), 157–174. DOI: 10.56201/jafm.v10.no5.2024.pg157.174

Ovharhe, O. H., & Chibuike, C. U. (2024b). Innovation accounting and frugal innovation. [WJIMT]. *World Journal of Innovation and Modern Technology*, *8*(2), 50–70. DOI: 10.56201/wjimt.v8.no2.2024.pg50.70

Ovharhe, O. H., & Chukwuemeka, S. P. (2023). Sustainable Development Goals: Therapeutic Entrepreneurship and Mental Health Conditions. *British Journal of Multidisciplinary and Advanced Studies*, *4*(1), 81–119. DOI: 10.37745/bjmas.2022.0107

Ovharhe, O. H., & Igbokwe, E. L. (2021). Analytical intervention of remote working correlates on risk culture and entrepreneurial adaptability in South-South Geopolitical Zone, Nigeria: Covid-19 Perspective. *Journal of Education and Practice, IISTE*, *12*(3), 34–44. DOI: 10.7176/JEP/12-34-05

Ovharhe, O. H., & Odepeli, S. (2024). Environmental pollution and maternal mortality among female entrepreneurs. [IJGEM]. *International Journal of Geography and Environmental Management*, *10*(2), 170–195. DOI: 10.56201/ijgem.v10.no3.2024.pg170.195

Ovharhe, O. H., Okolo, B. S., Woko, E. B., & Igbokwe, L. (2022). Light entrepreneurship and customer funded business model. *International Journal of Social Sciences and Management Research*, *8*(5), 87–106. DOI: 10.56201/ijssmr.v8.no5.2022.pg87.106

Ovharhe, O. H., & Woko, B. E. (2024a). Environmental pollution and life expectancy among Intrepreneurs. [IJMEPR]. *International Journal of Medical Evaluation and Physical Report*, *10*(2), 9–32. DOI: 10.56201/ijmepr.v8.no3.2024.pg9.32

Ovharhe, O. H., Woko, E. B., & Ezeocha, V. U. (2021). Remote working: Entrepreneurial risk and entrepreneurial survival in the micro firms in Niger-Delta, Nigeria (COVID-19 Pandemic Prospects). *International Journal of Small Business and Entrepreneurship Research*, *9*(4), 11–28. DOI: 10.37745/ijsber.2013/vol9n11-28

Ovharhe, Orugba Harry & Abada, A. M. (2024). Creative accounting and entrepreneurship opportunities. [JAFM]. *Journal of Accounting and Financial Management*, *10*(5), 175–190. DOI: 10.56201/jafm.v10.no5.2024.pg175.190

Özsungur, F. (2024). Generating entrepreneurial ideas with AI. IGI Global.com (ISBN: 9798369334980) DOI: 10.4018/979-8-3693-3498-0

Palmié, M., Zeschky, M., Winterhalter, S., Sauter, P. W., Haefner, N., & Gassmann, O. (2016). Coordination mechanisms for international innovation in SMEs: Effects on time-to-market and R&D task complexity as a moderator. *Small Business Economics*, *46*(2), 273–294. DOI: 10.1007/s11187-015-9683-8

Pansera, M., & Owen, R. (2015). Framing resource-constrained innovation at the 'bottom of the pyramid': Insights from an ethnographic case study in rural Bangladesh. Technol. *Technological Forecasting and Social Change*, *92*, 300–311. DOI: 10.1016/j.techfore.2014.10.004

Pansera, M., & Sarkar, S. (2016). Crafting sustainable development solutions: Frugal innovations of grassroots entrepreneurs. *Sustainability (Basel)*, *8*(1), 51. DOI: 10.3390/su8010051

Papadonikolaki, E., Krystallis, I., & Morgan, B. (2020). *Digital transformation in construction-Systematic literature review of evolving concepts.* London, Engineering Project Organization Conference (EPOC) 2020.

Papaoikonomou, E., & Alarcon, A. (2017). Revisiting consumer empowerment: An exploration of ethical consumption communities. *Journal of Macromarketing*, *37*(1), 40–56. DOI: 10.1177/0276146715619653

ParamparagatKrishiVikasYojana (PKVY). (n.d.). Ministry of Agriculture & Farmers Welfare. Retrieved from https://pib.gov.in/

Pareek, S. (2014, September 22). He designed a shoe for the visually impaired that vibrates to show them the right path. The Better India. Retrieved from https://thebetterindia.com/12631/man-designed-shoe-blind-will-let-navigate-without-help/

Park, S., Rosca, E., & Agarwal, N. (2022). Driving social impact at the bottom of the pyramid through the internet-of-things enabled frugal innovations. *Technovation*, *118*, 102381. DOI: 10.1016/j.technovation.2021.102381

Parwez, S., & Shekar, K. C. (2019). Understanding of grassroots innovations in India: evidence from the countryside. Society and Business Review., 10.1108, SBR-07-2018-0081.

Pawlowski, J. M. (2013). Towards born-Global innovation: The role of knowledge management and social software. *Proceedings of the European Conference on Knowledge Management,* ECKM, 2(January), 527–534.

Pelsmacker, P. D., Driesen, L., & Rayp, G. (2005). Do consumers care about ethics? Willingness to pay for fair-trade coffee. *The Journal of Consumer Affairs*, *39*(2), 363–385. DOI: 10.1111/j.1745-6606.2005.00019.x

Perera, C., Auger, P., & Klein, J. (2018). Green consumption practices among young environmentalists: A practice theory perspective. *Journal of Business Ethics*, *152*(3), 843–864. DOI: 10.1007/s10551-016-3376-3

Phelps, M., Owens, C., & Jordan, P. (2002). Technology delivery using a flex cam to cross the digital divide in rural Tennessee schools. *Society for Information Technology & Teacher Education International Conference* (pp. 1648-1649). Association for the Advancement of Computing in Education (AACE). Retrieved from https://www.learntechlib.org/p/6826/

Pisoni, A., Michelini, L., & Martignoni, G. (2018). Frugal approach to innovation: State of the art and future perspectives. *Journal of Cleaner Production*, *171*, 107–126. DOI: 10.1016/j.jclepro.2017.09.248

Ploeg, M., Knoben, J., Vermeulen, P., & van Beers, C. (2021). Rare gems or mundane practice? Resource constraints as drivers of frugal innovation. *Innovation (North Sydney, N.S.W.)*, *23*(1), 93–126. DOI: 10.1080/14479338.2020.1825089

Porfírio, J. A., Carrilho, T., Felício, J. A., & Jardim, J. (2021). Leadership characteristics and digital transformation. *Journal of Business Research*, *124*, 610–619.

Powell, S. (2017, November 7). An open door: OT finds out how the Aravind Eye Hospital in Tamil Nadu operates. Optometry Today. Retrieved from https://www.aop.org.uk/ot/professional-support/health-services/2017/11/07/an-open-door

Prabhu, J. (2017). Frugal innovation: Doing more with less for more. *Philosophical Transactions. Series A, Mathematical, Physical, and Engineering Sciences*, *375*(2095), 20160372. DOI: 10.1098/rsta.2016.0372 PMID: 28461436

Prabhu, J., & Jain, S. (2015). Innovation and entrepreneurship in India: Understanding jugaad. *Asia Pacific Journal of Management*, *32*(4), 843–868. DOI: 10.1007/s10490-015-9445-9

Prabhu, J., Tracey, P., & Hassan, M. (2017b). Marketing to the poor: An institutional model of exchange in emerging markets. *AMS Review*, *7*(3–4), 101–122. DOI: 10.1007/s13162-017-0100-0

Prahalad, C. K. (2012). Bottom of the pyramid as a source of breakthrough innovations. *Journal of Product Innovation Management*, *29*(1), 6–12. DOI: 10.1111/j.1540-5885.2011.00874.x

Prahalad, C. K., & Mashelkar, R. A. (2010). Innovation's Holy Grail. *Harvard Business Review*, *88*(7/8), 132–141.

Prahalad, C. K., & Mashelkar, R. A. (2010). *The New Age of Innovation: Driving Cocreated Value Through Global Networks*. McGraw-Hill Education.

Prakash, N., Sharma, S., & Jindal, P. (2024). Entrepreneurship and Frugal Innovation for Realising SDGs in Global Context. In *Sustainable Development Goals: The Impact of Sustainability Measures on Wellbeing* (pp. 167–182). Emerald Publishing Limited. DOI: 10.1108/S1569-375920240000113A010

Pratham. (2019). What We Do. Retrieved from https://www.pratham.org/

Prathap, G. (2014). The myth of frugal innovation in India. *Current Science*, *106*(3), 374–377.

Pulla, V. (2017). Strengths-based approach in social work: A distinct ethical advantage. International Journal of Innovation. *Creativity and Change*, *3*(2), 97–114.

PWC, (2018). *Digital Product Development 2025,* Na: PWC.

PWC. (2021). *A leadership agenda to take on tomorrow*. PWC.

Qin, W. (2024).How to unleash frugal innovation through internet of things and artificial intelligence: Moderating role of entrepreneurial knowledge and future challenges. 28(202) https://www.sciencedirect.com/science/article/pii/S0040162524000829 .https://doi.org/10.1016/j.techfore.2024.123286

Qin, W. (2024). How to unleash frugal innovation through internet of things and artificial intelligence: Moderating role of entrepreneurial knowledge and future challenges. *Technological Forecasting and Social Change*, *202*, 123286. DOI: 10.1016/j.techfore.2024.123286

Radjou N., Prabhu, J., & Ahuja, S. (2012). Jugaad innovation: Think frugal, be flexible, Generate breakthrough growth.

Radjou, N., & Prabhu, J. (2015). Frugal innovation: How to do more with less. The Economist.

Radjou, N., & Prabhu, J. (2013). *Frugal innovation: A new business paradigm*. INSEAD Knowledge.

Radjou, N., Prabhu, J., & Ahuja, S. (2012). *Jugaad innovation: Think frugal, be flexible, generate breakthrough growth*. John Wiley & Sons.

Radjou, N., Prabhu, J., & Ahuja, S. (2012). *Jugaad Innovation: Think Frugal, Be Flexible, Generate Breakthrough Growth*. Jossey-Bass.

Rahmanti, V. N., & Subandi, H. (2024). Redefining Social Entrepreneurship as a Strategy to Strengthen the Social Welfare of SDGs. *Migration Letters : An International Journal of Migration Studies*, *21*(S2), 110–132. https://migrationletters.com/index.php/ml/article/view/644

Rana, N. (2024). The Environmental Impact of Fashion. In *Threaded Harmony: A Sustainable Approach to Fashion* (pp. 5–16). Emerald Publishing Limited. DOI: 10.1108/978-1-83608-152-420241004

Rangan, V. K. (2007). Aravind Eye Care System: Providing total eye care to the rural population. Harvard Business School Case, 9-505-075.

Rani, R., & Srivastava, S. (2023). Grassroots innovation: A state of art literature review. Innovation The Research Concept, 8(2). ISSN: 2456-5474. Retrieved from http://www.socialresearchfoundation.com/innovation.php#8

Rao, B. C. (2013). How disruptive is frugal? *Technology in Society*, *35*(1), 65–73. DOI: 10.1016/j.techsoc.2013.03.003

Rao, B. C. (2018). Science is indispensable to frugal innovations. *Technology Innovation Management Review*, *8*(4).

Rasmussen, E., & Borch, O. J. (2010). University capabilities in facilitating entrepreneurship: A longitudinal study of spin-off ventures at mid-range universities. *Research Policy*, *39*(5), 602–612. DOI: 10.1016/j.respol.2010.02.002

Ravichandran, R., Kulshrestha, P., & Nadig, A. (2022). Frugal Innovation for Economic Development-A Perspective Study. *The Management Accountant Journal*, *57*(5), 53–57. DOI: 10.33516/maj.v57i5.53-57p

Ray, P. K., & Ray, S. (2011). Product Innovation for the People's Car in an Emerging Economy. *Technovation*, *31*(5-6), 216–227. DOI: 10.1016/j.technovation.2011.01.004

Rehman, K. U., Anwar, R. S., Antohi, V. M., Ali, U., Fortea, C., & Zlati, M. L. (2024). Driving frugal innovation in SMEs: How sustainable leadership, knowledge sources and information credibility make a difference. *Frontiers in Sociology*, *9*, 1344704. 1344704.doi.org/10.3389/fsoc.2024.1344704 DOI: 10.3389/fsoc.2024.1344704

Reis, J., Amorim, M., Melao, N., & Matos, P. (2018). Digital Transformation: A Literature Review and Guidelines for Future Research. In: Á. Rocha, H. Adeli, L. Paulo Reis & S. Costanzo, eds. *Trends and Advances in Information Systems and Technologies*. NA: Springer International Publishing, p. 1518. DOI: 10.1007/978-3-319-77703-0_41

Reniati, R., Yusnita, M., & Purwasih, R. (2022, July). MSMEs Scale Up Model Post Next Normal through Frugal Innovation, Transformational Leadership, Blue Ocean Strategy and Government Policies. In ICSST 2021: Proceedings of the 1st International Conference on Social, Science, and Technology, ICSST 2021, 25 November 2021, Tangerang, Indonesia (Vol. 428). European Alliance for Innovation.

Ries, E. (2011). *The lean startup: How today's entrepreneurs use continuous innovation to create radically successful businesses*. Crown Business.

Roehlkepartain, E. C. (2008). Beyond needs assessments: Identifying a community's resources and hopes. https://www.search-institute.org/downloadable/2008-Roehlkepartain-Beyond-Needs-SL-NSLC.pdf

Roger, T. A. (2002). *Yin and Yang", in encyclopedia of Chinese philosophy* (Cua, A. S., Ed.). Routledge.

Rooijen, M. V. (2024). Extrapreneurs: A more sensible form of entrepreneurship. https://www.europeanbusinessreview.com/extrapreneurs-a-more-sensible-form-of-entrepreneurship/

Rosário, A. T., Raimundo, R. J., & Cruz, S. P. (2022). Sustainable entrepreneurship: A literature review. *Sustainability (Basel)*, *14*(9), 5556. DOI: 10.3390/su14095556

Rosca, E., Arnold, M., & Bendul, J. C. (2017a). Business models for sustainable innovation – an empirical analysis of frugal products and services. *Journal of Cleaner Production*, *162*, S133–S145. DOI: 10.1016/j.jclepro.2016.02.050

Rosca, E., Reedy, J., & Bendul, J. C. (2018). Does frugal innovation enable sustainable development? A systematic literature review. *European Journal of Development Research*, *30*(1), 136–157. DOI: 10.1057/s41287-017-0106-3

Rovanto, S., & Finne, M. (2023). What motivates entrepreneurs into circular economy action? Evidence from Japan and Finland. *Journal of Business Ethics*, *184*(1), 71–91. DOI: 10.1007/s10551-022-05122-0

Sabo, B., & Trudeau, V. L. (2020). A strengths-based approach to mental health recovery. *Journal of Psychosocial Rehabilitation and Mental Health*, *7*(1), 69–79.

Sanger, D. E., & Perlroth, N. (2021). *Colonial Pipeline Hack Reveals Weaknesses in US Cybersecurity*. [Online] Available at: https://www.nytimes.com/2021/05/14/us/politics/pipeline-hack.html [Accessed 21 November 2021].

Sanger, D. E., & Perlroth, N. (2021). *Pipeline Attack Yields Urgent Lessons About U.S. Cybersecurity*. NewYork Times.

Sarasvathy, S. D. (2001). Causation and effectuation: Toward a theoretical shift from economic inevitability to entrepreneurial contingency. *Academy of Management Review*, *26*(2), 243–263. DOI: 10.2307/259121

Sarasvathy, S. D., & Dew, N. (2005). Entrepreneurial logics for a technology of foolishness. *Scandinavian Journal of Management*, *21*(4), 385–406. DOI: 10.1016/j.scaman.2005.09.009

Schaefer, K., Corner, P. D., & Kearins, K. (2015). Social, environmental and sustainable entrepreneurship research: What is needed for sustainability-as-flourishing? *Organization & Environment*, *28*(4), 394–413. DOI: 10.1177/1086026615621111

Schaltegger, S., & Ho¨risch, J. (2015). (in press). In search of the dominant rationale in sustainability management: Legitimacy-or profit-seeking? *Journal of Business Ethics*.

Schaltegger, S., & Wagner, M. (2011). Sustainable entrepreneurship and sustainability innovation: Categories and interactions. *Business Strategy and the Environment*, *20*(4), 222–237. DOI: 10.1002/bse.682

Scholderer, J., & Grunert, K. G. (2005). Consumers, food and convenience: The long way from resource constraints to actual consumption patterns. *Journal of Economic Psychology*, *26*(1), 105–128. DOI: 10.1016/j.joep.2002.08.001

Schulte, M., Balasubramanian, S., & Paris, C. M. (2021). Blood diamonds and ethical consumerism: An empirical investigation. *Sustainability (Basel)*, *13*(8), 4558. DOI: 10.3390/su13084558

Schwartz, M. S. (2016). Ethical decision-making theory: An integrated approach. *Journal of Business Ethics*, *139*(4), 755–776. DOI: 10.1007/s10551-015-2886-8

SELCO. (2019). Impact. Retrieved from https://www.selco-india.com/

SELCO. (2024, March 26.). SELCO India. Retrieved from https://selco-india.com/

Selwyn, N. (2014). *Digital technology and the contemporary university: Degrees of digitization*. Routledge. DOI: 10.4324/9781315768656

Shahhoseini, A., Heydari, S., & Pedrammehr, S. (2023). Manufacturing and Assembly for the Ease of Product Recycling: A Review. *Designs*, *7*(2), 42. DOI: 10.3390/designs7020042

Shahid, M. S., Hossain, M., Karami, M., & Anwar, T. (2023). Frugal entrepreneurship: A way to seize business opportunities for low-income customers. *Asia Pacific Journal of Management*, •••, 1–31.

Shahid, M. S., Hossain, M., Shahid, S., & Anwar, T. (2023). Frugal innovation as a source of sustainable entrepreneurship to tackle social and environmental challenges. *Journal of Cleaner Production*, *406*, 137050. DOI: 10.1016/j.jclepro.2023.137050

Sharma, A., & Iyer, G. R. (2012). Resource-constrained product development: Implications for green marketing and green supply chains. *Industrial Marketing Management*, *41*(4), 599–608. DOI: 10.1016/j.indmarman.2012.04.007

Sharma, R., Dubey, D., & Rana, G. (2024). Impact of team building on organizational performance. *Migration Letters : An International Journal of Migration Studies*, *21*(S7).

Shehzad, M. U., Zhang, J., Alam, S., & Cao, Z. (2022). Determining the role of sources of knowledge and IT resources for stimulating firm innovation capability: A PLS-SEM approach. *Business Process Management Journal*, *28*(4), 905–935. DOI: 10.1108/BPMJ-09-2021-0574

Shehzad, M. U., Zhang, J., Alam, S., Cao, Z., Boamah, F. A., & Ahmad, M. (2022). Knowledge management process as a mediator between collaborative culture and frugal innovation: The moderating role of perceived organizational support. *Journal of Business and Industrial Marketing*, *38*(7), 1424–1446. DOI: 10.1108/JBIM-01-2022-0016

Shen, B., Wang, Y., Lo, C. K., & Shum, M. (2012). The impact of ethical fashion on consumer purchase behavior. *Journal of Fashion Marketing and Management*, *16*(2), 234–245. DOI: 10.1108/13612021211222842

Shewale, R. (2024, January 10). YouTube Statistics For 2024 (Users, Facts & More). Demand Sage. Retrieved from https://www.demandsage.com/youtube-stats/

Shifana, M. (2024). What's the difference between an ultrapreneur and an entrepreneur? https://www.quora.com/What-s-the-difference-between-an-ultrapreneur-and-an-entrepreneur#:~:text=Ultrapreneurs%20can%20be%20seen%20as,entrepreneur%20who%20is%20comparatively%20restless

Singh, R. (2023, July 24). How PhysicsWallah solved the profitability equation. Forbes India. Retrieved from https://www.forbesindia.com/article/take-one-big-story-of-the-day/how-physicswallah-solved-the-profitability-equation/86915/1

Singh, A., & Hess, T. (2017). How Chief Digital Officers Promote the Digital Transformation of their Companies. *MIS Quarterly Executive*, *16*(1), 5.

Skinner, D., Delobelle, P., Pappin, M., Pieterse, D., Esterhuizen, T. M., Barron, P., & Dudley, L. (2018). User assessments and the use of information from MomConnect, a mobile phone text-based information service, by pregnant women and new mothers in South Africa. *BMJ Global Health, 3*(Suppl 2), e000561. DOI: 10.1136/bmjgh-2017-000561 PMID: 29713504

Smith, J. (2017). Strength-based interviews. PROSPECTS. Retrieved from https://www.prospects.ac.uk/careers-advice/interview-tips/strength-based-interviews

Soni, P., & Krishnan, R. T. (2014). Frugal Innovation: Aligning Theory, Practice, and Public Policy. *Journal of Indian Business Research, 6*(1), 29–47. DOI: 10.1108/JIBR-03-2013-0025

Soper, K. (2007). Re-thinking the Good Life: The Citizenship Dimension of Consumer Disaffection with Consumerism. *Journal of Consumer Culture, 7*(2), 205–229. DOI: 10.1177/1469540507077681

Stephan, F. (2016). *Religions in the modern world: traditions and transformations.* Routledge.

Strong, C. (1996). Features contributing to the growth of ethical consumerism-a preliminary investigation. *Marketing Intelligence & Planning, 14*(5), 5–13. DOI: 10.1108/02634509610127518

Suraksha, P. (2024). *ONDC's one-year journey touching the 50-million transactions mark.* Economic Times.

Tabrizi, B., Lam, E., Girard, K., & Irvin, V. 2019. *Digital Transformation Is Not About Technology.* [Online] Available at: https://hbr.org/2019/03/digital-transformation-is-not-about-technology [Accessed 02 October 2021].

Taneja, S., & Bhushan, B. (2017). Business models for frugal innovation in emerging markets: The role of pay-per-use schemes. *Technovation, 68*, 57–70.

Tata, R. N., & Matten, D. (2016) Corporate community involvement in the 21st century. In: D. Barton, D. Horva'th, M. Kipping (eds) Re-Imagining Capitalism: Towards a Responsible, Long-Term Model. Oxford University Press (Forthcoming). Available at *SSRN*: https://ssrn.com/abstract=2740687

Techment. (2021). *The Rising Heat On Digital Transformation In Healthcare And What Lies Ahead In 2021.* [Online] Available at: https://www.techment.com/the-rising-heat-on-digital-transformation-in-healthcare-and-what-lies-ahead-in-2021/ [Accessed 05 October 2021].

TEKSYSTEMS. (2021). *State of Digital Transformation (Building a Framework for Digital Success).* TEKSYSTEMS.

Tesfaye, L. A., & Fougère, M. (2022). Frugal innovation hijacked: The co-optive power of co-creation. *Journal of Business Ethics, 180*(2), 439–454. DOI: 10.1007/s10551-021-04883-4

Testa, F., Iraldo, F., & Frey, M. (2016). The effect of environmental regulation on firms' competitive performance: The case of the building & construction sector in some EU regions. *Journal of Environmental Management, 92*(9), 2136–2144. DOI: 10.1016/j.jenvman.2011.03.039 PMID: 21524840

Teubner, R. A., & Stockhinger, J. (2020). Literature review: Understanding information systems strategy in the digital era. *The Journal of Strategic Information Systems, 29*(4), 101642. DOI: 10.1016/j.jsis.2020.101642

Thangeni, F. (2022). *Digital leadership: towards developing an innovative technology-led culture of learning in rural Limpopo schools.* (MEd dissertation). University of Johannesburg. Retrieved from http://hdl.handle.net/102000/0002

Thiagarajan, K. (2018, July 9). The man who paves India's roads with old plastic. The Guardian. https://www.theguardian.com/world/2018/jul/09/the-man-who-paves-indias-roads-with-old-plastic

Thompson, N., Kiefer, K., & York, J. G. (2011). Distinctions not dichotomies: Exploring social, sustainable, and environmental entrepreneurship. In *Social and sustainable entrepreneurship* (pp. 201–229). Emerald Group Publishing Limited. DOI: 10.1108/S1074-7540(2011)0000013012

Thφgersen, J. (1999). The ethical consumer. Moral norms and packaging choice. *Journal of Consumer Policy, 22*(4), 439–460. DOI: 10.1023/A:1006225711603

Tiwari, R., & Herstatt, C. (2012). Frugal innovation: A global networks' perspective [Swiss Journal of Business Research and Practice]. *Die Unternehmung, 66*(3), 245–274. DOI: 10.5771/0042-059X-2012-3-245

Tiwari, R., & Herstatt, C. (2012a). Assessing India's lead market potential for cost-effective innovations. *Journal of Indian Business Research, 4*(2), 97–115. DOI: 10.1108/17554191211228029

Tondeur, J., Van Braak, J., Ertmer, P. A., & Ottenbreit-Leftwich, A. (2017). Understanding the relationship between teachers' pedagogical beliefs and technology use in education: A systematic review of qualitative evidence. *Educational Technology Research and Development, 65*(3), 555–575. DOI: 10.1007/s11423-016-9481-2

Trasciani, G., Petrella, F., & Richez-Battesti, N. (2024). Navigating Cross-Sector Partnerships: Innovative Strategies and Challenges for Work Integration Social Enterprises in France. *Journal of Social Entrepreneurship*, *15*(1), 1–22. Advance online publication. DOI: 10.1080/19420676.2024.2325706

Trucano, M., & Dykes, G. (2017). *Building and Sustaining National Educational Technology Agencies*. World Bank. Retrieved from https://openknowledge.worldbank.org/bitstream/10986/26507/1/114271-WP-PUBLIC-ADD-SABER-ICT-technical-paper-series.pdf

Tufts Gordon Institute. (2024). Jugaad & Frugal Innovation: Is doing more with less the future of innovation? https://gordon.tufts.edu/news-events/events/jugaad-frugal-innovation-doing-more-less-future-innovation

UCLA, Center For Health Policy Research. (2023). Asset Mapping. https://healthpolicy.ucla.edu/sites/default/files/2023-08/tw_cba20.pdf

UCMB. (2024). IoT & AI for Frugal innovation 2024. https://www.unicampus.it/corsi/offerta-formativa/ucbm-academy/bootcamp-overview/iot-and-ai-for-frugal-innovation-2024

UNESCO, I. (2009). Guide to measuring information and communication technologies (ICT) in education.

Unwin, T. (2017). *Reclaiming information and communication technologies for development*. Oxford University Press. DOI: 10.1093/oso/9780198795292.001.0001

Usman, F. O., Kess-Momoh, A. J., Ibeh, C. V., Elufioye, A. E., Ilojianya, V. I., & Oyeyemi, O. P.Favour Oluwadamilare Usman, & the Azeez Jason Kess-Momoh, & the Chidera Victoria Ibeh, & the Akinola Elumakin Elufioye, & the Valentine Ikenna Ilojianya, & the Oluwaseun Peter Oyeyemi. (2024). Entrepreneurial innovations and trends: A global review: Examining emerging trends, challenges, and opportunities in the field of entrepreneurship, with a focus on how technology and globalization are shaping new business ventures. *International Journal of Science and Research Archive*, *11*(01), 552–569. DOI: 10.30574/ijsra.2024.11.1.0079

Uusitalo, O., & Oksanen, R. (2004). Ethical consumerism: A view from Finland. *International Journal of Consumer Studies*, *28*(3), 214–221. DOI: 10.1111/j.1470-6431.2003.00339.x

van Beers, C., Knorringa, P., & Leliveld, A. (2020). Can frugal innovations be responsible innovations? In *Responsible Innovation in Large Technological Systems* (pp. 80–95). Routledge. DOI: 10.4324/9781003019930-6

Van Dijk, J. A. (2012). The evolution of the digital divide-the digital divide turns to inequality of skills and usage. In *Digital enlightenment yearbook* (pp. 57–75). IOS Press.

Varman, R., & Belk, R. W. (2009). Nationalism and ideology in an anticonsumption movement. *The Journal of Consumer Research*, *36*(4), 686–700. DOI: 10.1086/600486

Vasquez, A. V. (2019). *Increase Construction Safety With Digital Transformation.* [Online] Available at: http://constructionexec.com/article/increase-construction-safety-with-digital-transformation [Accessed 10 October 2023].

Vázquez-Pacho, M.G., & Payaud, M.A. (2024), "From strategy to impact: how MNCs innovate their business models for social value in BoP contexts?", Journal of Strategy and Management, Vol. ahead-of-print No. ahead-of-print. DOI: 10.1108/JSMA-06-2023-0145

Velananda, Y. V., Dissanayake, D. M. R., & Wickramasinghe, C. N. (2022). Application of frugal innovations in a global context. *Asian Basic and Applied Research Journal*, *6*(3), 17–28.

Verhoef, P. C., Broekhuizen, T., Bart, Y., Bhattacharya, A., Qi Dong, J., Fabian, N., & Haenlein, M. (2021). Digital transformation: A multidisciplinary reflection and research agenda. *Journal of Business Research*, *122*(1), 889–901. DOI: 10.1016/j.jbusres.2019.09.022

Vidergor, H. E., & Ben-Amram, P. (2020). Khan academy effectiveness: The case of math secondary students' perceptions. *Computers & Education*, *157*, 103985. DOI: 10.1016/j.compedu.2020.103985

Vierikko, K.. (2024). Unlocking potential for sustainable development in rural India: Lessons from frugal entrepreneurship. *Journal of Rural Studies*, *87*, 100–112.

Virmani, A., & Lépineux, F. (2016). Aravind Eye Care System as Transformational Entrepreneurship: Spiritual Roots, Multi-Dimensional Impact. *Philosophy of Management*, *15*(1), 83–94. DOI: 10.1007/s40926-016-0032-z

Vladova, A. Y. (2021). Regional Specifics of Digitalization the Oil Midstream Soil Monitoring. NA, Springer. DOI: 10.1007/978-3-030-73261-5_23

Webb, S. P. (2018). *Digitalization for Pipeline Construction.* [Online] Available at: https://metegrity.com/media/articles/digitalization-for-pipeline-construction [Accessed 10 October 2021].

West, J., & Bogers, M. (2014). Leveraging external sources of innovation: A review of research on open innovation. *Journal of Product Innovation Management, 31*(4), 814–831.

Weyrauch, T., & Herstatt, C. (2016). What is frugal innovation? Three defining criteria. *Weyrauch and Herstatt Journal of Frugal Innovation, 2*(1), 1. DOI: 10.1186/s40669-016-0005-y

Weyrauch, T., & Herstatt, C. (2017). Frugal innovation in emerging markets: The role of partnerships and co-creation. *International Journal of Technology Management, 75*(1-4), 23–42.

Weyrauch, T., & Herstatt, C. (2019). What is frugal innovation? In *Frugal Innovation* (pp. 3–39). Routledge. DOI: 10.4324/9780429025679-1

White, K., MacDonnell, R., & Ellard, J. H. (2012). Belief in a just world: Consumer intentions and behaviors toward ethical products. *Journal of Marketing, 76*(1), 103–118. DOI: 10.1509/jm.09.0581

Wightman, A.. (2021). *A leadership agenda*. PWC.

Willyard, C., Scudellari, M., & Nordling, L. (2018). Partners in science. *Nature, 562*(7725), 24–28. DOI: 10.1038/d41586-018-06858-4 PMID: 30283120

Winterhalter, S., Zeschky, M., Gassmann, O., & Weiblen, T. (2014, June). Business models for frugal innovation: the role of resource-constraints. *R&D Management Conference*, (pp. 3-6).

Winterhalter, S., Zeschky, M. B., & Gassmann, O. (2016). Managing dual business models in emerging markets: An ambidexterity perspective. *R & D Management, 46*(3), 464–479. DOI: 10.1111/radm.12151

Winterhalter, S., Zeschky, M. B., Neumann, L., & Gassmann, O. (2017). Business models for frugal innovation in emerging markets: The case of the medical device and laboratory equipment industry. *Technovation, 66*, 3–13. DOI: 10.1016/j.technovation.2017.07.002

Wiśniewska, M., & Roczniewska, M. (2017). Frugal Innovation in Education: Lessons from India. *International Journal of Educational Development, 53*, 128–136.

Witell, L., Gebauer, H., Jaakkola, E., Hammedi, W., Patricio, L., & Perks, H. (2017). A bricolage perspective on service innovation. *Journal of Business Research, 79*, 290–298. DOI: 10.1016/j.jbusres.2017.03.021

World Economic Forum. (2017). *Digital Transformation Initiative Oil and Gas Industry,* Geneva: World Economic Forum.

World Economic Forum. (2018). *Taking expectations of on-demand and quick services to healthcare.* [Online] Available at: https://reports.weforum.org/digital-transformation/pager/ [Accessed 24 November 2021].

Y. Y. et al. (2021). Detection and Numerical Simulation of Potential Hazard in Oil Pipeline Areas Based on UAV Surveys. *Frontiers of Earth Science*, *9*(1), 272.

Yela Aránega, A.. (2019). Frugal Innovation in Agriculture: Empowering Small-Scale Farmers in India. *Agricultural Systems*, *172*, 42–50.

Yin, E., & Prabhu, J. C. (2018). Innovation in China and India. Handbook of research on new product development, 146-170. DOI: 10.4337/9781784718152.00016

York, J. G., & Venkataraman, S. (2010). The entrepreneur–environment nexus: Uncertainty, Innovation, and allocation. *Journal of Business Venturing*, *25*(5), 449–463. DOI: 10.1016/j.jbusvent.2009.07.007

Yousaf, Z., Panait, M., Tanveer, U., Cretu, A., Hrebenciuc, A., & Zahid, S. M. (2022). Value creation through frugal innovation, innovation capability, and knowledge sharing in a circular economy. *Sustainability (Basel)*, *14*(14), 8504. DOI: 10.3390/su14148504

Yuqian, L. & Xun, X., (2019). Cloud-based manufacturing equipment and big data analytics to enable on-demand manufacturing services, *Science Direct,* June, Volume 57, pp. 92-102.

Zeschky, M. B., Winterhalter, S., & Gassmann, O. (2014b, June 8-11). "Resource-constrained innovation": Classification and implications for multinational firms. *XXV ISPIM Conference Proceedings* (pp. 1-19). Dublin: The International Society for Professional Innovation Management. Retrieved from https://www.alexandria.unisg.ch/handle/20.500.14171/86806

Zeschky, M., Winterhalter, S., & Gassmann, O. (2014a, June 3). What is frugal innovation?: Conceptualization and empirical evidence. Retrieved from https://www.alexandria.unisg.ch/handle/20.500.14171/86840

Zeschky, M., Widenmayer, B., & Gassmann, O. (2011). Frugal innovation in emerging markets. *Research Technology Management*, *54*(4), 38–45.

Zeschky, M., Widenmayer, B., & Gassmann, O. (2011). Frugal innovation in emerging markets. *Research Technology Management*, *54*(4), 38–45. DOI: 10.5437/08956308X5404007

Zeschky, M., Winterhalter, S., & Gassmann, O. (2014). From cost to frugal and reverse innovation: Mapping the field and implications for global competitiveness. *Research Technology Management*, *57*(4), 20–27.

Zhong, Z.-J. (2011). From access to usage: The divide of self-reported digital skills among adolescents. *Computers & Education*, *56*(3), 736–746. DOI: 10.1016/j.compedu.2010.10.016

Zhou,. H. A. et al., (2020). Towards a Digital Process Platform for Future Construction Sites. *2020 ITU Kaleidoscope: Industry-Driven Digital Transformation*

Zucchella, A., & Urban, S. (2019). *Circular entrepreneurship*. Springer International Publishing. DOI: 10.1007/978-3-030-18999-0

About the Contributors

Reshmi Manna, Associate Professor, Department of Business Analytics, MIT World Peace University, Pune. She was CEO of HR Knowledge Lab, New Delhi. She has worked with esteemed organisations like India Trade Promoting Organisation (ITPO), IBM, IGNOU, Gargi College (DU) and ICFAI University. Obtained her SRF Fellow post of doctorate, IIT Delhi, PhD and M.Sc. (Developmental Psychology) from Calcutta University, an MBA (HR) and a PGDM in Public Relations from Annamalai University. She has 22 years of experience in behavioural science, business analytics and people analytics. She is certified in Management and Leadership (Level 5) from the Chartered Management Institute (CMI), UK, and a Master Black Belt on Service Quality from Indian Statistic Institute, New Delhi. She has published industry-oriented research papers in international and national journals and is working on process automation patents.

Ankit Singh, Business Analyst, LINTL Clothing Private Limited. He obtained his Six Sigma green belt from the Indian Statistical Institute New Delhi and an MBA (HR) from ICFAI Business School Gurgaon. He has five years of experience in Human Resources with esteemed organisations like Aditya Birla Group, HR Knowledge Lab, and Indian Institute of Management Ahmedabad.

***

Angara S. V. Jayasri brings 24 years of experience in Teaching, Mentoring, and Industry. A former Project Manager at Wipro, she has worked with prominent clients such as Microsoft and HP and received the HERCULES Best Individual Contributor Award from Wipro Technologies. Dr. Jayasri holds a Ph.D. in Computer Science and an M.S. from BITS Pilani. She is dedicated to enhancing pedagogical techniques in programming, aiming to make learning both fun and effective.

Vinay Baburao is currently working as a Director, Digital Transformation at CRC Evans, Houston, Texas, United States at CRC Evans. He is alumnus of Liverpool Business School and Birla Institute of Technology and Science, Pilani. He has an MBA from Liverpool Business school and Master of technology from BITS, Pilani. He is in the industry for more than 15 years and has knowledge domain of Industrial products, Oil and Gas and Medical. He has 1 Patent ("Determining elevator car location using RFID) and co-authored a technical paper on using AI in identifying defects in welding using radiography images.

Subhajit Bhattacharya is now serving as Associate Professor, Marketing Area at XIM University Bhubaneswar (previously known as Xavier University Bhubaneswar). He is a Ph.D. in Business Administration from The University of Burdwan. He has more than 15 years of academic experience and teaches different courses in the marketing domain. His areas of experience and expertise include teaching Brand Management, Consumer Behaviour, Sales Distribution Management, and Customer Relation Management. Dr. Subhajit has published articles in a few international journals, mostly indexed in ABDC, Web of Science, and SCOPUS. Currently, he is researching the areas of Brand Management, Tourism Marketing, Online Consumer Brand Engagement, Political Marketing, Value-Based Distribution Equity, CSR-led Branding, Consumer Insight, and Pedagogical Issues in Marketing Education.

Yogesh Deshpande is a highly respected academician, psychologist, educationist, and corporate trainer with an illustrious career spanning multiple decades. He currently serves as the Professor and Head of the Department at Visvesvaraya National Institute of Technology (VNIT), Nagpur. With a unique blend of academic rigor, practical wisdom, and empathetic leadership, Dr. Deshpande has made significant contributions in the realms of psychology, education, and organizational behavior. His work has not only advanced academic knowledge but also inspired transformative educational practices across India.

Leila Goosen is a full professor in the Department of Science and Technology Education of the University of South Africa. She holds a C2 rating via the South African National Research Foundation. Prof. Goosen was an Associate Professor in the School of Computing, and the module leader and head designer of the fully online signature module for the College for Science, Engineering and Technology, rolled out to over 92,000 registered students since the first semester of 2013. She usually supervises around ten Masters and Doctoral students, and has successfully completed supervision of 43 students at postgraduate level. Previously, she was a Deputy Director at the South African national Department of Education. In this capacity, she was required to develop ICT strategies for implementation. Before that, she had been a lecturer of Information Technology (IT) in the Department for Science, Mathematics and Technology Education in the Faculty of Education of the University of Pretoria. Her research interests have included cooperative work in IT, effective teaching and learning of programming and teacher professional development.

Lekshmi Krishna S. is working as Assistant Professor, DC School of Management and Technology and Research Scholar of APJ Abdul Kalam Technological University, India.

Oly Mishra is an Assistant Professor at the Indian Institute of Foreign Trade in the Area of Marketing. She has publications in ABDC journals and book chapters. Her research areas include consumer behavior, social entrepreneurship, and frugal innovations. She has written case studies and also served as a reviewer for many journals.

Siddharth Misra has an experience of more than 16 years in the field of Research, Academics and Industry. He is presently working as Assistant Professor-I, School of Commerce, XIM University, Bhubaneswar, Odisha. He has served IIT Kharagpur, NIT Rourkela, Birla Global University, Biju Patnaik University, FM University, Bangalore North University, Jagdish Sheth School of Management (JAGSoM formerly known as IFIM BSchool), Bangalore and Central Institute of Petrochemicals Engineering and Technology (CIPET) in different academic and research positions. In the list of corporate he has served JCT Electronics Ltd, Gujarat, ICICI Bank Ltd, Bangalore and Accendere Knowledge Management Services Pvt. Ltd. (CL Educate Ltd.), Bangalore in managerial positions. To iterate about his qualification, he is a B.E from Biju Patnaik University (BPUT) in Electronics and Telecommunication, Post graduated from ICFAI University with a MBA in Marketing Management, completed his M.Tech degree from IIT Kharagpur and PhD. from National Institute of Technology, Rourkela in Marketing Management with an additional certificate of UGC NET in management. His major area of expertise is in business analytics and sustainable development. He has guided PhD scholars from National private universities and from Lincoln University College, Malaysia. He has published more than 30 articles in Scopus, WoS/SSCI/ESCI, ABDC journal, edited UGC Care listed journal and reviewer to ABDC Journals. He has also contributed and completed various Projects from ICSSR, NABARD, MCL, CYSD and Tata AIG business projects in different roles. His keen interest in research have motivated him to present his research ideas in 9 international conferences in India and Abroad. He has published an Indian patent in the field of Management and Data Security.

Ovharhe, Orugba Harry (Ph.D) is a prolific 'Entrepreneurship Therapist' and bona fide lecturer, consultant and practitioners in the field of entrepreneurship and innovation with various professional memberships. Harry was born and raised in Delta State, Nigeria. He is a renowned entrepreneur with practical guide in conferences, workshops, symposiums, seminars and simulation training and development with trend of multiple local and international awards. His international articles are streamlining value capture, even as an editor and reviewer. Harry is known for his innovation, invention, brain storming, branching network and creativity. He innovates and initiates "Champiopreneurship and Therapeutic Entrepreneurship" as means of rehabilitating entrepreneurs with disabilities and unpleasant conditions. He is currently exploring analytical research for possible remedies to the business world at large on "Seed Entrepreneurship, Agile Entrepreneurship, Lean Entrepreneurship, Entrepreneurship Code, Rainbow Entrepreneurship, Inclusive Entrepreneurship, Frugal Innovation and Frugal Entrepreneurship".

Prachita A. Patil an Assistant professor of Dr. Ambedkar Institute of Management Studies & Research, Deeskahbhoomi, Nagpur. is associated since last 3.0 years. She is currently handling Mentoring Records and Guest Lecture. She has worked for 2 years as an Executive in Operations at SBI Life Insurance, Nagpur. And then she worked as Teaching Assistant at SIBM, Nagpur for 1.5 years. She has completed BE (EXTC), MBA (HR. & Marketing) and Ph. D on the topic "Psychodynamics of Women Entrepreneurs: Issues and Concerns" from VNIT, Nagpur and currently pursuing M.com at (IGNOU). Besides this she cleared NET (National Eligibility Test) in 2015 and currently is a guide at ISTD, Nagpur and has guided 5 students since 2022. She has been delivering many lectures at MCED on the topics Entrepreneurship, Marketing, HR and OB. She has a fundamental contribution in the areas of HR & Entrepreneurship. She has been associated with various forums like VIA and MCED. She has written more than 25 research papers in International journals like Scopus, Sage, Taylor and Francis, Sage Open and includes 110 citations till now. She is currently reviewer of Sage Open, Sage, and Springer etc. She is an Editor in IIP Proceeding and Sage Open. Dr Patil's unique strength lies in her ability to blend academic perspective with industry relevance. A true and dedicated mentor, researcher, and academician she continues to contribute meaningfully to the growth of management education and industry-academia collaboration.

Smruti Patre is an Associate Professor & Program In-Charge at Symbiosis Institute of Business Management (SIBM), Nagpur. With over 17 years of academic excellence, Dr. Smruti Patre stands out as a distinguished academician, Program In-Charge at SIBM Nagpur, and an avid researcher in the field of management education. Known for her dynamic teaching style and strategic program leadership, she plays a pivotal role in shaping future business leaders. Dr. Patre holds a B.Tech in Textile Technology, an MBA in Human Resource Management, and a Ph.D. in Human Resource Management. Her educational journey reflects a strong interdisciplinary foundation that enhances her approach to teaching and research. She has published more than 25 research papers in reputed national and international journals, consistently contributing to contemporary discourses in human resource management, organizational behavior, and strategic leadership. Her academic work is recognized for its depth, relevance, and practical implications. In addition to her academic endeavors, Dr. Patre is also a corporate trainer, having delivered impactful training sessions for major public and private sector organizations including Power Grid Corporation of India, WCL (Western Coalfields Ltd.), MECL (Mineral Exploration & Consultancy Ltd.), and PHI (Public Health Institutes). Her training modules focus on leadership development, emotional intelligence, team effectiveness, and strategic HRM. Dr. Patre's unique strength lies in her ability to blend academic rigor with industry relevance. A true mentor, researcher, and leader, she continues to contribute meaningfully to the growth of management education and industry-academia collaboration.

Jayasankar Prasad C. is a Professor of Kerala University and ICFOSS, India. He is the founder CEO of Kerala Start Up Mission. He has three decades of experiences as COO and Directors of Various PSU by Kerala Government.

Premasish Roy is currently associated as Dean, Faculty of Management Studies, Bharati Vidyapeeth (Deemed to be University), Pune. He is also the Director - Department of Management Studies, Bharati Vidyapeeth (Deemed to be University), Navi Mumbai Campus. He is an alumnus of Jadavpur University, Kolkata. He has Ph.D (Management), PGDM (HR/OB specialization), PGDMC (Mass Communication), MA (English) with twenty-two years of full-time Teaching, Academic Administration, General Administration, Consultancy and Research experience in Business Schools & Universities in pan India location. He has guided two Ph.D scholars and 98 master thesis dissertations. He is currently supervising two doctoral research scholars. He has presented over 30 research papers in various International and National conferences. He has published around 22 articles in various journals of repute. He has published over 7 chapters in different edited books of repute. He is a Mentor to a startup working at one of the Atal Incubation Centres (Centre supported by NITI Aayog, Government of India). He is an Innovation Evangelist – organized 20 entrepreneurship boot camps & 01 training programme supported by DST, GoI.

Subrat Sarangi, Ph.D., brings over 25 years of industry, management consulting, teaching, and research experience. He has previously worked with IBM Global Services, Wipro Consulting, iGATE- Patni, and Beroe Inc. as Vice President, Market Intelligence. His research interests include marketing strategy, branding, and competitive dynamics in the B2B markets. Subrat is an Associate Professor at MICA (Ahmedabad), India. His research has been published in the Journal of Business Research, Growth and Change, Opsearch, and Journal of Marketing Channels, among others.

Ravi Saripalle, Professor of Entrepreneurship & Mentor, Venture Development Cell, previously served as Director, Centre for Innovation and Incubation, Gayatri Vidya Parishad CoE. He launched the Inspire to Innovate (I2I) Storytelling Movement, advocates Design Thinking among youth. A former Wipro executive (12 Y), he has advised startups, judged pitch competitions, and delivered talks globally. He holds Ph.D. in Innovation Management (JNTUK), GMP from IIMB, Masters from Andhra University.

Radhika Sharma is an Associate Professor and Head of the Department of Biotechnology and Microbiology at IIS (deemed to be a university) in Jaipur. She is also the Director of the International Cell at the university.

Supriya Singh is a research associate at MICA, Ahmedabad. She is a Post Graduate in Economics from BHU, India. She has research interests in sustainability, innovation, and development, especially in emerging economies.

Omar Vargas-Gonzalez, Professor, research assistant and former Head of Computer Systems Department at Tecnológico Nacional de México Campus Ciudad Guzmán, professor at Telematic Engineering at Centro Universitario del Sur Universidad de Guadalajara with a master degree in Computer Systems. Has been trained in Innovation and Multidisciplinary Entrepreneurship at Arizona State University (2018) and a Generation of Ecosystems of Innovation, Entrepreneurship and Sustainability for Jalisco course by Harvard University T.H. Chan School of Health. At present conduct research on diverse fields such as Entrepreneurship, Economy, Statistics, Mathematics and Information and Computer Sciences. Has collaborated in the publication of many scientific articles and conducted diverse Innovation and Technological Development projects.

Index

A

B

C

D

E

F

G

I

J

L

M

P

R

S

T

U

www.ingramcontent.com/pod-product-compliance
Lightning Source LLC
LaVergne TN
LVHW080606300926
849162LV00005B/1063
* 9 7 9 8 3 6 9 3 4 0 5 0 9 *